THE AMERICAN CONGRESS

Fifth Edition

The American Congress provides the most insightful, up-to-date treatment of congressional politics available in an undergraduate text. Informed by the authors' Capitol Hill experience and nationally recognized scholarship, this book presents a crisp introduction to all major features of Congress: its party and committee systems, leadership, and voting and floor activity. *The American Congress* has the most in-depth discussion of the place of the president, the courts, and interest groups in congressional policy making available in a text. The authors blend an emphasis on recent developments in congressional politics with a clear discussion of the rules of the game, the history of key features of Congress, and stories from recent Congresses that bring politics to life. No other text weaves into the discussion the important ideas of recent political science research. The book includes the most comprehensive list of suggested readings and Internet resources on Congress.

Steven S. Smith is Kate M. Gregg Professor of Social Sciences and Director of the Weidenbaum Center at Washington University in St. Louis. He has authored or coauthored seven books and many articles on congressional politics, including *Call to Order: Floor Politics in the House and Senate*, *Party Influence in Congress*, and *Politics or Principle: Filibustering in the U.S. Senate*, and has coauthored several articles and a book on Russian parliamentary politics. He is a former Senior Fellow at the Brookings Institution and has taught at the University of Minnesota, Northwestern University, and George Washington University.

Jason M. Roberts is Assistant Professor of Political Science at the University of Minnesota. His research interests include American politics, the U.S. Congress, elections, and Supreme Court nominations. He has published articles in the *American Journal of Political Science*, the *Journal of Politics*, and *Congress and the Presidency*.

Wielen is Assistant Professor of Political Science at Temple University. He was previously a Fellow in the Political Institutions and Public Choice program at Michigan State University and at the Weidenbaum Center at Washington University in St. Louis. He has recently been published in *Political Analysis* and *Loyola of Los Angeles Law Review*.

The American Congress

Fifth Edition

Steven S. Smith
Washington University in St. Louis

Jason M. Roberts
University of Minnesota

Ryan J. Vander Wielen
Temple University

CAMBRIDGE
UNIVERSITY PRESS

CAMBRIDGE UNIVERSITY PRESS
Cambridge, New York, Melbourne, Madrid, Cape Town, Singapore, São Paulo, Delhi

Cambridge University Press
32 Avenue of the Americas, New York, NY 10013-2473, USA

www.cambridge.org
Information on this title: www.cambridge.org/9780521708364

First published 2007

Printed in the United States of America

A catalog record for this publication is available from the British Library.

Library of Congress Cataloging in Publication Data

Smith, Steven S., 1953–
The American Congress / Steven S. Smith, Jason M. Roberts, Ryan J. Vander
Wielen. – 5th ed.
    p. cm.
Includes bibliographical references and index.
ISBN 978-0-521-70836-4 (pbk.)
1. United States. Congress.   2. Legislation–United States.   I. Roberts, Jason M.
II. Vander Wielen, Ryan J.   III. Title.
JK1041.S65   2008
328.73 – dc22   2007022860

ISBN   978-0-521-70836-4 paperback

Contents

Preface

The American Congress has long been one of the most powerful legislative bodies in the world. Congress is now struggling with momentous issues such as health care and worldwide environmental problems, funding new investments in America's economic infrastructure, shoring up the U.S. system of retirement security, the war against terrorism, and the place of the United States in the post–Cold War world. These issues present a serious challenge. They affect the interests of all Americans, they are highly controversial, and they involve technical subjects and complex public policies.

Major Features of *The American Congress*

Understanding the Place of Congress in American Democracy. Our primary goal in writing this edition is to instill in students and general readers an appreciation for the importance of a strong legislature in the American democracy. Such an appreciation requires an understanding of the constitutional setting in which Congress operates, the basic rules of the electoral and legislative processes, and the resources and strategies of members of Congress and other key players. Each chapter is designed to contribute to the reader's understanding by introducing key concepts, describing essential details of the process, and outlining general principles for understanding the subject.

The Changing Congress. In our efforts to introduce you to congressional politics, we emphasize the evolving nature of Congress. In writing a textbook, it is easy to describe current arrangements and create the impression that the rules and processes described have long been as described and are likely to stay that way for some time. We do not want to create that impression. Congress is created by its members and frequently changed by its members. Consequently, we emphasize the factors that influence legislators' thinking about their institution. Party conflict, competition with the executive branch, the drive for reelection, and other forces in congressional politics are discussed.

Important Ideas About Congress. We also highlight important ideas in recent public commentary and political science research about Congress and its members. While we do not organize our discussion around debates in the professional literature on Congress, we do not hesitate to observe differences of opinion among our colleagues in political science on important subjects. Political scientists have offered competing and insightful perspectives on the sources of the incumbency advantage, the importance and motivations of legislative parties, the power of committees, and other subjects. We provide an accessible and balanced discussion of the deserving perspectives.

A Starting Point for Your Research on Congress. We provide a starting point for most undergraduate research projects by including an extensive bibliography on congressional politics at the end of the book. The bibliography emphasizes both classic and recent books, includes major journal articles, and contains major Web sites that include useful information on Congress and related subjects. Because we have provided a lengthy bibliography, we have limited references to literature in the text.

We have not hidden our enthusiasm for congressional politics. To be sure, Congress is easy to dislike and often difficult to defend. The rough-and-tumble world of legislating is not orderly and civil, human frailties too often taint its membership, and legislative outcomes are often frustrating and ineffective. Still, we are not exaggerating when we say that Congress is essential to American democracy. We would not have survived as a nation without a Congress that represented the diverse interests of our society, conducted a public debate on the major issues, found compromises to resolve conflicts peacefully, and limited the power of our executive, military, and judicial institutions.

Organization of the Text

Chapter 1 begins with an overview of the condition of the modern Congress. The chapter gives the reader a look at the general trends in American politics that are shaping the character of congressional policy making. It also reviews recent developments that have changed partisan control of the institution and altered the distribution of power within the institution.

Chapters 2 and 7 survey both constitutional and internal legislative rules to give an integrated perspective on the legislative game. The special character of American national legislative politics is the product of the Constitution, which created three institutions – the House of Representatives, the

Senate, and the president – and set rules governing their interaction in the process of enacting public laws. In addition, the House and the Senate have developed complex rules and practices that have a substantial effect on public policy.

Chapter 3 focuses on congressional elections. It covers the fundamental rules that govern elections and details the advantages enjoyed by congressional incumbents in their efforts to stay in office. The chapter concludes by evaluating the importance of election outcomes for the policy choices made by Congress and the president.

Chapter 4 focuses on individual members. It begins by reviewing the variety of political goals that members pursue. It also considers the resources that members may mobilize in pursuit of their goals and the political actors who influence members' behavior. The chapter concludes by looking at the strategies that members pursue in the case of voting and policy leadership.

Chapters 5, 6, 7, and 8 concern the central components of the legislative process – parties, committees, and the chamber floors. Parties and committees are not mentioned in the Constitution, yet the interaction of parties and committees defines the decision-making process in the modern Congress. The emphasis is on both the development of congressional parties and committees and recent changes that have altered the character of congressional decision making in important ways. Chapter 8, while detailing the activity that takes place on the House and Senate floors, concludes with an overall perspective on how parties, committees, and the floors are related to each other.

Chapters 9, 10, and 11 consider the major institutions and organizations with which Congress interacts – the president and executive branch, the courts, and interest groups. In each case, the emphasis is on the way in which resources and strategies of the institution or organization affect its relations with Congress.

Budget politics and process are the concern of Chapter 12. Budget politics has become a nearly dominant feature of congressional politics, and many important procedural developments have occurred in recent years. This chapter emphasizes the importance of the evolving budget process for the distribution of power in Congress.

A Special Appendix

We have added an appendix on spatial theories of legislative politics. Spatial theory now plays a central role in the political science of legislative politics. Students at all levels benefit from understanding the basic ideas in spatial theory. We suggest that you read the relevant sections of the appendix along with the core chapters. We think it will enrich your understanding of the political strategies pursued by legislators and presidents and give you some basis for understanding the determinants of legislative outcomes.

Acknowledgments

We are very pleased to be publishing this edition of *The American Congress* with Cambridge University Press. Cambridge editor Ed Parsons has championed this project, provided wise advice to us, and shepherded the review and editorial processes with great skill.

This edition would not have been possible without the support and motivation provided by the Weidenbaum Center at Washington University in St. Louis. Chris Moseley provided superb administrative assistance.

We also thank our collaborators on various projects on congressional politics – Stanley Bach, Sarah Binder, Philip Frickey, Gerald Gamm, Eric Lawrence, Forrest Maltzman, and Elizabeth Rybicki – for their many contributions to our thinking about American politics. Many of our teachers and colleagues contributed to the scholarship underlying this book, including David Carlson, Aage Clausen, Joseph Cooper, Roger Davidson, Richard F. Fenno, Jr., William Flanigan, Robert Holt, John Kingdon, Virgil Kroeger, Donald Matthews, Norman Ornstein, the late William Riker, the late L. Earl Shaw, Kenneth Shepsle, Barbara Sinclair, and Barry Weingast.

Over the years, members of Congress have been remarkably generous with their time. Smith is particularly indebted to the late Speaker Thomas P. "Tip" O'Neill, with whom he spent a year under the auspices of the Congressional Fellowship Program of the American Political Science Association. He learned a great deal about congressional politics from Speaker O'Neill and his top aides, Ari Weiss and the late Spencer Smith.

We thank our many colleagues who teach about Congress for their encouragement.

Steven S. Smith, Jason M. Roberts, and Ryan J. Vander Wielen

Women Senators of the 109th and 110th Congress attend a bipartisan Senate Women Power Workshop in late 2006. From left are: U.S. Senators Susan Collins, (R-Maine); Mary Landrieu, (D-Louisiana); Hillary Clinton, (D-New York); Lisa Murkowski, (R-Arkansas); Barbara Boxer, (D-California); Patty Murray, (D-Washington); Mikulski; and Senator-elect Amy Klobuchar, (D-Minnesota), and Olympia Snowe, (R-Maine). Photo by Olivier Douliery/ABACAUSA

1

The American Congress: Modern Trends

C ONGRESS IS AN EXCITING PLACE. REAL POWER RESIDES IN ITS MEMBERS, real social conflicts are tamed or exacerbated by its actions, and thousands of people, most of them good public servants, walk its halls every day. Much good work is done there. In recent years, Congress has passed widely applauded bills that have, among other things, approved new security measures for airports and funding for the war against terrorism, granted important civil rights to women, minorities, and the disabled, given parents job protection so they can care for sick children, forced states to reduce barriers to voter registration and supported reforms of voting processes, expanded funding for college students, and limited what lobbyists can give to legislators.

Congress is a frustrating place as well. It is not easy to understand. Its sheer size – 535 members and more than 25,000 employees – is bewildering. Its system of parties, committees, and procedures, built up over 200 years, is remarkably complex and serves as an obstacle to public understanding. Perhaps most frustrating is that its work product, legislation, is the product of a process marked by controversy, partisanship, and bargaining. Even some members of Congress are uncomfortable with the sharp rhetoric and wheeling and dealing that are hallmarks of legislative politics.

But Congress is also important. No other national legislature has greater power than the Congress of the United States. Its daily actions affect the lives of all Americans and many people around the world. It checks the exercise of power by the president, the courts, and the bureaucracy. If you want to understand the forces influencing your welfare, you must understand Congress.

Congress is always changing. It changes because it is a remarkably permeable institution. New problems, whatever their source, invariably create new demands on Congress. Elections bring new members, who often alter

1

the balance of opinion in the House and Senate. Elections also frequently bring a change in majority party control of Congress, which leads to a transfer of agenda control on the floor and in committees from one party to another. And each new president asks for support for his policy program. Members of Congress often respond to these demands by passing new legislation. But as lawmakers pursue their personal political goals, compete with one another for control over policy, and react to pressure from presidents, their constituents, and lobbyists, they sometimes seek to gain advantage or to remove impediments to action by altering the procedures and organization of Congress itself. The result is nearly continuous change within the institution.

Explaining the ongoing changes in Congress is the central focus of this text. We begin in this chapter by highlighting several developments in American politics that have changed congressional politics. These developments – including changes in the way Congress is covered by the media, evolving standards for public ethics, the rise of plebiscitary politics and new information technologies, new forms of organized efforts to influence Congress, new kinds of issues, and the war on terrorism – have altered the context of congressional policy making in basic ways.

Low Public Confidence

The popularity of Congress ebbs and flows with the public's confidence in government generally. When the president's ratings and trust in government improved after the tragic events of September 11, 2001, Congress's approval ratings improved, too. Still, Congress's performance ratings are almost always below those of the president and the Supreme Court. The legislative process is easy to dislike – it often generates political posturing and grandstanding, it necessarily involves compromise, and it often leaves broken promises in its trail. Also, members of Congress often appear self-serving as they pursue their political careers and represent interests and reflect values that are controversial.

Scandals, even when they involve a single member, add to the public's frustration with Congress and have contributed to the institution's low ratings in opinion polls. Some of the highlights are provided in the box on page 3. A consequence is that Congress is a never-ending source of comic relief, like the joke about the senator who dozed off during a roll-call vote, was jerked awake when his name was called, and reflexively yelled out, "Not guilty." There also is the joke about the member who kept referring to the presiding officer as "Your Honor."[1] But seriously . . . it seems fair to say that a large majority of today's members behave ethically. It is even reasonable to argue

HIGHLIGHTS OF RECENT CONGRESSIONAL ETHICS SCANDALS

• In 1989, House Speaker James Wright (D-Texas) resigned after Republicans charged him with ethics violations for receiving extraordinarily large royalties on a book.

• In 1991, Senator David Durenburger (R-Minnesota) was condemned in a unanimously approved Senate resolution for a book deal and for seeking reimbursement for expenses for staying in a condo that he owned.

• The disclosure that many House members had repeatedly overdrawn their accounts at the House disbursement office led people to believe that members enjoyed special privileges.

• Questions about the propriety of campaign contributions were raised in the "Keating Five" affair, which concerned the relationship between five senators and a prominent savings-and-loan owner seeking to block an investigation of his financial dealings.

• In 1995, a long investigation of sexual harassment charges against Senator Robert Packwood (R-Oregon) led to his forced resignation from office.

• In 1995, Representative Dan Rostenkowski (D-Illinois), former chairman of the House Ways and Means Committee, was found guilty of illegally receiving cash for personal use from the House post office. He later served a prison term.

• In 1995, Representative Enid Waldholtze (R-Utah) retired after her husband was charged with felonies in conjunction with raising funds for her campaign.

• In 1997, Speaker Newt Gingrich (R-Georgia) agreed to pay $300,000 in fines based on charges that he used nonprofit organizations for political purposes and misled the House Committee on Standards of Official Conduct.

• In 1998, Representative Jay Kim (R-California) pleaded guilty to charges involving over $250,000 in illegal campaign contributions.

• In 2002, Representative James A. Traficant, Jr. (D-Ohio) was convicted of receiving bribes in exchange for helping businesses get government contracts and of engaging in a pattern of racketeering since taking office in 1985.

• In 2004, House Majority Leader Tom Delay (R-Texas) was issued letters of admonition by the House ethics committee for improperly promising to endorse the son of Representative Nick Smith (R-Michigan) in exchange for Smith's vote on a bill and for attending a fundraising event with lobbyists for a company that was lobbying him on pending legislation.

• In 2005, Representative Duke Cunningham (R-California) resigned and pleaded guilty to taking more than $2.4 million in bribes and related tax evasion and fraud, the largest financial sum involving an individual member.

• In 2006, Representative Tom Delay (R-Texas) resigned after being indicted in Texas for laundering money through a national party committee in his effort to redistrict Texas congressional districts.

(continued)

HIGHLIGHTS OF RECENT CONGRESSIONAL ETHICS SCANDALS (*continued*)

• In 2006, Representative William Jefferson (D-Louisiana) won reelection to the House but was denied a Ways and Means committee assignment after FBI agents videotaped him appearing to solicit a bribe and later found $90,000 of the marked cash in his freezer – making this the cold cash scandal. The prosecution continues at this writing.

• In 2006, Representative Mark Foley (R-Florida) resigned after it was disclosed that he sent sexually explicit email messages to underage House pages.

• In 2006, Representative Bob Ney (R-Ohio) pleaded guilty to making false statements and conspiracy in relation to receiving thousands of dollars in gifts from lobbyist Jack Abramoff. A Ney aide pleaded guilty for receiving gifts. Separately, Abramoff pleaded guilty to charges of conspiracy, fraud, and tax evasion.

that today's cohort of members is at least as ethical as any past cohort. No doubt the ethical standards applied by the public, the media, and Congress itself are higher today than at any other time. Yet, there is no denying that the disclosures and charges of the past few years have been unusually numerous and have harmed Congress's standing with the American people.

Congress suffers generally from low ratings, which some observers believe represents a long-term trend. Political scientist Norman Ornstein notes that changes in the electronic and print media have led to a greater emphasis on the negative and sensational side of Congress. He refers to this as the "tabloidization" of media coverage:

> The drive to emulate the *National Enquirer* and the *Star* has spread to the most respectable newspapers and magazines, while network news divisions have begun to compete with tabloids like "Inside Edition" and "Hard Copy" with their own tabloid shows like "Prime Time Live" and "Dateline: NBC," and with changed coverage on the nightly news.

Stories or rumors of scandal – both individual and institutional – have dominated news coverage of politics and politicians in recent decades more than at any time in modern history, and not just in terms of column inches or broadcast minutes, but in emphasis as well:

> The expansion of radio and cable television talk shows also seems to have increased the speed with which bad news about Congress is disseminated and the frequency with which bad news is repeated. On many of these programs, there is a premium on a quick wit and a good one-liner and little time for sober, balanced commentary.[2]

Groups supporting term limits for Congress and other reforms probably have influenced public opinion, too. They argue that congressional incumbents are a privileged class. Incumbents, in this view, have created a system in which various benefits of office – including biased districting, free use of official resources, fundraising leverage, cozy relations with lobbyists, and so on – give them an unfair advantage that can be overcome only through radical reform. The more extreme versions of this argument suggest that incumbents have been corrupted by their experience in Washington. Incumbents are said to have developed an "inside-the-beltway" mentality (reference to the freeway that encircles the District of Columbia and its inner suburbs) or suffer from "Potomac fever" (presumably a condition brought on by proximity to the famous river).

Politicians, of course, quickly latch on to themes that resonate with the public. As a result, running for Congress by running *against* Congress, an old art form in American politics, has gained an even more prominent place in recent campaigns. Indeed, many recent arrivals on Capitol Hill promised to end "business as usual" in Washington and to push through reforms to "fix" Congress – to end the system of congressional perks, to stop the influence of special interests, and so on. The repetition of anti-Congress themes undoubtedly contributes to the low ratings for Congress and its members in public opinion polls.

The public's generally low evaluations of Congress have been observed for years. The *Gallup Poll* has regularly asked the question, "Do you approve or disapprove of the way Congress is handling its job?" Figure 1.1 shows that less than a majority of the public approves of Congress's performance most of the time. In the last few decades, the only time Congress's approval rating reached significantly above 50 percent was in the months following the terrorist attacks of September 11, 2001, during which anti-terrorist legislation was quickly approved.

While Congress languishes with mediocre approval ratings, individual members of Congress continue to do quite well. Typically, Gallup finds that about 70 percent of the public approves of the way its own U.S. representative is handling his or her job. Running *for* Congress by running *against* Congress works well.

Plebiscitary Politics

Political scientist Robert Dahl argues that Congress suffers from the increasingly plebiscitary nature of American politics. By a movement toward plebiscitary politics, Dahl is referring to the trend toward more direct

FIGURE 1.1. Congress Job Performance Ratings, Gallup Poll, 1974–2006. *Source:* Poll Databank, The Roper Center for Public Opinion Research, University of Connecticut.

communication between the public and elected officials and the demise of intermediaries – such as parties and membership organizations – that once served to represent or express public opinion to elected officials. Directly observed, rather than mediated, public views are more important than ever – which could not be further from Madison's aspirations for the national legislature.[3]

Plebiscitary politics is facilitated by new technologies. Advances in transportation allow most members of Congress to be back home in their districts or states most weekends. Public opinion polls, which allow the public's views to be registered with legislators, have become more affordable because of advancements in digital technology. Leaders and parties sponsor focus groups to learn about nuances and shadings in public attitudes. Radio and television call-in shows enable nearly every constituent to talk directly to a member of Congress from time to time. Satellite technology allows members to communicate easily and inexpensively with groups in their home state or district from Washington.

Members of Congress, and certainly candidates for Congress, find the new information technologies irresistible and contribute to the trend. Members love to demonstrate their commitment to keeping in touch with their constituents by being among the first to use a new innovation in communications. To be sure, members face real problems reaching constituents in districts and states with ever-growing populations. The average House district is approaching 700,000 people, up from about 300,000 in 1940 and 400,000 in 1960. Still, the political value of appearing to be connected to constituents drives elected officials to exploit new technologies.

On its face, plebiscitary politics might seem to be a good thing: It seems better to have public opinion influencing members' decisions than to have highly paid lobbyists representing organized interests swaying their votes. But as Dahl notes, the effects of direct communication between the people and their representatives on Capitol Hill may not be so desirable. For one thing, elected officials and special interests might manipulate direct communication to their advantage. If the politicians are the ones who choose the time and place for direct communication, the process may create nothing more than a deceiving appearance of responsiveness.

More important, plebiscitary politics may undermine both representation and deliberation in legislative policy making. With respect to representation, the "public" that is likely to communicate directly to members may not be representative of members' larger constituencies. They will be people who are intensely interested in politics, generally or in a single issue, and can afford and know how to use new information technologies. If so, then members' impressions of public opinion may be distorted by such communication.

With respect to deliberation, direct communication with more constituents could lead members to make premature public commitments on more issues and reduce their flexibility in negotiating compromises in the legislative arena. The possible result is that demagoguery and grandstanding would take precedence over resolving conflicts and solving problems. Public opinion may win out over the public interest, just what Madison sought to avoid.

Governing as Campaigning

A close cousin to the rise of plebiscitary politics is the weakening distinction between governing and campaigning. Of course, we hope that there is a strong linkage between governing and campaigning. Elected officials' desire for reelection underpins our ability to hold them accountable. Broadly speaking, campaign promises are (and should be) related to governing, and election outcomes are (and should be) shaped by performance in office. Inevitably, then, the line between governing and campaigning becomes blurred.

In recent decades, campaigning has become more fully integrated with governing. No longer is governing done in Washington and campaigning done at home. The daily routines of members and top leaders are now geared to the demands of campaigning.

Few members retire from Congress without complaining about how much it costs to mount a campaign for reelection. Returning members may not have time to complain. In recent years, the average victor in a Senate race spent over $8 million, and the average House victor spent over a million dollars. Many races were far more expensive. For an incumbent seeking reelection, that is an average of more than $25,000 for each week served during a six-year Senate term and almost $10,000 for each week served during a two-year House term. These sums do not include additional millions spent by parties and independent groups on congressional campaigns. Competitive pressures, between incumbents and challengers and between the two parties, have produced a never-ending search for cash.

Congressional leaders have changed their ways, too. To assist their party colleagues, most party leaders spend many evenings and weekends at fundraising events. Many leaders have developed their own political action committees (leadership PACs, they have been called) to raise and distribute money. Leaders have formed public relations task forces within their parties, and the campaign committees of the congressional parties have greatly expanded their activities. Perhaps most important, congressional leaders now often use technology developed for campaigning in legislative battles. Professional consultants and pollsters help fashion legislative priorities and tactics. Opposition research – digging up dirt on your election opponent – is now conducted by the congressional campaign committees against congressional incumbents of the opposite party. Media campaigns are now planned for major legislative proposals with the assistance of television advertising specialists. Money, media, and partisanship feed on each other.

New Forms of Organized Influence

The number of interest groups in Washington and the rest of the country multiplied many times in the last half century. By one count, the number of groups increased from about 1,000 in the late 1940s to well more than 7,000 in the early 1980s.[4] Due to new lobbying registration requirements that were enacted in 1995, we now know that the number of registered lobbyists has more than doubled since 2000 to more than 35,000. This increase is primarily a by-product of the expanding scope of the federal government's

Congressionally Speaking...

Each Congress has a two-year life span. Federal law sets the date for federal elections, but the Constitution specifies the starting date for each Congress. Before 1935, congressional elections in November of an even-numbered year preceded the convening of a new Congress the following March. Since 1935, after the ratification of the Twentieth Amendment to the Constitution, a new Congress convenes on January 3 unless Congress otherwise provides by law, as it often does to avoid weekends. Each two-year Congress is given a number – the 110th Congress convened in January 2007 – and is divided into two one-year sessions. Congressional documents are often numbered 110–1 or 110–2 to combine the Congress and session numbers.

activity – as more interests were affected by federal programs, tax policies, and regulation, more interests sought representation in Washington. Technological developments in transportation, information management, and communications have enabled scattered people, corporations, and even state and local governments to easily organize, raise money, and set up offices and staff in Washington. The process feeds on itself, with new groups forming to counter the influence of other recently formed groups. The result has been a tremendous increase in the demands placed on members of Congress by lobbyists from organized groups.

Not only have interest groups proliferated, they have also become more diverse. Economic interests – corporations, trade associations, labor groups – greatly outnumber other sectors among lobbyists. In addition, many groups represent new industries, "citizens" groups sprouted in the 1960s and 1970s and continue to grow in number. These groups are often outgrowths of national movements – such as those for civil rights, women's rights, children's rights, the elimination of hunger, consumers' rights, welfare rights, gay rights, environmental protection, the homeless, and so on. Many of these groups now enjoy memberships numbering in the hundreds of thousands.

Along with their increasing number and diversity, groups have become more skilled in camouflaging their true identity. For most major legislative battles, coalitions of interests form and take all-American names, pool their resources to fund mass media campaigns, and often dissolve as fast as they were created. Many of the coalitions are the handiwork of entrepreneurs in law firms, consulting outfits, and public relations shops who are paid to coordinate the activity of the coalitions they spearheaded.

The roots have been taken out of grassroots lobbying. New technologies provide the ability to make highly targeted, highly efficient appeals to stimulate constituency demands on Washington. By the late 1980s, computerized telephone messages allowed groups to communicate with many thousands of people within a few hours. Technology now allows a group to telephone its own members, a targeted group (such as one House member's constituency), or the general public, briefly interview the respondents about their views on a subject, and, for respondents who favor the group's position, provide a few more facts to reinforce their views, solicit them to write letters to members of Congress, and quickly transfer the calls to the appropriate Capitol Hill offices before the respondents hang up. Several groups have developed television programs – some shown on the many cable television channels that are available in most communities – as a way of reaching specific audiences. Lobbyists exploit email and interactive video technologies to motivate citizens to flood Congress with messages. As a result, for a group with money, the absence of a large membership is not much of an obstacle to generating public pressure on members of Congress.

New Issues

New issues – such as the war against terrorism and global warming – always present some difficulty for Congress. They often create problems for congressional committees, whose official jurisdictions were defined years earlier when the new issues were not anticipated. Committees scramble to assert jurisdiction, and committee leaders or the parent chambers are asked to referee. After some amount of infighting and delay, committees eventually manage to adjust. In the view of some observers, however, Congress's ability to adjust in a timely way is becoming more and more strained.

It is nearly hackneyed to say that the issues facing Congress are becoming more technical and complex, but it is true. Increasingly, expertise in science, engineering, economics, or other fields is required to understand policy problems and alternatives. Congress often solves this problem by setting broad policy goals and delegating the power to make the necessary technical decisions to experts in the executive branch.[5] In this way, Congress is able to respond to demands for action. However, it does so at the cost of enhancing the executive branch's power over the details of public policy. At other times, Congress seeks to legislate the technical details. The cost then is that only a few members and staff assistants can understand the legislation and participate effectively in making important decisions. Scientific and

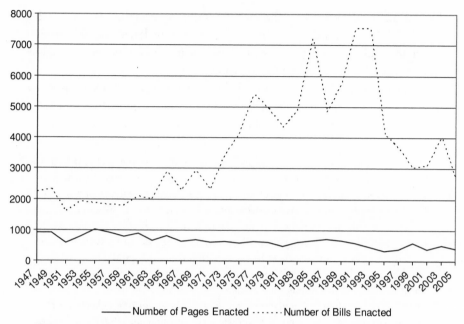

FIGURE 1.2. Number of Bills Enacted and Pages Enacted. *Source: United States Code 2000 Edition,* Vol. 29, Tables (Washington, D.C.: U.S. Government Printing Office, 2001); http://www. gpoaccess.gov/plaws/index.html.

medical research, defense programs, environmental protection, the regulation of financial institutions, international trade, and many other fields of public policy are no longer within the common experiences of elected officials. Thus, most members must look to competing interpretations of proposed legislation offered by staff specialists, lobbyists, and a wide array of outside experts.

The new policy challenges result from an increasingly complex American society coupled with the integration of international and domestic economies. Fewer major policies can be debated in isolation from other major policies. Health care reform, for example, concerns employer-employee relations, economic growth, welfare reform, and tax policy, among other things. This complexity leads Congress to craft unwieldy bills, often written by multiple committees, laden with technical language, and reaching several hundred pages in length. Figure 1.2 shows the increasing length of the average bill enacted by Congress in recent decades, at least until the Republicans gained congressional majorities in 1994. Between 1995 and 2006, the total number of bills and the number of pages enacted into law declined sharply, but the average length of a bill remained several times as

long as for the 1950s. More than issue complexity underlies the increasing
length of bills, as we will see in later chapters, but the length of bills presents
a serious challenge to legislators who might want to understand the legislation on which they are asked to cast votes.

Political scientist Lawrence Dodd believes that Congress, at least as it now
operates, cannot cope with the important issues of our time. In his view, the
problem lies in the relationship between members and their constituents:

> The voters may see the decay of urban infrastructure, sense the declining educa-
> tional and job opportunities of their children, acknowledge the ecological dam-
> age of industrial pollution, and worry about the long-term effects of a mount-
> ing deficit. But as they consider their vote for senator and representative, the
> citizens override any broad concerns they may have with collective issues and
> vote in accord with ensuring immediate benefits; they do so by voting for the
> powerful local incumbent who can assist with a desired local defense contract
> or who can help them with their veterans claim or Medicare benefits. They
> do so because of the immediate influence that a powerful incumbent legisla-
> tor can have on their particularized interests . . . The emerging collective prob-
> lems of the new era thus go unacknowledged and tear away at the fabric of
> society.[6]

If Dodd is right, then the public's ratings of congressional performance will
continue to be low while incumbent legislators will continue to be routinely
reelected.

Congress's tendency is to allow the president to define solutions to
the nation's problems and then to criticize those solutions from narrow,
often parochial perspectives. Unfortunately, plebiscitary politics, the proliferation of interest groups, and the new ways of influencing members
of Congress of interest groups, and the new ways of influencing members of Congress reinforce this tendency. Modern politics puts more pressure than ever on members to explain themselves in terms that are readily
understood by the folks back home. Scholar and congressman David Price
(D-North Carolina) observes, "Members must constantly explain themselves and their actions in terms of ordinary knowledge. A decision that does
not lend itself to such an explanation often has a heavy burden of proof
against it. In the era of television journalism, of thirty-second ads and negative advertising, a defensive deference to ordinary knowledge has probably become more important in congressional behavior than it was before."[7]
The gap between what legislators do and what they can explain seems to be
widening.

Congressionally Speaking...

Every 10 years, the Census Bureau counts the number of people living in the United States. On the basis of that count, the Census Bureau allocates seats in the U.S. House of Representatives to each of the states according to a formula set in law. This allocation is called *apportionment.* States then draw the boundaries of districts for the House of Representatives, a process known as *districting.* Districting is controversial because it may advantage one of the parties or certain incumbent legislators. Districting was very controversial in Texas following the 2000 census. The original districting plan enacted by a Democratic majority in the state legislature was replaced by a plan enacted by a later Republican majority in the legislature. As the Republicans hoped, the new districting plan helped to elect more Republicans to the U.S. House of Representatives in 2004.

Changing Membership

Regional Shifts

In recent decades, demographic and social changes in American society have altered the composition of Congress in important ways. One important change has been in the allocation of House seats to the states. The 435 seats of the House are reapportioned every 10 years to reflect changes in the distribution of the nation's population across the states. A formula established by law guides the Census Bureau, which calculates the number of districts for each state every 10 years after the decennial census. Population shifts have allowed certain states in the South and West to gain seats in the House of Representatives at the expense of several eastern and midwestern states. The regional shifts are visible in Table 1.1. The South and West gained even more seats after the national census in the year 2000 – again at the expense of the industrial Northeast and Midwest.

The redistribution of seats away from the northern industrial states has reduced those states' political clout at a time when they could use it. The need for infrastructure repairs, worker retraining, low-income housing, and other government services is severe in the old industrial states, but the declining influence of these states is reducing their ability to acquire financial assistance from the federal government. Indeed, the shift of power to the more conservative regions of the country has undercut congressional

TABLE 1.1. Changes in the Apportionment of House
Seats, by Region, 1960–2000.

Region	1960 seats	2000 seats	Difference
East	108	83	−25
Midwest	125	100	−25
South	133	154	21
West	69	98	29
Total	435	435	

Source: Census Bureau.

support for a major federal role in the rehabilitation of the industrial cities
of the northern-tier states.

The population growth in the South and West is the result of that region's
economic growth, an influx of workers from the older industrial states
and other countries, and the expansion of the region's middle class. The
most obvious consequence of these developments is that the South is no
longer a one-party region, as it was just three decades ago. Republicans
are now competitive in Senate races throughout the South and hold many
House seats as well. As recently as 1960, Republicans held no Senate
seats and only six of 104 House seats in the states of the old Confederacy. After the 1992 elections, Republicans held 13 of the 22 Senate seats
and 48 of the 125 House seats in the region, with the largest numbers in
Florida and Texas. The southern Senate seats were critical to Republicans
between 1981 and 1986, when they controlled the Senate, and again after
1994.

Women and Minorities

Beyond the changes in regional representation and partisan composition
in Congress, Capitol Hill has also acquired a sizable contingent of women
and minorities. The growing strength of women's and minority groups, the
acquisition of political experience by women and minority politicians in
state and local government, and new voting laws have contributed to the
recent improvement in these groups' representation in Congress. In 1993,
the Senate gained its first Native American, Ben Nighthorse Campbell
(D-Colorado), who later switched parties, and its first black woman, Carol
Moseley-Braun (D-Illinois). Table 1.2 shows the gains that women, African
Americans, and Hispanics have made in Congress in recent years, and even

TABLE 1.2. Number of Women and Minorities in the House and Senate, 1971–2007.

Congress (first year)	Women		African Americans		Hispanic Americans	
	House	Senate	House	Senate	House	Senate
92d (1971)	12	1	12	1	5	1
93d (1973)	14	0	15	1	5	1
94th (1975)	18	0	16	1	5	1
95th (1977)	18	0	16	1	5	0
96th (1979)	16	1	16	0	6	0
97th (1981)	19	2	16	0	6	0
98th (1983)	21	2	20	0	10	0
99th (1985)	22	2	19	0	11	0
100th (1987)	23	2	22	0	11	0
101st (1989)	25	2	23	0	11	0
102d (1991)	29	2	25	0	10	0
103d (1993)	48	6	38	1	17	0
104th (1995)	49	8	39	1	18	0
105th (1997)	51	9	37	1	18	0
106th (1999)	58	9	39	0	19	0
107th (2001)	59	13	36	0	21	0
108th (2003)	62	14	39	0	21	0
109th (2005)	68	14	42	1	24	2
110th (2007)	67	16	40	1	23	3

Source: *Vital Statistics on American Politics* (Washington, D.C.: Congressional Quarterly Press, 2000), p. 201; entries for the 107th–110th Congresses collected by the authors. Numbers reflect membership at the start of the Congress.

more – many more – women and minorities have been running for Congress. More than 100 women have been major party candidates for Congress in each election since 1992. In 2006, 139 women ran for the House. Only three Native Americans have served in the Senate.

Women and minorities are still underrepresented in Congress relative to their proportions in the population, but few doubt that women and minority lawmakers have already had a substantial impact. Most obviously, the Congressional Caucus for Women's Issues, the Congressional Black Caucus, and, to a lesser extent, the Congressional Hispanic Caucus have become important factions within the House Democratic Party. Women and blacks comprise about 20 percent of the House Democratic Caucus. The 2007 Senate began with 16 women, three Hispanics, and one black member. In fact, in winning his 2004 bid for a Senate seat from Illinois, Democrat Barack Obama became only the third African American popularly elected to the Senate since the early twentieth century when the Seventeenth Amendment to the Constitution, providing for direct election to the Senate, was ratified. Only one Native American, Tom Cole (R-Oklahoma), a member of the Chickasaw Nation, remained in Congress in 2007. Cole was elected chair of the National Republican Congressional Committee, his party's campaign committee, in late 2006.

The presence of more women and minorities has changed the mix of voices heard in congressional debates. Social and economic problems seem to be more frequently discussed in the first person today – that is, more members refer to their personal experience when addressing their colleagues and constituents. In addition, more legislation reflecting the issues that are given greater emphasis by women and minorities is introduced. Generally, issues important to these groups have been given higher priority by party leaders, particularly Democratic leaders.

Only one woman, Rep. Nancy Pelosi (D-California), has been elected the top leader of a congressional party. Pelosi was elected Speaker in 2007 after the Democrats won a majority of House seats in the 2006 elections. She had been elected the Democrats' Minority Leader in late 2002 after serving in the number two position, Democratic Whip, for two years. Rep. Deborah Pryce of Ohio served as House Republican Conference chair during 2002–2006. Other women have held second-tier party positions. They include House Republican Conference Vice Chair Kay Granger (R-Texas), who was elected to her post in late 2006, former Senate Republican Conference Vice Chair Kay Bailey Hutchison (R-Texas), former National Republican Senatorial Committee chair Elizabeth Dole (R-North Carolina), and Senate Democratic Conference Secretary Patty Murray (D-Washington). Many women have gained sufficient seniority to chair important committees and subcommittees.

Only two African Americans have served in one of the top three leadership positions in a congressional party. J. C. Watts of Oklahoma served as House Republican Conference chair in 1998–2002, but he retired from Congress in 2002. James Clyburn of South Carolina was elected the House Democratic caucus vice chairman and chairman in 2002 and 2004, respectively, and was elected Democratic Whip in 2006. When Rep. Robert Menendez of New Jersey became the House Democratic Caucus chair in 2002, he became the highest ranking Hispanic legislator in the history of Congress. Menendez was appointed to fill a Senate vacancy in late 2005 and was elected to the seat in 2006.

For many Washingtonians, the influence of congressional women and minorities was symbolized by Senator Moseley-Braun's (D-Illinois) successful effort in 1993 to reverse a Senate vote extending a government design patent for an organizational insignia that many minorities found deeply offensive. The Senate Judiciary Committee, at the senator's request, turned down a request from the United Daughters of the Confederacy to renew the design patent for the group's insignia – the flag of the Confederacy, encircled by a wreath. Senator Jesse Helms (R-North Carolina) then sought Senate approval of a floor amendment that would have granted the patent extension. With few senators giving the amendment much thought, the Senate approved a preliminary motion, 52 to 48. The action outraged Moseley-Braun, who came to the floor and delivered a blistering attack on the amendment. Threatening to filibuster if the Senate did not reject the Helms amendment, Moseley-Braun asserted that "the issue is whether or not Americans such as myself who believe in the promise of this country . . . will have to suffer the indignity of being reminded time and time again that at one point in this country's history we were human chattel."[8]

Senator Moseley-Braun's speech and her later exchanges with other senators captured the attention of the entire Senate and of many congressional observers. Senators' reactions were unusually emotional, and several of them commented on how important it was to have Moseley-Braun in the Senate. The Senate then voted 75 to 25 to set aside the Helms amendment. Moseley-Braun later observed that she had "given the Senate some hope that we can break out of the kind of business-as-usual mode that this institution has so long been known for."[9] After serving one term, Moseley-Braun was defeated in her bid for reelection in 1998.

Previous Occupations

Notable changes have occurred in members' occupational profiles. Congress is still dominated by lawyers and business people, with nearly 220 lawyers and 200 business types in the House and Senate in 2005. The number of farmers has declined – down from about 75 in the 1950s to two dozen in recent Congresses. Educators have become more numerous. Overall, the occupational backgrounds of members are now somewhat more diverse than they were three or four decades ago.

These trends in the membership of Congress – the shift to the Sunbelt, the increasing numbers of women and minority members, and the greater diversity in members' previous experience – are likely to continue well into the next century. They are likely to continue as sources of change in the

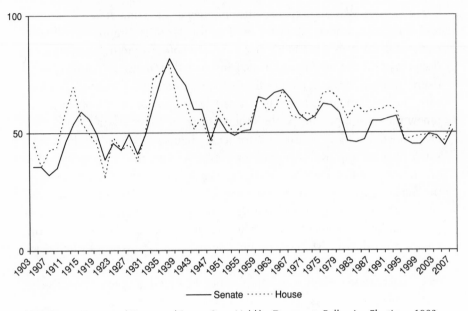

FIGURE 1.3. Percent of House and Senate Seats Held by Democrats Following Elections, 1903–2007.

way Congress conducts its business and in the policy choices Congress makes.

Changing Party Control

Perhaps the most conspicuous changes in Congress in recent years were the changes in party control. During the 1955–1980 period, Democrats enjoyed majorities in both the House and Senate. In 1980, the Republicans gained a Senate majority but lost their majority in 1986. In 1994, Republicans won majorities in both houses, which they maintained until 2001 when Senator James Jeffords of Vermont gave up his Republican affiliation and created a short-lived Democratic majority. Republican victories in the 2002 elections produced Republican majorities in both chambers, which they retained and expanded in the 2004 elections. Democrats won narrow majorities in both houses in the 2006 elections. With an evenly divided electorate, we have experienced a prolonged period of narrow majorities in both chambers of Congress in the last decade (see Figure 1.3).

Political scientist Richard F. Fenno, Jr., argues that frequent changes in party control keep the arrogance of the majority party in check.[10] Fenno contends that the uncertainties created by frequent change in majority control reduce the temptation for a new majority to overreach itself once in office. According to Fenno, because the Democrats had dominated the House for 40 years, when the Republicans took over in 1994, they were both inexperienced and impatient. The Republicans overstated their mandate from the 1994 elections, translated that inflated mandate into rigid and ultimately unsuccessful legislative strategies, and perhaps contributed to the reelection of Democrat Bill Clinton to the presidency in 1996.

Fenno also observes that the long era of Democratic rule led the Republicans, prior to their 1994 takeover, to adopt radical measures to end it. The Republicans assumed an uncompromising stance in Congress, making legislating more difficult and intensifying partisanship. After the Republicans gained control, Speaker Gingrich led a rhetorical assault on the very institution his party had fought to control, contributing to a further loss of public support for Congress.

If Fenno is right, then alternating control of Congress produces greater flexibility in party policy positions, more pragmatic party strategies, greater civility in political discourse, and perhaps greater public support for the institution. Early evidence may have supported his argument. In late 1996, hoping to do well in the upcoming elections, a House Democratic leader was quoted as saying, "Our themes will be to make the institution look reasonable, to take moderate steps for average Americans and to make sure that the public understands what we are doing."[11] In 1997, after experiencing a lopsided defeat in the presidential election and a scare in the House elections of 1996, congressional Republicans proved considerably more willing to bargain with the president over the single most important matter before Congress, the budget (see Chapter 12). After the 2006 elections, leaders of both parties promised to turn down the level of partisanship. A political "uncertainty principle" – that an uncertain electoral future breeds political moderation – seems to contribute to these proclamations.

The moderating effect appears to have a very short half-life. By many accounts, the Congress has been more partisan since the turn of the new century than it had been for a hundred years. Poor personal relations among leaders of the two parties, the exclusion of minority party legislators from some conference committee meetings, minority obstructionism on judicial nominations, personal campaigning against incumbents of the opposite party, and other developments are cited by insiders as evidence of deteriorating relations across party lines. Moreover, after 10 years of Republican control of the House, many Democrats asserted that they need to follow the approach of the Republicans of the late 1980s and 1990s, that is, to better define differences between the parties, intensify public relations campaigns against the majority party, and gear legislative tactics to winning a majority in the next election. With new Democratic majorities in Congress, the Fenno hypothesis will get another test.

The War on Terrorism and Congressional Power

Perhaps the most serious challenge to Congress's role in the American constitutional system is secret government necessitated by national security. The war against terrorism has revived fears that secrecy in the national security agencies of government will threaten Americans' civil liberties and undermine Congress's ability to influence the direction of policy, to oversee the expenditure of public funds, and to hold executive officials accountable. Executive branch officials are hesitant to reveal certain information to members of Congress because they do not trust legislators to keep the information secret. For their part, legislators cannot know what information is being withheld from Congress, so secret government tends to breed distrust on Capitol Hill.

In the 1970s, in the aftermath of the Vietnam War and disclosures of misdeeds by intelligence agencies, Congress enacted a variety of laws to require notification of Congress, and sometimes to grant the power to approve or disapprove to Congress, for the commitment of armed forces abroad, arms sales, and covert operations. Congress also created intelligence committees and established other mechanisms for handling classified information. Presidents of both parties have not liked to be constrained by these laws, at times arguing that the laws unconstitutionally impinge on the president's powers. Many members of Congress, on the other hand, have been unwilling to assume some responsibility for national security policy by exploiting new laws or insisting on presidential cooperation. The result is continuing uncertainty about when congressional approval is required. Congressional participation in national security policy making varies from case to case, driven by political calculations as well as legal and national security considerations.

The fight against terrorism poses special challenges for members of Congress. More classified activity, more covert action, and a bewildering array of technologies are involved. More domestic police activity is conducted under the umbrella of national security. The need for quick, coordinated, multi-agency action is intensified. Congress is not capable of effectively checking such executive action. Congress is open and slow, its division of labor among committees is not well matched to the executive agencies involved, and its members are hesitant to challenge the executive branch on high-risk policies and in areas where the public is likely to defer to the president.

Congressional participation in policy making related to the war against terrorism tends to be limited to a few members. The president consults with top party leaders, while agency officials brief members of the intelligence and defense committees. Average members are not regularly informed about developments in the war. They are asked to support funding for the war without access to all relevant information.

With Republican majorities during most of the period since the 9/11 attack, Congress did not actively pursue oversight hearings and investigations of Republican administration's conduct of the war against terrorists or the war in Iraq. Democrats, after winning majorities in both houses in the 2006 elections, promised to be more active.

Tempered Decentralization within Congress

The partisanship, concentration on budget, and national security issues have produced a Congress that behaves differently from what was predicted in the 1970s, when Congress last changed its organization and rules in major ways. Political scientists call this period the "post-reform" era. This term requires some explanation.

The House and Senate went through a period of reform in the early 1970s that led observers of the day to warn about the dangers of fragmentation in congressional policy making. In the House, new chamber and party rules were adopted to guarantee that committees operated more democratically and that subcommittee chairs were given greater independence from full committee chairs in setting their agendas and proposing legislation. Power appeared to be flowing away from central party and committee leaders and toward subcommittees and individual members. In the view of some members and outside observers, Congress seemed to be losing whatever ability it had to enact coherent policy. All of this happened at a time when the pressures brought by new interest groups, new lobbying strategies, and new issues were mounting. Although Congress had become a more open and democratic institution, its capacity to manage the nation's affairs seemed diminished.

By the mid-1980s, however, Congress – particularly the House – had not turned out as many observers had expected. Individualism had moderated a little, the congressional agenda had become more focused, party leaders and party organizations showed signs of revitalization, and the decentralization of power to the subcommittees had been tempered. Although Congress did not revert to its old ways, it acquired a new mix of characteristics that justified a new label – the "post-reform Congress." A brief review of the

characteristics of the post-reform Congress serves as an introduction to
many of the topics addressed in later chapters.

Tempered Individualism

Whatever other changes occurred after the 1970s, the entrepreneurial spirit
of individual members remained strong. In fact, it is almost a cliché to call
members of today's Congress political entrepreneurs. The term is used to
indicate members' relative independence from local and national parties.
Candidates for congressional office now develop their own campaign organizations, raise their own money, and set their own campaign strategies. This
independence from the national political parties tends to carry over when
the winners take office. Once in office, members use official resources and
exploit their relationships with interest groups and political action committees for political advantage. Knowing that they are on their own when it
comes to getting reelected, they take full advantage of taxpayer-supported
travel opportunities and communications technologies to maintain a high
profile at home. These topics are addressed in Chapters 3 and 5.

By the late 1970s, members had become weary of the surge in committee
and floor activity that was the by-product of reforms and unchecked individualism. Part of the concern was that members were spending longer days
on Capitol Hill, away from their families and their home states and districts.
And part of the concern was political – members faced more numerous and
more hazardous political choices as their colleagues forced recorded votes
on more legislative proposals. In the House, some members, even some of
those responsible for the reforms, began to ask committee and party leaders
to reassert some control. The most conspicuous response was to put more
restrictions on floor-amending activity in the House, a topic that is addressed
in Chapters 7 and 8. But more generally, both representatives and senators
now seem to appreciate leaders who are willing to set some direction, narrow
the agenda, and reduce scheduling and political uncertainties. Individualism
appears to have tempered somewhat.

Budget Constraints

The large federal budget deficit was a dominant force in legislative politics
during the period from 1979 to 1995 and again since 2001. Other than
in national security, few new federal programs were initiated, and much,
if not most, of the period's important legislation consisted of large budget
bills, particularly budget reconciliation bills. These bills, which are discussed

in Chapter 12, are the handiwork of many congressional committees and affect the full range of federal programs over multiple years. This emphasis on large, all-encompassing budget bills further reduced the ability of committees and individual members to pursue policy initiatives.

During the same period, many members turned from wanting to claim credit for legislative accomplishments to avoiding blame for making unpopular choices. Not only did this avoidance reduce comity on Capitol Hill and make service in Congress less enjoyable, it changed lawmakers' basic approach to policy making. Major decisions were made in closed-door sessions between top party and budget leaders and top administration officials rather than in open meetings in dozens of committees and subcommittees. The desire to avoid blame was also evident in the policy choices Congress made. Instead of considering the merits of individual programs, lawmakers passed broad spending caps or across-the-board spending freezes. The House voted to increase the national debt ceiling rather than try to peg it at a specific level or reduce it. When faced with politically sensitive issues, such as congressional salary increases and choosing which military bases to close, Congress created outside commissions to deal with the problem.

Until late 2001, it appeared that the federal budget would be in balance for the foreseeable future and that the politics of blame may be supplanted by a politics of claiming credit. At the start of 1998, the Congressional Budget Office, Congress's budget and economic forecasting agency projected no deficits and measurable surpluses to the year 2008. Predictably, new policy initiatives were proposed by Democratic president Bill Clinton, but few stood a chance of passage with the Republican majority in the House. After George W. Bush was elected in 2000, Republicans urged more tax cuts and a few initiatives of their own. A major tax cut bill was passed in 2001, one that seemed quite affordable to many observers until a recession settled in the economy and the terrorist acts of September 11, 2001, motivated large spending initiatives for New York, the war against terrorism, and the war in Iraq. Suddenly, the president and Congress were facing long-term deficits once again. With the exception of the war against terrorism, few new sizable programmatic initiatives seem likely. Even the new Democratic majorities in Congress, which have a new agenda for federal initiatives, are likely to find budget constraints severe.

Revitalized Parties

In the post-reform era, parties and their leaders have taken on greater importance than was predicted in the 1970s. Frustrations with unrestrained individualism and an emphasis on balancing the budget – issues that had long divided the parties – also contributed to the assertiveness of top party leaders since the 1980s. The replacement of some conservative southern Democrats by conservative Republicans made the Democratic cohort in Congress more liberal on balance and reinforced the conservatism of congressional Republicans. Divided party control of Congress and the presidency seemed to intensify partisanship in the 1980s, as each institution and party tried to avoid blame for ballooning deficits, unmet demands for action on social problems, and economic hard times. Top party leaders began to speak more authoritatively for their parties, and party regulars looked to their top leaders to promote party views in the media. For a year or so after the Republicans gained a majority of House seats in 1994, Speaker Gingrich came to be recognized as the most powerful Speaker since Joseph Cannon (R-Illinois) in the first decade of the twentieth century. Gingrich's successor, Speaker Dennis Hastert (R-Illinois) remained remarkably active in all major policy decisions and Speaker Nancy Pelosi (D-California) promises to be even more pro-active in structuring the Democrats' legislative program. These developments are detailed in Chapter 5.

Less Autonomous Committees

Chapter 6 details the substantial changes that have occurred in the role of the congressional committees in making law. Multiyear budget pacts, more assertive party leaders, and less deferential parent chambers have altered the place of committees and their subcommittees in the policy-making process. When committees may act and the kinds of legislation they may propose are now more highly constrained, and when they do act, committees are quite likely to be second-guessed by members when their legislation reaches the floor. Although committees remain central features of congressional policy making, they do not enjoy the autonomy that they once did.

The Changing Congress

The ways in which representation and lawmaking are pursued in Congress have evolved in important ways in recent decades. As this chapter has implied, not all of these developments have improved representation or lawmaking. In the chapters that follow, many of these developments are given a closer look. However serious we judge the problems of today's Congress to be, we should remember that Congress is a remarkably resilient institution. Its place in the political process is not threatened. It is rich in resources; critics even charge that it is too strong. Despite any attacks on Congress from critics, the legitimacy of its decisions is not seriously questioned by the chief executive, the courts, the states, or the American people.

POLITICAL PASSIONS LEAD TO VIOLENCE IN CONGRESS
Above: The caning of Charles Sumner (R-Massachusetts) by Preston Brooks (D-South Carolina). Brooks was upset by Sumner's speech against slavery.
Below: Cartoonist rendition of the first brawl on the House floor between Matthew Lyon (Democratic-Republican-Vermont) and Roger Griswold (Federalist-Connecticut). Lyon allegedly spit in Griswold's face after a heated debate, Griswold responded by attacking Lyon with a cane. Mayhem ensued as Lyon fought back with a fireplace poker as other House members look on.

2

Representation and Lawmaking in Congress: The Constitutional and Historical Context

I N REPRESENTATION AND LAWMAKING, RULES MATTER. THE CONSTITUTION creates both a system of representation and a process for making law through two houses of Congress and a president. One constitutional rule determines the official constituencies of representatives and senators; another determines how members of Congress are elected and how long they serve. Other constitutional rules outline the elements of the legislative process – generally the House, Senate, and president must agree on legislation before it can become law, unless a two-thirds majority of each chamber can override a presidential veto. More detailed rules about the electoral and legislative processes are left for federal statutes, state laws, and internal rules of the House and Senate.

While the constitutional rules governing representation and lawmaking have changed in only a few ways since Congress first convened in 1789, other features of congressional politics have changed in many ways. The Constitution says nothing about congressional parties and committees, yet most legislation in the modern Congress is written in committees, committees are appointed through the parties, and party leaders schedule legislation for consideration on the floor. In this chapter, we describe the basic elements of the representation and lawmaking processes and provide an overview of the development of the key components of the modern legislative process.

Representation and Lawmaking

Congress serves two, not always compatible, purposes – representation and lawmaking. Members of the House and Senate serve individual districts or states, yet they must act collectively to make laws for the nation as a whole. Collective action on divisive issues entails bargaining and compromise – among the members of each house, between the House and the Senate, and between Congress and the president. For compromise to be possible, members sometimes must retreat from their commitments to their individual states and districts. Determining who must compromise – and how to get them to do so – is the essence of legislative politics. The process can be messy, even distasteful, but, if it is to serve the nation, it is unavoidable.

Congress can be properly evaluated only by understanding our own conflicting expectations about the institution and about the politicians who work within it. To sort out the issues, we begin with a brief introduction explaining how representation and lawmaking occur in practice on Capitol Hill. As we shall see, achieving both perfect representation and perfect lawmaking, in the ways we desire each of them, is impossible.

Representation

REPRESENTATION BY INDIVIDUAL LAWMAKERS. Members of the House and Senate are expected to be *representatives* of their constituents back home. That is not a very precise job description. We might think that a representative's job is to faithfully present the views of his or her district or state in Congress – that is, to serve as a *delegate* for his or her constituents. But a delegate-legislator would not have an easy job because constituents often have conflicting or ambiguous views (or none at all) about the issues before Congress. Alternatively, a member of Congress might be considered a *trustee* – representing his or her constituents by exercising independent judgment about the interests of district, state, or nation. But it is impossible to be a both a faithful delegate and a true trustee.

A third possibility is to see the representative as a *politico* – one who behaves as a delegate on issues that are important to his or her constituents but on other issues has leeway in setting a personal policy priorities and casting votes. Unfortunately for many members of Congress, constituents are not likely to agree either about which issues are important or about when legislators should act as delegates and when they should exercise their own discretion. The challenge of the politician is to balance these legitimate but often competing expectations.

REPRESENTATION BY CONGRESS. Even if individual legislators can be considered good representatives for their own constituents, we might still wonder whether Congress can adequately represent the nation as a whole. Congress could be considered a delegate or trustee of the nation. As a delegate institution, Congress would be expected to enact policies reflecting nationwide public opinion, but public opinion often is as conflicted,

TABLE 2.1. Two Forms of Aggregating Policy Preferences in the Public and in Congress.

District	District's policy position on a 5-point scale	Legislator's policy position on a 5-point scale	Difference between district and legislator
A	5	1	4
B	4	2	2
C	3	3	0
D	2	4	−2
E	1	5	−4
	3.0	3.0	0.0

Adapted from Robert S. Weissberg, "Collective vs. Dyadic Representation in Congress," *American Political Science Review* 72 (1978): 535–7. Available at http://www.jstor.org.

ambiguous, or undeveloped as public opinion within individual districts and states. As a trustee institution, Congress would be expected to formulate policy in a manner consistent with its members' collective judgment about the nation's interests, whatever the state of public opinion. Members regularly invoke public opinion (a delegate perspective) or claim that Congress must do what is right (a trustee perspective) in their arguments for or against specific legislation.

COLLECTIVE VERSUS DYADIC REPRESENTATION. In practice, the correspondence between the quality of representation at the district or state level and that at the national level might be quite weak. To see this, imagine an issue on which five legislators from different districts take varying positions. As Table 2.1 illustrates, even if the legislators are not well matched to their districts, they can collectively represent the nation well. That is, *collective* representation can be good even when *dyadic* representation is not. Congruence between policy and public opinion may be poor at the state or district level but perfect at the national level. As a general rule, a legislative body will be at least as good a delegate for the nation as are individual members for their district or state.[1]

The logic of Table 2.1 does not guarantee that the House, the Senate, and the president will be able to agree on legislation. Indeed, James Madison, the chief architect of the Constitution, hoped not. Madison argued that policy should not necessarily reflect the majority's views. He justified the creation of an independent executive branch (the presidency) and a bicameral legislature (the two houses of Congress) on the grounds that policy should not simply reflect majority public opinion. He gave the president and the members of the two houses terms of different lengths, specified different means of selecting them, and gave the president the power to sign or veto legislation. Madison expected the two houses and the president to reflect different interests, which would reduce the chances that a majority could capture all three institutions and impose its will on a minority.

PARTY AND GROUP REPRESENTATION. We often think of political parties and other groups as representing parts of the nation. Nearly all members of Congress are recognized as either Democrats or Republicans and often are identified with other groups based on their gender, race, occupation, age, and other personal characteristics. Legislators, presidents, and the public usually see Congress in terms of its party composition. We speak of a "Republican Congress" or a "Democratic Congress," reflecting the importance of party control of the institution. Although voters choose between congressional candidates only in a single district or state, and no one votes directly for a Republican or Democratic majority in Congress as a whole, the party of the candidates and voters' views about which party should control Congress influence many voters and election outcomes. In turn, legislators tend to join with others of their own party to enact or block legislation, to develop and maintain a good reputation with the public, and to seek or retain majority control. Plainly, a great deal of representation occurs through the party mechanisms.

Although we do not often speak of a white-male, lawyer-dominated Congress, many people are conscious of the composition of Congress beyond its partisan or ideological makeup. A farming background is important for candidates in many areas of the country, whereas a union background is important in other areas. Organized caucuses of women, blacks, Hispanics, and other groups have formed among members of Congress, and groups outside Congress have developed to aid the election of more members from one group or another. It is said that increasing the number of women and minorities in Congress is essential because legislators' personal experiences shape their policy agendas. Moreover, the presence of role models in Congress may help motivate other members of these groups to seek public office.

THE TRADEOFFS OF REPRESENTATION. We cannot hope for perfect representation in Congress. Our multiple expectations for representation can all be met only if Americans hold uniform views on questions of public policy. They do not. Tradeoffs and compromise between the different forms and levels of representation are unavoidable. Neither the individual legislators nor the institution as a whole can simultaneously be a perfect delegate and a perfect trustee. In practice, we muddle through with mixed and changing forms of representation.

Lawmaking

For Madison, representative government – also known as republican government – served two purposes. One was to make the law broadly responsive to the people. The other was to allow representatives, not the people themselves, to make law. This second purpose was, and still is, controversial. Madison explained in *Federalist No. 10* that he hoped representatives would rise above the inevitable influence of public *opinion* to make policy in the public *interest*.

THE UNITARY DEMOCRACY MODEL. Madison's argument assumes that the common or public interest can be discovered by an elected representative through deliberation. In this view, the purpose of the legislative process is to discover those common interests through a process in which legislators share information, offer policy alternatives, and move toward a consensus on action to be taken. Building a consensus, rather than resolving conflicts by force of majority vote, is the object of this process. The emphasis on a common interest has led scholars to label this decision-making process *unitary democracy*.[2]

THE ADVERSARIAL DEMOCRACY MODEL. Madison's view may not be reasonable. Inherently conflicting interests may lead legislators to articulate those interests and decide controversies by the power of a larger number of votes. Deliberation may be viewed as needless delay to a majority that has no interest in compromise and has the votes to impose policies of its choosing. The majority naturally emphasizes the importance of efficiency and majority rule. The presence of conflicting interests leads us to call this decision-making process *adversarial democracy*.

THE TRADEOFFS OF LAWMAKING. Congress cannot easily harmonize the ideals of both adversarial and unitary democracy. Deliberation and consensus building may seem to be the preferred model of decision making, but time and the give-and-take required will frustrate a majority eager to act. In practice, as for representation, Congress will make tradeoffs among the ideal forms of lawmaking. Congress sometimes looks quite deliberative but will be pushed by majorities to be more efficient and look, at least to outsiders, as quite adversarial and partisan. Moreover, the two houses of Congress need not make the same tradeoffs. As we will see in later chapters, the smaller Senate continues to look more deliberative than the larger House – due in large part to significant differences in the rules that the two houses have adopted over the decades to govern themselves.

The struggle to balance alternative models of representation and lawmaking never ends. Contending forces in American politics usually favor different models as they seek to define democratic processes that give them an advantage. An implication of our discussion is that most sides can find theoretical justification for their positions – to better represent Americans in Washington (usually meaning to increase the influence of one group or another) or to reform lawmaking processes (also usually meaning to increase the influence of one group or another). This is not to say that common interests do not sometimes exist or that the nation as a whole cannot be better represented at times. It is to argue that the history of Congress is not one of smooth progress toward "better" representation and lawmaking processes. Rather, it is a history of political conflict as parties and ambitious politicians sought to appeal for votes and determine policy choices.

The Predecessors of Congress

The First Congress convened on March 4, 1789, under the Constitution drafted in Philadelphia in the summer of 1787. Despite the newness of their institution, the members of the First Congress were not new to legislative politics. The American Congress shares the same roots as Great Britain's parliament. The colonists brought with them British parliamentary practices and quickly established legislatures that governed in conjunction with governors appointed by the British crown. Beginning with Virginia's House of Burgesses in 1619, the colonial legislatures became both elected representative bodies and important lawmaking institutions almost immediately. Most of the legislatures followed procedures similar to those used in Parliament. Representation and lawmaking were well-accepted features of self-governance long before the Constitutional Convention of 1787. Eventually, the usurpation by British governors of the powers of the colonial legislatures became a critical motivation for the Revolutionary War.

Besides their experience from the colonial era, the members of the First Congress had more recent legislative experience from participating in the Continental Congress and in their state legislatures in the years after independence. The first Continental Congress met in 1774, at the time of the

Boston Tea Party and British assertion of military and political control over Massachusetts, as a step toward jointly working out differences between the colonies and the British government. The Continental Congress was not intended to be a permanent body but rather a temporary convention of delegates from the colonies. The crisis with Britain extended its life into the Revolutionary War, and its role in the new nation was formalized in 1781 with the ratification of the Articles of Confederation.

The Continental Congress was severely handicapped by its own rules. Very open floor procedures and a weak presiding officer undermined efforts to coordinate the diverse interests of the states and encouraged factionalism.[3] The Articles of Confederation did nothing to change that. Although they legitimated the national government that the Continental Congress symbolized, the articles gave the Congress little power. The Continental Congress could not regulate commerce or raise taxes, and without executive and judicial institutions to implement and enforce the laws it passed, it was wholly dependent on the willingness of state governments to carry out its policies.

In contrast to the weak Continental Congress, most state legislatures were very powerful. The new state constitutions adopted after independence gave the legislatures the power to appoint the state governors, guaranteeing that these officers, once appointed by the British crown, would serve at the pleasure of the egalitarian, popularly elected branch. The new governors were not granted the power to veto legislation, and most were denied the power to make executive branch appointments, which were left to the legislature. Governors, it was hoped, would be mere administrators. But soon legislative tyranny came to be viewed as a major problem. In the 1780s, an economic depression led debtors to demand relief from their creditors, and because debtors greatly outnumbered creditors, the legislatures obliged them. This undermined financial institutions, creating instability. Thomas Jefferson referred to the situation in Virginia as "elective despotism." Majority rule itself came to be questioned, and people began to wonder whether republican government was viable.[4]

The practice of having a bicameral, or two-house, legislature was well-established in the states by the time the Constitution was written in 1787. Britain had evolved a bicameral parliament based on its social class system, with the different classes represented in the House of Commons and the House of Lords. All of the American colonies except for Pennsylvania and Georgia had bicameral legislatures in 1776. Even after the Revolutionary War, when the British model was called into question, most states continued with a bicameral legislature. Debate over the proper relationship between

---

Congressionally Speaking...

The terms *unicameral* and *bicameral* come from the Latin word *camera*, which means "chamber." Under the Articles of Confederation, the national Congress was unicameral – one chamber – but many state legislatures were bicameral. The Constitution, of course, provided for a bicameral Congress. Among today's American state legislatures, only Nebraska's legislature is unicameral. Nebraska adopted the unicameral form in 1934 after using the bicameral form until then.

---

the two houses was frequent, and the states experimented with different means for electing their senates. Representing different classes in different institutions had lost its appeal, but the idea of preventing one house from becoming too powerful was widely discussed. By 1787, most political observers were keenly aware of the strengths and weaknesses of bicameral systems.[5]

The Constitution's Rules of the Game

Against the backdrop of an ineffectual Continental Congress and often tyrannical state legislatures, the framers of the Constitution sought a new balance in 1787. They constructed a stronger national government with a powerful Congress whose actions could be checked by the president and the Supreme Court.

For the making of public law, the Constitution establishes a specific process, involving three institutions of government, with a limited number of basic rules. The House of Representatives, the Senate, and the president must all agree to enact a new law, with the House and Senate expressing their agreement by simple majority vote. If the president vetoes the measure, two-thirds of the members of the House and of the Senate must agree to override the veto. If any of the three players withholds consent or if a presidential veto is upheld, the legislation dies.

The Constitution also provides for the election of members of Congress and the president, prohibits legislation of certain kinds, specifies the size of majority required in Congress for specific actions, and identifies the player who must make the first or last moves in certain circumstances. In addition, the Constitution allows the Supreme Court to determine whether Congress and the president abide by its rules.

The framers of the Constitution gave Congress tremendous political power. Article I, Section 8 of the Constitution grants to Congress broad discretion to "provide for the common defense and general welfare of the United States." It also specifies the basic powers of the national government and grants to Congress the authority to make laws to implement those powers. This general grant of power is supplemented by more specific provisions. Congress is given the power to tax, to regulate the economy to create courts under the Supreme Court, to create and regulate military forces, and to declare war. Section 9 grants Congress control over government spending: "No money shall be drawn from the treasury, but in consequence of appropriations made by law."

The Constitution entrusts the Senate with the authority to ratify treaties and confirm presidential nominations to executive and judicial offices. Congress can regulate congressional and presidential elections and must approve agreements between individual states and between states and foreign governments. The breadth of Congress's powers is reinforced in the "elastic clause," which provides that Congress can "make all laws which shall be necessary and proper for carrying into execution" the powers enumerated in the Constitution.

To protect members of Congress from personal intimidation by executive, judicial, or local officials, the framers of the Constitution devised several important clauses. First, beyond the age and citizenship requirements, the Constitution leaves to each house of Congress the authority to judge the qualifications of its members, to rule on contested election outcomes, and to punish or expel members for inappropriate behavior. Second, the Constitution protects members from arrest during and en route to and from sessions of Congress. And third, no member may be questioned by prosecutors, a court, or others about any congressional speech or debate. Members may be arrested and tried for treason, felonies, and breach of the peace, but they cannot be held personally liable by other government officials for their official actions as members of Congress.

Legislative Procedures

With respect to the details of the legislative process, the Constitution offers little guidance, with a few important exceptions. First, the framers of the Constitution were careful to provide that each house keep a journal recording its actions (Article 1, Section 5). Further, they required that the votes of individual members on any matter be recorded in the journal upon the request of one-fifth of the members present. A successful request of one-fifth of the members is known as "ordering the yeas and nays." In the Senate, the yeas and nays are taken by having a clerk call out each member's

THE LEGACY OF 9–11 FOR THE CONSTITUTION, STATUTES, AND HOUSE RULES

The terrorist attacks of September 11, 2001, led members of Congress and other congressional observers to worry about how the institution would function if an attack on the Capitol complex killed a large number of legislators. In 2002, the resolution providing for the adjournment of the 107th Congress provided that representatives and senators designated by the Speaker and Senate majority leader be allowed to call Congress into session in the event that those two leaders were killed or incapacitated. Without the provision, only the president could have called the Congress into special session, as the Constitution provides, but legislators believed that Congress should be prepared to act as an independent branch of government. In 2003, the House adopted three rules to address such a possibility. One rule requires the Speaker to establish a list of members who, in order, could serve as Speaker Pro Tem if the Speaker died or was incapacitated. This provision would allow the House to convene to elect a new Speaker. A second rule allows the Speaker to recess the House if there is an imminent threat to members' safety. Previously, the Speaker was not allowed to recess the House if business was pending. A third rule allows the Speaker to lower the number of members counted for the purposes of a quorum when a member dies, resigns, or is expelled. Without the change, a majority of the 435 possible members would have to be present for the House to conduct business. The new rule allows the total possible to be reduced to the number of seats that are currently filled.

In the view of some observers, the measures taken to date are inadequate. The Senate took no action on the more radical House-passed bill to order special House elections of substitute legislators within 45 days of a deadly attack. In 2005, the House adopted a rule that allows the House to act temporarily without a full quorum by empowering the Speaker (or his designee) to reduce the number required for a quorum after a series of lengthy quorum calls. Many observers doubt that this rule is constitutional because it appears to violate Article I, Section 5, of the Constitution, which provides that "a majority of each shall constitute a quorum to do business." A private study group recommended an amendment to the Constitution that would provide for quick and temporary appointment of replacements by state governors in the event of the death or incapacity of the incumbent, or by declaration of a national emergency by the House. The proposed amendment received only 63 votes in the House in 2004 and has not received a vote in the Senate.

The Senate is less of a problem. In nearly all states, governors are authorized by law to appoint replacement senators upon the death of the incumbents. Still, senators have expressed concern that the inability to gain a quorum in a national emergency would incapacitate the Senate. Legislation has been introduced to provide for temporary appointments if the majority and minority leaders jointly determine that the absence of a quorum to conduct business was caused by the inability of senators to discharge the duties of their office. States would determine how the temporary appointments would be made. No action has been taken on the proposal, which its sponsors recognized would have to be preceded by a constitutional amendment authorizing the process.

name and recording the response by hand. In the House, the yeas and nays have been recorded by an electronic system since 1973.

Second, the framers wanted tax bills to originate in the House. Because the Senate was originally to be selected by state legislatures, with only the House directly elected by the people, it was thought that the initiative for imposing taxes should lie with the House. The Constitution provides that "all bills for raising revenue shall originate in the House of Representatives; but the Senate may propose or concur with amendments as on other bills." The Senate has used a variety of gimmicks to circumvent this restriction, but the House generally has jealously guarded its constitutional prerogatives and spurned Senate efforts to initiate action on tax bills.

Third, the Constitution requires that "a majority of each [house] shall constitute a quorum to do business" (Article 1, Section 5). In principle, a majority of the members of a house must be present at all times, but like many other rules, this one is not enforced unless a member raises a point of order – that is, unless a member asks the chair for a ruling that a quorum is not present. This is sometimes used as a dilatory tactic. In the Senate, quorum calls have become a routine way to take a time-out – while the clerk calls the roll of senators' names, senators can confer in private or wait for colleagues to arrive. The most important implication of this constitutional provision is that a majority of members must be present and vote on a measure for the vote to count. To prevent absence from being used as an obstructionist ploy, the Constitution further provides that each house "may be authorized to compel the attendance of absent members."

Finally, the framers outlined the process of presidential approval or disapproval of legislation (Article 1, Section 7). After each house has passed a bill, it must be presented to the president, whose options vary depending on whether Congress has adjourned in the meantime. Congress has an opportunity to override a president's veto only if Congress remains in session (see box, "Constitutional Procedures for Presidential Approval or Disapproval of Legislation"). If Congress adjourns, the president can kill a bill by either vetoing it or taking no action on it (which is known as a pocket veto). Congress may pass a new bill if the president successfully kills a bill.

Constraints on Congressional Power

Although the framers of the Constitution intended Congress to be a powerful policy-making body, they also feared the exercise of that power. This concern produced (1) explicit restrictions on the use of legislative power; (2) a system of three separate institutions that share legislative powers; (3) a system of direct and indirect representation of the people, in Congress and by the presidency; and (4) a Supreme Court that judges the constitutionality of legislation and interprets ambiguities in legislative outcomes. The result is a legislative process that cannot address certain subjects, is motivated by political considerations, is likely to involve bargaining, and is biased against enacting new legislation.

EXPLICIT RESTRICTIONS. A list of powers explicitly denied Congress is provided in Article I, Section 9 of the Constitution. For example, Congress may not tax state exports, pass bills of attainder (pronouncing guilt and sentencing someone without a trial), or adopt *ex post facto* laws (altering the legal standing of a past action). The list of explicit limitations was extended by the 1791 ratification of the first ten amendments to the Constitution – the Bill of Rights. Among other things, the Bill of Rights prohibits laws that abridge freedom of speech, freedom of the press, and the freedom to peaceably assemble (Amendment 1) and preserves the right to a jury trial in certain cases (Amendments 6 and 7). And the Bill of Rights reserves to the states, or to the people, powers not delegated to the national government by the Constitution (Amendment 10).

In practice, the boundary between allowed and disallowed legislative acts is often fuzzy. Efforts by Congress to exercise its powers have often conflicted with individual rights or with powers asserted by the president and the states. The Supreme Court has resolved many ambiguities about where the lines should be drawn around the powers of Congress, but many remain for future court consideration. In some cases, particularly in the foreign policy realm, the Supreme Court has left the ambiguities to be worked out between Congress and the president.

SEPARATE INSTITUTIONS SHARING POWER. Rather than creating a single legislature that represents the people and determines laws, the framers of the Constitution created three institutions – the House, the Senate, and the presidency – that share legislative powers. Formally, legislation may originate in either the House or the Senate, with the exception of bills raising revenue. The president may call Congress into special session and is required to recommend measures to Congress from time to time. The president's

CONSTITUTIONAL PROCEDURES FOR PRESIDENTIAL APPROVAL OR DISAPPROVAL OF LEGISLATION

If Congress remains in session, the president may sign a bill into law, veto the bill and send it with a statement of his objections back to the house in which the bill originated, or do nothing. If the president vetoes the bill, two-thirds of both houses must vote to approve the bill (and thus override the veto) for it to become law. If he does nothing by the end of 10 days (excluding Sundays), the bill becomes law.

If Congress adjourns before 10 days, the president may sign the bill into law, veto it, or do nothing. Because Congress has adjourned, it cannot consider overriding a veto, so a vetoed bill will die. Likewise, if the president takes no action by the end of 10 days (excluding Sundays), the bill will die. Killing a bill by failing to take action on it before Congress adjourns has come to be known as making a pocket veto.

There have been disputes between Congress and recent presidents about the meaning of a temporary congressional recess. Presidents have argued that they may pocket veto a measure while Congress is in recess for a holiday or another purpose, even though Congress has not adjourned *sine die* (formally adjourned at the end of a two-year Congress). Many members of Congress disagree. Lower courts have ruled against the presidents' position, but the Supreme Court has not written a definitive opinion on the issue.

recommendations carry great weight, but the president cannot formally introduce legislation or compel Congress to act on his recommendations. Legislative measures are formally initiated in Congress, and once passed by both houses, they must be sent to the president for approval or veto.

A special arrangement was established for treaties with foreign governments, which also have the force of law. The Constitution (Article II, Section 2) provides that the president "shall have power, by and with the advice and consent of the Senate to make treaties, provided two-thirds of the senators present concur." Thus, the president formally initiates legislative action on a treaty by submitting it to the Senate, and an extraordinary majority of the Senate must approve it for the treaty to be ratified. The House is excluded from formal participation. Nevertheless, the House participates in foreign policy making by sharing with the Senate the power to restrict the uses of the federal treasury, to declare war, and to regulate foreign commerce.

Just as the president is an integral part of legislating, the Congress is central to implementing laws. The Constitution obligates the president to "take care that the laws be faithfully executed" and grants to the president the authority to appoint "officers" of the United States. But the Constitution requires that the president's appointees be confirmed by the Senate, allows Congress to establish executive departments by law and to establish means for appointing "inferior" officers of the executive branch, and grants Congress the authority to remove the president or other officers for "treason, bribery, or other high crimes and misdemeanors."

Interdependence, then, not exclusivity, characterizes the powers of the House, Senate, and president.

DIRECT AND INDIRECT REPRESENTATION. The framers of the Constitution wanted the government to be responsive to popular opinion, but they also wanted to limit the possibility that some faction could gain simultaneous control of the House, Senate, and presidency and then legislate to violate the rights of others. Only members of the House of Representatives were to be directly elected by the people. Senators were to be chosen by state legislatures, and the president was to be chosen by an electoral college composed of individuals elected in the states. Furthermore, House, Senate, and presidential elections were put on different timetables: The entire House is elected every two years, senators serve six-year terms (with one-third of the seats up for election every two years), and presidents stand for election every four years.

The result was a mix of constraints and opportunities for the legislative players. By providing for direct or indirect election of members of Congress and the president, the framers of the Constitution increased the likelihood that electoral considerations would play an important part in shaping legislative outcomes. Political competition could be expected to motivate much legislative action. But the framers hoped that indirect election of senators and presidents, along with their longer terms of office, would desensitize them to narrow interests and rapid shifts in public opinion. This safeguard was considered to be particularly important in the case of treaties and major appointments to the executive agencies and the judiciary, which are left to the president and the Senate.

Concern about the responsiveness of senators to public opinion led to the adoption in 1913 of the Seventeenth Amendment to the Constitution, which provided for direct election of senators. Direct election of senators reduced the difference between the House and the Senate in terms of their link to the electorate, as has the nearly automatic translation of the popular vote into state electoral college votes for president. Nevertheless, because senators represent whole states, presidents are elected nationally, and representatives are selected from small districts regulated by size, along with the differences in term of office, it continues to be likely that the three institutions will have different preferences about public policy. Variations in policy preferences among the players, combined with their procedural inter-dependence, increase the difficulty of adopting new laws. This bias against change reduces, but does not eliminate, the probability that legislative power will be used to the advantage of a narrow interest and increases the probabil-ity that successful legislation will represent a compromise among competing views.

JUDICIAL REVIEW AND STATUTORY INTERPRETATION. The constitu-tional provisions empowering Congress and setting limits on legislative power are enforced by the federal courts. Since 1803, when the Supreme Court issued its opinion in *Marbury v. Madison*, the federal courts have assumed the power to review the acts of Congress and the president and to determine their constitutionality. This power of judicial review gives the courts, and ultimately the Supreme Court, the final authority to judge and interpret the meaning of the Constitution. The courts' interpretations of the Constitution serve to limit the policy options that can be considered by Congress and the president. For example, the Supreme Court's interpreta-tion of the freedom of speech provision of the First Amendment bars policies restricting how much of her own money a candidate for elective office can spend on her campaign.

In addition, the federal courts interpret the meaning of laws passed by Congress – statutory interpretation. Individuals, organizations, and govern-ments that are disadvantaged by executive branch interpretations of laws often file suit in federal courts. The courts are asked to resolve ambiguities or conflicting provisions in statutes. For guidance about congressional inten-tions, the courts rely on previous cases, congressional committee reports, the records of floor debate, and other sources on the legislative history of a statute. Court interpretations are often anticipated by legislative players and subsequently shape the legislative language employed by these players. Legislators, in turn, often take court rulings into account when drafting leg-islation.

The powers of judicial review and statutory interpretation are exercised by federal judges who themselves are partially dependent on the legislative players. The Constitution provides that the president appoint judges to the Supreme Court with the consent of the Senate and that Congress may estab-lish federal courts below the Supreme Court. Congress also has required that lower court judges be nominated by the president and confirmed by the Senate. But to protect federal judges from the influence of presidents and members of Congress, the Constitution insulates them from potential

sources of presidential and congressional manipulation by granting them
life terms (although they may be removed by Congress for treason, bribery,
or other high crimes and misdemeanors) and preventing Congress and the
president from reducing their salaries. The effects of these provisions are
discussed in Chapter 10.

Congressional Development

Since the ratification of the Constitution, the United States has been transformed from a small, agrarian nation with little significance in international
affairs to the world's largest industrial power and sole military and political
superpower. The most rapid changes occurred during the industrial revolution of the late nineteenth century, when industry was transformed by new
technologies, many new states were added to the union, modern political
parties took form, and federal policies gained greater significance. These
conditions changed public demands on members of Congress, who in turn
changed their expectations of their institution. By the early twentieth century, many features of the modern Congress had taken form.

The Constitution provided only limited guidance to the House and Senate
concerning how they should organize themselves. The House, according to
the Constitution, shall elect a Speaker to preside, whereas the vice president
shall serve as the Senate's president. The Senate is also authorized to elect
a president pro tempore (or "pro tem") to preside in the absence of the vice
president. And the Constitution requires that the House and Senate pass
legislation by majority vote.

The Constitution says nothing about how legislation is to be prepared for
a vote. Instead, it grants each house the authority to establish its own rules.
Since their origin in 1789, the two houses of Congress have each accumulated rules, procedural precedents, and informally accepted practices that
add up to their own unique legislative process. Because both houses evolved
in the same political environment but each is empowered to establish its
own rules, the two houses have developed similar but not identical legislative processes.

The modern Congress has parties and committees that organize nearly
all of its activities. Nearly all legislation passes through one or more committees in each house. Members of those committees take a leading role in
writing the details of bills, dominate floor debate on those measures, and
represent their house in conference committee negotiations with the other
house. Parties appoint members to committees, give order to floor debate,
and are given proportional representation on conference committees. The
majority party in each house takes the lead in setting the agenda. But the

Congressionally Speaking...

In the context of the legislative process, *rules* can be a confusing term. While the Constitution outlines the basic features of the legislative process, each house of Congress has lengthy rules governing their internal affairs. In addition, Congress has placed rules governing its proceedings in many statutes, such as the Budget Act, which sets a timetable and special procedures for considering budget measures. Standing committees have their own rules, such as rules establishing subcommittees and providing procedures for committee meetings and hearings. Each of the four congressional party organizations (House Democrats and Republicans, Senate Democrats and Republicans) has its own rules to govern the election of party leaders, create party committees, and govern meetings. Chamber, committee, and party rules have been elaborated in many ways in recent decades as reformers have sought to reduce arbitrary rule by committee and party leaders.

Constitution is silent on the role of parties and committees in Congress. Both were created to meet the political needs of the members.

Parties

We now assume that the presiding officer of the House, the Speaker, will be the leader of the majority party and will be responsible for setting the legislative agenda of the House. Similarly, we assume that the Senate's majority leader will set the agenda for that house. But in the early Congresses, no formally recognized party leaders existed. In fact, it took nearly a century for the House to develop something like its modern party-based leadership structure, and the Senate took even longer. The Constitution, of course, is silent on the role of parties in Congress. Congressional parties developed only gradually, as parties outside Congress formed to compete in elections. Politicians and others seeking to get elected or to elect others have always taken the lead in forming political parties. Congressional party organizations have formed among newly elected members of the same party or, as has happened a few times, when sitting members form new parties to compete for reelection. They have varied in strength and influence as the degree of consensus about policy goals and political strategies has varied among their members.

EARLY FOUNDATIONS. Groups of members have collaborated to influence policy outcomes from the beginning. By the time of the Third Congress, shifting coalitions within the legislature had settled into polarized partisan groups, which began making organized efforts to get like-minded individuals elected. These groups were at first led by opposing cabinet officers in the Washington administration (Jefferson and Madison versus Hamilton). For a generation, the parties remained groups of elites, largely members of Congress and executive branch officials who shared party labels – at first, Republicans and Federalists. The congressional and presidential elections of 1800 initiated a period of Republican dominance that lasted until 1824. During that period, when the Federalist party faded away, members had clear party affiliations and gradually developed party caucuses to coordinate party activities. But there were still no formal party leadership posts in the House or Senate.

Speaker Henry Clay (R-Kentucky) was an effective leader, largely by force of personality, during his six nonconsecutive terms (the first starting in 1811). Remarkably, Clay gained the speakership, during his first term, which reflects as much on the weakness of the position as on Clay's popularity among his colleagues. But party factionalism, and sometimes assertive presidents, kept Speakers relatively weak; indeed, small shifts in the balance of power among factions often led to the election of a new Speaker. After Clay, strong personalities and factional leaders served as informally recognized leaders in both houses. Speakers enjoyed the power to make committee assignments, but this ability was insufficient to provide a foundation for party leadership, since the most coveted committee assignments were promised in advance during the multicandidate contests for the speakership itself.

The Senate did not have party leadership positions at all, except for caucus chairmen, whose duties and powers amounted to little more than presiding over caucus meetings. Strong regional leaders, like John C. Calhoun (D-South Carolina), Clay, and Daniel Webster (Whig-Massachusetts), tended to dominate Senate parties without holding formal leadership positions. But the first steps toward more party-based control of the chamber were taken in the middle of the nineteenth century. Conflict over control of standing committees led the parties in 1845 to rely on caucus meetings to prepare committee lists, and in 1847 the Democrats created a "committee on committees" to coordinate the task of making committee assignments for the party. In late 1859, the new Republican party formed its own committee on committees.

PARTY GOVERNMENT. The Civil War was an important turning point in the organization of the parties in Congress. Republicans became the dominant party during the war and began to use task forces and steering committees to coordinate the work of the House and Senate. After the war, the two major parties – now the Republicans and the Democrats – settled into broad regional divisions, with the Republicans powerful in the Northeast and the Midwest and the Democrats dominating the South. House Speakers during the 1860s and 1870s were not particularly strong, but they were the leaders of their parties.

In the early 1890s, under Speaker Thomas Brackett Reed (R-Maine), rulings of the Speaker and new House rules gave the Speaker more power to prevent obstructionism and allowed House majorities to act. These changes, stimulated in part by intensifying partisanship on major issues, firmly established party-based governance in the House. For the next two decades, House decision making was highly centralized and under the control of the majority party's leader, the Speaker. Speakers Reed and "Uncle Joe" Cannon so firmly controlled the flow of legislative business that they were known as "czars." By the end of the first decade of the twentieth century, the press referred to Cannon's heavy-handed style as "Cannonism."

In the Senate, the presiding officer – the vice president – may not share the same party affiliation as the Senate majority and so was never granted powers similar to those of the House speaker. During most of the 1800s, the parties had caucus chairmen but they did not acquire genuine leadership duties until very late in the century. Arthur Pue Gorman (D-Maryland), the Democratic caucus chairman, emerged as his party's floor leader in the 1890s, but Republicans did not follow his example. Instead, by the late 1890s and into the new century, a group of four Republican senators, led by Finance Committee chairman Nelson Aldrich (R-Rhode Island) dominated the party.

"Aldrichism" was sometimes paired with Cannonism in the press, but the absence of rules limiting debate or amendments in the Senate prevented the majority party from changing rules to bolster the authority of its leaders. As a result, minority-party obstructionism was not overcome, as it was in the House. Any change in the rules that disadvantaged the minority party could be filibustered – that is, the minority could prevent a vote on a proposal to change the rules by refusing to conclude debate. Efforts by Aldrich and others to limit filibusters were themselves filibustered. Consequently the ability of even the strongest majority party leaders to bring legislation to a vote was severely constrained by the possibility of a filibuster (see Chapter 7).

THE TWENTIETH CENTURY PATTERN. In the first decade of the twentieth century, a fragmenting Republican party altered congressional party politics for decades to come. Republican reformers in and out of Congress challenged Cannonism and Aldrichism. In 1910, a coalition of insurgent

Republicans and minority-party Democrats forced changes in House rules that substantially reduced the power of the Speaker. The Speaker was stripped of the chairmanship of and power to make appointments to the Rules Committee, which controlled resolutions that put important bills in order on the floor. In the next Congress, with a new Democratic majority, the Speaker's power to make committee assignments was turned over to a party committee.

In the Senate, with few formal chamber or party rules relating to leadership, the fading of Aldrichism was more gradual than was the revolt against Cannon. By the time the Democrats had gained a majority in 1913, no leader dominated either party, although Gorman and his successors as caucus chairs were known as the top party leaders. At a time when his party and the new president, Woodrow Wilson, wanted firmer Senate leadership, John Kern was elected Democratic caucus chairman and, in that capacity, also became known as majority leader, the first recognized majority leader in the Senate. Soon afterward, the Republicans created the position of minority leader, and both parties appointed "whips" to assist the top leaders in managing their parties' business on the floor.

For decades, neither House Speakers nor Senate majority leaders enjoyed the level of influence that Speaker Cannon and Senator Aldrich had possessed at the turn of the century. Committees became more important, as neither party, when in the majority, seriously challenged committee decisions. With a few short-lived exceptions, top party leaders fell into a pattern of supporting and serving the needs of committees more than trying to lead them.

Committees

Members of the first Congresses were influenced by their experiences in the Continental Congress and in their colonial and state legislatures. They devised mechanisms to allow congressional majorities to express their will, while maintaining the equality of all legislators. They preferred that each chamber, as a whole, determine general policy through discussion before entrusting a subgroup of the membership with the responsibility of devising detailed legislation. Because legislators feared that committees with substantial policy discretion and permanence might distort the will of the majority, House committees in the first eight or nine Congresses usually took the form of special or select committees that dissolved when their tasks were completed.

EARLY FOUNDATIONS. The House took the lead in developing the foundations of a standing committee system. By 1810, the House had created 10 standing committees for routine policy areas and for several complex policy areas requiring regular investigation. The practice of referring legislation to a select committee gradually declined thereafter.

In its formative years, the Senate used select committees exclusively on legislative matters; it created only four standing committees to address internal housekeeping matters. A smaller membership, more flexible floor procedures, and a much lighter workload – with the Senate always waiting for the House to act first on legislation – permitted the Senate to use select committees in a wider variety of ways than did the House and still maintain full control over legislation. But beginning in 1806, the Senate adopted the practice of referring to the same committee all matters relating to the subject for which the committee had originally been formed, creating implicit jurisdictions for select committees.

In the 50-year period before the Civil War, the standing committee systems of both houses became institutional fixtures. Both houses of Congress began to rely on standing committees and regularly increased their number. In the House, the number of standing committees increased from 10 to 28 between 1810 and 1825 and to 39 by the beginning of the Civil War. The Senate established its first major standing committees in 1816, when it created 12. It added 10 more by the Civil War.

The expansion of the standing committee systems had roots in both chamber and party needs. A growing workload and regular congressional interaction with an increasing number of executive departments combined to induce committee growth. And the House began to outgrow a floor-centered, decision-making process. The House grew from 64 members in 1789 to 241 in 1833, which made open-ended floor debate quite chaotic.

In the House, partisan considerations were also important. Henry Clay transformed the speakership into a position of policy leadership and increased the partisan significance of committee activity. Rather than allowing the full House to conduct a preliminary debate, Clay preferred to have a reliable group of friendly committee members write legislation. The Speaker's control of committee appointments made this possible. During Clay's era, two procedural changes transformed committees' places in the sequence of the House bill process and further enhanced their value to the Speaker. First, the practice of allowing standing committees to report at their own discretion was codified into the rules of the House in 1822 for a few committees. Second, Clay made referral of legislation to a committee before floor debate the norm. By the late 1830s, after Clay had left the House, all House committees could introduce new legislation and report it to the floor at will. Preliminary debate by the House came to be viewed as a useless procedure. In fact, in 1880 the House adopted a formal rule that required newly introduced legislation to be referred to committee, which meant that the participation of the full membership was reserved for review of committee recommendations.

Changes to the Senate's committee system came at a slower pace. The Senate tended to wait for the House to act first on a bill before it took up a matter, so its workload was not as heavy as the House workload. Additionally, the Senate did not grow as quickly as the House. In 1835, the Senate had only 48 members, fewer members than the House had during the First Congress, and, in sharp contrast to the House, factionalism led senators and their weak party leaders to distrust committees and avoid referral to unfriendly committees. As a result, the Senate's standing committees, with one or two important exceptions, played a relatively insignificant role in the legislative process before the Civil War, and the Senate retained a more floor-centered process.

PARTY CONTROL. In the half-century after the Civil War, the role of committees was strongly influenced by new issues associated with dramatic growth in the size of the nation, further development of American political parties, and the increasing careerism of members. Both houses had a strong tendency to respond to new issues by creating new committees rather than enlarging or reorganizing existing committee jurisdictions. When dealing with important issues, party leaders often liked the opportunity to appoint friendly members to a new committee within their jurisdiction. And committee chairs, who acquired offices and clerks when they were appointed, resisted efforts to eliminate committees. By 1918, the House had acquired nearly 60 committees and the Senate had 74. Nearly half of them had no legislative or investigative business.

These did not lead to a more decentralized Congress. Because of the stabilization of the two-party system and the cohesiveness of the majority-party Republicans in the late 1800s, majority-party leaders of both houses used the established committee systems as tools for asserting control over policy choices. In the House, the period between the Civil War and 1910 brought a series of activist Speakers who aggressively used committee appointments to stack important committees with friendly members, sought and received new bill referral powers, and gave the Rules Committee, which the Speaker chaired, the authority to report resolutions that set the floor agenda. With these powers, the Speaker gained the ability to grant a right-of-way to certain legislation and block other legislation.

Senate organization in the years after the Civil War was dictated by Republicans, who controlled that chamber for all but two Congresses between 1860 and 1913. The Republicans emerged from the war with no party leader or faction capable of controlling the Senate. Relatively independent committees and committee chairs became the dominant force in Senate deliberations. By the late 1890s, however, elections had made the Senate Republicans a smaller but more homogeneous group, with a coterie of like-minded members ascending to leadership positions. This group controlled the chamber's Committee on Committees, which made committee assignments, and the Steering Committee, which controlled floor scheduling. These developments made Senate committees agents of a small set of party leaders.

Party dominance did not last, however. After the revolt against Speaker Cannon in 1910, party cohesiveness and party leaders' ability to direct the legislative process declined substantially. With less central coordination and weaker party leaders, the bloated, fragmented committee systems became intolerable. Besides, the more independent members began to acquire small personal staffs in the 1920s and no longer needed the clerical assistance that came with a committee chair. As a result, both houses eliminated a large number of committees, most of which had been inactive for some time. Some formal links between party leaders and committees were broken as well. Because of reforms within the House Republican party organizations and similar policies adopted by the Democrats, the majority leader no longer chaired a major committee, chairs of major committees could not serve on the party's Steering Committee, and no committee chair could sit on the Rules Committee.

THE MODERN SYSTEM. The broad outline of the modern committee system was determined by the Legislative Reorganization Act of 1946. By 1945, most members shared concerns about the increasing size and expanding power of the executive branch that had come with the New Deal programs of the 1930s and then World War II. Critics noted that the large number of committees and their overlapping jurisdictions resulted in unequal distributions of work and participation among members, caused difficulties in coordination between the House and the Senate, and made oversight of executive agencies difficult. Committees also lacked adequate staff assistance to conduct studies of policy problems and executive branch activities.

The 1946 act reduced the number of standing committees to 19 in the House and 15 in the Senate, by consolidating the jurisdictions of several groups of committees. The standing committees in each house were made nearly equal in size, and the number of committee assignments was reduced to one for most House members and two for most senators. Provisions dealing with regular committee meetings, proxy voting, and committee reports constrained chairs in some ways. But the clear winners were the chairs of the new committees who benefited from expanded committee jurisdictions and the addition of more committee staff, which they would direct. Chairs also continued to control their committees' agendas, subcommittee appointments, the referral of legislation to subcommittees, the management of committee legislation on the floor, and conference delegations.

Committees appeared to be quite autonomous in both chambers for the next decade and a half. Committee chairs exhibited great longevity. More than 60 percent of committee chairs serving between 1947 and 1964 held their position for more than five years, including approximately two dozen who served more than a decade. And, by virtue of southern Democrats' seniority, chairs were disproportionately conservative. Southern Democrats, along with most Republicans, constituted a conservative coalition that used committees to block legislation favored by congressional and administration liberals.

A set of strong, informal norms seemed to govern individual behavior in the 1940s and 1950s. Two norms directly affected committees. First, members were expected to specialize in matters that came before their committees. Second, new members were expected to serve an apprenticeship period, during which they would listen and learn from senior members and refrain from actively participating in committee or floor deliberations. These norms emphasized the development of expertise in the affairs of one's own committee and deference to the assumed expertise of other committees. The collective justification for these norms was that the development of, and deference to, expertise would promote quality legislation. By the mid-1960s, new cohorts of members, particularly liberals, proved unwilling to serve apprenticeships and to defer to conservative committee chairs. Many members began to demand major reforms in congressional operations.

A five-year effort yielded the Legislative Reorganization Act of 1970. It required committees to make public all recorded votes, limited proxy votes, allowed a majority of members to call meetings, and encouraged committees to hold open hearings and meetings. House floor procedures were also affected – primarily by permitting recorded teller votes during the amending process and by authorizing (rather than requiring) the use of electronic voting. These changes made it more difficult for House and Senate committee chairs to camouflage their power in legislative jargon and hide their domination behind closed doors. As we will see, however, the reform movement did not end with the 1970 act. Indeed, the act only set the stage for two decades of change in the role of committees in congressional policy making. The developments of the last two decades are discussed in Chapter 6.

Conclusion

Congress's place in the constitutional scheme of representation and law-making was shaped by the experience with the Continental Congress and the state governments in the years following the Revolutionary War. The Constitution made Congress more powerful than the Continental Congress had been, but it also limited its power by dividing the policy-making process among the two chambers and the presidency and by imposing explicit constraints on the kinds of law that can be made. The Constitution provided only the most rudimentary instructions on how the two houses of Congress were to organize themselves to make law. Gradually, as members struggled to control policy choices and to meet changing demands, legislators created the key features of the modern Congress:

- legislative parties, which gather legislators with common political interests;
- committees, which write the details of most legislation;
- leadership positions in both parties and committees, which are held by elected and appointed legislators who organize most legislative business; and
- rules, which are now very complex and govern the activities of individual legislators, parties, committees, and the parent chambers.

By the 1920s, Congress had taken its modern form, with a full complement of party leaders and standing committees.

Above: Democratic Congressional Campaign Committee Chairman, Rep. Rahm Emanuel (D-Illinois), and Democratic Senatorial Campaign Committee Chairman, Sen. Charles Schumer (D-New York), hold a press conference on election day results before a Democratic rally at a hotel on Capitol Hill in Washington, Tuesday, November 7, 2006. (Chuck Kennedy/MCT)
Below: U.S. Senator-elect Jim Webb (D-Virginia) celebrates during a victory news conference November 9, 2006 in Arlington, Virginia. Webb defeated incumbent U.S. Senator George Allen in the U.S. Senate race for Virginia and helped the Democrats gain control of the Senate

3

Congressional Elections and Policy Alignments

T HE YEAR 2006 WAS A DIFFICULT YEAR FOR CONGRESSIONAL REPUBLICANS. Midterm elections are traditionally tough for the president's party in Congress – especially those occurring in a president's second term. Complicating matters further for Republicans was the very slim majorities that they held in each chamber and the declining popularity of President Bush, based in large part on the public's declining view of the war in Iraq. Additionally, the Republicans had presided over a worsening budget deficit and a lobbying scandal that allegedly involved numerous high-ranking members of the Republican Party. It all added up to a perfect storm blowing strongly in the face of Republican candidates nationwide. Republicans were not without their defenses or "firewalls" as many strategists labeled them. Many endangered Republicans were able to outspend their opponents and the party had a get out the vote (GOTV) campaign that was the envy of the Democratic Party. Ultimately, it was not enough. When the dust settled and the election returns were in, the Democratic Party had added 30 seats in the House and six seats in the Senate – gaining a narrow majority in each chamber for the first time since the 103rd Congress (1993–94) and starting a new period of divided government in the country.

The general policy preferences of the three major institutional players – the House, the Senate, and the president – are a product of elections. Elections are selection devices. They are intended to be competitive processes in which some candidates win and others lose. The winners arrive in Washington with certain personal policy views and an idea of what their supporters expect of them. Collectively, the winners give shape to the balance of policy preferences within the House and Senate and determine the broad contours of agreement and disagreement among the House, the Senate, and the president. Policy alignments change to some degree with each congressional and presidential election.

The connection between elections and policy is far from perfect. For one thing, election outcomes are influenced by factors other than the policy views of voters and candidates – such as personalities and scandals. For another, forces beyond constituency opinion and members' personal views are at work on most issues before Congress. Organized interest groups, expert and editorial opinion, and vote trading can influence policy choices. Moreover, most of the specific policy questions faced by Congress and the president do not arise in election campaigns, yet elections determine whether the same party controls the House, the Senate, and the White House, whether they lean in a liberal or conservative direction, and whether they are likely to agree on major policy questions.

Elections influence the legislative game beyond the party affiliations and policy positions of members of Congress and presidents. Most members seek reelection, and they seek legislative opportunities and resources that will further that goal. As we see in later chapters, the structure and function of virtually every major feature of Congress – committees, parties, rules, personal offices, and staffs – reflect the influence of electoral considerations. As political scientist David Mayhew wrote in 1974, and it is surely more true today, "[I]f a group of planners sat down and tried to design a pair of American national assemblies with the goal of serving members' reelection needs year in and year out, they would be hard pressed to improve on what exists."

Modern candidates for Congress face an electoral system that is highly decentralized and candidate-centered. The system is governed as much by state law as by federal law. Political parties endorse candidates for Congress, but they do not formally control the selection of candidates to run in the general election. Rather, any person who meets basic eligibility requirements may run in a primary election to gain a place on the general election ballot under a party's name. With few exceptions, candidates build their own campaign organizations, raise their own campaign money, and set their own campaign strategies. They do so in 435 different districts and 50 different states, each with a unique blend of economic, social, and political conditions. The winning candidates often emerge from their campaigns with strong individualistic tendencies, which they bring with them to the halls of Congress.

In this chapter we describe the formal rules and informal practices that shape congressional election outcomes. We then look at different types of candidates and at the advantages of incumbency. Next, we will consider national patterns in congressional elections, including the forces underlying divided party control of Congress and the presidency. Finally, we discuss the effect of elections on policy.

The Rules Governing Congressional Elections

More than 2,000 candidates run in congressional primary and general elections in any single election cycle. Their candidacies are governed by a web of rules provided by the Constitution, federal and state law, and, for incumbents, House and Senate rules. The rules have become increasingly complex as Congress and state legislatures, as well as the federal courts, have sought to prevent election fraud, to keep elections fair, and (on occasion) to tilt the rules in favor of one type of candidate or another. The rules concern eligibility for office, filing requirements, campaign finance restrictions, use of congressional staff, and many other matters. By shaping the strategies of candidates seeking election or reelection to Congress, these rules influence election outcomes and the political composition of the House and Senate.

The Constitution: Eligibility, Voting Rights, and Chamber Size

ELIGIBILITY. The Constitution requires that members of both chambers be citizens of the state from which they are elected, though this rule does not always prevent individuals from running to represent states that are not their primary residence. For example, Elizabeth Dole (R-North Carolina) had not lived in the state in decades before winning a Senate seat there in 2002. Members of the House must be 25 years old and must have been a citizen of the United States for seven years, while members of the Senate must be 30 years old and must have been a U.S. citizen for nine years. Candidates may be younger than the age requirements at the time they run for office, although they must have reached the required age before being sworn into office. House members must reside in the state but not necessarily in the district they represent, though most do. Representatives serve two-year terms. Senators serve staggered, six-year terms, with one-third of the seats up for election every second year. Representatives' and senators' terms begin at noon on January 3 following each election or as soon thereafter as the House and Senate may determine by law.

VOTING RIGHTS. The Constitution leaves the "times, places, and manner of holding elections for senators and representatives" to the states, although Congress may enact (and has) certain federal regulations concerning elections. For example, in 1845 Congress fixed the date for congressional and presidential elections as the Tuesday following the first Monday in November, although this change was not fully implemented until 1880. Constitutional amendments have added several rules limiting the ability of states

REPLACING CANDIDATES ON THE BALLOT: VARIATIONS IN STATE LAW

Article I, Section 4 of the U.S. Constitution leaves the "times, places, and manner of holding elections for senators and representatives" to the state legislatures. As a result of this, ballot access laws vary considerably by state. These differences have come to light in recent years as a result of tragedies and scandals affecting ongoing Senate election campaigns.

In Minnesota, tragedy struck on October 25, 2002, as Senator Paul Wellstone, his wife, and several staff members were killed in a plane crash. Senator Wellstone's death occurred less than two weeks before the 2002 general election in which he was seeking reelection to Senate. Minnesota law allows parties to fill ballot vacancies caused by death up to four days prior to the general election. In this case, the Minnesota Democrats' central committee nominated former Senator and Vice President Walter F. Mondale to take Wellstone's place on the ballot. Rather than printing new ballots to reflect the change in the Senate race, Minnesota used a supplementary ballot for the Senate race that had to be counted by hand. This change caused considerable controversy over how to deal with absentee ballots returned prior to Senator Wellstone's death that was settled by the state Supreme Court. Mondale ultimately lost the race to former St. Paul, Minnesota mayor, Norm Coleman.

In Texas, Rep. Tom DeLay (R-Texas) resigned his seat in June 2006 and decided not to seek re-election in 2006. This decision came after he had won the Republican primary in March of 2006, but in the face of declining popularity due to his indictment for fraudulent campaign fundraising. Texas Republicans and DeLay then sought to replace his name on the general election ballot. Texas law did not allow him to be replaced, so DeLay tried to disqualify himself by changing his official residence from Texas to Virginia. A federal court ruled that DeLay could not prove he would not be a resident of Texas and denied his claim. Eventually, DeLay succeeded in getting his name removed from the ballot, but Texas Republicans were not able to name a replacement. Instead, they encouraged voters to cast a write-in ballot for Shelley Sekula-Gibbs. This unconventional name proved difficult for many voters and former Rep. Nick Lampson (D-Texas) won the seat with 51 percent of the vote.

In Florida, Rep. Mark Foley (R-Florida) resigned in late September 2006 and announced he would not seek reelection in 2006 amid charges that he had engaged in improper communications with several congressional pages. Florida law did not permit Foley's name to be removed from the ballot, but it did allow the Republican Party to name a replacement candidate – Joe Negron – who would be credited with all the votes cast for Foley. Having Foley's name on the ballot proved to be too much of an obstacle for Negron and the Republicans lost their hold on the seat despite Negron's "Punch Foley for Joe!" campaign slogan.

to regulate the right to vote in federal elections. The Fourteenth Amendment (ratified in 1868) bars restrictions based on race, color, or previous condition of servitude (slavery); the Nineteenth Amendment (ratified in 1920) bars restrictions based on gender; and the Twenty-fourth Amendment (ratified in 1964) prohibits poll taxes (a tax that must be paid before a person can vote). Most recently, the Twenty-sixth Amendment (ratified in 1971) guaranteed the right to vote to persons 18 years of age or older.

CHAMBER SIZE. By implication, the Constitution sets the size of the Senate – each state has two senators. Since the late 1950s, when Alaska and Hawaii joined the union, the Senate has had 100 members. The Constitution guarantees at least one representative for each state, but the specific size of the House is not dictated by the Constitution and instead is set by law. For more than a century, the House grew as the country's population grew and states were added to the union. Since 1911, federal law has left the House at 435 voting members. With the House's size fixed, a growing population has produced districts of growing size – most districts now contain more than 600,000 citizens, a far cry from the 30,000 originally provided by the Constitution. A House vacancy because of death or any other cause must be filled by a special election, which is called by the state's governor. A Senate vacancy, according to the Seventeenth Amendment, may be filled by election or appointment by the state's governor, as determined by state law. Generally, state laws provide for a temporary appointment followed by an election at the time of the next regularly scheduled federal election to fill the remainder of the term. These appointments can be controversial. Senator Frank Murkowski (R-Alaska) resigned from the Senate upon winning the governorship of Alaska. He subsequently appointed his daughter, Lisa Murkowski, to fill the remaining two years of his term. Charges of nepotism surrounded Ms. Murkowski throughout the remainder of her father's term and her own campaign for the seat in 2004, but she was able to secure a full term for herself by narrowly defeating her Democratic opponent.

Federal Law: Apportionment and Campaign Finance

APPORTIONMENT. After each decennial census, changes in the distribution of population among the states must be reflected in the allocation of House seats. Fifty seats are allocated automatically because of the requirement that each state have at least one representative. But the constitutional requirement that seats "be apportioned among the several states according to their respective numbers" leaves ambiguous how to handle fractions when allocating all other seats. Congress, by law, establishes the formula for apportioning the seats. Population shifts over the past half-century have resulted in a redistribution of power from the industrial Midwest and Northeast to the South and Southwest (see Chapter 1). In addition, since 1967 federal law has required that states with more than one House seat must create districts from which only one representative is elected (single-member districts).

CAMPAIGN FINANCE. The Federal Election Campaign Act (FECA) of 1971, and important amendments to it in 1974 and 1976 created the Federal Election Commission (FEC) and established limits and disclosure requirements for contributions to congressional campaigns. The regulations were a response to scandals involving secret contributions to presidential candidates of large sums of money from wealthy individuals and corporations, some of which was used for underhanded activity. FECA restricted the size of contributions that individuals, parties, and political action committees (PACs) could make to candidates for Congress. FECA created no restrictions on how much congressional candidates may spend, and the Supreme Court has barred limits on how much a candidate or family members may contribute to their own cause. The law required groups and candidates to report contributions and expenditures to the FEC.

Under the law, membership organizations, corporations, and labor unions may create PACs to collect money from organization employees or members in order to pad resources for campaign contributions. Because PACs may contribute more than individuals, there is a strong incentive to create PACs, which grew in number from 608 in late 1974 to more than 4,000 in the mid-1980s and was just over 4,000 in 2003. The largest growth was in PACs tied to corporations, which numbered 1,552 in mid-2003, but growth has occurred in all categories – labor union PACs, trade association PACs, PACs formed by cooperatives, and PACs not connected to any organization.

The limits on contributions reflect a judgment that contributions from the wealthy and corporations may be harmful to the system and that party participation is more desirable. The basic rules on contributions provide that

- individuals may contribute larger sums to candidates and parties than to PACs;
- parties may contribute larger sums directly to candidates than may PACs;
- parties may coordinate a certain amount of spending with candidates, while PACs cannot.

The law emphasizes public disclosure of contributions and expenditures by candidates, parties, and PACs. Full disclosure of all contributions must be made in reports to the FEC, all contributions of more than $50 must be individually recorded, and the identity of donors of $100 or more must be provided. Detailed reports on expenditures are required as well.

FECA has plenty of loopholes, however. Contributions may be bundled, for example, by gathering many individual or PAC contributions and offering them as a package to a candidate. Lobbyists and other interest-group leaders can use bundling, without violating the limits on the size of individual contributions, to make very conspicuous contributions to candidates who might not pay much attention to much smaller, separate contributions. Furthermore, the law did not regulate "soft money" contributions, which by the late 1990s had taken on increasing importance in congressional and presidential campaigns. Soft money was contributed by wealthy individuals and corporations to political parties, to be used for television ads for the party (not specific candidates), party staff and office expenses, voter registration and GOTV efforts, and other purposes that are not directed by, but obviously benefit, the party's candidates. This loophole allowed individuals and PACs that had reached their limit in direct contributions to a candidate's campaign to contribute money to a party organization that can work on the candidate's behalf.

By the late 1990s, many had come to believe that the soft money loophole was allowing candidates, parties, and donors to circumvent the rules established by FECA. After almost a decade of bitter debate, proponents of campaign finance reform, including Senators John McCain (R-Arizona) and Russ Feingold (D-Wisconsin), succeeded in convincing Congress to ban most uses of "soft money" with the Bipartisan Campaign Reform Act of 2002 (BCRA) – sometimes known as "McCain-Feingold." In addition to the ban on soft money, the BCRA increased the amount of hard money that individuals could contribute to campaigns, created exceptions to the hard money limits for candidates facing self-financed candidates, and restricted "issue advocacy" by independent groups in the 60 days prior to an election (see Table 3.1).

A separate loophole was generated by a 1996 Supreme Court ruling that eliminated limits on how much parties could spend on congressional campaigns, as long as the spending was not coordinated with individual candidates' campaigns. The ruling paved the way for a sharp increase in fundraising and spending by the congressional campaign committees. The Senate Republicans immediately set up a special unit to raise funds for these "independent" expenditures. Total expenditures by the parties' congressional and senatorial campaign committees exceeded $900 million for the 2006 election cycle, which was up from just over $500 million in 2004.

TABLE 3.1. Congressional Campaign Contribution Limits under the Bipartisan Campaign Reform Act of 2002, for the 2007–2008 Cycle.

Type of contributor	Limits	Additional provisions and explanations

Limits on Contributions from Individuals	• $2,300 per candidate for primaries
	• $2,300 per candidate for runoff
	• $2,300 per candidate for general election
	• $108,200 total per two-year election cycle
	  ○ $42,700 to candidates
	  ○ $65,500 to parties and PACs
	• unlimited independent
		The $2,300 limit on contributions to a candidate for the general election triples if a House candidate faces a self-financed opponent. A more complex formula raises the limit for Senate races.
		Independent spending is spending by an individual or political action committee for or against candidates without coordinating with a candidate

Limits on Contributions from Political Parties	• $10,000 per House Candidate (Combined National, State, Local) • $39,900 per Senate candidate • Parties can either spend independently or in coordination with a candidate, but not both • National party committees have no limits on donations to state &local party committees ○ 2 cents per voting-age person in the state in coordinated spending.	The Senate limit of $39,900 applies to House candidates in single-district states. Coordinated spending is party spending for services provided to a candidate without coordinating
Limits on Contributions from Political Action Committees (PACs)	• $5,000 per candidate for primaries • $5,000 per candidate for general election • $15,000 per calendar year to a political party ○ unlimited independent spending	Independent spending is spending by an individual or political action committee for or against candidates with a candidate

Source: Federal Election Commission, www.fec.gov.

There are many legal obstacles for any new campaign finance reform law. The Supreme Court ruled in *Buckley v. Valeo* (1976) that the free speech clause of the First Amendment to the Constitution applies to campaign spending. The argument is that individuals and groups must be free to spend money to express themselves. Many observers thought that this interpretation of the First Amendment meant that the Court would not let stand the BCRA restrictions on when groups can spend money to advocate issues. However, the Court initially did just that in *McConnell v. FEC* (2003), on the grounds that the restriction of free speech was minimal and justified by the government's interest in curbing corrupt practices. However, the Court reversed itself in *FEC v. Wisconsin Right to Life* (2007). In a bitterly divided 5–4 opinion, a majority held that the restriction of so called "issue ads" in the weeks prior to an election amounted to unconstitutional censorship. This ruling is likely to increase the amount of corporate and union money used to indirectly campaign for or against candidates – which could effectively circumvent the soft money ban in the BCRA.

Even before the Court gutted many of the restrictions on advertising prior to a campaign, other loopholes in the BCRA had been exploited. Most notably, a number of so called "527" and "501(c)3" groups, named for the section of the tax code that permits their existence, formed during the 2004 election cycle. These groups, with names such as "MoveOn.org," "American Coming Together," and the "Media Fund" spent hundreds of millions of dollars seeking to influence the outcome of the 2004 and 2006 elections. In many ways, these groups filled in the void left by the soft money ban in the BCRA. Much of this money was spent on the 2004 presidential election, but 527 groups spent more than $200 million during the 2006 congressional elections.

THE "MILLIONAIRES' AMENDMENT". The Supreme Court's ruling in *Buckley v. Valeo* (1976) that money spent on gaining political office is protected speech invalidated restrictions on candidates' use of personal wealth that were contained in FECA. In recent years, many candidates for Congress and other offices have spent a considerable amount of their personal fortunes in their quests for office. Jon Corzine (D-New Jersey) is the most notable, having spent in excess of $60 million in his successful quest for the Senate. However, he is not alone. Maria Cantwell (D-Washington), Mark Dayton (D-Minnesota), and Peter Fitzgerald (R-Illinois) each spent in excess of $10 million from personal sources in their successful bids against Senate incumbents. Despite the fact that most self-financed candidates are not successful – Blair Hull spent more than $28 million in a losing effort to capture the Democratic Senate nomination from Illinois in 2004 – many observers have raised questions about the impact of self-financing on the electoral process. Critics argue that self-financing allows the wealthy to "buy elections," thus excluding citizens of more modest means from elective office. For their part, self-financed candidates often argue that by paying for their own campaigns they assure the public that they are not influenced by campaign contributions from organized interests.

The Bipartisan Campaign Reform Act of 2002 (BCRA) addressed the issue of self-financed candidates in the so called "millionaires' amendment." First, the act restricts the amount candidates can raise to repay themselves to $250,000 for loans to their campaign. Advocates of this restriction argue that candidates will be discouraged from self-financing if they cannot repay themselves later. Second, the act allows candidates running against self-financed candidates to raise additional hard money. Under the BCRA, candidates can only accept donations of $2,300 per election from an individual donor, yet if they are facing a self-financed candidate this limit triples for House races and possibly more for Senate races. Advocates point out that this provision will "level the playing field" for candidates facing self-financed opponents.

It is unclear whether these provisions of the BCRA will deter self-financing, as most candidates do not seek repayment for loans made to their campaign, nor is it clear if the provision increasing hard money limits for candidates facing wealthy opponents will withstand legal challenges that it does not treat all candidates equally. It does seem likely, however, that the millionaires' amendment will alter the strategic calculus faced by both wealthy candidates and their potential opponents.

State Law: Redistricting and Primaries

State laws continue to regulate many aspects of congressional elections. They exhibit a bewildering array of provisions. Two sets of state laws – those governing the drawing of district lines and those governing the process of gaining a place on the ballot – are particularly important.

REDISTRICTING. Among the most sensitive issues governed by state laws is the drawing of district lines for House seats. Because the composition of House districts can make the difference between winning and losing, the two major parties and individual politicians, particularly incumbents, often fight fierce battles in state legislatures over the alignment of districts. These battles are renewed at least every 10 years, after the decennial census.

Following the 2000 census, the seven least populous states – Alaska, Delaare, Montana, North Dakota, South Dakota, Vermont, and Wyoming – were each allocated a single at-large House district, so redistricting was not an issue. Of the other states, 37 began by using the normal process of having the state legislature enact redistricting legislation. But in response to the controversial character of redistricting decisions, the other states adopted some special procedures – an independent commission, a combination of commission and legislative action, or some other special rules. Incumbent members of Congress often seek to influence state redistricting decisions, but their influence varies. Redistricting is likely to be most controversial when a state loses one or more seats and must pit incumbent members against one another in consolidated districts.

States face two significant constraints when drawing district lines. First, federal law – the Voting Rights Act – requires certain states to submit their plans to the U.S. Department of Justice or a federal district court for approval before implementing them. These are states where discriminatory barriers to voting were or now may be a problem – a total of 16 in 2001. Since 1982, the Voting Rights Act has barred districting plans that have the effect of diluting the voting power of racial minorities by splitting their vote among districts, even if there is no evidence of deliberate discrimination.

Second, the Supreme Court has moved to set standards to limit certain kinds of gerrymandering – the manipulation of district lines for political purposes – as well as some unintentional districting outcomes. The clearest court directive is that House districts must be equal in population – within a very narrow margin. In addition, the Court indicated in 1986 that districting plans designed to advantage one political group (such as a party) over another may be unconstitutional. But just what constitutes impermissible "political gerrymandering" remains unclear as of the Court's latest decision on the topic, *Vieth v. Jubelirer* (2004), in which the Court did not intervene in the case because it recognized that it could not offer a concise solution.

Racial gerrymandering is another matter. Following the 1990 census, the federal courts at first let stand very oddly shaped congressional districts created to give racial minorities a voting majority. These new districts were critical to the election of more African-Americans and Hispanics to the House of Representatives in 1992. But between 1993 and 2001, the Court made a series of confusing rulings concerning the constitutionality of districts drawn with racial motives. The decisions have forced federal courts to determine whether other factors justified the redrawing of those districts' lines. By 2001, following the new Supreme Court rulings, courts had ordered "majority-minority" districts to be redrawn in Florida, Georgia, Louisiana, New York, North Carolina, Texas, and Virginia.

Political and legal complications abound in redistricting. Failure to adopt a timely redistricting plan or to meet legal standards often leads a federal district court to design and impose a plan. After the 2000 census, federal courts became involved in redistricting in at least 10 states, and state courts became involved in several others. Several states did not have settled district lines until the summer of 2002, forcing some of them to extend the filing deadline for congressional candidates for the 2002 elections.

PRIMARIES. State laws that govern the placement of candidates on the November general election ballot are remarkably varied. All states provide for primary elections as the means for choosing candidates from the two major parties for the November ballot. In 2006, the earliest standard primary elections for House and Senate seats were in California on March 7. The last standard primary was in Hawaii on September 23. But 10 states require that a candidate receive a specified percentage of the primary vote (more than 50 percent in most cases) before being placed on the November ballot; if no candidate wins the specified percentage, a run-off primary election is held soon thereafter.

Furthermore, states vary in the way they regulate voting in primary elections. Most states have closed primaries: Voters must register in advance as either a Republican or a Democrat and may vote only in that party's primary. Open primaries, used in nine states, allow voters to choose to vote in either party's primary at the polling place on election day.

Nearly all states have a system of plurality voting in the general election. That is, the candidate with the most votes wins, even if that candidate receives less than a majority of the total vote. Consequently, if more than two candidates are on the ballot (usually a candidate from each major party, plus minor party candidates), the winner may receive far less than half of the votes.

Louisiana has the most distinctive system. It puts all candidates for a House or Senate seat, regardless of party, in a single primary election. Prior to 1997 this primary occurred in October, and if a candidate received more than 50 percent of the vote, they were elected to office without a general election. If no candidate won a majority, the two candidates with the highest votes share, regardless of party, were placed on the ballot in the November general election. Because only two candidates would compete in the general election, if a general election were necessary, one candidate would win a majority (in the absence of a tie). In late 1997, the Supreme Court struck down the Louisiana primary election law. Because a candidate could be, and often was, elected in the October primary, the Court ruled that the Louisiana law conflicted with the federal law setting the date for congressional elections as the Tuesday following the first Monday of November. Following

THE CHANGING CONGRESS: REDISTRICTING EFFORTS HIGHLIGHT NEW PARTY STRATEGIES

Republicans in the Texas legislature found themselves in the majority for the first time in over 100 years when they convened in 2003. With some urging from then U. S. House Representative Tom DeLay (R-Texas), Texas Republicans began considering various plans to redraw the state's U.S. House districts to increase the number of districts likely to elect Republicans.

The drawing of House district lines is one of the most controversial and partisan issues faced by state legislatures, and the ensuing Texas episode was no exception. Aside from the requirements of equal population and certain restrictions found in the Voting Rights Act, states are free to draw their congressional district lines as they see fit. For much of the early part of the twentieth century, states redrew lines infrequently, if at all. Following the Supreme Court's decision requiring equal population in *Wesberry v. Sanders* (1964), redistricting became a decennial event in states, occurring prior to election years ending in *"2."* Nothing in federal law prohibits states from redrawing districts more frequently; in fact, in the late nineteenth century, states often redrew lines after each legislative election. Ohio, for example, once had six different sets of lines in six consecutive elections.

In the Texas case, Democrats fought the redistricting efforts for much of 2003. On two separate occasions, Senate Democrats fled the state to prevent the quorum necessary to enact the plan. After months of delay, a quorum was eventually attained after one of the Democratic senators relented and came back to Texas. After a skirmish among themselves, Texas Republicans eventually enacted a plan that significantly altered the partisan composition of many districts. The results were drastic for the Texas delegation. In the 108th Congress (2003–2004), Texas sent 17 Democrats and 15 Republicans to the House. Under the new districting system, the 109th Congress began with 20 Republicans and 12 Democrats, a net gain of five seats for the Republican Party.

In the wake of the Texas "re-redistricting" Colorado and Georgia enacted new districting plans. Colorado Republicans attempted to enact a plan that would have increased the proportion of Republicans in their U.S. House delegation, but were rebuffed when the Colorado Supreme Court ruled, and the U.S. Supreme Court affirmed, that Colorado law only permitted redistricting once per decade, while the new Georgia planned produced less net change in their congressional delegation.

this ruling, Louisiana shifted the primary to the date for the general election with a runoff following if no candidate attains a majority.

ELECTION PRACTICE REFORM. In the wake of the 2000 presidential election controversy, Congress sought to expand the federal role in national elections by making it "easier to vote and harder to cheat." Congress enacted legislation in 2002, the Help America Vote Act (HAVA), which authorized almost $4 billion to aid states in improving the mechanics of the election process. Close to $1 billion of this authorization was to assist states in replacing the infamous "punch card" voting machines that were the source of controversy in Florida in 2000, as well as replacing other outdated voting technology. The law also required that states must allow voters to cast "provisional ballots" in federal elections if their registration status is unclear. Upon demonstrating that the voter is properly registered, these provisional ballots are then to be counted as actual votes. The law seeks to reduce voter fraud by requiring identification for first-time voters, and a state-issued identification is now required in order to register to vote.

House and Senate Rules: Office Accounts, Staff, and the Frank

The House and Senate have established rules to limit incumbents' use of their official offices, accounts, staffs, and other privileges for campaign purposes. Generally, incumbents may not use their offices or staffs for campaign purposes. For example, they may not accept campaign contributions in their official offices. Staff members are required to take leave without pay to work on their bosses' campaigns.

Dating back to the first Congress, members have been permitted free use of the mail by using their signatures in place of stamps. The use of their signature, called the frank, is now regulated by a 1973 law that prohibits the use of the frank for purposes "unrelated to the official business, activities, and duties of members" and for "mail matter which specifically solicits political support...or a vote or financial assistance for any candidate for any political office." In 1989, the House limited the number of district wide "postal-patron" mailings that could be sent. The rules forbid explicit partisan and campaign references and allow only a limited number of references to the member per page.

The rules also bar mass mailings within 60 days of a primary or general election in the Senate and within 90 days in the House. Many members still use the frank within the 60-day period for multiple batches of mailings of fewer than 500 pieces each to target certain groups within their districts or states, and members still use the frank more in election years than non-election years. However, the 1989 rule change combined with a further tightening of member allowances in 1995 have reduced the amount of money spent on franked mail from over $100 million in 1988 to less than $20 million in 1999.

Until 1992, House members could send mass mailings at taxpayer expense to individuals living outside their district. Responding to a court ruling of that year, the House banned all mailings to more than 500 persons outside a member's district. The restriction is a problem for members whose districts are redrawn in an election year and seek to quickly communicate with their new constituents. The restriction also constrains members who are contemplating running for a statewide office, such as a Senate seat or governorship, who want to reach a larger electorate.

The Candidates

Personal ambition, more than any other factor, seems to drive people to run for Congress in the modern era. In recent years, party organizations have become very active in recruiting candidates. Interest groups, ranging from environmental groups to women's groups to manufacturing associations, seek candidates who reflect their viewpoint to run for Congress as well. Nevertheless, the initiative for the vast majority of candidacies rests with the candidates themselves. They are self-starters – independent political entrepreneurs who personally assess the costs and benefits then assume the risks of running for Congress.

Conventional wisdom suggests that Congress is an ossified institution filled with well-entrenched incumbents. As usual, conventional wisdom is half right and half wrong. Incumbents are advantaged and usually win reelection when they seek it. But it does not take very many voluntary retirements and electoral defeats in each election for substantial change in the membership to occur over just a few elections. Despite the fact that 90 percent or more of incumbents seek reelection, it takes only a few years for substantial turnover in the membership to occur. In 2003, for example, 245 of the 435 members of the House had been first elected in 1994 or later. In the Senate, 45 of the 100 senators serving in the 107th Congress (2001–2002) had served less than one full six-year term.

Three types of congressional candidates should be distinguished: incumbents seeking reelection, challengers to incumbents, and candidates running in districts or states with an open seat (that is, where the incumbent chose not to run or was defeated in the primary). As Figure 3.1 illustrates, several clear patterns have emerged in recent decades:

- most incumbents run for reelection and win;
- House incumbents are more successful than Senate incumbents in the typical election;

FIGURE 3.1. House and Senate Reelection Rates, 1948–2006. *Sources:* Ornstein et al. Vital Statistics on Congress, 2001–2002; Abramson, Aldrich, and Rohde, Change and Continuity in the 2000 and 2002 Elections. 2004–2006 calculated by the authors. Note: The percentage includes only those seeking reelection.

- in the House, the percentage of incumbents who successfully seek reelection has reached new highs in recent elections.

Clearly, the odds are stacked against challengers, although challengers for Senate seats are more successful as a group than are challengers for House seats. The high rate of success for incumbents seeking reelection has led observers to note an incumbency advantage – something intrinsic to incumbent officeholders, their office and campaign resources, or the electorate that gives incumbents a built-in advantage over challengers.

One indicator of the strength of incumbents' advantage is the percentage of incumbents reelected with at least 60 percent of the vote. As Figure 3.2 indicates, this percentage was higher in the 1980s than in the previous three decades. The percentage dipped in the 1990s when incumbent Democrats suffered losses, but in 2002 and 2004, the percentage was back to levels seen in the late 1980s. This measure can be misleading. Any national shift in voter preferences favoring or hurting the majority party will affect most incumbents' margin of victory even if nothing associated with incumbency played a role – this appears to have been the case in 2006.

A better measure would provide a statistical adjustment for how well the candidate did in the last election and how advantaged or disadvantaged his

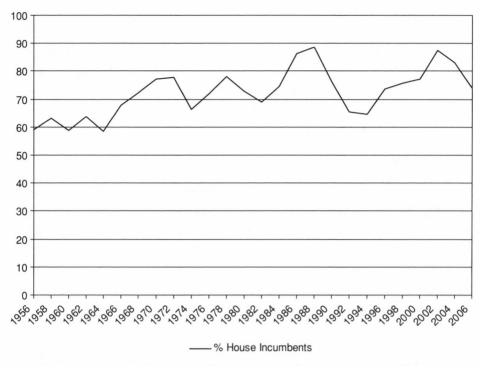

— % House Incumbents

FIGURE 3.2. Percentage of House Incumbents Winning with At Least 60 Percent of the Major Party Vote, 1956–2006. *Source: Collected by authors.*

or her party is nationwide. Such a measure indicates the advantage of incumbency corrected for the local and national advantages enjoyed by the incumbent and his or her party. Using a more refined measure, the House incumbency advantage shifted upward from 1964 to 1966. In the 1950s and early 1960s, the incumbency advantage was something less than five percentage points in most elections. Since then, the incumbency advantage has averaged close to 10 percentage points.

Senators' constituencies are often larger and more diverse than representatives' constituencies, and thus Senate races are often more competitive than House races. Incumbent senators find it more difficult than do incumbent House members to build a large base of support that will sustain them from election to election. The long six-year term may contribute to the inter-election variability in support for senators. Whatever the reason, Senate incumbents face a much higher probability of defeat than do their House counterparts.

In contrast to the pattern in elections involving incumbents, contests for open seats have become more competitive in recent decades. Between 1946 and 1964, only 20.3 percent of House open-seat contests produced a change in the party that controlled the seat; between 1966 and 2000, the percentage rose to close to 30. The trend is sharper in Senate open-seat races – 41.3 percent yielded party change between 1954 and 1964, and more than 50 percent did so between 1966 and 2000. In 2004, seven of the eight open Senate seats saw a change in party control.

Explaining the Incumbency Advantage

Political scientists have worked hard to identify the causes of the declining competition for seats held by incumbents and have discovered that many factors contribute to it. Influences include the declining importance of party identification in voting, an expanding incumbent advantage in campaign resources, more nonpartisan constituency service, imbalances in campaign funding, the quality of the candidates challenging incumbents, and more contact with voters.

The Decline of Party Identification

A major factor in incumbents' success is that their party holds the advantage in the district or state they represent. Democratic constituencies tend to elect and reelect Democrats; Republican constituencies tend to elect and reelect Republicans. For House districts, according to one estimate, the expected vote for incumbents, subtracting the vote attributable to their incumbency has varied from between 55 and 60 percent for most of the period since the late 1940s.

But party is a major element of the story of incumbency. The decline of party identification in the general electorate in the latter half of the twentieth century probably contributed to incumbents' advantage. As voters' psychological attachment to a major party weakened, the proportion of the electorate voting for congressional candidates in a reflexive, partisan way declined. This enlarged pool of "floating" voters and weak partisans produced more ticket splitting. The proportion of the electorate voting for the candidate of one party for one office and the candidate of the other party for another office – whether measured for House-Senate splits or House-president splits – nearly tripled from the 1950s through the 1980s, before declining in recent election cycles.

For congressional incumbents, weak partisanship and ticket splitting presented both danger and opportunity. The danger was that incumbents' natural base of support among fellow partisans was weakened, as there are fewer votes guaranteed for their party. This shift made the electorate more unpredictable. Indeed, for much of the 1960s–1980s there was more election-to-election volatility in incumbents' vote margins than there was in the 1950s – so much more that it nearly offsets the average incumbent's margin of victory. The increase in volatility accounts for the fact that incumbents were receiving a larger share of the vote but not actually winning at a much higher rate.

Expanded Perquisites of Office

The decline in party loyalty in the 1960s–1980s certainly contributed to the incumbency advantage, but incumbents have continued winning even in this era of renewed partisanship. Another important factor is that incumbents exploit their individual resources to combat electorate volatility and expand their base of support into the enlarged pool of independent voters. Their resources, which are discussed in Chapter 4, include a sizable personal staff distributed between their Washington and home offices, their committee staffs, office and stationery budgets, the use of the frank, a travel allowance, access to and influence over the White House and executive agencies, access to the media, and the expertise of the congressional support agencies.

All of these resources have grown since the 1960s and legislators can use them to attract favorable publicity at home. Staff members, often with the assistance of experts in support agencies, help members write legislation and timely amendments that are popular at home. Committee and subcommittee staffs assist their bosses in organizing hearings, some of which are held away from Washington and many of which attract media attention. Stationery allowances and the frank permit members to send mass mailings directly to their districts or states. Travel allowances make it easier for members to return home more frequently to appear before groups. And Congress's own radio and television facilities now permit members to make live and taped appearances on local television more frequently.

Expanded Constituency Service

Incumbents' official resources also can be used to improve their personal standing with their constituents. Additional staff and home offices have allowed members to provide personal services to constituents. Many of these services fall under the heading of "casework" – efforts to solve constituents' and local governments' problems with federal agencies. Perhaps the most common problem involves a constituent's eligibility for social security

Congressionally Speaking...

Political scientists often use the *swing ratio* to gauge the bias of an electoral system. The swing ratio is the percentage change in seats won by a party for a 1 percent increase in its average nationwide vote. In a system of perfect proportional representation, the number of seats a party wins is proportional to the number of votes received, so the swing ratio is 1.0. A party winning 55 percent of the vote, for instance, would win 55 percent of the seats.

For single-member districts, a small percentage increase in the vote for a party may produce a large increase in the number of seats it wins (narrow defeats might be turned into narrow victories). The swing ratio for House elections has been about 2.0 in the twentieth century, indicating that a party gains two seats for each additional one percent of the nationwide vote it gains. The increasing incumbency advantage has reduced the House swing ratio in recent decades. Incumbents, who average more than 60 percent of the vote, can lose 5 or 10 percent of the vote and still retain their seats. This means that the system is less responsive – seat changes are smaller for the same change in nationwide vote.

benefits. The expansion of federal programs since the mid-1960s has fostered this ombudsman role for members. Unlike legislating, which forces legislators to take sides on controversial issues, casework is a nonpartisan activity for which members can gain credit. The emphasis on personal service and de-emphasis on controversial issues facilitate more candidate-oriented and less party-oriented campaign.

Of course, the expansion of members' resources and the growth of constituency service have another side. In a large country with a large, complex federal bureaucracy, members perform a genuine service on behalf of constituents with real problems with government agencies. Legislators often justify their resources on the grounds that they are meeting the needs and expectations of their constituents. It is not surprising that members advertise their good works and get credit from voters for doing them.

Redistricting

One seemingly obvious explanation for the increase in the incumbency advantage is redistricting. With the Supreme Court ruling in *Wesberry v. Sanders* (1964) that districts had to approximate a "one person one vote" standard, many states had to redistrict for the first time in decades. In 1962, Michigan's largest district contained more than 800,000 residents, while the smallest contained less than 200,000. This massive wave of redistricting in the wake of *Wesberry*, is timed almost perfectly with the increase in the incumbency advantage.

For many years political scientists were unable to demonstrate that redistricting in the aftermath of *Wesberry v. Sanders* was responsible for the increased incumbency advantage. Recently, political scientists Gary Cox and Jonathan Katz have demonstrated that redistricting in the 1960s played a significant role. They point out that redistricting was dominated by Democrat-controlled state legislatures and federal courts staffed by Democratic judges. These authorities "packed" Republican voters into a few overwhelmingly Republican districts while spreading Democratic voters across more districts so as to increase the number of seats Democrats could be expected to win. This packing of Republicans produced a large number of seats that were virtually guaranteed to elect Republican members, but decreased competition in many other seats that were controlled by Democrats. Thus, they conclude that the increase in incumbency advantage was largely attributable to this increase in the number of safe Republican seats.

The post-2000 census redistricting has surely contributed to the lack of electoral competition in the 2002 and 2004 elections and helped prevent further Republican losses in 2006. In addition to locking in more Republican seats, this round of redistricting considerably reduced the number of districts with a competitive party balance. By one count, 75 percent of the seats that had been competitive in 2000 were no longer competitive after redistricting. The most extreme of these "incumbency protection acts" was the new districting system in California, where all 53 districts had at least an eight percentage point registration advantage for one party.

Biased Campaign Funding

Changes in campaign finance laws and the introduction of PACs have been a mixed blessing for incumbents. The expanded resources and activities of party committees and PACs create a potential threat to incumbents. By recruiting, funding, and providing campaign services to challengers and even organizing mass mailings and media campaigns against incumbents, PACs and party committees can neutralize some of the advantages of incumbents. Republicans have proved to be especially adept at this strategy, but the Democratic party successfully used this strategy against them in 2006. Rep. Rahm Emmanuel (D-Illinois) and Sen. Charles Schumer (D-New York) successfully recruited and raised funds for many of the candidates who were key to the Democrats gaining a majority in the 2006 elections.

Of course, incumbents generally do not sit idly by as potential challengers are recruited and trained. In fact, by using their committee and subcommittee chairmanships, party posts, and other sources of influence, incumbents have done a good job of staying ahead of challengers. The incumbency advantage over challengers in PAC contributions, as well as in total contributions, is huge and has been growing since the 1970s.

Further, as the competition over majority control in Congress has intensified, the parties themselves have turned more attention to bolstering the resources of their own incumbents. Following the controversy surrounding the impeachment of President Clinton in 1998–99, House Majority Whip Tom DeLay (R-Texas) created a fundraising plan dubbed ROMP (Retain Our Majority Program) in which incumbent Republicans donated over $1.5 million to the campaign funds of Republicans who were thought to be vulnerable during the 2000 election cycle. The stated goal of ROMP was to insure that vulnerable incumbents had enough money to "scare off potential challengers." Democrats instituted a similar program in 2004 called Frontline, which sought to funnel money from members in safe seats to endangered Democratic incumbents. In attempting to keep their newly won majority beyond the 110th Congress (2007–2008), the Democratic party had already identified 29 endangered incumbents for the Frontline program by March of 2007 – more than 18 months ahead of the 2008 election!

The flip side of contributions is expenditures. Figure 3.3 shows the historical record of spending by congressional candidates. The incumbent-challenger spending ratio increased from 1.5:1 in 1978 to 3.7:1 in 1990 for House races and from 1.9:1 to 2.1:1 in Senate races for the same years. By the year 2000, challengers improved their competitiveness, reducing the ratio to 2.2:1 in House contests and 1.6:1 in Senate contests, but in both 2004 and 2006 the ratios were over 4.5. In Senate campaigns, the gap between incumbents and challengers has grown, but generally it is not quite as large as the gap for House campaigns. Expenditures by open-seat candidates for the House show increases that parallel those of incumbents. In fact, open-seat candidate spending consistently runs ahead of incumbent spending. Without an incumbent to scare away candidates, open seat races tend to attract quality candidates and stimulate more spending on both sides.

The fundraising capacity of incumbents gives them a tremendous advantage over challengers. Indeed, incumbents now raise large sums early to deter potential opponents from entering the next race and to protect against unforeseen challenges. Incumbents' emphasis on deterrence and risk avoidance is evidenced in their efforts to raise far more money than they end up

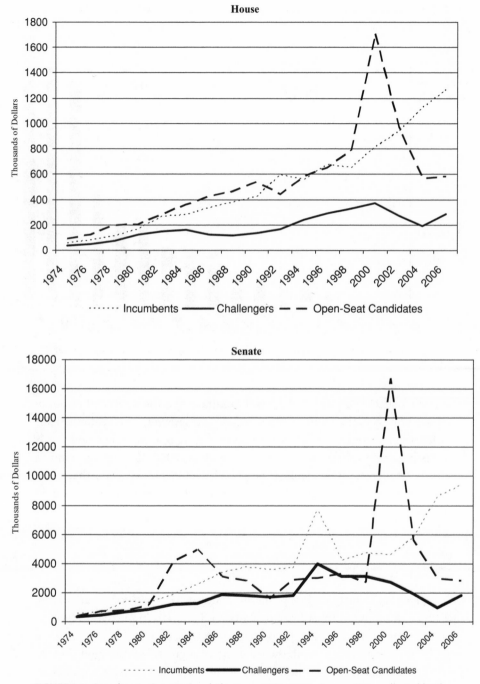

FIGURE 3.3. Spending in Congressional Elections, 1974–2006. *Source:* Data collected by the authors from FEC data and the Center for Responsive Politics.

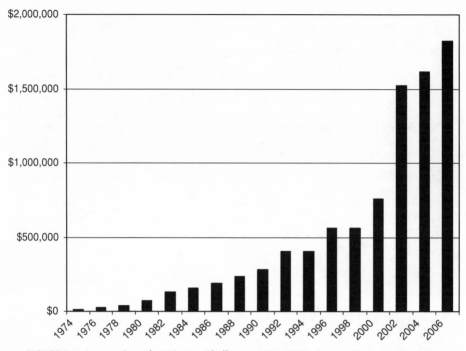

FIGURE 3.4. Average Spent by Winning Challenger, 1974–2006. *Source: Opensecrets.org.*

spending. These surpluses, along with fundraising efforts initiated just after an election, give the incumbents a huge – and growing – head start on any potential challengers for the next election. Figure 3.4 shows just how costly it has become to defeat a House incumbent. In 2000, the average winning House challenger spent approximately $750,000, but by 2006 that number had more than doubled to $1,800,000 – an increase of more than $1 million!

Candidate Quality

Congressional elections are primarily contests between local candidates, each of whom has a mix of personal and political attributes that influences voters' evaluations of them. If one party fails to field a quality candidate, or perhaps any candidate at all, the other party is greatly advantaged. In fact, candidate quality, as measured by candidates' previous political experience, is strongly related to electoral success for both challengers and open-seat candidates. Members of Congress have always known this.

Declining quality among challengers may underpin incumbents' increasing margins of victory in recent decades. Over the past four decades, the quality of challengers has declined, which may be a partial explanation for the growth of incumbent vote margins. Contributors, quite naturally, may have been less willing to give money to candidates who seemed unlikely to win. The party with the best set of challengers typically does a much better job of winning elections in the aggregate. Republicans attracted far more quality candidates to challenge Democratic incumbents in 1994, when they dislodged the Democrats as the majority party, but Democrats were able to turn the tables on them in the 2006 election cycle.

The record in House open-seat contests, in which no incumbents are present to scare off potential opponents, is very different. In recent decades, the quality of open-seat candidates in general elections has improved. By one estimate, the number of high-quality, open-seat candidates (those with experience in elective office) has nearly doubled since the 1950s. This pattern, which contrasts sharply with the pattern for challengers, helps explain why open-seat races have become more competitive as races between incumbents and their challengers have become less competitive.

Contact with Voters

Incumbents' increasing advantage appears to be the product of several mutually reinforcing developments in the electorate's partisanship, incumbents' resources and behavior, campaign finance practices, and the decisions of potential candidates. Note also that scholars have eliminated several other possible explanations for incumbents' increasing vote margins.

The incumbency advantage, the competitiveness of open-seat elections, and House-Senate differences are all revealed by patterns in voters' contacts with candidates. Voters have somewhat more contact with small state Senate incumbents than with House incumbents, but the big difference lies between House and Senate challengers. Voters report far less contact with House challengers than with most Senate challengers, reflecting the vast difference in visibility and campaign resources for challengers at the two levels. In fact, Senate challengers do not lag much behind Senate incumbents in voter contact. One reason for this is the notoriety of many Senate challengers. People of wealth, celebrities, and well-known politicians make up a larger proportion of Senate challengers than House challengers. Many Senate challengers simply have a head start on their House counterparts.

The form of voter contact for which incumbents enjoy the biggest advantage over challengers is contact through the mail. This is true of both House and Senate incumbents, which suggests that incumbents' franking privilege and funding for mass mailings give them an important edge over the competition. Open-seat candidates have more contact with voters than do challengers, but have less contact than do incumbents. This is expected. After all, in comparison with challengers, open-seat candidates tend to be better qualified, more familiar to voters, and more successful at raising campaign funds. For the same reasons, Senate open-seat candidates are more successful than House open-seat candidates in reaching voters.

National Patterns in Congressional Elections

Although the local candidates and their personal and political characteristics are the major determinants of congressional election outcomes, national forces appear to be an influence worth at least several percentage points in some congressional races. Such a small effect may seem quite unimportant, but it is more than enough to determine the outcome in many close contests. The state of the national economy, the public's evaluation of the president's performance, and the public's tendency to be conservative are typically strongly related to which party is most successful in congressional elections. When the economy is weak, the president's performance ratings are low. When the public mood is out of sync with administration policy, candidates of the incumbent president's party are less successful. By influencing the outcome in at least a few races, such forces can shape the partisan and ideological balance in the House and Senate.

National forces may be felt in congressional elections in several ways. Voters and financial contributors sometimes reward or punish congressional candidates for national conditions. To the extent that they do, potential candidates have reason to assess the odds of winning. In any given year, potential candidates of one party may decide to stay out of congressional races when conditions do not seem favorable, reducing the pool of quality candidates that the party is able to field. Weak candidates, of course, attract few contributions, build ineffective campaigns, and are not likely to win. Thus, anticipated and actual choices made by voters, contributors, and potential and actual candidates combine to reward the candidacies of the party credited with good times and to punish the party blamed for bad times.

This description of the influence of national forces has one serious weakness: It cannot account for the frequency of divided party control between Congress and the presidency. The influence of national conditions generally pushes voters in the same direction for congressional and presidential elections. To be sure, idiosyncratic factors – a presidential scandal, for example – might occasionally produce a Congress and president of different parties. And yet, in 17 of the 28 two-year Congresses between 1952 and 2006, divided party control existed. All of the Republican presidents in that period, except George W. Bush, served with a Democratic House and, usually, a Democratic Senate. In 1995–2000, Democratic president Clinton served with a Republican Congress.

It turns out that the effects of national forces, including presidential popularity, on congressional elections are not invariant. In fact, important changes have occurred in recent decades.

Presidential Election Years and the Coattail Effect

The "coattail effect" refers to the ability of popular candidates at the top of the ticket to attract voters to candidates of the same party for other offices. The coattail effect is thought by some to be generated by a spillover process – the popularity of the top candidate becomes associated with all candidates from the same party in the minds of voters. Such coattail effects may amount to rewarding all candidates of the same party for good times (or blaming all candidates of a party for bad times). Or perhaps the party of a strong top candidate, whose strength may come from favorable economic conditions, attracts better candidates for lower offices. Conversely, the pull might actually be in the other direction – popular congressional candidates draw support to their party's presidential candidate. Whatever the mechanism at work, coattails, when they exist, have an important consequence: They produce a change in voting in the same partisan direction for presidential and congressional elections, and they encourage the election of a president and congressional majorities of the same party. The best evidence mustered by political scientists indicates that the presidential coattail effect is irregular but has declined since the mid-twentieth century.

The weakened coattail effect is consistent with the expanded incumbency advantage. Incumbents may have been able to insulate themselves from negative public evaluations of presidents of their own party. They do so by working hard to associate themselves with the needs of their local district or state, distancing themselves from party labels, and advertising their personal attributes. How much they can divorce themselves from their party is limited, however, because they are listed with a party label on most state ballots, and challengers work hard to show the connection when it is advantageous to do so.

Midterm Elections

For congressional elections held in the middle of a presidential term – called midterm elections – there is no concurrent presidential contest. Yet for House midterm races, the number of congressional seats the two parties win is predicted well by the state of the economy and the public's evaluation of the president's performance. But candidates of the president's party are not credited or blamed for economic conditions in midterm contests as much as they are in presidential election years, when the choice of a presidential candidate is also on voters' minds. In Senate midterm elections, economic conditions are even more weakly related to partisan seat gains or losses than they are in the House.

Midterm elections are distinctive for two reasons. First, turnout among voters is lower in midterm elections than in presidential elections. Without the stimulus of a highly visible presidential contest, turnout is often 10 to 15 percentage points lower in a midterm election. In recent midterm elections, less than 40 percent of the nation's adult population has voted. Turnover varies widely among states and districts, however, and surges in midterm election turnout are related to the competitiveness of congressional races. Incumbents must be wary of challengers who can stimulate turnout and create uncertainties about the size and composition of the November electorate in midterm elections.

Second, for most of the twentieth century political scientists could safely predict that the president's party would gain seats in Congress in presidential election years, but lose seats in midterm elections. This pattern held for House seats in every midterm election from 1938–1994 and for Senate seats in all but three midterm elections during the same period. In 1990, for example, the Republicans lost a net of eight House seats and one Senate seat. Between 1946 and 1996, the president's party suffered an average loss of about 24 seats in midterm elections, compared with an average gain of about nine seats in presidential election years.

The election outcomes in 1998 and 2002 bucked this familiar trend. In 1998, Democrats managed to win a net gain of five House seats and lost no Senate seats, whereas in 2002 Republicans gained seven House seats and three Senate seats. The common thread running through both of these elections is that both occurred while the president enjoyed extraordinarily high public approval ratings.

Furthermore, the president's party tends to lose more House seats in the midterm election of the president's second term than in the president's first term. By one estimate, which took into account other factors that influence House elections, the president's party does about twice as poorly in the second term as in the first term. The 2006 election is an excellent example of this as the Republicans, weighed down by an unpopular president, lost 30 seats in the House and 6 in the Senate.

A reasonable explanation of the difficulty confronted by the president's party in midterm elections is the exposure thesis. This thesis holds that the more a party gains in one election above its average or natural level for recent decades, the more seats it is likely to be holding in states and districts that generally favor the other party. The party that gains in a presidential election year becomes vulnerable to losing seats two years later in the midterm election. The number of seats won in the presidential election year that are above the party's average indicates how "exposed" the party will be to seat losses at the midterm. Actual results are influenced by national conditions and the president's popularity.

Congressional Elections and Policy Alignments

Assessing the effects of elections on public policy is tricky. We can never be sure what kinds of policies would have been enacted had the cast of players within Congress and the White House been different. Moreover, some of the factors that influence election outcomes, such as changing public attitudes, directly affect both old and new decision makers and might produce policy changes even if little turnover in Congress occurs. To complicate matters further, we usually cannot determine the policy preferences of members until they cast roll-call votes. This means that we usually cannot distinguish members' policy views immediately after an election from positions they take later on, which are influenced by new events, presidential demands, interest group lobbying, and other political forces.

Even when election results appear to predict future policy directions, there is no simple one-to-one correspondence between election outcomes, the ideological alignment of the three lawmaking institutions, and eventual policy outcomes. For example, the 1986 elections clearly produced a more liberal Senate – Republicans lost eight seats and gave up majority control. But the White House remained in the hands of Ronald Reagan, a conservative Republican president, whose concurrence was required to get liberal legislation favored by Congress enacted into law. Thus, although the Constitution provides the means (elections) for changing the policy views represented in Congress and the White House, it also established rules for the electoral and legislative systems that reduce the chances that changing views will be translated directly and immediately into new public policy.

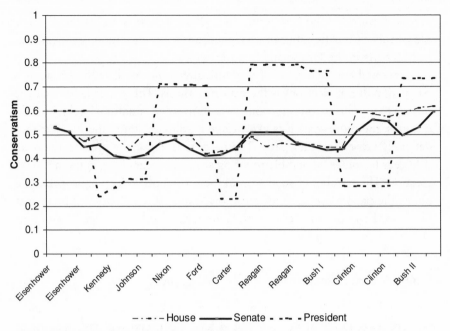

FIGURE 3.5. House, Senate, and Presidential Conservatism, 1955–2006. *Source: Data provided by Keith Poole and Howard Rosenthal,* http://www.pooleandrosenthal.com.

Ideological Outlook

Figure 3.5 demonstrates the effect of elections on the changing ideological position of the House, the Senate, and the presidency in recent decades.[1] High scores indicate a conservative outlook, and low scores indicate a liberal outlook. Not surprisingly, the line for the presidency varies widely as it moves back and forth between Democratic and Republican control. Democratic presidents take a more liberal position than the typical member of the House or Senate, and Republican presidents take a more conservative position. In contrast, the ideological positions of the House and Senate are more stable, which reflects the tendency of single elections to produce only a small change in the overall membership of Congress.

The patterns revealed in Figure 3.5 are consistent with what might be expected. During most of the period since the 1950s, all presidents have faced challenges in gaining cooperation from the two chambers of Congress. As we might expect, Republican presidents Nixon (after his first two years), Ford, Reagan, and Bush differed from the Democratic houses of Congress by a larger margin than did Democratic presidents Kennedy, Johnson, and Carter. Republican President Eisenhower, however, did not differ a great deal from the Democratic Congresses that he faced in the late 1950s.

Moreover, the 1980 and 1986 elections, which produced a change in party control of the Senate, are associated with changes in the ideological placement of the Senate relative to the House and the presidency. The Senate became more like the Republican White House after the 1980 elections, although still not as conservative as the administration. After the 1986 elections, the Senate reverted to its usual place, close to the House, with Presidents Reagan and Bush taking far more conservative positions.

The patterns in Figure 3.5 are important because they show that elections shift the ideological alignment of the three institutional players. They indicate that the House and Senate are usually not too distant from each other, and the president is often the outlier. If left to their own devices, presidents probably would produce more radical shifts in policy than they are allowed to do in the three-player game. Nevertheless, important shifts do occur within Congress as well. For example, Congress moved considerably farther away from President Clinton following the 1994 election, leading to a conflict-ridden six years of divided government, while the 107th through 109th Congresses were very sympathetic to President Bush's legislative agenda. If early indications hold, the 110th Congress will produce two years of acrimony between President Bush and congressional Democrats.

The extended period of divided party control of government under Presidents Ronald Reagan, George H. W. Bush, Bill Clinton, and George W. Bush have rekindled a debate about the policy consequences of divided control of government. Many observers have characterized the period as one of political deadlock: Conservative presidents have checked the initiatives of a liberal Congress, and the liberal Congress has blocked the proposals of conservative presidents (and, under Clinton, vice versa).

Partisan competition exacerbates the already difficult task of gaining agreement among the House, the Senate, and the president. This depiction of the state of American national government has led many critics to recommend radical reforms, so we must know whether it is accurate. Does divided party control of government make any difference?

The Divided-Government Debate

THE MAYHEW THESIS. Political scientist David Mayhew investigated the question of divided control in his book *Divided We Govern*. He examined the frequency of major congressional investigations of the executive branch and the enactment of major legislation for the period between 1947 and 1990. During that period, one party controlled both houses of Congress and the presidency for 18 years and neither party controlled both houses and the presidency for 26 years (including 1981 to 1986, when Republicans

TABLE 3.2. Presidential Success on Roll-Call Votes: The Effect of Divided
Government, 1953–2006.

Unified Government	76.6
	(16)
Divided Government	65.4
	(38)

Percentages reflect average success rates of presidents on roll-calls that they took positions on. Data collected by the authors from *Congressional Quarterly Weekly Report*.

controlled the Senate and White House but not the House). He found that
"unified as opposed to divided control has not made an important difference in recent times" with respect to either the undertaking of high-profile
investigations or the rate at which important laws are enacted. Mayhew concluded that "it does not seem to make all that much difference whether party
control of the American government happens to be unified or divided."

Mayhew's somewhat surprising findings call attention to the forces in
American politics that lead to cooperation between the House, the Senate, and the president. All three institutions must respond to the same
national problems, and they share many constituents. Furthermore, members of Congress and presidents both have strong electoral incentives to
establish a positive record of accomplishment. And even if public opinion
varies greatly among different congressional constituencies, shifts in public mood, which are produced by changing conditions and events, tend to
propel all elected officials in the same direction.

OTHER EVIDENCE. Nevertheless, evidence seems to show that divided
party control does make some difference. To make sense of patterns in the
direction of public policy over time, we must take into account the ideological distance between the House, the Senate, and the president at specific points in time. After all, divided control may not always cause a large
gap between the policy positions of the president and the two chambers
of Congress, nor is it true that unified control insures ideological alignment
between the president and Congress. We have seen that ideological distance
between the House, the Senate, and the president is related to party control. In addition, we can examine direct measures of policy agreement and
disagreement among the three institutions. In fact, three such measures –
the rate of success for presidential proposals, presidential success on congressional roll-call votes (see Table 3.2), and presidential vetoes – show the
expected differences between unified and divided control. The president's
recommendations are adopted less frequently under divided party control,

the president's position on roll-call votes wins less frequently, and the president resorts to the veto more frequently under divided control than under unified control.

Others have pointed out that differences between the president and Congress are not the only causes of legislative gridlock. Factors such as the level of consensus between the two chambers of Congress and within each chamber of Congress, along with the strength of congressional parties are also important determinates of legislative productivity. Scholars have also pointed out that many institutional features of the lawmaking process, such as the bicameral nature of Congress and the two-thirds majority required to override presidential vetoes, impact the lawmaking process as much if not more than partisan affiliation of the players.

A fair conclusion is that the party balance in Congress, a direct product of elections, is an important force among the many different forces that shape relations between the House, the Senate, and the president. Because party control is related, albeit imperfectly, to ideological distance, it affects the degree to which the president's policies are accepted by Congress and vice versa. Other forces are at work as well, and many of them push the House, Senate, and president in the same direction even when partisanship divides the three institutional players.

Conclusion

The electoral arena has changed in important ways in recent decades. New laws and court decisions have greatly complicated the rules governing congressional elections and are sure to continue to do so in the coming years. The power of the president's coattails has declined, PACs have blossomed and gained a critical role in financing campaigns, and parties have taken on a greater role in financing campaigns. Campaigns have become more candidate-centered and less party-oriented, with candidates often spending large sums of their own money to gain a seat. Perhaps most importantly, congressional incumbents, particularly House incumbents, have gained important advantages over challengers.

Although congressional elections are primarily contests between local candidates, they have had critical national consequences. Time and again, national conditions and elections have altered the ideological alignment between the House, the Senate, and the president. Since the mid-twentieth century, elections have regularly produced divided party control of government, which has increased conflict between the branches of government and has made it more difficult to assign credit and blame for government performance.

Above: Newly elected House members pose on the Capitol steps for their freshman class photo following the 2006 elections.
Below: Staff works late into the evening in the Hart Senate Office Building

4

Members, Goals, Resources, and Strategies

I N TODAY'S WORLD, WE MAKE SEVERAL REASONABLE ASSUMPTIONS ABOUT members of Congress. We assume that most of them will seek reelection, and, if they don't, it is because they are seeking another elective office or are retiring. We expect that legislators have the ability to get back to their districts and states on most weekends to attend civic functions and meet with constituents. We take for granted that legislators can answer the mail, deal with the government problems of constituents, and address the policy concerns of House districts that average about 675,000 people and states that average nearly 6 million people.

These assumptions are fairly accurate, but Congress has not always been this way. Only in the last few decades have nearly all legislators sought reelection. In the late 1800s, it was common for two-thirds or less of House members to run for reelection. Even in the 1940s, two out of 10 legislators sat out the next election. But in recent Congresses, 90–95 percent of incumbents sought reelection. Moreover, the technology, resources, and staff required to make frequent trips home and to be responsive to ever-expanding constituencies are of recent vintage. Since the 1950s, office budgets have quadrupled and personal staffs have doubled in size.

This chapter takes a look at Congress from the members' perspective. Legislators exhibit a range of personal goals, but most modern legislators see politics as a career and view reelection as essential to the achievement of their goals. They have granted themselves the resources to pursue their electoral, policy, and other objectives simultaneously. Still, legislators do not pursue all goals all the time, but rather they exploit resources and opportunities selectively. We will see that there are important patterns and generalizations that can be made.

Setting Personal Priorities

Legislators have well-established policy attitudes by the time they arrive in Washington for the first time. For example, most of them can be characterized as liberals, moderates, or conservatives, with some variation on specific issues. Those attitudes are the product of many factors – personal experience, a track record in politics, the necessities of the campaign, and so on. In general, therefore, the voting behavior of most members is quite predictable. And yet members face many decisions for which their general ideological outlook offers little guidance – how to vote on hundreds of roll-call votes on narrow issues, which committee assignments to request, how to allocate staff, which issues to emphasize, and how much time to spend in Washington versus the home state or district. Members' choices about these matters mold their legislative careers.

Members have wide latitude in setting their personal priorities and choosing strategies for pursuing their goals. No party leader or president dictates how members vote, what issues members pursue, how much time members spend in their home districts and states, or how members organize their staffs. To be sure, members are subjected to pressure from leaders, presidents, and many other people and groups, but members of the modern Congress are remarkably free to shape their priorities and determine their own strategies.

There is a catch. Time, staff, and budgets are limited so members must exercise care in allocating their resources. New members face the most difficult choices. They must worry about organizing a staff, selecting and arranging new offices, requesting committee assignments, and responding to appeals from senior members competing for leadership posts – all while trying to find a place to live in a new city. Members do these things with incomplete information. In requesting committee assignments, for example, a member might like to know the career plans of committee and subcommittee leaders: Whether they plan to retire soon or to run for higher office will affect how quickly the member might rise to chair a committee or subcommittee. In hiring staff, a member might like to know what issues will be hot in the coming years so that he or she can appoint people with relevant expertise. In nearly every aspect of setting priorities, a member would like to know who future opponents are likely to be and whether economic and world conditions will favor his or her party. And most members would like to know if and when opportunities to run for higher office will arise. With the passage of time, members gradually resolve some uncertainties, acclimate themselves to others, and settle into routines that reflect their personal priorities, campaign experience, and style.

Members' Goals

Members of Congress tend to be quite purposeful in their professional activities as elected officials. Most of what they do as legislators is connected to some goal or goals – political scientists would label this *instrumental* behavior. They do not always articulate their goals, but they usually can explain how particular decisions affect their own political objectives. Moreover, they usually see connections between their goals and what they do every day. They try to use their limited resources effectively, if not always efficiently, and consciously move toward achieving their personal political goals. To be sure, not every move is calculated, but members generally think and act in ways that make it reasonable to characterize them as strategic politicians.

What are members' goals? For our purposes, focusing on the political goals that members mention when explaining their many decisions makes sense. Political scientist Richard Fenno, in studying differences among members sitting on different committees, found that three categories – reelection, good public policy, and influence – accounted for most of the goals expressed by members.

Reelection

Members of Congress are like the rest of us – most of them want to keep their jobs. They gain personal satisfaction from making contributions to public policy and serving the interests of people they care about, as well as from the prestige of holding high public office. Perhaps a few members like the income, have a craving for power, enjoy the attention given to them by lobbyists and others, or simply like to see themselves on television.

Members face a test for retaining their jobs that the rest of us do not. Periodically, at times fixed by law, they must seek the approval of a very large number of citizens they do not know personally. The opinion voters hold of their representatives and senators can turn on factors beyond the members' personal control. And campaigning, even for members who have won by wide margins in the past, involves a large commitment of time, money, and energy. Most of the rest of us do not face such an extraordinary test to retain our jobs once we have established a career.

We should not be surprised that many, if not most, members make obtaining reelection a high priority in their daily activities. In the view of critics, members care too much about reelection. Some critics assert that members ignore the general welfare of the country while pursuing the narrow interests of financial contributors, the special interests of organized groups, and the parochial interests of their home constituents. Furthermore, critics contend that the reelection drive has become more intense in recent years. Supporters of term limits, in particular, claim that members have become obsessed by reelection, have become excessively insular in their political outlook, and have built up staffs and perks – the resources that come with their office – that virtually ensure their reelection.

Even scholars often assume, at least for the sake of argument, that members are single-minded seekers of reelection. And for good reason: In recent decades nearly all members of Congress seek reelection, and much of what members do is best explained by the drive for reelection. Requesting assignment to committees with jurisdictions affecting their constituents, introducing popular legislation, winning federal funds for projects in their states and districts, solving constituents' problems with federal agencies, evaluating legislation for its impact on their constituencies, and soliciting media attention are common activities that members pursue to enhance their chances of reelection. Political scientist David Mayhew neatly summarized these activities as credit claiming, position taking, and advertising. And political scientist R. Douglas Arnold has shown how congressional leaders take into account the electoral calculations of members when designing strategies for building majority coalitions.

Still, great care must be exercised in declaring reelection to be the sole motivating force of congressional action. Reelection is probably better viewed as a means to an end than as an end in itself. As we see it, people seek election and reelection to Congress primarily because they value membership in Congress in some way. If other goals were not served by membership, or if running for office were too onerous, few people would make the effort. Those other goals, whatever they may be, surely influence members' daily activities as well.

Moreover, reelection plays little role in many decisions and activities of members of Congress. Many committee and floor votes have no consequences for reelection, and actively advocating legislation and building coalitions involves much activity that is unseen and unappreciated at home. David Price, a political scientist and a Democratic representative from North Carolina, explains that "most members of Congress, most of the time, have a great deal of latitude as to how they define their roles and what kind of job they wish to do. If they do not have the latitude, they can often create it, for they have a great deal of control over how their actions are perceived and interpreted."[1]

One way a member gains latitude is to earn the trust of constituents. Political scientist Richard Fenno observes that trust is earned only over time, as a member's constituents come to see him or her as qualified, as a person who

Congressionally Speaking . . .

The *pork barrel* is the term used in politics for local projects funded by Congress. The term is thought to originate in the pre-Civil War practice of serving slaves salted pork in large barrels. When the pork barrels were set out, slaves would rush to grab as much of the pork as possible. In the early twentieth century, journalists began to comment that members of Congress behaved similarly in an effort to distribute pet projects to their constituents.

Each year Congress approves funding for hundreds of local projects ranging from a university building to a youth center to a new dam or bridge. Legislators take credit for the projects by issuing press releases, including stories in their newsletters, and appearing at ground-breaking and opening ceremonies. As nonpartisan public works, almost everyone at home appreciates the "pork" projects and the legislators' efforts, a perfect combination for legislators eager to please voters.

Earmarks are provisions in bills or committee reports that direct funding to individual projects. A 2007 House rule requires committees and other sponsors of legislation to list earmarks and their sponsors in accompanying reports. House members are required to certify that they do not have a personal financial interest at stake in an earmark they sponsor. The Senate voted for similar rules but the ethics reform legislation in which the new rules were placed was not enacted by this writing.

identifies and empathizes with them, and as someone who can defend his or her actions in Washington credibly. In seeking to develop such trust, members develop distinctive "home styles," tailored to their own personalities and skills as well as to the nature of their constituencies.

For one member of the House, Barney Frank (D-Massachusetts), wit has become a trademark. During his reelection campaign of 1992, a year in which a large number of members retired from office, Frank wrote a letter to supporters saying that

> I feel somewhat apologetic about what I am going to tell you: I do not plan to quit Congress. As I read the praise which the media lavishes on my colleagues who are retiring, I'm afraid my eagerness to keep working on a broad range of public policy issues may be taken as a character defect. So I hope that as character defects go, this one will be considered sufficiently minor for you to overlook.[2]

Apparently, it was. Frank was reelected in 1992 with 72 percent of the vote and has been reelected every two years since then.

Nearly all members of Congress seek reelection, so it is reasonable to assume that concern about reelection plays a part in many, if not most, decisions that legislators make. Because it is a goal that must be achieved periodically if a legislator is to continue pursuing other goals in public office, it is not too surprising that reelection dominates all other considerations. Yet for most members, reelection does not explain everything.

Good Public Policy

Among the other goals members pursue is to make good public policy. The cynics are wrong: Most, if not all, members care about the country's future. Many members come to Congress with preexisting policy interests and often are deeply committed to certain policy views. These commitments influence members' committee preferences, staffing decisions, and legislative activities.

A good illustration of a legislator's background shaping his or her legislative interests is Representative Carolyn McCarthy (D-New York), who has developed a national reputation as a staunch advocate of gun control. In 1993, McCarthy's husband was killed and her son seriously injured by a gunman on the Long Island Railroad. When McCarthy's representative, Dan Frisa (R-New York), voted against a federal ban on assault weapons, she decided to run for office. Despite being a lifelong Republican, she ran under the Democratic label in 1996 and won by a decisive margin. Since her initial election to office, McCarthy has fought for stricter gun control laws. She has sponsored or cosponsored dozens of bills proposing more stringent regulation of guns and ammunition. She won reelection five times – with 65 percent of the vote in 2006.

Political scientists have shown that personal experience motivates involvement in the legislative process. For example, studies demonstrate that African American members of the House of Representatives devote more legislative effort to the issues that are particularly important to black Americans even when the composition of their home districts is taken into account. Similar findings are reported for women, although, on the whole, their behavior is not as distinctive as African Americans in Congress. More casual observations about other groups – farmers, veterans, business leaders, and so on – are made with some frequency, too.

Many legislators acquire policy interests, sometimes quite accidentally, while serving in Congress. It could hardly be otherwise. Members are introduced to many subjects in the process of listening to constituents, sitting through committee hearings, and discussing issues with colleagues, staff, and outside experts.

Political Influence

Many members also want political influence. Influence may be an end in itself, or it may be a means for pursuing certain policy goals, constituency interests, or even reelection. Most members try to develop a base of power within Congress so that they have more influence than other members do.

Influence can be acquired in many ways, but earning formal party and committee positions is particularly important in Congress. Party and committee leaders often enjoy certain procedural prerogatives and additional staff, both of which may give them an edge in influencing policy outcomes. Members striving for broad influence pursue party leadership posts by first seeking appointment or election to low-level party positions, in the hope of gaining a top post in the future. Holders of committee and subcommittee chairs also are advantaged, at least within the jurisdiction of their committees and subcommittees. Members also might try to gain a seat on committees with broad and important jurisdictions, such as House Appropriations and Ways and Means. Because the work of these types of committees is important to all members of Congress, and many special interests, a spot on one of them puts a player in a position to help fellow members. As Representative Norm Dicks (D-Washington) described the House Appropriations Committee, "It's where the money is. And money is where the clout is."[3]

Serving Constituents

Many members feel a strong obligation to look out for the interests of their home constituents, even when doing so has little effect on their reelection prospects or when there is little connection between their constituents' needs and their own policy interests. Political scientists have sometimes called the duty to behave in accordance with the wishes of constituents the delegate role. The delegate role is often contrasted with the trustee role, in which the member exercises independent judgment about questions of public policy. Of course, members seldom make a conscious philosophical judgment about whether to act as a delegate or as a trustee. For many members, behaving as a delegate comes naturally, at least on many issues. After all, most members grew up in the districts or states they serve. They often identify and empathize with their constituents, and believe that their constituents deserve good representation. But because their constituents have opinions about only a small fraction of the many policy questions Congress must confront, every member must behave like a trustee much of the time, no matter how committed he or she is to serving constituents' interests.

Political scientist Christopher Cooper and Representative Daniel Lipinski (D-Illinois), a former professor of political science, suggest that members are strategic in communicating to constituents their adherence to the delegate role. Members use rhetoric to signal the extent to which they are a delegate or trustee, although the signal conveyed need not correspond perfectly to legislative behavior. The use of this rhetoric appears to be systematic. Members are more likely to emphasize the delegate role when they are in their first term or when they represent a district that contains a large percentage of blue collar workers, senior citizens, or friendly partisan voters – groups that appear to prefer a more home-oriented form of representation.

Not all constituents are of equal importance to members. It goes without saying that virtually every member would prefer a happy constituent to an unhappy one, but members know that they are choosing which constituents to give priority to when they select their committee assignments, set their personal policy emphases, and cast votes on divisive issues. Members naturally give priority to constituents who supported them when they were forced to make tough choices, and this makes it difficult for the outside observer to distinguish between members who are genuinely committed to their constituents' interests and members who are motivated by reelection alone.

Higher Office

Higher office is on the minds of many members of Congress. They may not see their current position solely as a stepping stone to higher office, but many members are clearly ambitious. In 2006, for example, 11 sitting House members left their seat to run for the Senate or governor. At first glance, this may not appear to be a significant number, but the number accumulates quickly over several elections. Moreover, this number doesn't take into account the number of members who considered running for higher office and decided not to do so, at least for the time being. By one count, a total of 199 House members ran for the Senate between 1960 and 2002. Table 4.1 details the political background of members of the 110th Congress (2007–2008). Progressive ambition is quite apparent. In both chambers, the vast majority of members bring to their current positions experience in elective office. Nearly half of all senators served in the House. And ambition does not stop with

TABLE 4.1. Previous Elective Office of Representatives and Senators, 110th Congress (2007–2008).

Current office	Previous Elective Office						Percent with previous elective office
	U.S. representative	U.S. senator	Governor	State legislator	Mayor	Other elective office	
House of Representatives	–	0	1	222	13	49	65.5
Senate	48	–	7	8	3	17	83.0

Source: Congressional Biographical Directory. Coding done by authors.

the Senate: For the general elections between 1960 and 2004, 24 of the 44 major-party candidates for president and vice president had served in the Senate.

Several factors contribute to a member's decision to run for higher office – comparative value of the higher seat, probability of winning the higher seat, and cost of running for the higher seat. The relative value of seats is obvious in the senators' decisions about future office. Incumbent senators seldom run for small-state governorships but sometimes do run for large-state governorships. The probability of winning is a factor that is frequently illustrated after the redistricting of House seats. House members who find their district lines changed radically anticipate that gaining reelection to their seat may be difficult and often choose to run for higher office.

Legislating

The work of legislating seems to have an intrinsic appeal to many legislators. The legislative game can be fun. Formulating strategies, mastering complicated issues, learning the complexities of the policy-making process, building majority coalitions against talented opponents, making a lasting contribution to public policy, and associating with other bright and energetic people appear to motivate many members. Former senator Dan Quayle (R-Indiana) is a case in point. A close observer of Quayle reports that "in recounting his first year's activities [as a senator] he exuded enthusiasm for legislative work in general. 'I had fun on all of them,' he said after canvassing his first-year interests. 'There was no one highlight. The highlight is getting involved and accomplishing a whole lot of things.' "[4]

Multiple Goals

Most members appear to be motivated by more than one goal. In fact, much of what they do is consistent with pursuing several goals. After all, the more goals served by a particular activity or decision, the more valuable it is likely to be. For example, using a committee hearing to draw attention to a policy problem and to oneself may simultaneously further a member's reelection chances, prospects for higher office, and public policy objectives. Furthermore, the media attention generated by a hearing may help influence colleagues' views about the member's intelligence and leadership ability as well as their views on the issue at hand.

Members can pursue a multifaceted strategy to avoid having to select among competing goals. For example, Senator Norm Coleman (R-Minnesota), a former mayor of St. Paul, sought an assignment on the

Agriculture Committee, which has jurisdiction over farm programs important to large parts of his state, but also gained a seat on the Foreign Relations Committee, where he could pursue issues of personal and national interest.

With limited time, money, and staff, members often face making tradeoffs among goals. Generally, representatives face more severe tradeoffs than senators do. With fewer committee assignments, a smaller staff and office budget, and a shorter term of office, representatives must carefully allocate resources among the various activities they would like to pursue. Fortunately for them, over the past few decades, all members have benefited from an expanding base of resources.

Members' Resources

Pursuing goals requires resources. A member's most important resource is the power to vote – in subcommittee, in committee, on the floor, or in conference. Members also have many nonprocedural resources. As managers of numerous offices – personal, committee, and perhaps even party offices – with their sizable staffs and budgets, members might even be thought of as heading small political enterprises.

Over the long term, a member's resources may expand. As a legislator takes on more important party or committee leadership positions, he or she will gain more influence and additional budget and staff support. Because many committee leadership posts are allocated on the basis of seniority, these additional resources are acquired by winning reelection repeatedly. In this way, the value of a House or Senate seat – to the member and to home constituents – increases with time.

Personal Office and Staff Allowances

For the first time in 1893, the House voted to permit the use of government funds to hire personal staff assistants. Until then, members either paid for assistants with their own funds or relied on family members, usually wives and daughters. Even committee aides were rare until the mid-nineteenth century. Only after office buildings were built adjacent to the Capitol early in the twentieth century did rank-and-file members acquire personal offices. Before then, only top party leaders and committee chairs were given separate rooms in the Capitol.

In the modern Congress, a spending bill for the legislative branch is passed each year. It specifies a certain amount of money for members' personal offices. In recent decades, members in both chambers have been given more discretion over the use of these funds. In 1987, the Senate adopted reforms that consolidated senators' office and staff allowances into a single, fungible account called the Senators' Official Personnel and Office Expense Account (SOPOEA). Whereas the previous system limited the portion of a senator's total personal budget that he or she could allocate to staff or office expenses, the reforms lifted those constraints. Senators now receive a single allowance from which they can determine the mix of resources that best suits their needs. In 1996, the House followed the Senate's lead by putting into place the Members' Representational Allowance (MRA) system. Prior to the MRA, members were required to pay for resources from three separate accounts – the clerk-hire allowance, the official expenses allowance, and the official mail allowance. The MRA puts these allowances under a single, flexible account, and permits members to interchange funds freely.

Although members in both chambers have a single account, the different needs of the members require that components of the accounts be calculated separately. In the House, members are allocated identical amounts for personnel, and are entitled to hire up to 22 employees – 18 full-time and four part-time. That limit is up from eight in 1955, 10 in 1965, and 18 in 1975. Although there are a few restrictions on how office funds may be used, representatives are largely free to allocate staff as they see fit. Members adopt a wide range of strategies in choosing staff (see Table 4.2). The office and mailing expense components of the account vary from member to member depending on a variety factors, such as the cost of traveling to his or her district from Washington, long-distance phone costs to the district, and the cost of renting office space in the district. In 2003, the MRAs ranged from $701,136 to $1,636,750.

In the Senate, there is no explicit limit to the number of staff aides a senator can hire. Personal staff funding varies according to state population. Senators from large states have funding to hire many more staff assistants than do senators from small states. In addition, each senator receives an equal amount of funds above the clerk-hire allowance for the hire of three legislative assistants. Senators also have an official expense allowance to cover office, telephone, travel, and mailing costs. This allowance varies from one Senator to another, as it does in the House. In 2007, these accounts ranged from to $2,653,806 to $4,279,521.

In addition to their personal staffs, many members enjoy sizable staffs in their capacity as committee leaders – chairs or ranking minority members. Committee staffs are particularly important to senators, nearly all of whom are committee or subcommittee leaders. From time to time, members shift

TABLE 4.2. Frequency of Staff Titles in Personal Staff Offices and Location of Staff, 2006.

Position title	Mean number per office	Typical location of staff member
Chief of Staff	1.00	Capitol Hill Office
Counsel	0.05	Capitol Hill Office
Legislative Director	0.78	Capitol Hill Office
Senior Legislative Aide	0.55	Capitol Hill Office
Legislative Assistant	1.28	Capitol Hill Office
Legislative Correspondent	0.55	Capitol Hill Office
Office Manager	0.33	Capitol Hill Office
Press Secretary	0.68	Capitol Hill Office
Executive Assistant	0.23	Capitol Hill Office
Scheduler (D.C.)	0.36	Capitol Hill Office
Systems Administrator	0.13	Capitol Hill Office
Staff Assistant (D.C.)	0.68	Capitol Hill Office
Staff Assistant (District)	0.60	District Office
Constituent Services Representative	1.80	District Office
District Director	0.56	District Office
District Scheduler	0.27	District Office
Field Representative	0.80	District Office
Grants and Projects Coordinator	0.14	District Office

Source: "2006 House Compensation Study," Chief Administrative Officer, U.S. House of Representatives, 2006.

staff between their committee and personal offices in response to changing priorities. The combined personal and committee staffs responsible to a member can be quite large. A large-state senator who chairs a committee can have more than 100 staff assistants reporting to him or her.

The total number of congressional staff workers grew steadily between the 1930s and the 1980s. The 1960s and 1970s marked a period of particularly rapid expansion of personal and committee staff in both chambers. The numbers have remained relatively stable since the early 1980s, as shown in Figure 4.1. The Senate, having a smaller membership, employs fewer total staff, although senators have more personal and committee staff per capita than representatives. In fact, the per capita advantage held by senators is substantial. In 2001, for example, the average senator had approximately 2.4 times more personal staff than the average representative. And the average senator's committee staff was nearly three times as large as the average representative's.

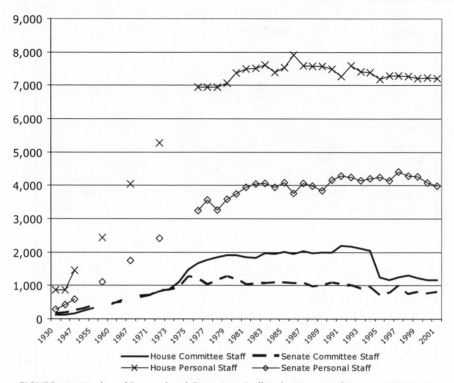

FIGURE 4.1. Number of Personal and Committee Staff in the House and Senate, 1930–2001. *Source:* Harold Stanley and Richard Niemi, *Vital Statistics on American Politics, 2005–2006.* Washington, D.C.: Congressional Quarterly Press. Note: Data unavailable for some years.

One of the first decisions new members face is how to divide their staff between their home and Washington offices. Since the 1960s, as the size of lawmakers' personal staffs has increased, more members have placed staff aides in their home district or state. New members led the way in exploiting larger staff allocations to develop a more visible presence at home. As seen in Figure 4.2, the percentage of personal staff working in district or state offices has gradually increased since 1970. In recent years, just under half of the personal staff of House members and about a third of the personal staff of senators have worked in district or state offices. Members have shifted more responsibility for constituency service to their home office staffs, allowing their Washington staffs to devote more time to legislative and policy work. Senators, with larger staffs, keep a larger percentage of their staff in Washington.

Enlarged staffs have helped members meet increased demands for casework while at the same time more vigorously pursuing their legislative activities in Washington. Of course, members still differ in how they allocate their

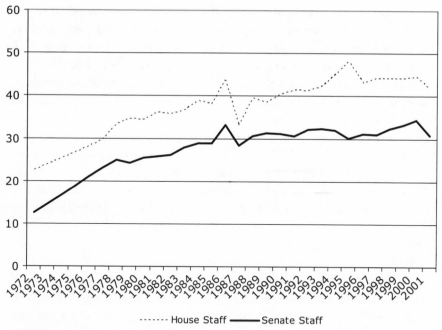

FIGURE 4.2. Percent of Personal Office Staff Located in District or State Offices, 1972–2001. *Source:* Norman Ornstein, Michael Malbin, and Thomas Mann, *Vital Statistics on Congress,* 2001–2002. Washington, D.C.: Congressional Quarterly Press. Updated by authors.

staff resources. First-term members seeking to solidify their hold on their seat often concentrate staff in their district. Senior members, who developed their staffing practices when members could not hire as many assistants and now have greater responsibilities in Washington, often are accustomed to having fewer local offices and tend to devote more staff resources to their Washington offices. In the House, a few committee and party leaders focus their personal staffs almost exclusively on constituency service and rely on committee or leadership staffs for their legislative work.

Travel and Recesses

Just as an increase in staff has reduced the severity of the tradeoffs members must make in setting priorities, expanded travel allowances and official recesses have enabled members to spend more time with constituents at home without fear of missing meetings or votes on Capitol Hill. Since the 1960s, the amount of time incumbents spend in their home districts and states has grown steadily. Before 1970, for example, House and Senate members averaged about two or three days per month at home. By 1980, House members were spending an average of about 10 days each month at home, and senators spent an average of six or seven days a month at home, a pace that they have maintained since then. In general, senior members spend less time in their districts, but members of both houses and at all levels of seniority make more trips home during an election year.

Both the House and the Senate have moved to accommodate members' need to travel to their home districts and states. The House, for example, rarely holds votes on Mondays or Fridays. Members are thus free to fly home on Thursday evenings and return to Washington in time for Tuesday votes. Members of the "Tuesday-Thursday club" can maximize their time at home among constituents without great cost to their performance in Washington. Many members of Congress do not even own or rent homes in the Washington area because they spend only two nights a week there. Several legislators have slept in their offices, sometimes for several years, before finding a residence in the D.C. area.

In both houses, the number of official recess days increased significantly in the late 1960s and has remained high since then. In most years, official recesses now consume more than 100 days, a number that does not include weekends. The houses are in session about as many hours as before, but they now concentrate their sessions into somewhat longer days. Leaders also are more careful in designating recess periods. No committee markups or floor sessions are held during recesses so members know that they are free to go home.

Congressional Mail

Mail is a resource members use to remain visible in their districts between elections. By placing their signature where a stamp would go on an envelope (the "frank"), members of Congress may send mail through the Postal Service. Congressional offices are given budgets for this specific purpose. Members can maintain a presence at home by sending their constituents franked mail at the taxpayers' expense. Since World War II, the amount of mail sent by House and Senate members has grown steadily. Mail totals surge during election years and then drop in off years, a pattern that reflects members' efforts to advertise themselves as elections draw near.

Some of the increase in mail from Capitol Hill in recent decades is due to an increase in opinion letters from constituents and in requests for assistance from congressional offices (casework). As the population grows and constituencies become larger, legislators must respond by mail to a larger volume of demands. But that's only part of the story. Members more actively solicit opinions and casework in their newsletters and personal

THOSE NASTY LETTERS FROM CONSTITUENTS[5]

Most famous among the many witty responses that members and their staff have devised for constituents is the standard reply to critical letters of Ohio Representative Wayne Hays:

Dear Sir:

Today I received a letter from some crackpot who signed your name to it. I thought you ought to know about this before it went further.

appearances – they are happy to be of service to voters. Moreover, most of the increase in outgoing mail is due to the vast increases in mass mailings from members' offices to their home districts and states. In fact, by one estimate, more than 90 percent of the mail sent by Congress consists of mass mailings of newsletters. Critics of congressional incumbents frequently cite the use of the frank for campaign-related publicity as an unfair incumbent advantage, and there is some evidence to support their view. Incumbents argue that newsletters are essential for keeping their constituents informed about members' activities as their representatives.

Other Resources: Party Organizations and Support Agencies

The resources made available to legislators (at public expense) have expanded in many dimensions. A very conspicuous development is the expansion of House and Senate radio and television studios. Legislators use satellite up-link equipment to make appearances on local stations without leaving Capitol Hill. The congressional parties have their own facilities, too. These facilities are used heavily – nearly four out of five House members send regular radio programs to district stations. These programs are aired mostly, if not exclusively, by small-town stations with limited budgets and staff to purchase or produce their own programming. In addition, members sometimes can convince local television stations to use video news releases beamed in from Washington.

The addition and expansion of congressional support agencies (see box, "The Changing Congress") have made more expertise available to members seeking assistance and advice on policy questions. The assistance of policy analysts, scholars, lawyers, and other professionals in the support agencies makes it easier for rank-and-file members without large committee staffs to write bills and amendments, conduct studies, and meet constituents' requests for information.

Members are further aided by the computerization of Capitol Hill. Information networks give members and their staff instant electronic access to the text of bills and amendments, legislative summaries and analyses prepared by the Congressional Research Service, and a variety of databases on economic and social conditions and government programs. Computers also allow members to transmit large volumes of information among their Washington and home offices.

The tremendous expansion of the interest group community in Washington has bolstered rank-and-file members' access to experts and information. By various counts, the number of lobbyists and others employed by interest groups doubled during the 1970s and 1980s, after having grown substantially in the preceding decades. Interest groups regularly distribute information favorable to their causes and make policy and legal expertise available to friendly members. Think tanks – non-profit organizations that produce studies and policy recommendations – also have expanded the availability of expert advice and assistance.

Influences on Members

Members act strategically. Their actions are not only a product of their own preferences and resources but also the actions and anticipated actions of others. Members care about other political actors – constituents, interest groups, party and committee leaders, presidents, and colleagues – because members rely on these players to achieve their goals. Similarly, those other players place demands on members of Congress because members have something those players want: influence over policy choices affecting them. The nature of the demands placed on members is the subject of this section.

Constituencies

Most members share the perspective of most constituents on important issues. This connection between legislators and their constituents is perhaps the most important force in congressional politics. It originates in the process by which legislators are selected. Voters tend to favor candidates whose views are close to their own. Liberal, Democratic districts tend to elect liberal Democrats to Congress, just as conservative, Republican districts tend to elect conservative Republicans. As a result, legislators represent their constituencies' views fairly well simply by following their own political dispositions. In this way, legislators' personal views, the views of their constituents,

THE CHANGING CONGRESS: CONGRESSIONAL SUPPORT AGENCIES

Congress has created a number of support agencies within the legislative branch to provide a variety of functions that are not conveniently provided by standing committees and their staffs. These units serve as nonpartisan servants of Congress and cost more than a half billion dollars each year.

Congressional Budget Office (CBO). Created in 1974, CBO provides economic forecasts, cost estimates for legislation, and other fiscal policy studies. CBO works most closely with the budget, appropriations, and tax committees and has more than 200 employees.

Congressional Research Service (CRS). Created in 1970 from the Legislative Reference Service, CRS provides policy research in nearly all policy areas and functions as a library reference service. CRS has over 700 employees. It responds to requests from committees and individual members and often lends policy experts to committees.

Government Accountability Office (GAO). Created in 1921 as the General Accounting Office, the GAO audits executive branch agencies, sets government accounting standards, settles certain claims against the government, gives legal opinions, and conducts policy studies as requested by formal acts of Congress, committees, and individual members. The GAO was renamed in 2004 (previously the Government Accounting Office) and has over 3,200 employees.

After the Republicans gained new House and Senate majorities in the 1994 elections, Congress closed the Office of Technology Assessment (OTA). OTA, with nearly 150 employees, was created in 1972 to provide analysis of scientific and technical issues.

and even partisanship tend to be mutually reinforcing influences on members' decisions.

Nonetheless, constituents' views are an important parameter in most members' decision-making calculus. Constituents, and more specifically voters, have something members want: votes in the next election. Unfortunately, defining members' constituencies is difficult. After all, the public rarely speaks with one voice and is rarely attuned to what is going on in Congress. Fenno proposes that members' perceive constituents in four categories that can be conceptualized as concentric circles (see box, "Members' Perceived Constituencies"). A member's strongest political friends (intimates) are at the center, and they are encircled by a larger group of constituents who support the member in primary elections. Next is an even larger group that supports the member in general elections, but

MEMBERS' PERCEIVED CONSTITUENCIES

Political scientist Richard F. Fenno, Jr., observes that many members view their
constituencies as a set of concentric circles, ranging from their closest political
confidants (the intimates) to their strongest supporters in the electorate (the
primary constituency), to voters who vote for them (the reelection
constituency), to their whole state or district (the geographic constituency). A
great source of uncertainty for members is the variable composition of the
primary and reelection constituencies.[6]

whose support is more tenuous. The entire district population stands as
the fourth, or geographic, constituency. Fenno observes that legislators
develop styles – home styles, he calls them – for relating to each of these
constituencies.

Concern about how activities in Washington will play at home often pre-
occupies legislators. Members have to anticipate whether a roll-call vote or
other public action will come back to haunt them in a future campaign. Party
and coalition leaders, lobbyists, and presidents seeking support from a member must consider how that member's vote will be regarded back home. All
participants know that high-profile issues – abortion, tax increases, social
security, and congressional pay raises – always attract a more attentive public, whose views must be considered. On some issues, only a narrow constituency takes an interest, but its interest may be so intense that members
are compelled to pay attention to it. On other issues – perhaps, even on most
matters that come before Congress – members need not be overly concerned
about the electoral consequences of their decisions. Still, the uncertainty of
electoral consequences may keep some members guessing about the political costs and benefits at home of their actions.

Representatives and senators have several ways to gauge constituents'
opinions. When a particularly controversial issue comes up, a wave of letters,
phone calls, and emails is likely to flood members' district and Washington
offices. Much of the incoming post takes the form of preprinted letters or

cards supplied by lobbying groups. Because it takes little effort to send that kind of mail, legislators may not put much stock in it. Still, members are attentive to groups of constituents with intensely held preferences. In such cases, members usually take note of where the letters are coming from and bear in mind the level of interest expressed.

Members also learn constituents' opinions from interacting with them at home and in Washington. Most members hold town meetings or other forums in their district to give constituents a way to express their views. While at home, attentive members are almost always asking questions of and listening to their constituents. And in Washington, many members schedule regular events, such as weekly coffee, to provide an additional outlet for constituents to voice their opinions. The internet has facilitated the interaction between members and constituents by reducing the need for the two to communicate in person (see box, "Changing Congress"). With increasing frequency, legislators commission public opinion polls with campaign funds, most often at campaign time.

Interest Groups and Lobbyists

For many people, lobbyists and interest groups represent the unseemly, even corrupt, side of congressional politics. "Money talks," "the best Congress money can buy," and "the golden rule of politics – whoever has the gold rules" – are among the clichés that capture common fears about who really runs Congress. Just where the line between legitimate representation and bribery falls is one of the ambiguities confronting every democratic system of government. On the one hand, lobbying is protected by constitutional guarantees of free speech, free association, and the right to petition the government for redress of grievances. Lobbying often involves building support for a position by bargaining, providing assistance to legislators, and even providing timely campaign contributions. On the other hand, lobbying can cross the line into bribery when cash or other material considerations are traded for certain official actions, such as introducing a bill or casting a particular vote. The whole business of lobbying seems tainted to many.

Perhaps the most important change in Washington in recent decades has been the great expansion and fragmentation of Washington's interest group community. The best study of the subject indicates that most interest groups were formed after World War II, that the formation of groups has accelerated in recent decades, and that more and more groups are locating in Washington, D.C. (see Chapter 11). Many single-issue groups have been created and nearly every industry group has professional representation in Congress. In the health care industry, for example, the older American

THE CHANGING CONGRESS: MEMBERS AND THE WORLD WIDE WEB

The Internet has become an invaluable resource to members of Congress, as it provides a relatively low cost means of interacting with constituents. In addition, it offers members another platform for disseminating an image or message. Member websites have proliferated over a reasonably short period of time. Today, every member of Congress has a website and many of them are quite sophisticated. While there is considerable variation in website features, a common feature is an email form for constituents to communicate with their member.

Not surprisingly, large volumes of e-mail pour into Capitol Hill computer networks every day. Each house receives more than 100 million e-mails directed to legislators' personal offices each year. When email became popular in the 1990s, congressional offices were not prepared to deal with it. Most offices sent automatic responses saying that they could not respond to email, and the writer should send a letter by regular mail. That has changed. According to a 2001 survey of House offices, more than a quarter of members' offices were responding to email with individualized email responses.

Medical Association is joined by associations for hospitals, medical schools, medical equipment manufacturers, health insurance companies, and a variety of professional associations of nurses, dentists, and others.

Particularly noteworthy is the rise of "citizens' groups" or "public interest groups," groups organized around a general cause rather than a narrow economic interest. Good-government groups such as Common Cause, environmental groups such as the Sierra Club, and consumer product groups such as the Consumers' Union are examples. About one-fifth of all lobbying groups counted in 1980 were citizens' groups. In addition, more corporations, state and local governments, universities, and other organizations have established Washington offices for in-house lobbyists. By one estimate, the number of corporations with Washington offices increased tenfold between 1961 and 1982. One consequence of this expansion in Washington-based representation of organized interests is that the clout of individual lobbyists and groups has actually declined. Often, large coalitions of lobbyists and interest groups pool their resources to overcome the fragmentation in the interest group community.

Party Leaders

Party pressures in congressional politics are weaker in the United States than in most other national legislatures. Representatives and senators rarely are dependent on party organizations – national or local – to secure reelection. Moreover, party leaders in Congress have relatively few ways to compel rank-and-file members to comply with their wishes. Indeed, party leaders generally want their party colleagues to pursue legislative strategies that will enhance their chances of reelection. When members of a congressional party vote in unison, it is due more to their shared policy views and similar constituency expectations than to pressure from party leaders.

Still, partisan pressures are ever-present in Congress. Many decisions members make have no direct electoral consequences so members are free to meet the demands of party leaders. The high level of party loyalty on procedural matters provides some evidence of this. Moreover, much of the influence of party on legislators' behavior is indirect. For example, party leaders set the floor agenda and, particularly in the House, shape the alternatives from which members must choose. But occasionally, particularly on close votes, the direct pressure of party leaders can be critical. Even then, the leaders target just a few members whose votes will make the difference between winning and losing.

The President

Presidents need support from legislators for their own legislative programs, and they can wield considerable influence in their efforts to gain it. Much of the support presidents get from lawmakers comes from their partisan ties to members. Because members' own electoral fortunes are affected by the popularity of the president, members of the president's party have a stake in the president's success and thus provide a natural base of support. The size of that base of support depends on past congressional election outcomes, the diversity within party coalitions, and the president's popularity. Every member must decide when to stick with the president and when it is safe to ignore the president's wishes.

Presidents also influence members' choices by influencing the congressional agenda. By pushing major legislative proposals, presidents can help define the issues that dominate the congressional agenda and how the major alternatives are debated. A successful president draws the attention of the media, the public, and legislators away from issues that hurt him and toward issues that help him. An effective president also knows that his influence over the congressional agenda is tenuous. Presidents, after all, cannot require either house of Congress to vote on their proposals, or to even take their proposals seriously.

The task of presidents is primarily one of persuasion. Presidents have a variety of tools for influencing individual legislators (see Chapter 9).

Presidents' primary source of influence is their formal power to sign or veto legislation, which gives them a source of leverage over members who want to see their own legislation enacted into law. Presidents' ease of access to the media gives them an advantage over members and other players in shaping public opinion. In addition, their influence on agency decisions that affect many interests gives presidents more clout. That clout can be used to coax interest groups to work in support of presidents' legislative proposals or to prod legislators whose constituents are affected by executive branch decisions.

Staff

A popular theory is that members of Congress have been captured by their staffs. Michael Malbin's book, *Unelected Representatives*, lends credence to this view. Malbin, a political scientist who worked for many years as a Capitol Hill reporter and staff member, argues that "the staffs – individually well educated, hard working, and, in general, devoted to what they perceive to be the public good – collectively create a situation in which many of the elected members fear they are becoming insulated administrators in a bureaucratized organization that leaves them no better able to cope than they were when they did all the work themselves."[7] Malbin observes that staff assistants do a good job of representing their bosses, but, he continues, members delegate to their aides too much authority to initiate legislation, negotiate compromises, and narrow the range of policy choices offered to them. Staff assistants have created more work for members, distanced members from one another, and turned members into office managers. Staff influence is pervasive: It is felt both in the early stages of the legislative process, in the setting of members' and committees' agendas and at the late stages when the final details of legislation are worked out (see accompanying box for more information on types of congressional staff).

Choosing Strategies

Political scientists have no comprehensive theory to explain how members' goals, resources, and political environment combine to produce their strategies. Nevertheless, they have done a reasonably good job of describing and explaining members' behavior in one decision-making arena: roll-call voting on the floor. A newer area of research looks at policy leaders' coalition-building strategies, which focuses on how members solicit support from their colleagues. This section briefly reviews what we know about the typical

TYPES OF CONGRESSIONAL STAFF

There are numerous types of congressional staff. Because legislators organize their own office staffs, there is tremendous variation in organization and titles. Some positions (i.e., legislative counsel) are quite rare in personal offices but quite common in committee staffs. Among the most common types of staff positions on Capitol Hill are chief of staff, legislative director (LD), legislative assistant (LA), constituent services representative or caseworker, and legislative correspondent (LC).

The top personal aide to a member is usually a chief of staff or administrative assistant (AA). This position oversees the entire operation and manages all staff. The legislative director supervises the policy staff and typically works closely with the member to devise legislative strategies. Legislative assistants are responsible for the legislator's work on specified policy areas and assist with committee work. Those charged with responding to constituent communications are often given the title of legislative correspondent.

All personal offices have constituent service representatives or caseworkers. These assistants are primarily dedicated to *casework*, the term used to describe constituents' problems that members are asked to solve. Casework ranges from getting a problem with social security checks solved to arranging for a leave for a soldier who just had a death in the family. These assistants usually are located in district or state offices where they can deal with constituents directly. They communicate electronically with federal agencies and the Capitol Hill office. Most legislators consider an effective caseworker essential to building a good reputation.

member's approach to roll-call voting and coalition leadership and contrasts the strategies in these two areas of legislative activity.

Roll-Call Voting on the Floor

Casting roll-call votes is one activity members consider mandatory. Members want a good attendance record so that future opponents will not be able to charge that they are shirking their responsibilities. Maintaining a good attendance record is not easy, and maintaining a perfect record is nearly impossible. In recent Congresses, the average member voted on about 95 percent of the roll-call votes held, which have numbered between 500 and 1,000 per Congress. Plainly, members are forced to cast votes with such frequency that they cannot possibly study each issue with care. Yet, they are aware that they may have to explain a vote to some constituents, perhaps in response to a challenger's charges in some future campaign, or to some party or committee leader. Therefore, most members develop a general strategy for how to approach roll-call voting.

From time to time, members are confronted with particularly difficult choices. Representative Robin Hayes (R-North Carolina) encountered such a situation in 2005 during consideration of the Central American Free Trade Agreement (CAFTA). The textile industry, a leading industry in Hayes' district, had been hit hard throughout North Carolina in recent years. Many observers blamed the industry's hardships on the earlier North American Free Trade Agreement (NAFTA). Further trade liberalization was viewed by many, including Hayes, as a detriment to the already struggling textile industry. A week before the vote on CAFTA Hayes emphatically stated, "It's not in the best interests of the core constituency I represent. Every time I drive through Kannapolis and see those empty plants, I know there is no way I could vote for CAFTA."[8]

When the vote over CAFTA took place on the House floor, Hayes immediately voted against the measure. After the official 15-minute time limit on the vote had ended, Republican leaders realized that they were going to come up short on votes. A loss on the legislation would hand the Republican administration an embarrassing defeat, as CAFTA was a White House priority. Holding the vote open for roughly one hour, Republican leaders proceeded to put intense pressure on Hayes to switch his vote. Then-Speaker Hastert (R-Illinois) cornered Hayes telling him, "We have to have your vote."[9] The circumstances forced Hayes to make an uncomfortable choice between his party and constituents. Despite the earlier promises made, the noticeably distraught Hayes switched his vote to hand the Republicans a 217–215 victory. The great drama of Hayes' predicament is not a common occurrence, but members are sometimes called on to cast difficult votes.

Political scientist John Kingdon conducted an ingenious study of the vote decision. Kingdon interviewed members about how they had made up their minds on a series of fairly important votes on controversial issues that had been the subject of substantial political activity. Kingdon asked a simple question about each vote: "How did you go about making up your mind?" He then noted whether the members mentioned their constituencies spontaneously, only in response to a follow-up question, or not at all. For most members, the votes concerned issues that fell under the jurisdiction of committees on which they did not sit. Thus, most members interviewed by Kingdon had not had the benefit of listening to expert testimony in hearings.

TABLE 4.3. The Frequency with which Legislators Mentioned Political Actors as Factors in Their Voting Decisions (Percent of Voting Decisions).

| | Political actors involved in vote decision | | | | |
	Constituency	Fellow members	Interest groups	Administration	Party leaders
Mentioned Spontaneously	37	40	31	25	10
Mentioned in response to a question	50	35	35	14	28
Not Mentioned	13	25	35	60	62

Source: Kingdon, John. 1981. *Congressmen's Voting Decisions*, 2nd ed. New York: Harper & Row.

Members' responses to Kingdon's questions show several important patterns (see Table 4.3). First, constituency considerations are frequently involved but are not always the most important factor. Members mentioned constituencies spontaneously 37 percent of the time. While members spontaneously mentioned fellow members more frequently than constituents, constituents ranked above every other group in this category. Members mentioned constituencies in response to probes 50 percent of the time and failed to mention constituencies altogether only 13 percent of the time.

Kingdon also found that the more salient the issue, the more likely members were to consider constituents' wishes to be of major importance in making their decisions. Consequently, they were more likely to vote in agreement with the constituency opinion they identified. Nevertheless, even on issues of low or medium salience, members were likely to give weight to, and vote in agreement with, constituency opinion. On most issues, members rely on trusted colleagues for cues about how to vote. In response to Kingdon's questions about their voting decisions, members mentioned their colleagues either spontaneously or after prompting 75 percent of the time (Table 4.3). As one member noted, "On a run-of-the-mill vote, on an obscure bill, you need some guidance. You don't know what's in it, and don't have time to find out."[10] Fellow members serve as informants who reduce uncertainty about the policy and political implications of a roll-call vote.

With so many staff assistants and lobbyists circulating on Capitol Hill, why do members rely so heavily on one another? Members turn to certain colleagues because they trust that their fellow representatives and senators, professional politicians with problems similar to their own, will make comparable calculations about which course of action to pursue. Indeed, members tend to rely on colleagues from the same party, state, and region – colleagues who can help them assess the political consequences of their votes – and committee members who know the issue well. Fellow legislators also are in the right place at the right time – on the floor as roll-call votes are being conducted.

Members obtain guidance from fellow members in many ways. One way is to read the "Dear Colleague" letters that are routinely sent to all members, explaining bills and soliciting support for amendments. These letters are usually concise arguments in favor of a bill, and they often explain how a bill's opponents plan to distort the bill's true intent. For more detailed information on a bill, members or their staffs are likely to turn to the written reports that accompany most bills when they are reported by committee.

After constituents and fellow members, interest groups and the administration rank as the most important influences on members' voting decisions. Most interest group influence, Kingdon found, came from groups connected to members' constituencies. For example, farm groups played an important role for members from agricultural districts. Presidential influence is greater for members of the president's party – members who are politically connected to the president and have the highest stakes in the president's success.

Finally, party leaders and staff aides appear to have influence only at the margins. In more recent years, party leaders probably have become more important than Kingdon found in the late 1960s, when he conducted his study (Chapter 5 describes the revitalization of party leadership in Congress). Similarly, as roll-call votes have become more numerous, other burdens on members' time have grown, and staffs have expanded in the decades since Kingdon's study. Thus, members may have become more dependent on staff assistants for guidance.

In summary, members adopt strategies in response to the unique character of individual voting decisions. Roll-call voting is repetitive, very public, consumes little time and few resources, is well documented, and is considered politically compulsory. Members rely on cues from colleagues to simplify their decision-making process and assess the political risks of specific votes. Members appear to be heavily influenced by constituency opinion and electoral considerations, which they assess by seeking advice from trusted colleagues and information from interest groups. At the same time, constituency considerations are seldom the sole or even the decisive influence on members' votes.

Coalition Leadership

Serving as a coalition leader on a legislative issue lies at the other end of the spectrum of legislative activities. In contrast to roll-call voting, assuming a leadership role on an issue may not be very visible to the general public, is difficult to document, consumes more time and resources, and is normally discretionary. Consequently, the strategies of policy leaders may be shaped by a different mix of considerations than are voting decisions.

Political scientist David Mayhew observes that the goal of reelection, although nearly universally held by members, motivates little leadership activity within Congress. The effort to mobilize colleagues for or against legislation is worthwhile for a reelection-oriented member only if constituents or important financial contributors are paying close attention to the member's behavior. On most matters, merely advertising one's position and token efforts – citing speeches made, legislation introduced, and amendments offered – may be all that is required to receive maximum electoral benefit from an issue. Certainly, members do not actually have to win legislative battles as long as the people who affect their reelection prospects – people with votes, money, or endorsements – believe they have put up a good fight.

If Mayhew is right, most genuine leadership is motivated by goals beyond reelection. A member aspiring to higher office may seek special distinction and media attention by championing a legislative cause. A committee chair, seeking to preserve a reputation for influence, may assume the lead in writing legislation and soliciting support simply to avoid being overshadowed by a rank-and-file member who would otherwise take over. That same rank-and-file member may pursue a policy leadership role because no one else seems equally committed to his or her policy views.

Senator Pete Domenici (R-New Mexico), who is a prominent legislator in budgeting and fiscal policy, is a good example of a policy leader motivated by objectives beyond reelection. Fenno, in his book about Domenici's rise as a Senate leader, explains:

> From the beginning of his Washington career, Pete Domenici's most transparent goal was to become a policy-making "player" inside the Senate. The chairmanship [of the Budget Committee] brought him that influence. His first two years in that position, he said later, "made me a senator." He wanted to keep or expand the policy influence he had gained. A second goal – institutional maintenance – has been imposed on him by this chairmanship. And Domenici adopted that one, too – to protect and to preserve the budget process itself. The two goals did not always lead to the same decision.... In the two years ahead, he would

often be forced to choose between his desire for inside policy influence and his desire to keep the budget process alive.[11]

Domenici's reelection prospects, Fenno recounts, were greatly enhanced by his prominence in the Senate. He won reelection easily in 1984, 1990, 1996, and again in 2002, with vote shares of at least 65 percent. Domenici's success as Budget Committee chair led him to run for party leader in late 1985, but Robert Dole won the post.

Domenici's story seems typical in many respects. Electoral concerns did not seem to drive his leadership activity in Washington, even though that activity paid dividends at home. Similarly, Domenici's run for the top party leadership spot did not appear to drive his strategies as Budget chair, although his service as chair positioned him for the leadership race. Thus, partly by good fortune and partly by personal skill and dedication, Domenici's multiple goals of obtaining influence, making good public policy, and gaining reelection were served by his leadership activities. And yet his goal of reelection cannot account for the priority he gave to his chairmanship and the legislative tactics he pursued as chairman.

Some relevant evidence about members' goals in pursuing leadership responsibilities is available. In one study, a political scientist asked top legislative aides of a sample of 121 members of both houses to identify issues on which their boss had taken a central leadership role and to offer explanations for their boss's involvement in those issues.[12] All aides reported that their boss had taken a leading role on some issue, large or small. But few members had taken on more than two or three issues at one time. Senators' aides tended to mention more issues than did representatives' aides, reflecting important differences between the two chambers. In the Senate, members have more committee assignments and staff, and they receive more demands from larger, more diverse constituencies.

For each issue the aides mentioned, the researcher asked them, "Why did (Senator/Representative----) take the lead on this issue?" They often mentioned several reasons. For 52 percent of the issues mentioned, they noted the importance of the issue to the member's district or state, although for only 17 percent was reelection or some other constituency-related reason the sole motivation mentioned. For 72 percent of the instances of policy leadership described, the aides mentioned their boss's personal interest or policy commitments as a motivating factor. In addition, 28 percent of the issues pursued by members were related to their responsibilities as committee or subcommittee leaders. Only 3 percent of the instances of policy leadership were described as being connected to a member's pursuit of higher office.

We are led to this conjecture: Leaders – whether they are party, committee, or self-identified coalition leaders – are motivated by more than reelection, whereas their followers are motivated primarily by reelection. Followers, most of whom are not sufficiently motivated to assume a leadership role on most issues, allow their default goal – reelection – to orient their behavior. Of course, if members' reelection prospects seem unaffected by a particular issue, as they often are, they are free to pursue policy positions for other reasons. Nevertheless, it seems fair to say, coalition building on most important issues typically involves interaction between policy- or influence-oriented leaders and reelection-oriented followers.

Concluding that members ignore their reelection interests when they pursue other objectives would be a mistake. On the contrary, members often discover issues that fit them well – issues that allow them to pursue multiple goals simultaneously, including reelection. Indeed, 47 percent of the staff assistants in the study readily identified more than one goal served by their boss's policy leadership activities. Forty-eight percent reported that reelection in combination with some other goal, usually good public policy, motivated policy leadership activities.

A good example of a member who discovered an issue that fit is former senator Dan Quayle (R-Indiana), who was vice president under President George Bush (1989–1992). In the mid-1980s, congressional liberals were pushing legislation designed to reduce the effect of political influence on decisions about the acquisition of military equipment, to introduce more competition into the process of bidding for defense contracts, and to limit the ability of former Department of Defense officials to take jobs in defense industries. Quayle was chair of the Senate Armed Services Subcommittee on Defense Acquisition Policy, so the task of resisting the liberal onslaught and developing legislation acceptable to the Republican administration fell to him. Quayle had become the chair of the procurement subcommittee in 1983 because more senior Republicans had chosen other subcommittee chairmanships.

Two considerations appeared to motivate Quayle's initial eagerness to take on procurement reform. The first was his concern that bad publicity about procurement practices might undermine the nation's commitment to defense spending, which he had worked to increase in the early 1980s. The issue was getting some media attention because of a few highly publicized cases of wasteful defense spending (a $700 toilet seat for a military transport plane, for example). The second was his interest in reinforcing his developing reputation as an effective legislator. He saw an opportunity to assume a leading role on an emerging issue and he took it. Quayle asked the Armed

Services Committee chairman, John Tower (R-Texas), to create a task force on procurement, which he then chaired and later turned into a regular subcommittee. Taking the lead and being reasonably successful were important to Quayle for reasons beyond his reelection prospects. He devoted considerable personal time, as well as the time and energy of his senior aides, to the issue.

Quayle soon saw new angles to the procurement reform issue. Developing his own reform legislation was a good way to score political points at home. Quayle also realized that Indiana had a number of defense contractors and subcontractors whose business might be affected by radical reforms. By working to protect Indiana businesses and jobs, Quayle was doing himself a favor. In a press release issued just before the 1986 election, Quayle's press secretary listed eight major accomplishments of Quayle's first term. The seventh was this:

> Senator Quayle had consistently supported the long-overdue strengthening of our national defense to meet the threat to our freedom. The help he has provided Indiana defense contractors and subcontractors in their dealings with Congress and the Pentagon has contributed substantially to the Hoosier State's economic development over the past six years; during that period, Indiana's share of defense procurement dollars has more than doubled – from $1.43 billion in FY 1980 to $3.16 billion in FY 1985. Quayle also succeeded in protecting the jobs of more than 800 federal workers in the drive to reform the Pentagon's purchasing practices to make sure our essential investment in national security is prudently managed.[13]

Pairing support for more defense spending with the procurement reform effort allowed Quayle to deflect Democratic criticism that he and other Republicans were throwing money at defense. The paired issues were mentioned in radio and television ads as well. The procurement issue was not given the highest priority in Quayle's advertising, but he obviously found a way to use his Washington activity effectively at home. In addition, taking the lead on more moderate reforms than those proposed by liberal Democrats yielded an influx of campaign contributions from defense contractors.

Just as important, Quayle developed a personal interest in procurement politics and policies. Mastering procurement procedures, mediating bureaucratic battles within the Department of Defense, and dealing with powerful defense contractors proved challenging. He appeared to develop a personal commitment to devising good reform legislation.

Assuming a policy leadership role, then, is far more discretionary than casting a roll-call vote. In addition, taking a leadership role on an issue requires an investment of resources far in excess of those involved in casting

a vote. Members cannot afford to take on more than a handful of issues at
a time. Because such efforts may have only small direct electoral benefits
and take up time and resources that could be devoted to other activities,
the potential value of the effort must be high in terms of policy objectives,
personal influence or reputation, or other goals.

Conclusion

In this chapter, we have viewed the legislative process from the perspective of the individual member. Members' goals, resources, and strategies
combine to shape their policy positions and political careers. We have seen
how those goals, resources, and strategies evolve as a function of members'
own choices, changes in members' institutional positions, and the evolution
of Congress's political environment.

The roll-call voting and policy leadership examples in this chapter illustrate
the two broad political purposes of members' strategies – avoiding blame and
claiming credit. Avoiding blame seems to be the dominant situation in roll-
call voting. The fact that roll-call voting is politically mandatory creates many
hazards for members. Particularly in the House, where individual members
have little control over the issues on which they must vote, members must
frequently choose between groups of constituents in casting their votes. In
contrast, claiming credit is the more dominant motivator in policy leadership. Senator Quayle's experience with procurement reform illustrates how
goals, resources, and strategies can be combined opportunistically and give
a member more control over the choices he or she confronts.

Since the late 1970s, members' opportunities for policy leadership have
declined as budget constraints have limited new policy initiatives. Most
members have not been as lucky as Senator Quayle. As a result, members
have found that it is more difficult to counter the inevitable criticisms associated with voting by promoting one's own legislative successes. It certainly
has contributed to the greater dissatisfaction with service in Congress that
members have expressed in recent years and has intensified pressure on leaders to structure floor decision making more carefully.

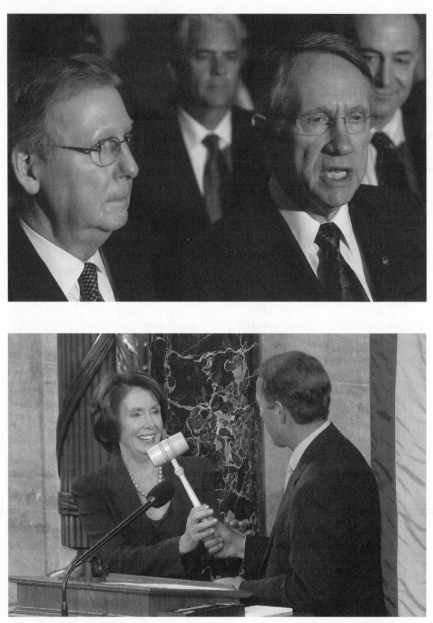

Above: U.S. Senate Majority Leader Harry Reid (D-Nevada) answers questions from the news media as (L-R) incoming Minority Leader Mitch McConnell (R-Kentucky), Sen. John Ensign (R-Nevada), and Sen. Charles Schumer (D-New York) look on.
Below: Speaker of the House Nancy Pelosi (D-California) receives the Speaker's gavel from Minority Leader John Boehner (R-Ohio) after being elected as the first woman Speaker during a swearing in ceremony in 2007.

5

Parties and Leaders

ELECTION OUTCOMES OFTEN MOTIVATE CHANGE IN THE ORGANIZATION and strategies of congressional parties. After the 2006 elections, in which Republicans lost their majorities in the House and Senate, new Republican leaders were elected. In the House, Speaker Dennis Hastert (R-Illinois), who was blamed for excessive partisanship and ineffectiveness in some quarters, quickly announced his retirement from leadership. In the Senate, Senator Bill Frist (R-Tennessee) had earlier announced his retirement from the Congress. Spirited leadership contests followed the elections in which candidates for the Republican leadership offered diagnoses of their party's failings and new approaches to legislating and public relations. The newly elected leaders of the two houses promised joint meetings, a unified communications strategy, and a common legislative program. Republican leaders promised to coordinate their efforts to reestablish an attractive "Republican brand," as one leader defined the task. At the same time, Senate Democratic leader Harry Reid (D-Nevada) created a new post, conference vice chairman, to reward Senator Charles Schumer (D-New York) for leading the Democratic Senatorial Campaign Committee during the 2006 campaign and to bring Schumer into the legislative leadership circle.

The parties' adjustments in strategies and leadership are typical of congressional parties throughout history. Unhappiness with the party's popularity, more than anything else, motivates legislators to seek change in party strategy, organization, and even leadership. And when one party's innovations seem to be successful, the other party tends to follow. Over time, the two parties in each house of Congress have developed more elaborate organizations – and they tend to look alike.

In recent years, congressional parties have become more important avenues of participation for members and their leaders have been more active in shaping policy outcomes. This chapter considers the nature of congressional parties, outlines their organization, and describes the activities and resources of congressional party leaders and their organizations. It concludes with a discussion of the factors contributing to the intensified partisanship of recent years.

The Nature of Congressional Parties

Congressional parties exist to serve the interests of their members. The Constitution does not mention congressional parties. Just as candidates and their supporters created electoral parties outside of Congress to effectively compete in elections, legislators created congressional parties to serve their ends. The four congressional parties (House Democrats, House Republicans, Senate Democrats, and Senate Republicans) convene separately before each new Congress begins, and they meet with some frequency while Congress is in session. No formal joint organization of House and Senate Democrats or House and Senate Republicans exists, although party leaders of the two houses often discuss matters of mutual concern.

Congressional party organizations are independent of the national and state political parties. Members of Congress have chaired and served in other capacities on the parties' national committees, but the four congressional parties have no formal relationship with the national party committees. Moreover, members of Congress usually are considered important party leaders in their home districts and states, but they are seldom officials of their local party organizations. Members' candidacy for office usually is endorsed by the local party organizations, but, as members know, winning the party primary, not the endorsement, gets them on the general election ballot in November. The bond between the local party and an incumbent representative or senator can be weak. National committees, congressional party organizations, and local party organizations do not directly control who gets nominated through primaries and eventually elected to Congress. Party organizations may recruit candidates, contribute money, and offer campaign advice and expertise. They do not have the power to prevent someone from running in party primaries and gaining a seat in Congress.

A reasonable characterization of congressional parties is that they are relatively stable, but loose, coalitions of legislators that exist to serve the common interests of their members. Both electoral and policy interests appear to motivate party activity.

Common Electoral Interests

Members of each congressional party share a party label – a political "brand name." The party labels hold meaning for voters and influence their decisions at the polls, so members of the same party have an incentive to build and maintain a positive reputation for their party. This collective interest encourages legislators to develop party organizations and select party leaders who work to enhance the party's image. Leaders choose issues to emphasize, develop public relations strategies, and work with presidents and committee leaders to shape the content of legislation. They also work more directly to aid election campaigns by raising and contributing money, making appearances at fundraising and campaign events, disseminating information, and playing a role in recruiting candidates. In election years, top leaders spend several weeks traveling to support the electoral efforts of fellow partisans.

By building a favorable party reputation, leaders help their colleagues get reelected and help their party gain and maintain majority party status. A majority party controls committee and subcommittee chairmanships, which legislators covet, has more influence over the agenda, and, with more votes, is more likely to win legislative battles. Electoral failures have caused the defeat or led to the resignation of several party leaders (see box, "Electoral Trouble for Leaders").

Leaders are expected to promote their party's electoral interests, but tensions sometimes arise between leaders and rank-and-file members whose personal or political interests motivate them to vote differently than leaders and other party colleagues would like. Even congressional party leaders, whose job it is to rally support for their party's policy positions, are sensitive to the personal political needs of deviant colleagues. After all, most party leaders would prefer to give a deviant party member some leeway to vote as he or she chooses rather than lose that member's seat to the other party. Imperfect support for party positions is the typical pattern for most members. These differences in members' home constituencies are an important source of conflict over party strategy within all congressional parties.

Shared Policy Preferences

Members of each party hold distinctive views on most important policy questions. The shared policy views among legislators of the same party

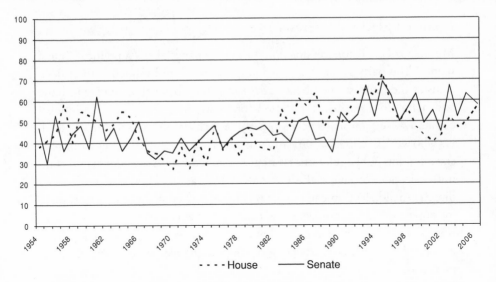

FIGURE 5.1. Percent of All Votes that Were Party Votes, 1954–2006. *Source:* Congressional
Quarterly Weekly Report, January 1, 2007, p. 39.

are grounded in the similarities in the views of their home constituencies.
Liberal-leaning districts tend to elect more Democrats than conservative-
leaning districts, which elect more Republicans. Shared policy views create
an incentive for members to choose leaders and coordinate their strategies.

Majorities of the parties have taken opposing positions on roll-call votes
about half of the time in most recent Congresses. Figure 5.1 indicates the
percentage of roll-call votes that were party votes – those on which a majority
of Democrats voted against a majority of Republicans. In the recent past,
party voting has tended to be higher in odd-numbered years than in even-
numbered years, particularly in the House. This trend may reflect political
pressures associated with the two-year electoral cycle of the House. In the
odd-numbered years immediately after congressional elections, the winning
side may feel emboldened to push a partisan agenda. But as another election
approaches, members and party leaders may avoid issues that polarize the
parties and create problems at home for some members.

The percentage of party votes was relatively high in the late 1980s and
1990s. We consider this trend later in this chapter. But why aren't more votes
in Congress aligned along party lines? The primary reason is that Congress
addresses many programs and issues that do not involve partisan considerations, such as the merchant marine, veterans' health programs, and flood
insurance. Congress considers a greater volume of legislation – and more
detailed legislation – than do most other national legislatures. Most of the

ELECTORAL TROUBLE FOR LEADERS

Members of Congress expect their leaders to guide their parties to electoral success. Major failures, or even unexpected losses, as well as other embarrassing developments, can lead to the demise of a leader, as is evident in several episodes.

After his party suffered unexpected losses in the 1998 elections, Speaker Newt Gingrich (R-Georgia) took the extraordinary step of resigning from the speakership and Congress. His party had lost five seats in the House of Representatives, narrowing the Republican advantage to 223, just five more than a majority of 218. Rarely does the party opposing the president lose seats in a midterm election. In fact, 1934 is the only other midterm election of the twentieth century in which the president's party won additional seats. Gingrich was blamed for failing to provide needed leadership.

In 2002, just after his party failed to win seats in the midterm election, Democratic Minority Leader Dick Gephardt chose not to seek reelection as the party leader. Gephardt soon announced his intention to run for president, but many viewed his decision to retire from the post a wise move. Gephardt had served as party leader since 1994, when House Democrats lost their majority for the first time since 1954, yet he had not managed to lead the party back to majority status.

After his party regained a majority of Senate seats in the 2002 elections, Senate Republican Minority Leader Trent Lott (R-Mississippi) was expecting to become the majority leader as soon as the new Congress convened in January 2003. However, in December a video recording of Lott's comments at a birthday party for retiring Senator Strom Thurmond (R-South Carolina) were aired on television. The recording showed Lott saying that the country would have been better off if Thurmond had won the presidency when he ran in 1948. Thurmond was the pro-segregationist candidate of the Dixiecrats in 1948. It was soon learned that Lott had made similar comments two decades earlier. The public uproar caused by these disclosures led many of Lott's colleagues to conclude that he had to step down as party leader. He did (although he remained in the Senate).

In 2006, after his party lost its House majority, Speaker Dennis Hastert (R-Illinois) stepped down as his party's leader.

legislation enacted into law each year is routine or concerns matters of little political interest. The parties are not motivated to play a role in shaping such legislation.

Even on votes that generate partisan divisions, the two parties are seldom perfectly cohesive. In most recent Congresses, an average of 70 to

FACTIONALISM WITHIN CONGRESSIONAL PARTIES

Intra-party factionalism in Congress is reflected in the presence of named groups. In the Senate, owing to its smaller size, members appear to see less benefit and some cost in becoming associated with formally organized factions. In recent years, a handful of Senate Democratic liberals formed the Democratic Study Group and a bipartisan group of moderates formed the bipartisan Senate Centrist Coalition. Only the Steering Committee, the informal organization of Republican conservatives, has been in existence for long.

In the House, factions representing liberals, moderates, and conservatives have formed and reformed in both parties. The most venerable factional group is the Democratic Study Group, which was organized in the late 1950s to pursue liberal causes but expanded to provide such good informational and research services that most House Democrats eventually joined it. Of more recent vintage is the New Democratic Coalition, organized in 1998 by a group of about 65 self-proclaimed centrists. The Blue Dog Coalition is an organization of conservative or moderate Democrats. The most liberal Democrats comprise the Progressive Caucus. In addition, the Congressional Black Caucus and Hispanics Caucus represent Democrats who generally are liberal.

On the Republican side in the House, the Republican Study Committee is the major faction and comprised of about 110 conservatives – a majority of the party. In recent years, Republican moderates organized the Main Street Coalition and the Tuesday Group. Both the Republican Study Committee and the Tuesday Group hired staff aides to assist the groups.

80 percent of members have voted with a majority of their party on party votes – meaning that a 20 to 30 percent rate of defection is common even when party majorities oppose each other. Indeed, nothing in the way that members are elected or reelected guarantees that members of the same party will agree with one another on important issues or that Democrats and Republicans will take opposing views. To the contrary, variation in political views of members' constituencies promotes variation in the voting behavior of members of the same party. Factionalism often has made it difficult to use the party organizations to promote policy ideas and solicit support.

Party Identification

Most members, like most political activists and many citizens of the United States, identify with their parties – they have a psychological and emotional attachment to their parties. This attachment reinforces a sense of group identification and enhances group cohesiveness. These bonds lead members to turn to party colleagues for cues on how to vote and for other forms of assistance and advice. Party leaders further strengthen party bonds by emphasizing common loyalties, policy commitments, and personal ties in their appeals for support from their colleagues. Furthermore, most members of Congress face another reality: Legislators are dependent on voters who, for the most part, share the same partisan affiliation and vote in party primaries. Members who vote against their party's position on major issues or, even worse, actively work to undermine their party's institutional position may face challenges from within their party in a primary. Few members are willing to take such a risk. In this way, the partisan connection between a member and his or her electoral base constrains members who might otherwise work to form inter-party coalitions within their chamber.

Most Common Coalitions

Although congressional parties are not perfectly cohesive, they have an important advantage over other groups that might seek to influence legislative outcomes: They are the most common basis for building majority coalitions. Because party-based coalitions are so common, members have an incentive to organize formal party organizations and identify leaders to work on behalf of their common interests. That is, over the long run, members believe that they are better off joining an enduring party organization than operating as freelance legislators. Once established, parties acquire important institutional advantages that make it difficult for other coalitions to establish formal organizations in Congress. By using their procedural and appointment powers, as well as by making a few concessions to dissident factions, majority party leaders have been able to defuse the few intra-party disputes that have threatened party control of their chambers.

Stable but Loose Coalitions

For all of these reasons, the House and Senate depend on party leaders to perform many basic organizational functions, but do not give them too much independent power. Members of the *majority* party choose the presiding officers of both chambers (the Speaker of the House and, to preside in the absence of the Vice President, the Senate President Pro Tempore), select committee leaders, and assume responsibility for scheduling activity at all stages of the legislative process. The parties assign members to standing committees and subcommittees as well as to all select, joint, and conference committees. The majority party in each house reserves for itself the majority of seats on nearly all committees. And within the committees, most activity is organized by party – the questioning of witnesses at hearings, the hiring of staff, even the arrangement of seats in committee rooms. Seating on the House and Senate floors is also arranged by party: The Democrats are on the left and the Republicans are on the right when facing the front desk. All in all, partisan elements pervade the organization of the modern Congress and have done so since the first half of the nineteenth century.

Yet, American congressional parties are not as strong as parties in many other national legislatures. Congressional parties in the United States usually are not as cohesive on questions of public policy as are parties in other systems. U.S. congressional party leaders have little power over who is elected under their party's label and few resources to compel loyalty from members once they are in office. Equally important, state and national party leaders have no formal authority over legislators sharing their party label.

Congressional party leaders sometimes struggle to balance the diverse policy and electoral interests of their party colleagues. In their efforts to do so, they may delay action on a bill until the timing is more convenient for a legislator or urge their colleagues to be tolerant of a legislator whose political circumstances necessitate a vote against the party position. Still, there are situations when leaders seek the vote of every party member. Such situations usually involve legislation that is a high priority of a president of the same party, whose success or failure will reflect on the party, and for which there are not enough supportive members of the opposition party to muster a majority. Leaders may seek to accommodate some members by compromising provisions of the legislation or by promising certain actions on unrelated legislation. Explicit or implicit threats of retribution for disloyal behavior are sometimes issued, typically in the form of warnings about future committee chairmanship or appointment decisions made by party committees and leaders. These tradeoffs reflect the loose organization and discipline of congressional parties and the long-term importance of party affiliations to members.

Party Organizations

Each of the four congressional parties (two in each house) has three major organizational features: a caucus (or conference) comprised of all party members in the chamber, party committees, and elected and appointed leaders. All four party caucuses meet in late November or early December after each election to organize for the new Congress, which begins in January. They elect their leaders, may adopt and revise their rules, and begin to make assignments to standing committees. In recent Congresses, all four caucuses have met weekly or biweekly while Congress is in session. These meetings

---

Congressionally Speaking . . .

Among the four congressional parties, only House Democrats call their organization a *caucus.* House Republicans, Senate Democrats, and Senate Republicans call their organizations *conferences.* The difference in labels dates to the 1910s, when the House Democrats used their caucus, the so-called King Caucus, to make policy decisions and required party members to support those positions. The Democrats' binding caucus was so distasteful to House Republicans that they chose an entirely different label for their organization. Senate parties followed suit.

---

usually serve as forums for the discussion of party strategies. To facilitate candid discussion and avoid media reports of party infighting, caucus meetings are generally not open to the public or the press.

Each party has a set of committees (see Table 5.1). The policy committees discuss (and, infrequently, endorse) policy positions; the campaign committees provide advice and money to party incumbents and candidates; the committees on committees assign party members to standing committees. For several decades, the policy committees of the House and Senate Republicans have sponsored weekly luncheons that serve as forums on matters important to the party. Senate Democrats adopted the practice of weekly luncheons in 1990.

Party staffs provide a wide range of services to members. Services include timely reports on floor activity, briefing papers on major issues, media advice and technical assistance, newspaper-clipping services, recorded messages on current floor activity, personnel services, and limited research assistance. The Senate parties operate closed-circuit television channels that provide senators and their staffs with informative details about floor action. They also provide radio and television studios that allow senators to appear live on home-state stations. Over the last two decades, most new party leaders have found additional services to promise and deliver to the membership. As a result, the party staffs have become large and expensive, with nearly all of the funding provided through appropriations.

Party Leaders

The Constitution provides for presiding officers in Congress but says nothing about parties or leaders. It provides that the members of the House "shall choose their Speaker," makes the vice president of the United States the president of the Senate, and requires that the Senate select a president pro

TABLE 5.1. Party Committees, 110th Congress (January 2007).

House Democrats

Steering and Policy	Makes committee assignments; sometimes endorses policy positions; discusses party strategy
Democratic Congressional Campaign Committee	Provides money and other assistance to Democratic House candidates
Organization, Study, and Review	Recommends changes in party organization and rules

House Republicans

Steering	Makes committee assignments
Policy	Discusses and recommends policy proposals
National Republican Congressional Committee	Provides money and other assistance to Republican House candidates

Senate Democrats

Steering and Outreach	Makes committee assignments; formulates political strategy
Policy	Recommends policy priorities; provides a forum for conference discussion; staff provides research
Democratic Senatorial Campaign Committee	Provides money and other assistance to Democratic Senate candidates

Senate Republicans

Committee on Committees	Makes committee assignments
Policy	Discusses and recommends policy proposals; staff provides research
National Republican Senatorial Campaign	Provides money and other assistance to Republican Senate candidates

Source: Collected by authors.

tempore ("president for the time being") to preside over the Senate in the absence of the vice president. Although the Constitution does not explicitly require the Speaker or the Senate president pro tempore to be members of Congress, all have been.

Only in the House is the presiding officer, the Speaker, also the leader of the majority party. At the start of each Congress, the majority and minority parties nominate their top leaders for Speaker. The majority party leader is then elected on a party-line vote. In the Senate, presiding over daily sessions is normally a routine activity, so the vice president is seldom present. Since

TABLE 5.2. Top Party Leaders, 110th Congress (January 2007).

House Democrats

Speaker	Nancy Pelosi, California
Majority Leader	Steny Hoyer, Maryland
Majority Whip	James Clyburn, South Carolina
Caucus Chair	Rahm Emanuel, Illinois
Caucus Vice Chair	John Larson, Connecticut

House Republicans

Minority Leader	John Boehner, Ohio
Minority Whip	Roy Blunt, Missouri
Conference Chair	Adam Putnam, Florida
Conference Vice Chairman	Jack Kingston, Georgia

Senate Democrats

Majority Leader (and Conference Chair)	Harry Reid, Nevada
Assistant Floor Leader (Whip)	Dick Durbin, Illinois
Conference Vice Chair	Charles Schumer, New York
Conference Secretary	Patty Murray, Washington

Senate Republicans

Minority Leader	Mitch McConnell, Kentucky
Assistant Floor Leader (Whip)	Trent Lott, Mississippi
Conference Chairman	Jon Kyl, Arizona
Conference Vice Chairman	John Cornyn, Texas

Source: Collected by authors.

the 1940s, the majority party has named its most senior member president pro tempore. The president pro tempore is usually busy as a committee chair and assigns the duty of presiding over the Senate to junior senators of the same party. All four parties choose a floor leader (known as a majority or minority leader), assistant floor leader (or whip), conference chair, and other leaders.

Major Responsibilities of Party Leaders

No specific statements about party leaders' jobs can be found in chamber or party rules. Rather, leaders' responsibilities have developed in response to their colleagues' expectations that leaders must promote the common electoral and policy interests of their parties. These responsibilities are primarily assigned to the top leader in each party, although the burden is shared among the top three or four leaders in each party.

BUILDING COALITIONS ON MAJOR LEGISLATION. Building coalitions in support of party policy positions is a large part of the job of leaders. Because the majority party is often divided to some degree on controversial issues, such majorities do not automatically materialize. Rather, leaders carefully count votes, craft legislation, and use various means of persuasion to try to unify their own party and attract votes from members of the opposition party to pass or block legislation. Leaders also work to build majority coalitions in committees and conference committees from time to time, but they tend to be deferential to committee leaders at those stages. Party leaders are most active on the floor.

Extra-large majorities must often be mustered as well. In the Senate, 60 votes must be secured to invoke cloture on a filibuster, unless the matter concerns the Senate's standing rules, in which case a two-thirds vote (67, if all senators vote) is required. On a few other occasions in the Senate, such as to waive a budget restriction, a 60-vote majority must be found. In both chambers, a two-thirds majority of members present and voting is required to override a presidential veto. In such cases, support from at least a few minority members is usually required for the majority party leaders to win.

MANAGING THE FLOOR. Managing floor activity is primarily the responsibility of the majority party leadership. This responsibility includes scheduling sessions of the houses and arranging for the consideration of individual pieces of legislation. The stark differences between House and Senate floor scheduling practices are noted in Chapter 7. In the Senate, minority members' power to obstruct proceedings requires that the majority leader work closely with the minority leader. In fact, nearly continuous consultation between the two leaders and their staffs is typical in the Senate in midsession. A much more distant relationship between the majority and minority party leaders is found in the House. As a result, the Senate majority leader has more difficulty gaining a tactical edge by careful scheduling than does the House Speaker.

SERVING AS INTERMEDIARY WITH THE PRESIDENT. Serving as intermediaries between the congressional party and the president has been a regular duty of party leaders since the early twentieth century. Leaders of the president's party normally meet with the president once a week while Congress is in session, and they often report on those meetings at party luncheons or caucuses. On matters central to the president's legislative agenda, the leaders work closely with executive branch officials to build majority support in Congress.

Congressional leaders of the president's party often have divided loyalties. Their most immediate obligation is to their congressional colleagues, but they also feel an obligation to support the president. Tensions frequently arise as congressional leaders seek to balance the competing demands of the president and their congressional party colleagues.

Leaders of the out-party – the party that does not control the presidency – meet sporadically with the president, usually to be briefed on foreign policy matters. The relationship between a president and out-party leaders is not often one of genuine consultation, for obvious reasons. Occasionally, political circumstances or personal friendship may strengthen the bond. Senate Republican leader Everett Dirksen, for example, was a confidant of Democratic president Lyndon Johnson during the 1960s, and Dirksen's support for Johnson's civil rights and Vietnam War policies was crucial to the president's legislative success.

ENHANCING THE PARTY'S REPUTATION. Publicizing party views has become a central leadership responsibility in recent decades. Skillfully managing media relations is now considered an essential element of a good legislative strategy. The objectives are to win public support for legislative positions, to persuade undecided legislators of the political support for party positions, and to win elections.

Media skills were seldom a major consideration in leadership selection in the 1950s, 1960s, and early 1970s. Service to colleagues, mastery of the mechanics of the legislative game, and position among party factions were given greater weight. Perhaps because of their weak institutional position and lack of national media coverage, only House Republicans made media skills much of an issue in leadership contests. In general, party leaders took a back seat to committee leaders as opinion leaders on matters of policy. In fact, the leading studies on party leadership of the 1960s did not catalog service as party spokesperson or anything similar among the major functions or techniques of leaders.

Expectations have changed. The increasing importance of television as a medium of political communication, presidents' domination of television news, and the larger number of news programs seem to have intensified demand for telegenic leaders. Since the mid-1960s, out-party congressional leaders have sought and been granted time on the television networks to respond to presidential addresses. By the early 1980s, the role of party spokesperson had become so prominent as to warrant listing it among leaders' primary responsibilities.

Congressional party leaders realize that to compete with the president, television pundits, interest group leaders, radio talk show hosts, and other

REPLICATING SUCCESSFUL INNOVATIONS

In preparation for the 1994 elections, House Republican leaders prepared a 10-point legislative agenda – known as the "Contract With America" – that they promised to pass in the first 100 days of the new Congress if they gained a majority of seats. Republicans won a House majority in the 1994 elections for the first time since the 1952 elections and credited the new Speaker, Newt Gingrich, for enhancing the importance of national issues in House contests and ultimately for their success.

Ten years later in 2004, the House Democratic leader, Nancy Pelosi (D-California), organized a similar effort for her party. Drawing on the advice of outside consultants and citing the need for a clear message like the Contract With America, the Democratic leaders produced the "New Partnership for America's Future" in which they identified their party's six "core values." The effort did not lead to a new Democratic majority, at least not in the 2004 elections. In 2006, when the Democrats won back a House majority, Pelosi and the Democrats prepared a "Six for '06" agenda that included six legislative initiatives that were passed in the first 100 hours of legislative session in 2007.

opinion leaders, all of whom actively court public opinion in an effort to generate pressure on legislators, they need media strategies of their own. All top leaders have daily contact with print, radio, and television reporters. The House Speaker and Senate leaders usually have brief press conferences before their chambers' daily sessions. They employ experienced press secretaries and speechwriters. They sometimes commission their own public opinion polls to gauge how well their party's message is being received. On a few major issues, they even create special party task forces charged with carrying out a media strategy.

CAMPAIGNING. Providing campaign support to colleagues is a regular part of leaders' activity. All modern leaders help their colleagues raise money and join them at campaign events. Such an extensive effort is now the norm for top party leaders. Leaders' efforts are not altruistic, of course. Party leaders want to see party colleagues reelected in order to maintain or gain a majority for their party, and they hope that their kindness will be repaid in loyalty. Even candidates for top leadership posts now spend time and money on their colleagues' campaign to attract support and demonstrate the kind of leaders they will be. All leaders, and most aspirants for leadership posts, form political action committees so they may receive contributions that can, in turn, be contributed to the campaigns of their colleagues.

SWITCHING PARTIES, CHANGING PARTY CONTROL

In late May 2001, Senator Jim Jeffords (I-Vermont) announced that he was leaving the Republican Conference, becoming an independent, and joining with the Democrats for the purpose of organizing the Senate. Since the 1880s, there have been 25 instances of party switching in the Senate, but Jeffords' move was the first time that such a switch caused a party to lose majority status in either chamber. The Senate had been divided 50–50 between Democrats and Republicans; the Republican Vice President Dick Cheney allowed the Republicans to be considered the majority party, for the Republican floor leader to be recognized by the presiding officer as the majority leader, and for the Republicans to control the committee chairmanships. Republicans attempted to keep Jeffords in the party by offering more money for education, his favorite cause, giving him a seat in the leadership circle, and granting him an exemption to the party conference rule limiting the number of terms he could serve as chair of the Health, Education, Labor, and Pensions Committee. The new Democratic majority gave Jeffords a committee chairmanship. In the 2002 elections the Republicans gained additional seats and reassumed majority status. Jeffords lost his chairmanship. There have been 81 instances of party switching in the House since the 1880s. Jeffords announced in early 2005 that he would not seek reelection in 2006.

MANAGING THE PARTY AND THE CHAMBER. Organizing the party and chamber is an important duty of party leaders. Obvious political aspects of this job include making committee assignments and appointments to various party positions. More administrative in character are the selection and supervision of chamber officers and other employees. For example, the majority party leaders in the two houses nominate the chief clerks and sergeants at arms, who then must be approved by the houses, and they share responsibility for choosing a director for the Congressional Budget Office.

Selection of Leaders

The party caucuses elect their top leaders. The leaders are not chosen on the basis of seniority, although most recent leaders have been very experienced members. A candidate's place among factions and regional groups within the party, record of service to colleagues, personal friendships, intelligence and policy expertise, and other factors play a role in leadership contests. As noted, skill in managing relations with the media has become increasingly important. Members who have been serving in lower party posts may be advantaged because they have been in a position to demonstrate their skills and to perform favors for colleagues.

Only in the ascension to House Speaker is there much routine in leadership selection. A vacancy in the speakership is typically filled by the previous floor leader – the majority or minority leader – without opposition. The majority or minority leader generally has already won several leadership elections and has substantial support for the move to Speaker. Challenging the heir apparent would be pointless. Contests for the speakership have not occurred since the 1800s.

The election of Republican Speaker Dennis Hastert in early 1999 was a special case. After Speaker Gingrich announced his resignation shortly after the 1998 elections, in which the Republicans did unexpectedly poorly, the immediate favorite to replace Gingrich was Rep. Bob Livingston (R-Louisiana). But, after the media disclosed that Livingston had an extramarital affair years earlier, Livingston chose to resign from the House. Somewhat anxious to find a new leader, House Republicans asked Hastert, who had held only low appointive positions in the party and was not well known. Hastert was replaced by Nancy Pelosi after the Democrats won a House majority in 2006.

For other party offices, hotly contested races are common, usually to fill vacancies. As contests among fellow partisans, the races are often filled with intrigue. They involve intense campaigns as the candidates make personal appeals to colleagues to solicit support. Organized factions sometimes choose a favorite; in fact, faction leaders often are the candidates. Wild speculation, personal grudges, and conspiracy are the standard fare. The behind-closed-doors campaigning and secret-ballot voting always generate a great deal of speculation and second-guessing among Washington insiders. A potentially close outcome heightens the suspense.

Challenges to incumbent leaders occur only occasionally. Most incumbent leaders do the kind of job their party colleagues expect. Challenges to an incumbent tend to be particularly divisive, and even disgruntled members usually try to avoid a fight within the party family. Of course, taking on an incumbent may be risky. Leadership contests are expensive in terms of time and effort. Running and losing may undermine future leadership hopes, to say nothing of incurring the wrath of the winner.

House Party Leaders

Today's House party leaders are much more visible and active than were their predecessors of the 1960s and 1970s. Personality is one reason, but more important are the power of television and demands of rank-and-file party members for aggressive, media-oriented leadership. Partly for those reasons, somewhat younger and more assertive members have been promoted to top leadership spots in recent years. Greater party cohesiveness has liberated leaders to be more pugnacious and partisan without alienating major factions within the party.

The Speaker of the House

The Speaker of the House possesses more formal authority than does any other member of Congress. House rules and precedents grant the Speaker important prerogatives concerning floor scheduling and procedures, bill referrals, and appointments to select and conference committees and to various commissions. One of the Speaker's newest prerogatives is the power to remove a member from a conference committee delegation and replace him or her without the approval of the House, a power that is intended to make majority party members of a conference delegation accountable to their party's top leader. In addition to the rules of the House, both parties' internal rules give their top leaders control over the party's appointments to the Rules Committee, extra influence over other committee assignments, and power to make appointments to party committees. It is the combination of powers granted under House and party rules that make the Speaker more powerful than the Senate's majority leader, who enjoys few special powers under Senate rules.

The Speaker's most important source of power is his or her control of the flow of business on the House floor. By precedent, the Speaker has the power to recognize members on the House floor. That means that the Speaker may choose to ignore members who seek recognition to call up legislation that the Speaker prefers to consider later or to block. Scheduling prerogatives give the Speaker control over the timing of floor action, which may affect the legislative outcomes and political impact of House votes. Among other things, the Speaker can keep from the floor legislation he or she opposes or wishes to delay. Also, the Speaker may use scheduling to reward or punish legislators.

As presiding officer and the majority party's top leader, the Speaker must exercise great discretion in making public appearances and statements. For example, Speakers make floor speeches on only a few occasions each year, for important issues and close votes. On the momentous occasions when a Speaker does speak on the floor, nearly all members are in attendance and the galleries are packed. Speakers are granted the privilege of speaking last.

TERM LIMITS FOR LEADERS

Since the early 1990s, term limits for party leaders and committee chairs have been a popular reform proposal. Congressional Republicans have moved farther in adopting limits than Democrats. The known limits on leaders' service in key positions appear to have stimulated ambitious legislators to announce their candidacy for leadership posts earlier.

House Republicans led the way among congressional parties to set limits on the number of terms a legislator could serve in a particular leadership post. Soon after they gained a majority in the 1994 elections, the House Republicans limited all party leaders to six-year terms in any given office, with the exception of the speakership for which an eight-year limit was established. They eliminated the limit on the Speaker in 2003 and Democrats did not reimpose a term for the Speaker when they gained a House majority in 2007.

Senate Republicans followed their House counterparts by setting a six-year limit for holding any leadership position with the exceptions of floor leader and President Pro Tempore for which no limit was set.

House Democrats limit their caucus chair, caucus vice chair, and elected regional whips to two consecutive terms, but do not set term limits for other party leaders.

Senate Democrats have not imposed term limits of any kind on party or committee leadership posts.

Recent Speakers – Thomas P. "Tip" O'Neill (1977–1986), James Wright (1987–1989), Thomas Foley (1989–1994), Newt Gingrich (1995–1998), Dennis Hastert (1999–2006), and Nancy Pelosi (2007–present) – have been more active in using their formal powers than were the Speakers of the middle decades of the twentieth century. The speakership gained particularly high visibility after the 1980 elections, in which Republican Ronald Reagan was elected to the White House and the Republicans gained a majority in the Senate. O'Neill, as the highest elected Democrat, became the chief strategist and spokesperson for his party. After Reagan's initial year of great legislative success, the Democrats united in opposition to the president's conservative agenda, with O'Neill taking the lead in challenging Reagan's program and presenting Democratic alternatives. In doing so, O'Neill was responding to the demands for leadership from the frustrated liberal rank-and-file members of his party.

O'Neill's activism paled in comparison with the boldness of his successor, James Wright, however. Upon gaining the speakership, Wright bullied committees to act quickly on a range of domestic legislation, leading Republicans to complain about a new House dictatorship. In the foreign policy arena, Wright broke through unwritten limits on congressional involvement by negotiating directly with representatives of the contending governments and factions in Central America.

Wright resigned from the House in 1989 after the House Committee on Standards of Official Conduct charged him with several violations of House ethics rules. Thomas Foley, who succeeded Wright, had been caucus chair, whip, and majority leader. Compared with Wright, he was less assertive, more deferential to committees, and less inclined to make partisan attacks on Republican leaders. Like O'Neill, Wright was unlikely to take the lead on controversial issues unless a consensus had already crystallized within his party.

Republican Newt Gingrich became the most proactive Speaker since the first decade of the twentieth century after he was elected to the post in January 1995. A well-developed agenda, called the Contract With America, provided an unusually concise 10-point policy platform for Gingrich. Gingrich was given much of the credit for these developments – he had championed aggressive Republican strategies in the House, coauthored the Contract With America, raised money, and recruited candidates to challenge the incumbent Democratic majority. Gingrich, backed by his House Republican colleagues, became the leading spokesman for his party, dominated the selection of committee leaders and other committee appointments, directed the actions of committees, set the floor agenda, and pushed legislation associated with the Contract With America through the House in the first 100 days of the 104th Congress (1995–1996).

Gingrich's speakership was a lightning rod for partisanship and ended in political tragedy. Gingrich had leveled the initial charges against Jim Wright that eventually led to Wright's resignation and later, as Speaker, was at least as aggressive as Wright in leading the majority party. His political downfall began with his 1995 strategy to hold hostage debt ceiling increases and funding for executive departments in order to get President Bill Clinton's approval of the Republican's budget plan. Clinton refused to budge and eventually the Republican Congress accepted Clinton's compromise legislation. The episode produced sharply weaker approval ratings for Gingrich in public opinion polls and much stronger ratings for Clinton. After that point, Gingrich became far less aggressive, setting aside his confrontational strategies. Following Clinton's reelection in 1996, Gingrich maintained a low public profile and appeared to be somewhat less heavy-handed in directing the work of the House, an approach that has received mixed reviews from his colleagues. In the summer of 1997 there was serious discussion among senior Republicans of replacing him. Gingrich continued to be subject to criticism for ineffective leadership, and he eventually resigned his post when challenged by Bob Livingston in the aftermath of the 1998 elections.

In 1995, the Republicans instituted a new House rule limiting the number of consecutive terms that a member could serve as Speaker. In December 1994, newly elected Republicans proposed a three-term limit for the Speaker, just as they proposed for committee chairs. At Gingrich's insistence, they approved a four-term limit instead, which was incorporated into the House rules in January 1995. Gingrich did not survive long enough for the rule to apply.

Hastert's style contrasted sharply with Gingrich's, at least at first. Hastert consulted more frequently with his fellow partisans and granted more independence to committee chairs. He successfully healed some of the rifts among Republicans left from the Gingrich years, and, for a while, he held regular meetings with the Democratic leader. He campaigned endlessly for his colleagues, earning their respect and indebtedness, and, in the view of some observers, used this support to gain the upper hand with other party and committee leaders.

However welcome Hastert's more accommodating style was initially, by late 2002 Hastert became more aggressive in his enforcement of party loyalty. He denied committee chairmanships and choice committee assignments to several Republicans who had opposed the leadership position on campaign finance reform, patients' bill of rights, and other issues. He endorsed Majority Leader Tom Delay's (R-Texas) proclamation that a Republican member of the party's organization who voted against the party on any procedural matter be excused from service. In 2003, the Republicans' package of House rules changes dropped the eight-year term limit for a Speaker. Democrats did not reimpose a term limit for the Speaker when they gained a majority in 2007.

After the Democrats won a majority of House seats in the 2006 elections, they elected their floor leader, Nancy Pelosi, the first woman Speaker. Pelosi, a liberal Democrat from San Francisco, had worked hard as minority leader to build support among moderate and conservative Democrats. During her first few months in the speakership, she proved to be an aggressive leader who set the agenda for her party and showed a willingness to work around committee chairs who were not in sync with her agenda. While she worked hard to win the support of fellow partisans on controversial issues, she created more opportunities for the minority party to offer alternatives and gave her own partisans somewhat more freedom to vote as they chose.

House Floor Leaders

Both House parties elect a floor leader – that is, a majority leader or a minority leader – at the start of each Congress. As the label suggests, floor leaders are the chief spokespersons for their parties on the House floor. The majority leader is considered the second-ranking leader of the party, just behind the Speaker. The minority leader is the minority party's top leader and is always that party's (losing) nominee for Speaker at the beginning of each Congress.

There are few duties formally assigned to the majority leader in party rules. Recent Speakers have relied on the floor leader to receive and screen requests to schedule legislation for floor consideration. The majority leader consults with the Speaker (normally several times a day), works with the Speaker and others to promote party unity, and increasingly serves as a party spokesperson. Recent majority leaders have been loyal to the Speaker and have seldom publicly disagreed with him or her. As the person who is next in line to become Speaker, and an individual with a strong voice in scheduling and all other leadership decisions, the majority leader is considered very powerful.

The minority leader generally is the minority party's chief spokesperson and strategist. The minority leader sometimes consults with the majority leader about the floor schedule, although more often he or she is merely informed of the majority leadership's scheduling decisions. Keeping the minority party united and attracting majority party votes are the central tasks of the minority leader's job. The job is made easier when the minority leader's party controls the White House, and the president's resources can be drawn upon. The minority party can do little to obstruct a cohesive majority in the House, so the minority floor leader's job tends to be quite frustrating. The minority leader, like the Speaker, is an *ex officio* member of the Permanent Select Committee on Intelligence.

House Whips and Whip Organizations

The third-ranking majority party leader and second-ranking minority party leader in the House are the whips. Both whips are now elected, although the Democratic whip was appointed by the majority leader until late 1986 when the position was made elective. Both whips head large whip organizations, whose purpose is to collect information for the leadership and persuade colleagues to support party positions. To facilitate the communication process, the whip offices maintain systems of recorded messages about floor actions, issue whip notices about the upcoming schedule, and use automated

---

Congressionally Speaking . . .

The term *whip* originated in the British House of Commons. It is derived from the term whipper-in – the fellow who keeps the dogs in line during an English foxhunt. In the American Congress, the use of the term reflected the responsibility of the whip to get party members to the floor on time. Today the term is often used as a verb – as in "the undecided members were whipped" – to refer to the process of persuasion and arm-twisting.

---

telephone and paging systems to reach members about pending votes. Whips also try to keep track of the whereabouts of members, particularly on days when important, close floor votes are expected.

The Democratic whip organization has been large for many years. In recent Congresses, the House Democrats had as many as seven chief deputy whips, 12 deputy whips, and 70 at-large whips, all appointed by the party leader. In addition, there have been 24 regional whips elected by groups of Democrats from specific regions and one ex officio whip (the ranking Democrat on the Rules Committee), for a total of 88 whips. The whip system has grown rapidly as the top leaders have responded to demands for whip appointments from party factions and individual members.

The Democratic leaders often appoint task forces to collect information and generate support on specific issues. This approach has been called a "strategy of inclusion," because it gives a large number of members an opportunity to work closely with the leadership. By working hand in hand with the party rank-and-file, party leaders are able to persuade some members who otherwise might oppose the leadership to join the team.

The House Republicans have a more modest whip system, although it also has expanded in recent years. The Republican whip system has been comprised of a chief deputy whip and about 17 deputy whips – all appointed – and nearly 50 assistant whips elected by groups for regions of the country. The Republican whips meet irregularly. The Republicans maintain several subcommittees on their Policy Committee that serve purposes similar to Democratic caucus task forces.

Appointment or election as a whip, policy subcommittee, or task force member gives a member some prestige, an additional office to add to his or her letterhead, and access to informative weekly whip meetings. For some members, service in these party posts provides an opportunity to prove their leadership abilities to their colleagues, which can be important to a member who aspires to the top leadership posts. For all members, these posts provide

EVOLVING PARTY ORGANIZATIONS

Congressional party organizations have become much more elaborate in the past generation, a result of competitive pressures and the desire to include more members in party activities. A good example is the elaboration of the Senate Democratic leadership following the 2006 elections. Senator Charles Schumer (D-New York) was praised by his party colleagues for recruiting candidates, raising money, and aiding in the creation of a new Democratic majority. He was rewarded by Majority Leader Harry Reid (D-Nevada) with an appointment to a new party position, conference vice chairman, that Reid created for him. Reid said the position would be the third-ranking leadership post under the majority leader and assistant majority leader (whip).

an opportunity to learn more about the politics of key issues and of their party. Nearly all members advertise their assumption of these "leadership" positions at home.

Senate Party Leaders

Traditionally, the Senate's smaller party organizations have had fewer formal leadership posts, committees, and staff than have their House counterparts, although Senate party organizations have become more elaborate in recent years. The Senate's chief leaders are the majority leader and minority leader. These two leaders have historically been prominent politicians, frequently mentioned in the newspapers and seen on television.

Senate Floor Leaders

The majority leader is the principal leader of the Senate. The majority leader sets the Senate's schedule and plans the order of business for the Senate floor. Critical to that function is a procedural advantage granted to the majority leader by precedent: the right of first recognition. The presiding officer recognizes the majority leader to speak or to offer a motion before recognizing any other senator, a practice that dates back to the 1930s.

Like House Speakers, Senate majority leaders vary in their assertiveness. Lyndon Johnson (D-Texas), who served as Democratic leader from 1955 to 1960, set the modern standard for aggressive leadership. Recent majority leaders of both parties have played a more important role in enacting major legislation – negotiating the content of many important bills, pushing committees to bring legislation to the floor, and taking a leading role in managing controversial legislation on the floor.

A majority leader's ability to set the floor agenda depends on the cooperation of his or her Senate colleagues. To call up a measure for consideration on the floor, the majority leader normally must gain approval of a "motion to proceed." Although the motion requires only a simple majority for approval, it also may be debated and so may be subject to a filibuster. Thus, on a controversial measure, the majority leader may require 60 votes to invoke cloture on the motion to proceed and get a measure to the floor for debate and amendment. Once the motion to proceed is adopted, the measure itself or any amendment to it may be filibustered. Consequently, the Senate's schedule is often quite unpredictable.

The majority leader usually seeks to limit debate and often seeks to limit amendments without going as far as invoking cloture. But to do so, the leader must receive unanimous consent – that is, the leader's request will be rejected if one senator objects. Objections are common from senators who want to protect their right to speak, do not want to give up opportunities to offer amendments, or simply do not want to be inconvenienced. Of course, leaders of both parties entertain requests from colleagues not to allow certain measures to be called up for consideration on the floor (see box, "Congressionally Speaking"). As a result, scheduling in the Senate is much less routine and more a process of negotiation than it is in the House.

The minority leader works closely with the majority leader on scheduling matters. The minority leader protects the parliamentary prerogatives of party members when the majority leader seeks unanimous consent to call up measures, schedule floor action, or limit debate and amendments. Like majority leaders, minority leaders differ in their aggressiveness, and their success depends on the size and cohesiveness of their parties. Unlike the House Speaker and floor leaders, the Senate floor leaders may retain committee assignments. Both Senate leaders are *ex officio* members of the Select Committee on Intelligence. Floor leaders do not hold full committee leadership positions, however.

In late 1996, Senate Republicans set a three-Congress term limit for party leadership positions except for the floor leader and President Pro Tempore. The term limit forced several leaders to give up their positions for the first time at the end of 2002. Senate Democrats are alone among the four congressional parties in not placing term limits on any leadership positions.

Senate Whips and Whip Organizations

Both Senate parties call their whips assistant floor leaders to reflect their chief responsibility: standing in for the floor leader in his or her absence.

Congressionally Speaking . . .

The predicament of the Senate majority leader is illustrated in the practice of holds. A *hold* is an objection to considering a measure on the Senate floor. Senators usually communicate their objections by letter to their party's floor leader. For several decades, these communications were considered confidential so the name of the senator placing the hold often is not known to his or her colleagues. When senators place holds on measures, they sometimes merely want advance warning of floor action, but at other times they seek to change or even prevent action. Working to remove holds is time consuming and involves bargaining with contending factions. Holds are not formally recognized in Senate or party rules, but rather are effective because they constitute notices to object to a unanimous consent request to move to the consideration of a bill or other measure. A leader may call the bluff of a colleague and seek to bring up a bill without clearing the hold, but leaders generally observe holds because they need the cooperation of their colleagues on other matters.

In 2006, a provision requiring public disclosure of the name of the senator placing a hold was included in the ethics reform legislation. The sponsors hope that disclosure will limit the practice and allow the public and fellow senators to hold accountable those senators who place holds.

The Senate whips conduct few head counts. One reason is that bill managers – committee leaders or others who take the lead in the floor debate – often do their own head counting, owing to the Senate's smaller size. Senate whips' specific duties depend on the needs of individual floor leaders. Senate party whips have sometimes named assistant or deputy whips to help with head counts and floor duties, but, as a general rule, the deputy whips have not played a regular or important role in the smaller Senate, where the top leaders, bill managers, and their staffs can manage most duties.

Party Leaders' Resources

The influence of the top congressional party leaders flows from their use of several important resources: (1) their parties' voting strength, (2) the procedural powers granted them by the formal rules of their chamber and party, (3) the tangible rewards that they can grant to members, (4) information, (5) their access to the media, and (6) their staffs. Generally, the combination of party strength and formal powers accorded to him or her makes the House Speaker the most powerful member of Congress, followed in descending order by the Senate majority leader, the Senate minority leader, and the House minority leader.

Party Strength

The relative size of the parties' delegations in Congress determines their majority or minority status and thus which party will enjoy the procedural advantages conferred to the majority. Figures 5.2 and 5.3 show the size of the two major parties in each house since 1900. But a party's ability to pass or block legislation involves more than its size. A majority party must also be fairly cohesive, or at least benefit from a fractured opposition, for its potential strength to be realized. Seldom are majority parties so large that they can afford to lose many votes from their own ranks and still win on the floor. Votes that require supermajorities, such as the two-thirds majority required to override presidential vetoes or the three-fifths majority required to overcome a Senate filibuster, are particularly troublesome for majority parties. As a general rule, there is uncertainty about a majority party's prospects of prevailing on important issues. Hard work is required to build winning coalitions on most important legislation. Not all party colleagues can be trusted to support their leadership, and ways of attracting support from members of the minority party often must be found.

Formal Rules

The standing rules of the House and Senate, as well as the written rules of the congressional parties, grant party leaders certain procedural advantages over other members. Of the four top leaders, the Speaker of the House is, by far, the most advantaged by standing rules and precedents. The Speaker enjoys powers that far exceed those of the most comparable Senate leader, the Senate majority leader. The Senate majority leader, by virtue of the right of first recognition and a few other privileges, comes in second behind the Speaker in formal powers, but the Senate minority leader is not far behind. The Senate's cloture rule and its reliance on unanimous consent agreements to organize its business require the Senate majority leader to consult and gain the consent of the minority leader on most scheduling matters. No such consultation is necessary in the House if the Speaker has the backing of his or her party, making the House minority leader the weakest of the top congressional leaders.

In 1974, the formal power of the House Speaker was bolstered under House rules by granting the Speaker the ability to refer legislation to multiple

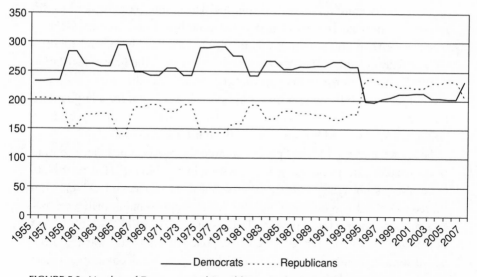

FIGURE 5.2. Number of Democrats and Republicans in the House of Representatives, 1955–2007. *Source:* house.gov.

committees or to propose the creation of an ad hoc or temporary committee. Previously, the Speaker was required to refer each measure to the single
committee that had predominant jurisdiction over it. The Speaker now may
send legislation to committees sequentially, with one committee identified

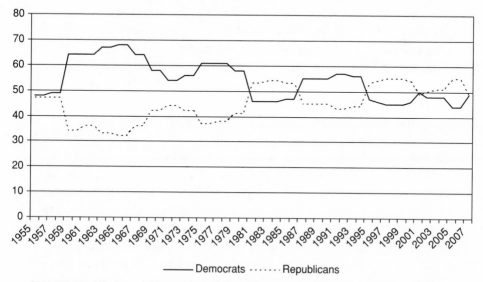

FIGURE 5.3. Number of Democrats and Republicans in the Senate, 1955–2007. *Source:* Senate.gov.

as the primary committee, or can split legislation into parts to send to different committees. The Speaker may set time limits on committee action when more than one committee is involved. This flexible referral rule has substantially enhanced the Speaker's ability to control the flow of legislation in the House – even to direct legislation toward friendly committees and away from unfriendly committees. On only one occasion, for a large multifaceted energy bill in 1977, whose content spanned the jurisdiction of many committees, has an ad hoc committee been used successfully.

The powers granted to the Speaker created the prospect of a more centralized, Speaker-driven, policy-making process in the House. That possibility certainly was not realized in the 1970s. Speakers Albert and O'Neill continued to defer to committees and did not attempt to manipulate committees by using their referral powers. To the contrary, the 1970s were a period of remarkably fragmented, decentralized policy making. This was the product of simultaneous reforms that diffused power from full committee chairs to subcommittee chairs (see Chapter 6). And it reflected the expectations of rank-and-file Democrats. Only in the last year or two of the 1970s did Speaker O'Neill begin to use his new referral powers with some vigor.

The power of the Speaker was enhanced in 1993 when the House, over the objections of minority party Republicans at the time, adopted a rule that allows the Speaker to remove members and appoint additional members to select and conference committees after initial appointments have been made. The new rule, which covers minority party appointees as well as majority party appointees, is aimed at majority party conferees who pursue positions that will obstruct outcomes favored by the leadership. Such conferees cannot be confident that their place on a prominent select committee or important conference committee will be protected once they have been appointed. Instead, the Speaker is free to correct errors in judgment made at the time of the initial appointments. In practice, the Speaker is likely to continue to defer to the minority leader on the appointment of minority party members to select and conference committees. The Republicans retained the rule once they became the majority party after the 1994 elections.

With respect to intra-party rules and practices, the House parties give their top leaders considerable power. They have a strong influence over their party colleagues' committee assignments, appoint their parties' members of the Rules Committee, and appoint members to a variety of party positions. Through the Rules Committee, the Speaker, the majority party's leader, controls the flow of major legislation to the floor. In combination, the powers granted under House and party rules make the Speaker exceptionally influential.

ANOTHER STORY OF SWITCHING PARTIES

In 2004, with no advance notice, freshman Democrat Rodney Alexander (then D-Louisiana) filed for reelection to his seat as a Republican. Not only were House Democratic leaders surprised, they soon became upset when Alexander did not promptly return about $70,000 in contributions that he had received from the political action committees of several Democratic colleagues. Democratic leaders threatened a lawsuit for fraud after failing to hear from Alexander for a month. Alexander began to refund the contributions about two months later, just a month before the November elections, which, at least one Democrat complained, was so late that it limited the value of redirecting the money to other campaigns. Alexander won the seat and was rewarded by his new party with a seat on the prestigious Appropriations Committee, a move up from the Committee on Agriculture and Committee on Transportation and Infrastructure assignments he had as a Democrat. Alexander was reelected in 2006 as a Republican.

Tangible Rewards

Party leaders have a few resources at their disposal that provide direct political benefits to their colleagues and can be used to reward friends and punish enemies. The power to influence committee assignments is the most prominent of these resources. An assignment to a committee with jurisdiction over legislation important to a member's home constituency or to well-financed special interests may be important to the member's electoral prospects. House party leaders play a major role in their parties' committees on committees, where committee assignments are made. Tangible rewards come in many other forms as well. The expanded use of task forces by the congressional parties has increased the number of opportunities for leaders to bestow special status on party colleagues. Leaders can appoint members to special commissions and approve international travel plans.

Leaders can be supportive of their colleagues' campaign efforts. They can influence the allocation of funds from the party campaign committees. In recent decades, party leaders have created political action committees of their own and contributed to colleagues' campaigns. Even candidates for leadership posts seek to demonstrate their leadership abilities by raising money that is directed to their colleagues' campaigns. And in recent years, leaders have become very active in attending the fund-raising events of their colleagues, sometimes even choosing not to attend an event to make clear their dissatisfaction with a member's behavior. In a few cases, leaders have intervened to discourage primary challenges to an incumbent colleague.

Information

Information is critical to legislative success. Devising effective legislative strategies requires information about the specific policy issues and alternatives that will arise during the Congress, the policy preferences of the membership, the administration, the other key players, and how others plan to act. Advantages from chamber or party rules, or even party strength, remain only potential sources of leadership power if they are not matched by useful and timely information.

The top leaders navigate in a sea of information. With the help of their staff, leaders collect and absorb information about committee schedules and actions, floor scheduling, presidential requests, members' political circumstances, and interest group activity. The top leaders do not have a monopoly over most kinds of information, of course, but they are uniquely placed to assimilate information from many different sources. Requests are made of them on such matters as scheduling, committee assignments, and campaign assistance, and leaders can sometimes pry information from members, lobbyists, and others who want something from them. The whip systems and party task forces are often activated to gather and disseminate information. And the time they spend on or near their chamber floor gives leaders and their staffs opportunities for casual conversations and informal exchanges of information.

Because information flows to the top leaders so readily, few other members can compete with party leaders as coalition builders. To be sure, committee leaders and bill sponsors master information relevant to their own legislation. But from time to time even committee leaders turn to party leaders for assistance in gathering and distributing information. By exercising care in granting access to their information, party leaders can affect the strategies of other important players.

Leaders' informational advantage is stronger in the House than in the Senate, owing to the House's larger size. In the House, the seemingly simple task of counting members planning to vote for or against something is onerous. For the majority party, this means reaching more than 218 members, many of whom might be away from Washington when the information is needed. Consequently, House bill managers often must rely on the services of the party leadership – whip offices and task forces – for timely information. In contrast, Senate bill managers are more self-reliant because they need to count fewer heads. Thus, Senate whip organizations are not critical to the collection and dissemination of information on most important matters.

The overall trend in recent decades has been toward a diffusion of information across Capitol Hill. Junior members have benefited from the expansion of committee, personal, and support agency staffs and from the growth of the interest group community and informal members' caucuses. Party leaders now have more competition in the market for information than they did just a few decades ago.

Access to the Media

Although top party leaders cannot compete with the president for media attention, they enjoy far better access to the media than do most other members. The media often turn to top leaders for their reactions to events or to presidential decisions or statements. This phenomenon is natural: Leaders are presumed to represent their parties and to be in a position to act on their views. Even when there is no breaking story, leaders' routine press conferences attract reporters on the chance that the leaders will say something newsworthy. Few other members can count on such attention. Thus, leaders gain media attention because they are powerful, and, at least in part, they are powerful because they gain media attention.

Party leaders' media access serves as an important resource in the legislative game. Leaders can share their access with colleagues: They can mention a colleague's legislation, invite a colleague to join in a press conference, or refer reporters and television producers to a colleague. They can selectively divulge information about the plans of friendly and unfriendly factions. They also can increase the ease or difficulty of reaching compromises by intensifying or softening the rhetoric of claiming credit and avoiding blame.

Until recently, Senate leaders generally had an advantage over House leaders in their access to the media. The greater public prestige of the Senate and greater public interest in senators than in representatives encouraged the national media to pay more attention to Senate leaders. The advent of televised floor sessions in the House in 1979, about seven years before the Senate permitted television coverage of its sessions, seemed to make little difference.

Recent House Speakers have been as visible as the top Senate leaders on network news programs. In the 1950s through the mid-1970s, Senate leaders were far more visible on television news programs than were House leaders. The Speaker of the House has gained prominence since the 1970s. For a couple years in the mid-1990s, Speaker Gingrich was second only to the president in media visibility. The House minority leader generally lags far behind other top leaders in media visibility, reflecting the relatively weak

formal powers and informal influence of most House minority leaders. In
contrast, the power of the Senate minority to obstruct bills, coupled with
the Senate's prestige, gives the Senate minority leader a big advantage over
his or her House counterpart in attracting media attention.

Recent party leaders in both houses have made a concerted effort to shape
the message communicated through the media to the general public. They
have expanded their press office operations, hired media specialists, consulted pollsters, created party committees or task forces to shape party messages, and sought new ways to communicate to the public. All recent top
leaders have sought to fashion coherent policy programs, to advertise their
programs, and to develop a common argument or theme for the parties on
major issues.

Leadership Staffs

Top leaders' staffs have expanded as leaders have sought to meet colleagues'
expectations and expand their own influence. These staffs now include policy specialists, public relations personnel, and even experts in parliamentary
procedures, as well as people who assist the leaders with daily chores. With
the help of expanded staffs, leaders can more carefully follow committee
deliberations, more rapidly respond to political events, and more frequently
take a leading role in the negotiation of legislative details.

Organizational arrangements for the staff of the four top party leaders
vary, reflecting both differences in the leaders' positions and historical accident. The House Speaker's leadership staff is spread between the Speaker's
office and the Steering and Policy Committee. Similarly, the Senate Democratic leader's staff is located primarily in the Policy Committee. The House
and Senate Republican leaders' staffs are housed within their leadership
offices. Both Senate leaders manage the activity of the party secretaries,
who are staff members, and the secretaries' assistants.

An Era of Reinvigorated Parties

The role of parties and their leaders in Congress is not written in stone.
Indeed, members of the early Congresses could not have envisioned modern
congressional parties. The development of congressional parties has
occurred in response to the changing needs and demands of members, who
elect the top party leaders and are free to write and rewrite the rules of
their chambers and party caucuses. New issues, turnover in the membership, new presidents, new political cleavages in American society, the nature

of electoral parties, and changing rules sometimes alter members' calculations about the kind of legislative party organization and leadership that will best serve their interests.

In recent decades, stronger parties and leaders have emerged. This development would have surprised most observers of the mid-1960s. At that time, the House and Senate caucuses of the majority party Democrats were inactive; today, all four congressional party caucuses (or conferences) are active. In the mid-1960s, the top Democratic leaders were deferential to committee and subcommittee chairs; today, party leaders frequently name party task forces, composed of members both on and off the standing committees of jurisdiction, to devise policy and strategy on major issues. In the mid-1960s, party leaders assumed that committee leaders would speak for the party on policy matters; today, party leaders themselves are clearly expected to assume a prominent role in the media on nearly all important matters. In the 1970s, extreme individualism was the most common description of Congress; during the last 20 years, unrestrained partisanship has been the dominant theme.

These developments appear to be the products of change in the several basic elements of the legislative game –what the issues are, who the players are and what they want, and the rules. Each of these elements contributed to forming the parties' coalitions inside and outside of Congress and deserves brief consideration.

The Issues

Large federal deficits in the 1980s and early 1990s dominated the policy agenda of Congress and exacerbated long-standing differences between the parties over the appropriate size and function of the federal government. Such matters as tax hikes and cuts, the allocation of money between defense and domestic programs, and government commitments to entitlement programs for the elderly, the sick, and the poor stimulated pitched battles between the parties. Few issues were perceived to have as direct a connection to electoral fortunes as aggregate spending and tax choices, so the incentives for the parties to seek credit and avoid blame were high. The partisan electoral consequences of fiscal politics produced demands on the top leaders to be more assertive in public relations and to work harder to bolster their parties' public images. Partisan differences over fiscal policy reemerged as a central issue after the 2000 elections and remain important.

Contributing to partisanship is the use of omnibus legislation for the federal budget. As a consequence of procedures authorized by the 1974 Budget

Act, budget policy was wrapped into two major pieces of legislation each year – a budget resolution and a reconciliation bill. The stakes are particularly high for reconciliation bills, which typically package the proposals for spending cuts of more than a dozen committees. These high-stakes bills force party leaders into all negotiations and encourage members and outside observers to judge outcomes in terms of party winners and losers.

To make matters worse, this high-stakes contest, between a Congress controlled by one party and a president of the other party, tended toward stalemate. Blaming the other party – and the other institution – for the lack of action became the chief political strategy. Only top party leaders and the president could overcome the gridlock, but that only increased the stakes and enhanced the perceived partisan consequences of the outcome.

In this environment, party leaders were expected to be aggressive and outspoken. Some leaders were not especially comfortable or capable in that role. Only after Jim Wright assumed the speakership in 1987 did House Democrats have a Speaker who relished a prominent place in the media. When Senator George Mitchell took over after Byrd relinquished his leadership post, also in 1987, Senate Democrats had a leader who saw being a party spokesperson as a high-priority responsibility. Since then, leaders of both parties and in both houses have aggressively promoted their party's views.

Contributing to a stronger role for party leaders have been issues that cut across the jurisdictions of multiple standing committees. When party interests dictate action on issues such as global warming and energy that fall under the jurisdiction of many committees, their chairs cannot be expected to act promptly and effectively to coordinate legislative action. The majority party's interests dictate that central party leaders coordinate the development of legislation, take the lead in finding compromises among party colleagues, devise public relations strategies to sell the legislation to the public, and concentrate the resources required to build majorities on the floor.

In recent years, foreign policy and the war in Iraq divided the parties. In 2007, efforts to limit or end the war produced some divisions among Democrats, but the unpopularity of President George W. Bush's Iraq policy with the public motivated strong centralized action by Democratic leaders in the House and Senate to set restrictions on war spending.

Members' Demands

Former Senate parliamentarian Floyd Riddick once observed that "the position of the floor leader is not that of an army general over a multitude of soldiers. Unlike army officers, the floor leaders must maintain continued support. They are subject to periodic reelection by the same persons they have been leading."[1] That is, party leaders are appropriately viewed as agents of their party colleagues, and their success depends largely on the cooperation of those colleagues. Consequently, leaders' goals and strategies are shaped by the demands and expectations of their party colleagues, whose own political goals and needs change over time.

Many observers have commented on the individualism that has characterized members of Congress in recent decades. This "new breed" of lawmaker, as it is often called, is a product of the 1960s. New-breed members are anti-establishment, intolerant of traditional norms and authority, and more national, or even worldly, in their orientation. They are more independent, outward-looking, issue-oriented, media-oriented, and entrepreneurial. Their individualism is encouraged by expanded opportunities outside Congress – a swelling interest group community, broader single-issue constituencies facilitated by new forms of electronic communication and greater ease in cross-continental and intercontinental travel, and the growth of computerized mass mailings and telephone solicitation techniques. In addition, individualism among legislators is encouraged by the necessity of personally raising large sums of money to gain reelection.

In the late 1960s, the Senate's new breed began to produce presidential candidates. In the 1970s, new-breed members contributed to a redistribution of power within House committees from full committee chairs to subcommittee chairs (see Chapter 6), the distribution of more resources to rank-and-file members in both chambers, and a surge in floor amending activity. They also contributed to the demise of such waning norms as deference to committee recommendations and serving a quiet apprenticeship period to learn the ropes before actively seeking to influence policy choices.

Unrestrained individualism created several problems for party leaders. Surveying, coordinating, and scheduling chamber activities became more complicated. No longer could majority party leaders rely on consultations with a few senior committee leaders. Individualism meant that leaders were less certain about who wanted to participate and who expected to be consulted, that committee leaders could expect more challenges to committee bills, and that floor sessions would be longer and less predictable. Of course, many bill managers faced difficulties because of their inexperience. In the House, individualism also meant less restrained tactics on the part of minority party members.

As members struggled to adapt to the new conditions, many majority party members turned to their party leaders for assistance. More and more

frequently, majority party leaders were called on to resolve intra-party conflicts that had once been negotiated or squelched by committee chairs. Even
before legislation was ready for floor action, conflicts between committees
and between committee members and nonmembers led some members to
ask top leaders to intervene. And majority party frustration with minority
party tactics – calls for votes, redundant amendments, and so on – resulted
in calls for a crackdown on the minority by the majority party leadership.
The Speaker responded with some rules changes and more creative use of
special rules to limit floor amendments. Ironically, then, from the chaos of
unrestrained individualism came demands for stronger central leadership.

Policy Alignments

At the same time that policy making was becoming further complicated by
individualism, members' positions on major policy questions became more
polarized by partisan affiliation. Electoral forces and changes in Congress's
policy agenda contributed to greater partisanship in voting during the 1980s.

The budget-oriented agenda produced intensified conflict among legislators. Large deficits increased the difficulty of finding funds for new or
expanded programs, and old programs became targets for budget cutters.
Consequently, legislation that in the past had seemed to produce far more
winners than losers, such as student aid and environmental protection measures, was evaluated less on its own merit and more on the basis of its impact
on the deficit during the next few years. Attention shifted from individual programs, which often attract support across party lines, to the overall
spending and taxation patterns of the federal government – just the kind of
issue that taps deeply held ideological beliefs and most differentiates the two
parties.

Electoral forces also contributed to party polarization. The largest changes
appeared in the South, where the expansion of the African American voting
base for Democrats and the suburban, white base for Republicans altered
the electoral coalitions for the two parties. Southern Democrats became
more moderate and sometimes quite liberal, making the Democratic contingents in the House and Senate more homogeneous. Southern Republicans,
a scarce breed before the 1970s, fit the traditional conservative Republican mold, so they reinforced the homogeneity of the Republican party in
Congress. Southern Republicans now hold many of their party's top leadership posts.

A change from less to more polarized parties has characterized developments in the House and Senate since the late 1970s. Increasing intra-party

LEADERSHIP IN ANOTHER ERA

Sam Rayburn (D-Texas) was the most beloved twentieth-century Speaker of the House. He served as Speaker from 1940 to 1961, with the exception of four years when Republicans controlled the House. Rayburn listened well and was always kind to his colleagues, and because he was sheepish about his bald head, he shied away from cameras. He exercised his power quietly. A Rayburn biographer reported an incident on the floor of the House that was typical of the way he ruled:

[W]hen a bill providing for a cooling-off period to stave off labor strikes came to the House floor, Rayburn wanted it debated fully. Experience and instinct told him that with feelings running high an attempt might be made to shut off debate and go directly to a vote. This proved correct when Jennings Randolph of West Virginia, a member of the Labor Committee, won recognition and started to make a motion to do this.

While he was still talking, Rayburn walked down from the dais and headed toward him. With each approaching step Randolph's voice grew weaker. Finally he stopped talking when Rayburn reached him and put a hand on his shoulder. For a short time, with his face set sternly, Rayburn spoke in a low, gruff tone to Randolph, whom he liked. Then still talking, he removed his hand, plunged it into his jacket pocket, and his body rocked back and forth from his heels to his toes. Then he turned suddenly and walked back to the rostrum.

Laughter swept the chamber as embarrassment crossed Randolph's face. When silence came, Randolph announced he was withdrawing his motion, and he added, "As a legislative son I am always willing to follow the advice of my legislative elders."

Rayburn was special, to be sure, but no recent Speaker, in an age of televised floor sessions and independent-minded members, would have dared embarrass a colleague in that way.

cohesiveness, reinforced by increasing inter-party conflict, has altered the demands placed on party leaders. That partisanship has led members to insist that their leaders actively pursue party interests, and at the same time it has reduced resistance to strong central leaders from the remaining but shrinking minority factions within the parties.

Rules of the Game

The reinforcement of the Speaker's powers, beginning in the early 1970s, represents an important development in the distribution of power in the House. The House party leaders appoint the members of the Rules Committee, which, in the case of the majority party, gives the Speaker effective control over the content of special rules governing the consideration of major legislation on the floor. Furthermore, the Speaker now has the power to refer legislation to multiple committees and set deadlines for committee action. In the House, therefore, the majority party leader can exercise a good deal of control over the process by which legislation is brought to the floor, debated, and subject to amendment.

In many cases, the House Speaker's new powers have been exercised in routine ways. The Speaker does not seek to influence most committee assignments, for example, because many committees have little relevance to partisan concerns or few members are competing for the available seats. For more routine legislation going through the Rules Committee, the committee relies on past experience to guide the design of rules, without consulting with the Speaker. Similarly, the parliamentarian makes recommendations on multiple referral based on established precedent and inter-committee agreements and the advice usually is followed. The Speaker seldom gets personally involved. The development of such standard operating practices is a natural product of the gradual accumulation of precedents under new rules and the desire of members and their staff to lend predictability to the process.

The new powers become a political tool only when the Speaker deliberately calls them into play. In the 1970s, Speakers Albert and O'Neill generally let their procedural tools sit idle. But since the late 1970s, the nature of the policy agenda and members' demands led speakers to employ their powers more often and aggressively. In fact, the speaker's bill referral and special rules prerogatives are a regular part of strategic calculations by most members on important, controversial legislation. As a result, the speaker frequently is brought into discussions about strategy by other members at early stages in their planning so that the speaker has regular opportunities to influence the policy directions taken by House committees and subcommittees.

Strategies of Adaptation

Party organizations and leaders are much more important to congressional policy making now than they were three decades ago. Four aspects of party responses to the changing conditions deserve summary.

EXPANDED SERVICES. Since the 1970s, congressional party organizations and leaders have greatly expanded the services they provide their members. Leaders and party committee staffs now provide quite varied services: publications on the chamber schedules, legislation, policy problems, and political matters; electronic mail communications; clearinghouses for job applicants; analyses of floor voting records; assistance in the production of newsletters and graphics material; and facilities and staff assistance for the production of radio and television messages and programs. In the Senate, the parties maintain in-house cable television systems to provide senators' offices with up-to-the-minute information on floor developments and satellite up-link equipment so that senators can make live appearances on local stations or at meetings away from Washington. On a personal basis, leaders work harder to meet the scheduling demands of party colleagues and to assist colleagues in fundraising, campaigning, and attracting media attention.

The expansion of services represents an effort on the part of top party leaders to incur the gratitude of party colleagues whose support they need on controversial legislation. Secondary leaders – whips, the chairs of the campaign, policy, and research committees, and conference chairs and secretaries – who, in their effort to demonstrate their fitness for even higher positions, have led the way by diversifying services. As members compete for votes to get elected to party posts, they solicit ideas for new services and move to expand services once elected. While doing so, secondary leaders expand party staffs that they control and extend their own reach to a broader range of issues.

STRATEGY OF INCLUSION. All leaders want fellow party members to feel that they have influence on party policy stances and tactics – a strategy of inclusion. All four party caucuses (or conferences) and many of the party committees meet regularly. Whip organizations have grown and task forces have multiplied to give more members an opportunity to participate in policy making beyond the confines of their assigned standing committees. Leaders also call together informal groups of members to solicit their views and encourage their participation through party channels. These developments contribute to leaders' efforts to gather information, promote a party spirit, solicit support, and build majority coalitions.

PROCEDURAL STRATEGIES. Leaders have expanded their repertoire of procedural strategies. The standard committee-to-floor-to-conference process remains, but variations on that process are now more common. Discussions in party councils are more likely to occur before action is taken in standing committees. Leaders more frequently engage in negotiations with committee and faction leaders after committees have reported legislation but before floor action. Party task forces have added a layer of party members who influence both the content of legislation and coalition-building strategy. At times, task forces even initiate legislation, and their proposals are taken directly to the floor by party leaders. Flexibility, not rigidity, characterizes the legislative process in recent Congresses.

Majority party leaders, particularly in the House where their formal powers are the strongest, use their procedural tools to set the agenda in a way that favors their party. This happens at two levels. On the first level, leaders more actively seek to set detailed policy agendas for their chamber, including a general schedule for action on major legislation. On the second level, leaders work harder to control the specific alternatives that are considered on the floor once legislation gets there. In the House, this is done through special rules written by the Rules Committee. Controlling alternatives is more difficult in the Senate, where unanimous consent must be obtained to structure the consideration of alternatives, a requirement that severely limits the ability of the majority leader to manipulate the floor agenda. Nevertheless, pressure to lend some structure to the process comes from members of both parties, all of whom have busy schedules and an interest in avoiding embarrassing or repetitious votes. At times, negotiating unanimous consent agreements becomes a full-time job for the majority leader.

PUBLIC RELATIONS. Leaders work harder to influence the image of their party that is communicated through the mass media. Such efforts are aimed at creating a climate of public opinion favorable to the party, which makes it easier for party members to support their leaders and explain their votes at home. If successful, leaders' media strategies produce support for party positions from independent-minded members who are not readily pressured.

Conclusion

As consequential as some recent developments have been, they have not made congressional parties capable of expeditious, centrally directed legislative action for an extended period of time. Congressional parties still lack the capacity to deny nomination or election to Congress and so have limited influence over their members, far less influence than exists in most other national legislatures. To be sure, the parties elect leadership, organize the standing committees, and structure floor and conference action. Moreover, congressional parties' internal organizations and staffs have become more elaborate. And in the last two decades leaders have been prime movers in the legislative process on major issues. Nevertheless, diverse constituency interests across a large, heterogeneous country, the weakness of the parties in candidate selection, the fragmentation of American party organizations across several levels of government, and the difficulty of coordinating House and Senate activities stand in the way of party-directed policy making over the long term.

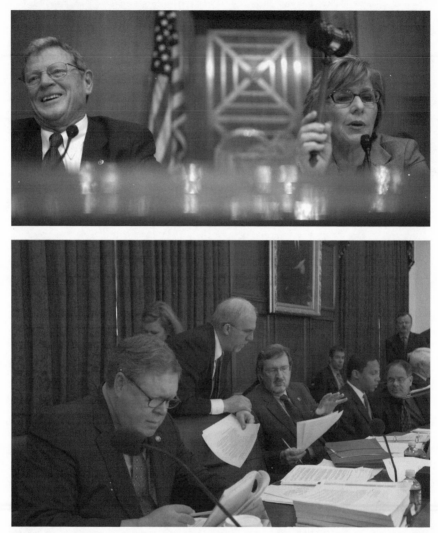

Above: Shortly after Democrats regained a majority in 2007, Chairwoman Barbara Boxer (D-California) reminds Sen. James Inhofe (R-Oklahoma) that he no longer wields the gavel of the Senate Environment and Public Works committee.

Below: Rep. Leonard Boswell (D-Iowa) speaks with Chairman David Obey (D-Wisconsin, sitting) during the House Appropriations Committee markup of the fiscal year 2007 Iraq/Afghanistan, Veterans, and Hurricane Katrina Supplemental Appropriations bill.

6

The Standing Committees

ONE OF THE MOST VISIBLE AND ENDURING FEATURES OF CONGRESS IS ITS committee system. From hearings to investigations to legislative activity, committees are the congressional darlings of the mass media. And considering the central role that committees play in modern-day lawmaking and oversight, there is little wonder why they garner so much attention. Most important legislation originates in a standing committee, most of the details of legislation are approved in committee, and standing committee members usually dominate floor and conference action. When legislation dies, it usually does so in committee.

The significance of standing committees in the policy-making process varies over time. In the mid-twentieth century, committees were often described as nearly autonomous policy makers (see Chapter 2). The tremendous growth in government and power of the presidency that characterized the New Deal and World War II era of the 1930s and 1940s led Congress to reevaluate the way it did business. The Legislative Reorganization Act of 1946 reduced the number of standing committees, provided detailed, written committee jurisdictions, guaranteed a professional staff for each committee, and directed committees to conduct oversight of executive agencies. As a result of the 1946 act, most of the key features of the modern committee system were put into place. Moreover, the leadership of the internally divided Democratic majority usually preferred to defer to committees rather than risk open divisions on the House and Senate floor. In fact, prescriptive norms – deference to committees and senior committee leaders – were articulated by leaders to bolster the power of committees.

In recent decades, committees have lost much of the autonomy they had gained in the middle of the twentieth century. A more assertive membership, increasingly polarized parties, stronger party leadership, and new checks on committee leadership, among other factors, reduced the level of independence once held by committees and their leaders. Still, committees retain a considerable amount of power within their issue domains; they process the vast majority of legislation that is approved by the House and Senate. In this chapter, we profile the House and Senate committee systems and then examine the foundations of committee power and how these powers have evolved over time.

Types of Committees

Modern congressional committees have two formal functions: (1) collecting information through hearings and investigations and (2) drafting and reporting legislation. Committee hearings are Congress's primary means for formally receiving the testimony of representatives of the executive branch, organized interest groups, independent experts, the general public, and, occasionally, movie stars. Congress usually relies on committees to investigate disasters (natural or human-made), scandals in government or elsewhere, or policy crises. Informally, congressional hearings provide opportunities for legislators to publicize causes and receive media attention. On the legislative side, the vast majority of bills and other legislation introduced by members are referred to the committee or committees with the appropriate jurisdiction. In committee meetings for considering legislation, called markups, the details of legislation are reviewed or written.

The House and Senate have developed several types of committees to perform these informational and legislative functions. All committees can hold hearings and investigate policy problems that fall within their jurisdiction. However, not all committees have the right to receive and report legislation, and not all committees are considered to be standing or permanent committees (Table 6.1).

Standing committees have legislative authority and permanent status (standing committee are listed in Table 6.2). Their legislative jurisdiction is specified in chamber rules and precedents, and they write and report legislation on any matter within their jurisdictions. Committee members, and particularly chairs, are territorial about their committees' jurisdictions and resist efforts to reduce or reallocate their jurisdictions. As a result, with a few important exceptions, change in the committee systems of the House and Senate has been incremental.

Ad hoc committees may be created and appointed to design and report legislation, but they are temporary and often dissolve either at a specified date or after reporting the legislation for which they were created. Since 1975,

TABLE 6.1. Types of Committees.

Permanent Status?	May report legislation to the floor?	
	Yes	No
Yes	standing committees	some select committees joint committees
No	conference committees most select committees ad hoc committees	

the Speaker of the House has been permitted to appoint ad hoc committees with House approval, but this authority has been used infrequently.

Conference committees are temporary and have legislative responsibilities. They are appointed to resolve the differences between House and Senate versions of legislation. The Constitution requires that legislation be approved in identical form by both houses before it is sent to the president. While the Constitution is silent as to how the two houses are to resolve their differences, conference committees were an almost immediate solution to this problem. Although inter-chamber differences can be resolved in other ways, conference committees are formed for most important legislation. Conference committees have wide, but not unlimited, discretion to redesign legislation in their efforts to gain House and Senate approval. In theory, conference committees are bound to the differences between the House and Senate legislation. In practice, however, it is not uncommon for conference committees to insert provisions into legislation that did not appear in either chamber's final legislation and remove provisions that were agreed upon by both chambers (see accompanying box). When a majority of House conferees and a majority of Senate conferees agree, a conference committee issues a report that must be approved by both houses for the bill to be sent to the president. Conference committees dissolve as soon as one house takes action on the conference report.

Joint committees are permanent but lack legislative authority. Joint committees are composed of members from both houses, and the chairs alternate between the houses from Congress to Congress. The Joint Economic Committee frequently conducts highly publicized hearings on economic affairs, and the Joint Committee on Taxation serves primarily as a holding company for a respected staff of economists whose economic forecasts and

TABLE 6.2. Standing Committees of the House and Senate, 2007–2008.

House of Representatives

Name (Number of Subcommittees)	Dems[c]	Reps[c]	Ratio[d]
Agriculture (6)	25	21	1.19:1
Appropriations (12)	37	29	1.28:1
Armed Services (7)	33	28	1.18:1
Budget (0)	22	17	1.29:1
Education and Labor (5)	27	21	1.29:1
Energy and Commerce (6)	31	26	1.19:1
Financial Services (5)	36	33	1.09:1
Foreign Relations (7)	26	22	1.18:1
Homeland Security (6)	17	15	1.13:1
House Administration (0)	6	3	2:1
Judiciary (5)	23	17	1.35:1
Natural Resources (5)	25	21	1.19:1
Oversight and Government Reform (5)	22	18	1.22:1
Rules (2)	9	4	2.25:1
Science and Technology (5)	23	20	1.15:1
Select Committee on Intelligence[a] (4)	12	9	1.33:1
Small Business (5)	18	15	1.2:1
Standards of Official Conduct[b] (0)	5	5	1:1
Transportation and Infrastructure (6)	40	34	1.18:1
Veterans' Affairs (4)	16	13	1.23:1
Ways and Means (6)	24	17	1.41:1

Senate

Name (Number of Subcommittees)	Dems[e]	Reps	Ratio[d]
Agriculture, Nutrition, and Forestry (4)	11	10	1.1:1
Appropriations (12)	15	14	1.07:1
Armed Services (6)	13	12	1.08:1
Banking, Housing, and Urban Affairs (5)	11	10	1.1:1
Budget (0)	12	11	1.09:1
Commerce, Science, and Transportation (7)	12	11	1.09:1
Energy and Natural Resources (4)	12	11	1.09:1
Environment and Public Works (6)	10	9	1.11:1
Finance (5)	11	10	1.1:1
Foreign Relations (7)	11	10	1.1:1
Health, Education, Labor, and Pensions (3)	11	10	1.1:1
Homeland Security and Governmental Affairs (5)	9	8	1.13:1
Indian Affairs (0)	8	7	1.14:1
Judiciary (7)	10	9	1.11:1
Rules and Administration (0)	10	9	1.11:1
Select Committee on Intelligence[a] (0)	8	7	1.14:1
Select Committee on Ethics[b] (0)	3	3	1:1
Small Business and Entrepreneurship (0)	10	9	1.11:1
Veterans' Affairs (0)	8	7	1.14:1

a = The two intelligence committees are officially named select committees but have authority to report legislation. b = The House Committee on Standards of Official Conduct may report legislation; the Senate Ethics Committee does not have legislative authority. c = Numbers include only full members of the chamber and vacant seats allotted to the party. d = Party ratio is (Democrats: Republicans). Ratios in House and Senate chambers are 1.15:1 and 1.04:1, respectively (counting the independent senators among the Democrats). e = Independent Senators Bernie Sanders (I-VT) and Joseph Lieberman (I-CT) are counted among the Democrats. *Source:* www.house.gov; www.senate.gov.

reports on fiscal policy matters are frequently cited. The Joint Committee on Printing performs the more ministerial duty of overseeing the Government Printing Office; the Joint Committee on the Library oversees the Library of Congress. Bills are not referred to joint committees, and joint committees cannot report legislation to the floor. The Joint Committee on Atomic Energy (1946–1977) was the only joint committee to date with authority to report legislation.

Select, or special, committees are, in principle, temporary committees without legislative authority. They may be used to study problems that fall under the jurisdiction of several standing committees, to symbolize Congress's commitment to major constituency groups, or simply to reward particular legislators. Select committees have been used for seven prominent investigations since 1970, including the Senate's 1973 investigation of the Watergate break-in and cover-up and the 1987 House and Senate investigation of the Iran-Contra affair. Major reforms of congressional rules and organization have originated in select committees.

Unfortunately, committee nomenclature can be misleading. For example, the House and Senate have each made their Select Intelligence Committee permanent and granted it the power to report legislation. Some select committees, such as the House Committee on Homeland Security, began as select committees and gained standing status later. In 1993, under pressure to streamline the legislative process and reduce spending, the House abolished its Select Committee on Aging, Hunger, Narcotics Abuse and Control and its Select Committee on Children, Youth and Families. The Senate maintains a Special Committee on Aging, which studies issues relevant to the elderly, in addition to the Select Committee on Ethics, which handles ethics violations of senators and staffs.

Standing committees are the primary concern of this chapter. In the modern Congress, standing committees originate most legislation, and their members manage the legislation on the floor and dominate conference committees. Unless otherwise indicated, the following discussion concerns standing committees.

The Nature of Congressional Committees

The Constitution makes no provision for committees. Yet, committees emerged early in congressional history. And across time the committee system has undergone considerable change. At different points in history the House and Senate have adopted rules to expand and reduce the number of committees, as well as to modify their structure and authority. Given the

CONFERENCE COMMITTEE OUTSIDE THE SCOPE OF CHAMBER DIFFERENCES

In the waning days of 2003, Congress was faced with a dilemma very similar to the one they had encountered a year earlier – the new fiscal year was underway and there was no end in sight to the ongoing appropriations process. As always, entering the fiscal year without passing all of the annual appropriations bills threatens the funding, and thus the continuation, of important programs and departments (see Chapter 12). For the majority party Republican leaders, however, this posed a particular quandary, having vowed to the public a few months earlier to run the process more smoothly and with greater discipline upon being given control of both chambers. The intensity of conflict over these bills made it clear to Republican leaders that the appropriations process would drag on for some time if they remained dedicated to passing the bills individually. In mid-December 2003, more than two months after fiscal 2004 had begun, Congress had failed to pass seven of the 13 annual appropriations measures.

The Republican leadership had hoped to pass each of the appropriations bills as free-standing legislation, but there appeared to be no simple means of resolving the disputes that persisted on the seven remaining bills. GOP leaders decided instead to turn their attention toward packaging the bills. The timing of conference negotiations for one of the bills (the agriculture spending bill) conveniently provided Republican leaders with a vehicle for constructing an omnibus appropriations bill.

In selecting conferees, Republican leaders in both chambers appointed a large number of conservative loyalists with close ties to the GOP leadership and White House. Even a cursory glance at the legislation that emerged from the conference suggests that the conferees had done a considerable amount of legislating outside the scope of chamber differences. Several provisions that had been agreed to by both chambers in the original bills were removed. For instance, the conferees decided to drop a provision that would lift the ban on Americans' travel to Cuba – a provision that had gathered strong support in both chambers. Moreover, a number of provisions that had not been agreed to by either chamber had been inserted as a favor to the administration. Many of these provisions, in fact, had little relevance to the appropriations bills themselves, but had been controversial measures that the administration was uncertain could pass on their own. One such measure was a highly contentious provision, backed by the National Rifle Association, that required the government to destroy background check records on gun purchasers within 24 hours, rather than 90 days as under existing law. In the end, the conference report marked a conservative shift in the legislation when compared with the original bills of the two houses.

Conferees were given a tremendous amount of leverage because failure to adopt the conference report would have resulted in an undesirable outcome in the eyes of most legislators. The conference report passed the House without any delays. And following a brief, symbolic gesture of opposition, the report also passed the Senate by a wide margin.

Source: "2003 Legislative Summary: Appropriations." *CQ Weekly*, December 13, 2003, 3095. Mary Clare Jalonick 2003. "Plethora of Partisan Issues Makes Agriculture Appropriations Vulnerable to Inclusion in Omnibus." *CQ Weekly*, November 8, 2003, 2778.

emergence and longevity of committees, it is clear that the division of labor that allows each house to pursue multiple hearings and legislative efforts simultaneously has proven useful.

To whom are committees responsible? What interests do committees serve? Such questions have motivated an important literature in political science. Three prominent perspectives offer rationale for the existence of committees – the information, distributive, and partisan perspectives.

Informational Politics: Committees Governed by Floor Majorities

A traditional view of congressional committees is that they are designed to meet legislators' need for information about policy problems and solutions. Given Congress' large workload and the complexity of issues, it is unrealistic to expect members to have the capacity to make informed decisions on all matters. By focusing on the issues before their own committees, legislators gain expertise that is applied in a committee setting to improve the fit of policy solutions to policy problems. The expertise serves the interest of the larger membership by generating information that is useful to all legislators in evaluating the recommendations of committees.

In this view, committee experts serve the interest of a majority of the parent house. If committee recommendations diverge too much from the preferences of the floor majority or prove misleading, floor majorities will reject committee recommendations and may even reform the committee system. Under normal circumstances, the better-informed arguments of committee experts will guide the behavior of other legislators.

Distributive Politics: Autonomous Committees

A distributive perspective suggests that committees exist to distribute the benefits of policy across constituencies with diverse interests. Committees are created to address the legislative interests of constituencies who are important to legislators' reelection efforts. The multiple committees of each

SOMETIMES A SENSE OF HUMOR IS REQUIRED

Senators do not always get their first choice of subcommittees. In an interview, Senator Amy Klobuchar (D-Minnesota) told a reporter about her first day on the Subcommittee on Oceans, Atmosphere, Fisheries, and Coast Guard:

Somehow I got placed on the Ocean Subcommittee. I didn't ask for that. But it does have jurisdiction over the Great Lakes, which is important, and so I can be a voice for the Great Lakes. But when I got there the first I realized all the other senators had an ocean. Olympia Snowe (R-Maine) was on there, John Kerry (D-Massachusetts) was on there. And I wrote a note to Frank Lautenberg (D-New Jersey) and I said, "I am the only senator on the Oceans Subcommittee without an ocean." And he wrote back, "Just come back next year and ask for one."

Source: http://blog.washingtonpost.com/sleuth/2007/06/post_1.html

house allow legislators to gain membership on the committee or committees most relevant to their own constituencies.

By empowering committees, each house gives legislators with the strongest constituency interest in a policy area the most influence over legislative action. Because members represent diverse constituencies, the committee system institutionalizes a mutually beneficial arrangement for legislators who want to do favors for home audiences. Public policy is then the product of a giant "logroll" – each committee of legislators getting what it wants.

From the perspective of distributive politics, committees serve the interests of individual legislators and their home constituencies (see box "Sometimes a Sense of Humor Is Required"). Therefore, the committee system reflects the pluralism of American politics and permits legislators to focus on the political interests that matter most to them. The distributive perspective considers committees to be relatively autonomous units to which parties and the parent chambers defer. Each committee operates in a community of executive branch agencies and interest groups with similar interests. The larger public interest may suffer as the demands of the disparate constituencies are addressed by committees.

Partisan Politics: Committees Governed by the Majority Party

The partisan perspective posits that parties create committees to better ensure the success of party programs. On committees whose jurisdictions matter to the majority party, party leaders make committee assignments to enhance the party's policy prospects. This, along with expectations of loyalty, constrains the behavior of committee members. And since the majority party has a numerical advantage on committees, it ultimately dictates the policies that emerge.

From this perspective, committee members serve the interests of the parties. While each house approves committee membership lists, each party determines which of its members are on each committee list. Parties structure the internal organization of committees – the majority party assumes the chairmanships and controls most staff. And the majority party leadership schedules committee legislation for action on the floor.

In Practice: Committees Governed by Multiple Principals

In practice, committee members must balance conflicting demands placed on them by their parent chambers, parties, and constituencies. While seeking to satisfy the expectations of constituents, they must stay on good terms with party colleagues to retain important committee positions and must meet chamber majorities' expectations to get legislation passed. Fortunate legislators find that the demands of constituents, party leaders, and the chamber majority are aligned most of the time, but real-world politics require many committee members to take risks, balance interests, and struggle with difficult choices.

The extent of independent committee influence over policy outcomes varies over time and across committees. Three sets of factors stand out for their impact on the relationship between committees and their principals: The character of the policy agenda, party strength, and institutional context.

SIZE AND SALIENCE OF THE POLICY AGENDA. The size and salience of the congressional agenda affects the importance of committees to the parties and all chamber members. A large policy workload requires the division of labor that a system of committees provides, but only issues that are salient to a large number of legislators will attract the attention of party leaders or rank-and-file members on the floor. Committees with jurisdictions that affect narrow constituencies are unlikely to be supervised by party leaders or given serious problems on the floor.

MAJORITY PARTY STRENGTH. Political scientists have observed that when parties lack cohesiveness because of internal divisions over policy, less authority is extended to party leaders to pursue partisan objectives. Under these conditions, strong-arm tactics are not tolerated and will alienate large numbers of partisans. Committee delegations will recognize party leaders' weakness and operate with little fear of retribution. In contrast, a cohesive majority party will expect its leaders to work pro-actively for party positions and pressure committee chairs and members to support the party.

INSTITUTIONAL CONTEXT. The House and Senate operate under very different rules. The larger, more unwieldy House has a stronger presiding officer and relies more heavily on formal rules than the Senate does. Senate rules protect each senator's right, on most legislation, to offer amendments on any subject and to conduct extended debate. In doing so, Senate rules protect individual initiative and create more opportunities to resist committee- or party-imposed policy choices. As a result, senators have more bargaining leverage with committee and party leaders than do representatives.

The Power of Modern Committees

Committees' power is expressly or implicitly granted to them by the parent houses and parties. Their continued existence and parliamentary privileges depend on the sufferance of the parent houses and parties. The parent chambers formally approve all committee assignments, but the parties construct the committee lists that are routinely ratified by the chambers. This function gives the parties a source of leverage with committee members and allows the parties – and, most important, the majority parties – to regulate the behavior of committee members through formal and informal rules. For the most part, committees must function procedurally and substantively in ways that are consistent with the expectations of their parent chambers and parties.

The Legislative Power of Committees

Evaluating the power of committees is difficult. It is very difficult to determine the influence of a committee on any given measure without knowing what the outcome would have been in the absence of committee involvement. Nevertheless, it is reasonable to infer that committees exercise real power in the modern Congress. Much of their power stems from the indifference of most members about the details of most legislation. Committees are extended considerable autonomy because most matters over which they have jurisdiction are of some importance to committee members and little, if any, importance to most other members. Parties and leaders focus on the few issues each year that are likely to affect the parties' reputations and electoral prospects. Members do not and cannot take an interest in the details of much, and probably even most, of the legislation that is considered on the floor.

Even when members are not indifferent, committees still have advantages that give their members disproportionate influence over policy outcomes. Mounting real challenges to their power can be difficult. Threats to strip a committee of jurisdiction, funding, or parliamentary privileges or to retract members' committee assignments usually are not credible, if for no other reason than such actions would set precedents that members of other committees would not like to see established (see box "A 'Heated' Dispute Over Committee Turf"). In this way an implicit, self-enforcing pact among members underpins committee power. The most practical means for keeping committees in check is to reject their policy recommendations.

It is convenient to consider two forms of committee power.

- Positive power is the ability of committees to gain the approval of legislation opposed by others.
- Negative power is the ability of committees to block legislation favored by others.

On both counts, committees have substantial advantages over other players.

POSITIVE POWER. At first glance, committees appear to have no positive power. Under the Constitution, legislation can be enacted only by the full House and Senate. Neither chamber has rules that permit a committee to act on the chamber's behalf with respect to final approval of legislation. Thus, positive power for committees must come from sources other than the explicit provisions of chamber rules.

Standing committees start with considerable discretion in writing and reporting legislation. They are free to act as they see fit on most legislation that is referred to them. They may simply refuse to act, hold hearings but take no legislative action, amend the legislation in any way, or accept the legislation without change. They may also write their own legislation, or they may vote to report legislation with a recommendation that it pass, with no recommendation, or with a recommendation that it be rejected.

Nevertheless, committees are not guaranteed that their legislation will receive favorable consideration on the House and Senate floors. To gain passage of legislation that might not otherwise pass, committees may exploit four sources of potential positive committee power: (1) *persuasion* on the basis of superior argument and information about the merits of legislation, (2) *leverage* acquired through threats of unfavorable action on members' bills if they fail to cooperate with a committee on its agenda, (3) *strategic*

A "HEATED" DISPUTE OVER COMMITTEE TURF

Early in 2007, Speaker Nancy Pelosi announced that she had plans to establish a special committee to design legislation for reducing greenhouse gases. This announcement was a step toward taking action on an issue that topped the Democratic agenda. The creation of such a committee would, however, encroach on the turf of two committees with jurisdiction over issues related to global warming – Energy and Commerce and Ways and Means. The reasonable speculation was that the special committee was necessary to avoid placing responsibility for the legislation in the hands of Energy and Commerce Committee Chairman John Dingell (D-Michigan), a champion of the auto industry who had been an opponent of mandating increases in fuel-economy standards for vehicles.

Despite the fact that most Democrats supported the notion of an aggressive stance on greenhouse gases, Pelosi's announcement made many House members exceedingly nervous. Such a maneuver could set a precedent that may someday jeopardize their own committee turf. House Judiciary Committee Chairman John Conyers (D-Michigan) described the tension between Pelosi and Democratic committee chairs as "palpable."

Given the unrest between Democratic leaders and committee chairs, it was unclear whether the party would be divided on the floor vote to approve the creation of a special committee. After three weeks of negotiation and some expressions of animosity, Pelosi and Dingell reached a compromise limiting the committee's powers. The special committee would have no legislative authority and would dissolve on October 28, 2008. Moreover, Pelosi assured Dingell that his committee will retain primary call on witnesses when there is a potential conflict between the committees and that the special committee must consult with the Speaker's office before issuing subpoenas.

Sources: Laura Litvan, "Pelosi Global Warming Plan is Latest Tussle with Panel Chiefs" *Bloomberg,* January 19, 2007. Jonathan E. Kaplan. "Pelosi, Dingell Reach Deal" *The Hill,* February 6, 2007.

packaging of unpopular legislative provisions with more popular provisions to win floor majorities, and (4) *domination of conference committees* to gain chamber endorsement of policy provisions favored by the committee. Each of these deserves a brief mention.

First, committees can usually gain a tactical edge by being better informed than their opponents. Committee members sit through hearings, participate in discussions with lobbyists and executive branch officials, and often have previous experience with the issues their committee deals with. Committees' large, expert staffs and their extensive networks of allies in the executive branch and interest group community further enhance their informational advantage over competitors. Traditional norms such as serving an apprenticeship before actively participating, developing expertise in the jurisdiction of one's committees, and deferring to committee specialists reflect the importance of informational advantages for committee power.

Second, the ability of committees to obstruct action on some legislation can be used to gain leverage with members whose support is needed on other legislation. Particularly in the House, where circumventing a committee is neither easy nor convenient, obstructing action on legislation can be used as a threat to win support for committee recommendations.

Third, within the bounds of their broad jurisdictions, committees may package provisions addressing multiple subjects in legislation. By doing so, they can combine the unpopular provisions with more popular provisions to win support for bills. In the House, this power is enhanced when a committee can acquire a special rule from the Rules Committee that limits amendments to the unpopular provisions when the legislation is considered on the floor.

Fourth, members of committees gain positive power through their domination of conference committees. Conference negotiations between the House and Senate give conferees considerable flexibility to alter chamber decisions. The conferees know that they are free to exercise such discretion provided that they can attract majority support for the conference report – which cannot be amended on the House or Senate floor – when it is returned to the two houses for final approval. The ability of conferees to choose any policy outcome that is at least as preferred to no bill by the two houses often renders opposition to the committee's preferences futile.

NEGATIVE POWER. The negative power of standing committees rests in their ability to control newly introduced legislation and to obstruct alternative routes to the floor. The ability to obstruct action is often called "gatekeeping" in theories of politics. Committees' negative power is much stronger in the House than the Senate.

In the House, negative power is supported by rules that give committees near-monopoly control over newly introduced legislation and make circumventing committees difficult. House Rule 10 requires that all legislation relating to a committee's jurisdiction be referred to that committee, a rule that has been in place since 1880. Before 1975, the single committee with the most relevant jurisdiction would receive the referral, a process

that often involved direct conflicts between committees with related jurisdictions. Since 1975, the rule has provided for multiple referral by granting
to the Speaker the authority to refer legislation to each committee with relevant jurisdiction. Monopoly control by single committees was broken by
the new rule, but the practice of referring nearly all legislation to committee
remains in place.

Committees' blocking power is enhanced by their domination of conference committees. The wide latitude extended to conferences to design the
final form of legislation gives committee members another opportunity to
wield negative powers. Committee members appointed to conference can,
and frequently do, delete provisions they find objectionable. Because conference reports cannot be amended when sent to the House and Senate floors,
it is difficult to reverse a conference committee's surgical removal of legislative provisions. Conferees also can take the more drastic step of refusing to
file a conference report, thus blocking the legislation in its entirety, at least
temporarily.

Circumventing House committees is difficult but not impossible under
House rules. The House operates under a germaneness rule that requires a
floor amendment to be relevant to the section of the bill or resolution it seeks
to modify. Thus, it is difficult to bring to the floor as an amendment a policy
proposal whose subject has not been addressed in legislation reported by a
committee. The germaneness rule can be waived, but only if a special rule
from the Rules Committee is approved by a majority on the House floor.
The Speaker's control of the Rules Committee means that this approach is
unlikely to work without the Speaker's cooperation.

House rules provide additional means for bringing legislation to the floor.
At certain times, members may move to suspend the rules to consider a
measure blocked by a committee. Going this route is usually not feasible
without the consent of the relevant committee because the member must
be recognized by the Speaker to make the motion and two-thirds of the
House must support it.

A second route is to gain a special rule from the Rules Committee to
discharge a measure from committee. This route requires Rules Committee
support and majority support in the House for the special rule. The Speaker's
cooperation is probably required to gain Rules Committee action on such a
rule.

Alternatively, party leaders occasionally circumvent committees by drafting legislation themselves or by delegating this responsibility to task forces or
special committees. Task forces are ad hoc panels typically created by party
leaders to carry out legislative duties. Party leaders may use task forces if

they are concerned that a committee with jurisdiction will perform unsatisfactorily. For example, they may fear that the committee will not reach an agreement in a timely fashion or that it will produce a bill that either cannot pass the chamber or will not satisfy majority party members. When legislation is drafted in a task force, party leaders determine which members are charged with drafting the legislation and, in the House, can and often do exclude minority party members from the process.

Finally, House members may seek to discharge a measure from a committee that fails to report it within thirty days of referral. Any member may file a discharge petition, which requires the signatures of 218 members. Once the petition receives the necessary number of signatures, it is placed on the Discharge Calendar for consideration on the second or fourth Monday of the month following a seven legislative day waiting period. Many members are hesitant to encourage the use of discharge petitions because doing so threatens the power of their own committees. Nevertheless, there has been more interest in discharge petitions since late 1993, when the House voted to make public the names of members who sign them. Public disclosure makes it easier to generate public or interest group pressure on members to sign petitions.

The discharge petition may appear to be the most promising route for circumventing committees because it does not require the assistance of the Rules Committee or the Speaker. In fact, between 1931 and 2002, 563 discharge petitions were filed, but the petitions gained the required number of signatures only 48 times. Of the 48 instances in which discharge petitions gained the necessary 218 signatures, only 19 times did the discharged measure go on to pass the House. However, the threatened use of discharge petitions, special rules, and suspension of the rules occasionally has stimulated committees to act in accordance with the floor majority's preferences. For example, between 1931 and 1994 there were 15 cases in which the needed 218 signatures were acquired on a discharge petition, but the majority leadership called up the legislation for consideration by other means.

The Senate's rules create weaker blocking power for its committees. Senate committees lack much of the negative power that House committees enjoy. Although measures are routinely referred to Senate committees upon their introduction, a senator can easily object to a referral and keep a measure on the calendar for floor consideration. Furthermore, the Senate lacks a germaneness rule for most measures, so senators are able to circumvent committees by offering whole bills as amendments to unrelated legislation. Senators often hesitate to support efforts to bypass a committee in this way, but it is a procedural route that is used much more frequently than are the

CIRCUMVENTING UNFRIENDLY COMMITTEES

For Senator Sam Brownback, a Republican from Kansas, banning human
cloning became a key legislative objective. Twice in the 107th Congress
(2001–2002), Brownback introduced legislation that fell into the unfriendly
jurisdiction of the Judiciary Committee. Senator Orrin Hatch (R-Utah), chair of
the Judiciary Committee, openly stated that he supported scientific endeavors
that could lead to finding cures for diseases.

On his third attempt at passing the legislation calling for a ban on human
cloning, however, Senator Brownback manipulated the legislation to
circumvent the Judiciary Committee. Knowing that Senator Judd Gregg (R-New
Hampshire), chair of the Health, Education, Labor, and Pension (HELP)
Committee, was supportive of his legislation, as were other HELP Committee
members, Brownback changed the legislation so that a different part of existing
law would be modified. Instead of calling upon the U.S. penal code, which
falls under the jurisdiction of Judiciary, Brownback altered the legislation so
that the ban would be enacted under the Public Service Act, which is under the
jurisdiction of the HELP Committee. In response to this maneuver, a GOP
senior aide said with understatement, "There are parliamentary conventions
that can be used or abused to ensure referral to a more friendly committee."

Source: Emily Pierce, "Leaders Circumvent Hatch," *Roll Call*, February 5, 2003.

more complicated House procedures for circumventing committees. Moreover, most conference reports are potentially subject to filibusters in the Senate, giving Senate minorities a source of bargaining leverage over committee
members at the conference stage that does not exist in the House.

Nevertheless, in practice, Senate committees do retain some blocking
power. Calling up a measure from the calendar requires the cooperation
of the majority leader, who usually sides with the committee chair on procedural matters. And if the majority leader cooperates, committee members,
like all senators, may filibuster or threaten to filibuster unfriendly legislation.
Consequently, successful circumvention of a committee on a controversial
matter often requires the support of at least 60 senators, the number needed
to invoke cloture.

Nongermane amendments are troublesome for Senate committees, but
they can often be set aside by a motion to table. A successful motion to table
kills the amendment. Because a tabling motion is not debatable (and therefore cannot be filibustered) and is a procedural question, it often attracts
more votes than would be cast against the amendment itself. Moreover, the
members of conference committees have an opportunity to drop adopted
nongermane amendments in conference.

In short, under most circumstances committees in both chambers – but especially in the House – exercise considerable negative power. Circumventing committees requires special effort and is usually possible only with the cooperation of the majority party leadership.

Oversight and the Investigative Power of Modern Committees

Central to the legislative power of committees and vital to the power of Congress as an institution is the ability of committees to oversee and investigate governmental or private activity that is or might be the subject of public policy. Courts have ruled that Congress's power to compel cooperation with its investigations is implicit in its constitutional functions of legislating and appropriating funds. Without broad powers to investigate and compel cooperation, Congress would not be able to exercise its legislative powers effectively.

Throughout the history of Congress, committees have been the vehicle for conducting congressional investigations. Select or special committees have been appointed for many important investigations. In the last three decades, important investigations of the Watergate break-in and cover-up, the involvement of the Central Intelligence Agency in assassinations, and the Iran-Contra affair were conducted by select committees.

Since the passage of the Legislative Reorganization Act of 1946, standing committees have been assigned the duty of maintaining "continuous watchfulness" over executive branch activities within their jurisdictions. The 1946 act also created two committees with governmentwide oversight duties, now called the House Committee on Oversight and Government Reform and the Senate Committee on Homeland Security and Governmental Affairs. Both committees attract members who want to participate in hearings on and investigations into a wide range of government activity.

The 1946 act was reinforced by stronger directives to committees in the Legislative Reorganization Act of 1970, which required most committees to write biennial reports on their oversight activities. Moreover, during the 1970s both houses assigned oversight responsibility for several broad policy areas to multiple committees to encourage oversight. Furthermore, the House instructed many committees to create oversight subcommittees and allowed them to add an oversight subcommittee beyond the limit for the number of subcommittees that would otherwise apply. With these developments, committee staffs devoted to oversight expanded greatly in the 1970s, which enabled committees and subcommittees to organize more hearings and more extensive investigations.

Congressionally Speaking...

As part of their oversight and investigative powers, committees and subcommittees are authorized by House and Senate rules to issue *subpoenas* – formal writs compelling a recipient to testify or produce documents (or both) to the committee or subcommittee from which they originated. Typically committees/subcommittees receive the information they need without forcing compliance. Should the President invoke executive privilege or an official simply refuse to cooperate, however, subpoenas help equip committees to carry out investigations.

The decision rules for issuing a subpoena vary across committees, as they are not codified by chamber rules and parent bodies extend considerable autonomy to committees in determining their internal proceedings. House rules only require that a quorum (majority) be present at the time that the subpoena is agreed to. House rules also allow the committee/subcommittee to delegate subpoena power to full committee chairs. Senate rules provide even less guidance. It is important to note, however, that federal courts have established basic requirements that subpoenas must satisfy in order to be recognized as legitimate.

Oversight became an increasingly important part of committee activity. In 1961, less than 10 percent of committee meetings and hearings were devoted to oversight; by 1983, more than 25 percent were devoted to oversight.[1] The biggest surge occurred in the 1970s and appears to have been the product of several factors: the new independence of subcommittee chairs to pursue oversight, the expanded capacity of larger committee and subcommittee staffs to conduct oversight activities, tensions between a Democratic Congress and a Republican administration, and a generally more assertive Congress. The proportion of meetings and hearings dedicated to oversight continued to rise throughout most of the 1990s, as congressional Republicans aggressively investigated the Clinton administration. By 1997, nearly 34 percent of all committee hearings and meetings were devoted to oversight.[2]

Declining Committee Autonomy

Committee power has been under siege since the early 1970s. Although committees continue to draft the details of nearly all legislation and their members remain central players in nearly all policy decisions, they have become less autonomous as their parent houses and parties have exercised more control over their operations and policy choices. Change has been most dramatic in the House of Representatives, where committees appeared to have dominated policy making during the middle decades of the twentieth century. The forces producing change in the role of committees in recent decades are similar to the forces that have been active throughout Congress's history – the policy agenda, strength of congressional parties, and the institutional context.

Changing Policy Agenda

Changes in the policy agenda have led to a decline in the autonomy of committees in recent decades. Many new and salient issues arose in the 1960s and 1970s, such as consumer protection, civil rights, and numerous others. Some of the emerging issues, like energy and the environment, were interconnected, sparked controversy, and stimulated the growth of interest groups. They energized outsiders to seek influence over committees' policy choices and pitted powerful committees against one another. As a result, more controversy spilled out of the committee rooms and onto the chamber floors. Since the late 1970s, the struggle with budget deficits led Congress to adopt rules that limited the policy discretion of most congressional committees. As we report in Chapter 12, the effect of the budget rules was a shift in emphasis from authorizing to appropriating committees and increased control over committee action by party and budget leaders.

Changing Party Strength

The increasing polarization of congressional parties (see Figure 6.1) has generated demands for central leaders to become more assertive. Thus, party leaders have clamped down on committee autonomy. Furthermore, the rank-and-file members of the parties, particularly in the House, have become less tolerant of committee and subcommittee chairs' deviating from party policy positions. Following the Republican takeover of 1994, Republican and Democratic majorities alike have been particularly aggressive in expressing their expectations of committee leaders.

The increase in activity by the party organizations and leaders during recent years is noted in Chapter 5. The party organizations now provide more opportunities for meaningful participation in policy making outside of members' assigned committees. The parties have provided forums, such as task forces, for those outside of committees to challenge the committees and their leaders and even to devise legislation for floor consideration. In the House, party leaders have frequently negotiated legislation after a

FIGURE 6.1. Party Polarization in the House and Senate, 1937–2006. *Source:* Common space scores from http://voteview.com/dwnl.htm. Calculations by the authors. Note: The measure of polarization is taken from Elizabeth Rybicki, Steven S. Smith, and Ryan Vander Wielen, "Congressional Committee Bias, 1963–2002." Paper presented at the 2003 meetings of the American Political Science Association.

committee has reported a bill and placed the negotiated provisions in the bill through use of a special rule from the Rules Committee.

Changing Institutional Context

Committee autonomy has been further undermined by rules changes that either directly regulated committee behavior or made it easier for members to challenge committee recommendations. These new rules were pursued by members who were unhappy with the nearly dictatorial control that some full committee chairs exercised over legislative proceedings. They reflected an effort to make committees – and especially committee leaders – more accountable to rank-and-file members of the parent chamber and to make members less dependent on committees for information and advice.

SUNSHINE RULES. Sunshine rules – rules that open congressional activity to public scrutiny – have contributed to the diminishing autonomy of standing committees. One such rule requires that roll-call votes cast in committee be recorded in documents that are open to the public. This rule was amended in 2007 to exclude votes taken in the Rules Committee. Another rule dictates that committee markups be held in public sessions (except for meetings concerned with national security matters) unless a majority of committee members cast a recorded vote in favor of closing a meeting. Even conference committees are required to hold their meetings in open sessions unless, as the House rule requires, a majority of the parent chamber approves the use of closed meetings. The rules were intended to make committee members more accountable, both to outside constituencies and to their colleagues. In recent Congresses, committees have voted more frequently to close meetings to the public, and they have become more creative in their efforts to sidestep the rules. In some cases, members appear to have allowed staff to negotiate legislative details to avoid holding official meetings subject to open-meeting rules. But party leaders have attempted to reinforce the sunshine rules by requiring that committees accommodate television and radio broadcasts and still photographers whenever a meeting is open to the public.

BILL REFERRAL RULES IN THE HOUSE. In 1974, the Speaker of the House was granted the authority to send legislation to committees jointly, sequentially, or in parts. Before 1974, the Speaker was required to assign legislation to the single committee that had the most relevant jurisdiction, a practice that guaranteed monopoly referral rights to a single committee in each policy area. Under the current rule, adopted in 1995, sending a bill jointly to more than one committee is no longer possible, but the Speaker may still establish a sequence of committees for consideration or split a bill into parts that are referred to different committees (sequential and split referral). In fact, in recent Congresses, about one-fourth of the workload for the average House committee has consisted of multiply referred legislation. In the Senate, all three forms of multiple referral are possible upon a joint motion of the majority and minority leaders. Multiple referral remains far less common in the Senate than in the House, perhaps because committees can more easily protect their jurisdictional interests by seeking to amend legislation on the floor.

Multiple referral in the House generates greater interdependence among committees and with the Speaker, reducing committee autonomy. Multiple referral creates more potential conflicts among committees and increases the number of legislators with some role in committee action on the affected bills. Sometimes the conflict among committees spills onto the House floor, where party leaders are asked to intercede. And, perhaps most important, multiple referral substantially strengthens the Speaker's influence over committee decisions. The Speaker determines, without appeal, the referral of legislation to multiple committees and may set deadlines for committee action in such cases. In designing such arrangements, the Speaker is in a position to advantage some committees, speed or delay committee action for strategic purposes, and send strong signals about his or her policy preferences.

VOTING RULES. Weakening committee autonomy and the demise of deference to committees are reflected in the record of floor amending activity since the mid-1950s. In terms of both the absolute number of floor amendments, the number of amendments per measure, and the proportion of measures amended on the floor, floor amending activity increased in both chambers during the 1950s and 1960s and surged upward in the 1970s. In the Senate, the number of floor amendments nearly tripled between the mid-1950s and late 1970s, with most of the increase occurring in the 1960s. The number of House floor amendments more than quadrupled between the mid-1950s and the late 1970s, with most of the increase occurring in the early 1970s after the introduction of recorded electronic voting. Previously, recorded votes were not possible on most amendments, which made it difficult to bring public pressure to bear and enhanced the influence of powerful insiders, particularly committee chairs.

Floor amending activity was perceived to be a more serious problem in the House and the House majority party could change its practices in response. The most important response was the expanded use of special rules to limit floor amendments. Most rules have not foreclosed floor amendments, but they have required that amendment sponsors notify the Rules Committee in advance, which permits the Rules Committee to arrange for their order of consideration and allows committee leaders to prepare against unfriendly amendments (see Chapters 7 and 8).

No effective constraints on floor amending activity for the purpose of enhancing committee autonomy are possible in the Senate. The minority would prevent a vote on any reform that would put it at a disadvantage. In only two areas, budget measures and certain trade agreements, has the Senate moved to limit debate and amendments. In general, therefore, a majority of senators have no way to insulate committee bills from unfriendly or nongermane amendments whose sponsors are committed to offering them.

CONFERENCE RULES. The ability of committees to control conference negotiations on behalf of their chambers has long been a vital source of power. In the House of the 1970s and 1980s, challenges to committee autonomy were accompanied by challenges to committees' monopoly over appointments to conference delegations. New rules were adopted imploring the Speaker to appoint delegations that represented House preferences, to include members who had sponsored major components of the legislation in question, and to require conferences to hold their meetings in public sessions. The rules were targeted at senior committee members who had dominated conferences for decades. The Speaker's control over conference delegations was reinforced in 1993 when the House adopted a rule giving the Speaker the power to remove a member from a conference delegation at any time. In spite of these rules, few members not sitting on the standing committees originating legislation are appointed to conference committees.

RANK-AND-FILE RESOURCES. Individual members now have far more sources of information at their disposal than they once did in the mid-twentieth century, so the traditional advantage enjoyed by committee members over rank-and-file members – greater access to expertise and staff assistance – has been reduced. Over the years, changes in House and Senate rules have allowed members to expand their personal staffs. Much of a member's personal staff is devoted to nonlegislative duties such as answering the mail and handling constituents' problems with the federal agencies. Nevertheless, the great expansion in members' personal staffs has allowed legislators to draw on staff for assistance in developing legislative proposals, making arguments, and soliciting support – often in opposition to committee positions. Furthermore, members may draw on the congressional support agencies. These agencies often conduct studies for or delegate staff to congressional committees, but they also respond to requests for information from individual members and their staffs. As a result of the increased availability of these varied sources of information, an enterprising member can equip himself or herself to challenge committee members' arguments. Thus, seldom does a committee now command deference on the basis of policy expertise alone.

Committee Membership

At the start of each new Congress, members of the House and new members of the Senate seek committee assignments that will shape their daily schedules and perhaps their electoral and legislative futures. Returning members are routinely reappointed to their former committees, following the "property right" norm, unless they seek to improve their situation by transferring to other committees, as a few always do. State delegations, intra-party factions, and lobbyists work to maximize their influence over policy by getting friendly members onto the right committees.

Committee Size and Party Ratios

Majority and minority party leaders negotiate the number of Democratic and Republican seats on each committee, with the majority leaders having the upper hand because of their ability to win a floor vote on the resolutions that provide for the allocation of seats to each party. With important exceptions in the House, seats on most committees are allocated roughly in proportion to the size of each party. The exceptions are the House Appropriations, Budget, Rules, and Ways and Means Committees – which are particularly important committees so the majority party reserves a larger-than-proportionate number of seats for themselves (see Table 6.2). The House and Senate ethics committees are the only committees on which there is an equal number of majority and minority party members.

Committee Assignments

In each chamber, committee seats are filled on the basis of recommendations from each party. For example, the House rule states that "the House shall fill a vacancy on a standing committee by election on the nomination of the respective party caucus or conference." To accomplish this, each House and Senate party has its own committee on committees (see box, page 185), which is responsible for making committee lists. Assignment decisions depend on the number of vacancies, the number of members competing for assignments, and rules on the number and type of assignments each member may hold. New members and returning members seeking new assignments must compete for support from the members of their party's committee on committees to gain assignment to the committees they want.

THE HOUSE. For the first time in 1995, as proposed by the new Republican majority that year, the House adopted a rule restricting the number of committee assignments its members may hold. The two parties had had internal rules, but the Republicans imposed the new rule and Democrats retained it after gaining a House majority in 2006. The rule prohibits a member from holding more than two standing committee assignments and more than four subcommittee assignments on standing committees. The two parties supplement this restriction by treating four committees (Appropriations, Energy and Commerce, Rules, and Ways and Means) as "exclusive" committees. Members serving on these committees are not permitted to hold seats on other committees. Both parties also identify "exempt"

COMMITTEES ON COMMITTEES, 2007

The *House Democratic Steering and Policy Committee* is comprised of 13 top party officials, three assistant chairs appointed by the Democratic leader, 12 regional representatives, five top committee leaders, a representative of the freshman class, the chair of the Democratic Caucus's Committee on Organization, Study, and Review (OSR), and 15 members appointed by the Democratic leader. Each of the members has one vote.

The *House Republican Steering Committee* has nine members from the party leadership, four committee leaders, 12 regional representatives, a representative of the freshman class, and a representative of the sophomore class. In the event that the regional representatives are from states that have four or more Republican members, a "small state" group is allowed to elect a member to the committee. The Speaker has five votes, the Majority Leader has two votes, and all others have one vote.

The *Senate Democratic Steering and Outreach Committee* is appointed by the floor leader. Each of the 19 members serving on the committee receives one vote.

The *Senate Republican Committee on Committees* is appointed by the chairman of the Republican Conference. Each of the approximately 10 members receives one vote.

committees (Select Committee on Intelligence and Standards of Official Conduct) that do not count against a member's committee membership limit.

In recent years, both House parties have become less inclined to grant exemptions to their limits on assignments. Traditionally, members have received exemptions with relative ease and have been allowed to maintain them indefinitely. But leaders of both House parties grew frustrated with the number of members who expected to receive exemptions and retain coveted extra seats. Upon becoming leader of the House Democrats at the end of 2002, Nancy Pelosi (D-California) strictly applied party rules limiting committee assignments. In 2005, Pelosi decided against granting John Larson (D-Connecticut) a waiver that would have allowed him to keep his position as ranking member on the House Administration Committee after having been chosen to sit on the Ways and Means Committee. House Republicans approved a party rule in 2004 that requires members who have received a waiver to committee assignment limits to reapply every two years. Moreover, the Republicans require members who wish to sit on multiple committees to receive the approval of the chairs of the committees involved in addition to the steering committee. For both parties, restricting exemptions allows party leaders to distribute desirable committee assignments to more members.

THE SENATE. Since the 1970s, Senate rules have restricted the number and type of committee assignments that senators may receive. A senator may sit on no more than two of the 12 most important committees ("A" committees) and is limited to an appointment to only one of five other standing committees, the Special Committee on Aging, or the Joint Economic Committee ("B" committees). There is no restriction for seats on the Select Committee on Ethics, the Committee on Indian Affairs, and the Joint Committee on Taxation ("C" committees). A senator may sit on no more than three subcommittees of any "A" committee (Appropriations members are exempt from this restriction) and no more than two subcommittees of any "B" committee. Both parties have adopted rules that further restrict membership on "A" committees. Senators are not permitted to sit on more than one of the "Super A" or "Big Four" committees, which include Appropriations, Armed Services, Finance, and Foreign Relations. The Senate occasionally grants exemptions to these assignment limitations at the request of the parties. Since the 1950s, both Senate parties have observed the practice of granting every senator a seat on one of the top four committees before any senator gets two such seats. The practice is called the "Johnson rule," after Lyndon Johnson (D-Texas), the Democratic leader who initiated the practice.

INFLUENCES ON ASSIGNMENTS. Many factors influence the committee assignment decisions of party leaders and the committees on committees. The legislators' political needs, claims by individual states or regions for representation on certain committees, geographic considerations, party loyalty, views on specific issues, and seniority are the most important factors. In the House, members supported by the largest state delegations are at a distinct advantage. For example, in 1992 New York's delegation lost all three of its members on House Appropriations through retirement or defeat, but it managed to regain all three seats (two Democratic and one Republican) for its members when new appointments were made. But there are few guarantees – New Jersey Democrats lost their representation on both Appropriations and Ways and Means (one seat each), but failed to gain a replacement.

Only for Senate Republicans has seniority historically been a decisive consideration. In fact, seniority has been the sole determinant in both the allocation of committee seats and the ascension of the committee hierarchy for Senate Republicans. In 2004, reflecting a desire to strengthen their leader's influence with party colleagues, Senate Republicans approved, by narrow margin, a change in party rules to grant the floor leader the authority to make influential committee appointments without regard to seniority. The rule permits the Republican leader to appoint at least half of the party's committee assignments on "A" committees. As a result, the leader has considerable say in the appointments to committees such as Agriculture, Appropriations, Armed Services, Finance, Foreign Relations, and Judiciary. For Senate Democrats, seniority has been an important, but less decisive, factor in committee assignment decisions.

Similar to the Senate Democrats, the House parties consider seniority along with many factors when making committee assignments. Having an established record of party loyalty, trustworthiness, and skill gives a more senior member an edge over newcomers. In recent Congresses, party leaders have increasingly taken into account members' contributions to party campaign efforts when distributing committee seats. Yet, particularly when a large class of new members enters Congress, party leaders make sure that a few freshmen are named to the top committees. The 104th Congress (1995–1996) was particularly unusual in having both a large class of new Republicans and a new Republican majority in the House. The change in party control gave the Republicans 31 new seats on the exclusive committees. The party allocated 19 of those seats to freshmen. In the years following the new Republican majority in 1995, it has become clear that the seniority norm has further weakened in the House.

LEADERSHIP PREROGATIVES. Assignments to the House Committee on Rules and the House Committee on House Administration are unique cases. The Rules Committee's primary function is to consider, devise, and report "special rules," resolutions that provide for the floor consideration of measures – usually reported by other committees – that would otherwise not receive timely consideration under the standing rules. In the 1960s and early 1970s, the independence of Rules Committee members was troubling to the majority party Democrats. Ultimately, both parties transferred the power to appoint Rules members to their top party leaders, making Rules Committee members agents of their party leadership.

In late 1994, both House parties also gave their top leaders similar power to name the members of the House Administration Committee. Because the House Administration Committee has jurisdiction over the internal administrative affairs of the House, including the way important resources are distributed to committees and members, the top leaders wanted to assert more control over it than they had in the past. The committee also has jurisdiction over election and campaign finance law – subjects of the highest partisan significance.

The Pecking Order

The appeal of committees to members varies. We can learn about the value of committees to members by examining the committees that members choose to leave and join. Because members have the ability to stay on the committee that they served on in the previous congress (because of the norm of "property rights"), we can assume that members transfer to more desirable committees. This is especially likely to be true because of the costs members incur for leaving a committee on which they had accumulated seniority. Table 6.3 shows the ranking of committee values for the House and Senate derived from the study of members' transfers off and on committees.

House Ways and Means (taxes, social security, trade), Appropriations (spending authority), Commerce (health, regulation of interstate commerce), and Rules (special rules) have jurisdictions of exceptional breadth and importance and attract the interest of many members. Competition for assignment to these committees is intense. Because of these committees' importance, party leaders expect loyalty from members assigned to them. In late 1992, a House insider reported that the Democratic leadership was holding applicants to Appropriations and Ways and Means to a high standard of loyalty. Leaders were telling members, "There may be a time your leader and your president will need your support. It may be difficult for you to vote for it. Will you be with us?"[3] Such anecdotal evidence illustrates the significant role of party as a cue to members on committees of prestige.

As a general rule, freshmen have difficulty gaining assignment to the top committees. Only when an extraordinary number of new members are elected does the leadership become eager to demonstrate a commitment to appointing a fair share of freshmen. And only when their numbers are large, are freshmen emboldened to demand their share of top assignments. At the start of the 103rd Congress (1993–1994), for example, the 63 Democratic freshmen and 47 Republican freshmen gained a total of 13 appointments to Appropriations, Ways and Means, and Commerce. Two years later, with an even larger class of Republican freshmen, 19 of the 31 available slots on the top four committees were given to freshmen by the Republican steering committee.

Beyond the common desire for assignment to one of the top committees, members vary widely in their preferences for committee assignments.

TABLE 6.3. Ranking of House and Senate Committee Values, 1979–2006.

Ranking	House Committees	Senate Committees
1	Ways and Means	Finance
2	Appropriations	Veterans Affairs
3	Energy and Commerce	Appropriations
4	Rules	Rules and Administration
5	International Relations	Armed Services
6	Armed Services	Foreign Relations
7	Intelligence	Intelligence
8	Judiciary	Judiciary
9	Homeland Security	Budget
10	Transportation and Infrastructure	Commerce, Science, and Transportation
11	District of Columbia	Indian Affairs
12	Government Reform and Oversight	Small Business and Entrepreneurship
13	Budget	Homeland Security and Governmental Affairs
14	Post Office and Civil Service	Agriculture, Nutrition, and Forestry
15	Financial Services	Health, Education, Labor, and Pensions
16	Science	Energy and Natural Resources
17	Resources	Environment and Natural Resources
18	House Administration	Banking, Housing, and Urban Affairs
19	Education and the Workplace	
20	Standards of Official Conduct	
21	Agriculture	
22	Veterans Affairs	
23	Merchant Marine and Fisheries	
24	Small Business	

Source: Keith M. Edwards and Charles Stewart III. "The Value of Committee Assignments in Congress Since 1994." Paper presented at the 2006 Annual Meeting of the Southern Political Science Association.

Differences among members reflect their personal interests and political goals. As a consequence of these differences, many committees are not very representative of their parent house. Sometimes this imbalance is manifest in the policy preferences held by committee members. For example, the House Armed Services Committee, which attracts members disproportionately from districts with military bases, has been more conservative than the House as a whole for many years. But many committees are distinguished from the rest of their chamber less by their policy views than by their degree of interest in the subject matter. The House Agriculture Committee, for example, attracts legislators from rural farming districts.

Committee Bias?

Differences in the policy preferences of committees and their parent chambers are not easy to measure, but it does appear that the political balance on some committees is quite different from the balance in their parent chamber. Committee medians on a liberal/conservative scale for the Republican-controlled Congress of 2005–2006 are shown in Figure 6.2. With Republican majorities, we would expect to observe conservative-leaning committees and they were, but there still is substantial variation among committees. Among House committees, those with a larger proportion of Republicans are among the most conservative – House Administration, Appropriations, Budget, Rules, and Ways and Means.

The biases of congressional committees, as well as subcommittees, are evident in the character of the witnesses they call to their hearings. A study of congressional hearings between 1945 and 1986 on four issues – nuclear power, drug abuse, smoking, and pesticides – found large, predictable bias in the mix of industry and public-interest group representatives appearing before them.[4] Committee majorities chose to listen to more witnesses that confirmed their views than opposed their views.

Committee Leaders

The most powerful member on most committees is the full committee chair. The chair exercises considerable control over the agenda, schedules meetings and hearings of the full committee, and, in recent Congresses, approves the scheduling of subcommittees' meetings and hearings. Furthermore, the committee chair controls the committee budget, offers party leaders recommendations regarding the composition conference committees for legislation falling under the committee's jurisdiction, supervises a sizable staff, and often serves as a spokesperson for the committee and party on issues under the committee's jurisdiction. The chair also reports legislation to the floor on behalf of the committee and makes requests of the majority leadership and, in the House, the Rules Committee to schedule the legislation for action on the floor. In exercising his or her formal powers, the chair benefits from years of experience in dealing with the policy problems and constituencies of the committee. Consequently, the support of the full committee chair can be critical to bill sponsors and opponents.

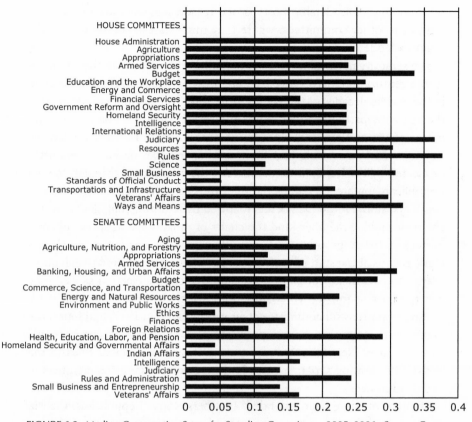

FIGURE 6.2. Median Conservative Score for Standing Committees, 2005–2006. *Source:* Common space scores from http://www.voteview.com. Committee medians calculated by authors.

However, full committee chairs no longer dominate their committees as they once did. Understanding why is important.

The Seniority System

Both the majority and minority parties designate a formal leader for each committee and subcommittee. The majority party names the chair of each committee and subcommittee, and the minority party appoints a ranking minority member for each committee and subcommittee. The seniority norm dictates that the party member with the longest continuous service on the committee serves as chair or ranking minority member, although there are limitations on the number and type of chairmanships a member may hold. Subcommittee chairs and ranking minority members are chosen, in most cases, on the basis of seniority within the committee. Accruing seniority toward leadership posts is one reason members are reluctant to transfer to other committees, where they must start at the bottom of the seniority ladder.

The seniority norm came to be recognized in the House in the late nineteenth century and was observed in both houses, virtually without exception, in the middle decades of the twentieth century. The norm was weakened in the 1970s by party rules that required a secret ballot election of full committee chairs and ranking minority members. Senate Republicans led the way in 1973 by requiring that their ranking member on each committee be elected by the Republican members of the committee, although the full Republican conference retains the right to reconsider a committee contingent's decision. House Democrats followed by requiring that all committee chairs or ranking members and the chairs or ranking members of subcommittees on the Appropriations Committee stand for election in the Democratic caucus at the start of each Congress. They later required the chairs of Ways and Means subcommittees to stand for caucus election as well. The new rules had an impact. Three full committee chairs were deposed in 1974, an Appropriations subcommittee chair was replaced in 1977, and four more Democratic committee chairs were ousted later. The other two congressional parties, House Republicans and Senate Democrats, adopted rules in the mid-1970s allowing separate votes on the ranking committee members in their conferences.

The reforms have been extended. In 1992, House Republicans, then in the minority, adopted a new party rule to limit the tenure of their full committee and subcommittee leaders to three consecutive Congresses, forcing rotation in the top committee posts every six years. In 1995, the Republicans made this a House rule for committee and subcommittee chairmanships and Democrats retained it after winning a majority in 2006. A Republican conference rule applies the term limits to ranking committee and subcommittee leaders when the party is in the minority. Since the adoption of the term limits, only one exemption has been granted – for David Drier (R-California) to remain the Rules committee chair for the duration of the 109th Congress. Chairs are permitted to move from one chairmanship to another.

Predictions that term limits would lead to more frequent departures from the seniority norm in selecting committee chairs proved accurate. In the first Congress to have forced turnover in committee chairs, the 107th Congress (2001–2002), six of the 13 vacant chairs were won by members who were not the most senior of the remaining members on their committees. In the next two Congresses, there were five vacancies compelled by the term limits and only two were filled by the most senior remaining member of the committee. In one instance, five Republicans with more seniority were skipped over to elect a chair.

In 1996, Senate Republicans adopted a six-year limit on committee chairs. Because the Republican majority status was interrupted in the 107th Congress (2001–2002) following Senator Jim Jeffords' decision to leave the Republican Party, the term limits were enforced for the first time at the beginning of the 109th Congress (2005–2006). The resulting vacancies led to a game of musical chairs, as four term-limited chairs went on to chair other committees. The Senate Democrats have not adopted term limits on committee leaders.

Senate Republicans also adopted a new rule governing the election of committee leaders. Rather than allowing the Republicans on each commit-tee to elect their committee chair or ranking minority member, as they had been doing for many years, the new rule requires secret ballot votes within each committee and then by the full Republican conference, making the chairs and ranking members more accountable to the full conference. The first use of this rule, in early 1997, produced no changes in committee chairs. Nevertheless, two senators, Mark Hatfield (R-Oregon) and Arlen Specter (R-Pennsylvania), had to overcome substantial opposition from within their party conference to retain or gain chairmanships.

Formal reforms have been reinforced by changes in practice. After the Republicans won a House majority in the 1994 elections, Speaker Newt Gingrich assumed responsibility for appointing committee chairs even before his conference had had an opportunity to meet. For three commit-tees, Gingrich bypassed the most senior committee Republican and backed a more assertive or conservative member as chair. At the same time, House Democratic leader Dick Gephardt chose a close political ally to be ranking member on the House Oversight Committee (now House Administration), dumping the former chairman, who had challenged Gephardt for his leader-ship post. Speaker Dennis Hastert followed Gingrich's lead by considering member loyalty to be an important element in the selection of committee chairs when vacancies occurred. Speaker Nancy Pelosi made it quite clear prior to the Democratic victory in 2006 that seniority would be only one of the factors considered in determining committee assignments. In fact, the Democratic caucus rules drafted by the House Democratic leaders stated that the Steering committee "shall consider all relevant factors, including but not limited to merit, seniority, length of service on the committee, degree of

THE CHANGING CONGRESS: REMOVING A HOUSE COMMITTEE CHAIR

The waning independence of committee chairs in the modern Congress is well exemplified by the 2004 decision of House Republicans to remove a sitting chair before his tenure had expired. Most members of the Republican Steering Committee, the party's committee on committees, opposed the reelection of Representative Chris Smith (R-New Jersey) to the chairmanship of the House Committee on Veterans' Affairs. Smith chaired the committee for only two terms and was supported by veterans groups for reelection to the post, but he was considered insufficiently loyal to the party and too aggressive in his support for more spending on veterans' programs. Representative Steve Buyer (R-Indiana), who campaigned for the position, was elected in Smith's place. A Republican leadership aide observed, "There will definitely be a perception out there that you need to be a team player if you want to succeed."[5]

commitment to Democratic principles and the Democratic agenda, and the diversity of the caucus."

Selecting Subcommittee Chairs

THE HOUSE. The means for selecting House subcommittee chairs have come full circle. Before the 1970s, full committee chairs appointed sub-committees and their chairs. That procedure was transformed into a more egalitarian one in the 1970s. Starting in the mid-1970s, House Democrats required that Democratic committee members bid for subcommittee leadership posts, chairs, or ranking minority member status in order of seniority and that appointments be ratified by a majority vote of the party members on the committee. Although seniority generally is observed, this procedure gives party members on a committee the right to reject the most senior member and elect someone else, as has happened more than a dozen times. House Democrats also bar full committee chairs or ranking members from serving as chair or ranking member of a subcommittee. To make the most important subcommittee leaders accountable to the party, House Democrats require subcommittee leaders of three committees – Appropriations, Energy and Commerce, and Ways and Means – to receive majority approval of the full House Democratic Caucus and, since early 2004, require those subcommittee leaders to first receive approval of the party's Steering and Policy Committee, which is chaired by the party leader.

In contrast, the House Republicans leave the appointment process to each committee's chair (or ranking minority member), although a majority of the Republican members on the full committee can override the chair's decisions. Like the House Democrats, the Republicans require that subcommittee leaders of the Appropriations Committee receive full approval of the party conference. In practice, nearly all of the Republican subcommittee leaders are selected on the basis of committee seniority. As a part of their late 1992 reforms, the House Republicans adopted a party rule prohibiting most chairs or ranking members of full committees from serving as chair or ranking member of any subcommittee. This party rule was made a rule of the House in 1995. These rules spread committee and subcommittee leadership posts among more members and limit the influence that any one member can enjoy by holding multiple leadership posts.

THE SENATE. Both Senate parties allow committee members to select their subcommittee chairs or ranking members in order of seniority. Less conflict over subcommittee chairs has arisen in the Senate than in the House, perhaps because nearly all senators can count on having at least one subcommittee leadership post. Senate rules merely prohibit any member from holding more than one chair on a single committee. With most senators serving on three standing committees, they may have up to three subcommittee chairs (or two if they hold a full committee chair on one of those standing committees). In the 110th Congress (2007–2008), roughly 80 percent of majority party members hold at least one subcommittee chair, and more than one-half hold two or three subcommittee leadership posts.

Limiting the Power of Full Committee Chairs

Compared with their predecessors of the 1950s and 1960s, today's full committee chairs face more effective competition for control over policy choices. Rank-and-file legislators are more likely to appeal to central party leaders and their party caucus to hold committee leaders accountable to them, and the parties have adopted changes in their rules to limit service of committee leaders and to force chairs to face party approval periodically. Moreover, as discussed earlier, rank-and-file legislators now have larger staffs and can turn to outside groups for assistance in challenging the handiwork and arguments of committees and their leaders.

House Committee Chairs

We have noted a few of the changes affecting the power of full committee chairs, but it is useful to review the two waves of reforms that altered the role of House committee chairs. First, the House Democratic majority of the early 1970s adopted rules to reduce the influence of full committee chairs over the decisions of their committees:

- Chairs were required to stand for election by the Democratic caucus at the start of each Congress,
- Committees with 15 or more members were required to form at least four subcommittees,
- Subcommittees were empowered with written jurisdictions and provided staffs,
- Proxy voting by chairs and ranking members was restricted (see box "Congressionally Speaking..."),
- The minority party contingents on committees were guaranteed staff,
- Committees were required to open their meetings to the public unless a majority of committee members agreed to close them,
- Committee members were empowered to call meetings (on a majority vote) so that chairs could no longer refuse to hold meetings, and
- Chairs were required to report legislation promptly after it was approved by their committees.

Furthermore, as discussed above, House Democrats adopted a new procedure for subcommittee assignments so that full committee chairs could no longer stack important subcommittees with their supporters. Thus, the ability of full committee chairs to block legislation favored by their committees was curtailed.

Second, following the Republican takeover in 1995, the House passed a series of reforms that would increase the power of the majority party at the expense of both committee and subcommittee chairs. First, and, perhaps most visible, House rules reduced the number of committees by three and the number of subcommittees by 28. The elimination of these committees and subcommittees resulted in a loss of 484 seats. Additional reforms were passed that placed the majority party leadership at the center of decision-making, and further constrained the behavior of committee chairs:

- Six-year term limits on committee chairs,
- Committees were limited to forming five subcommittees,
- Proxy voting was banned (see box "Congressionally Speaking..."),
- TV and radio coverage had to be accommodated for all committee meetings that were open to the public, and
- Overall committee staff budgets were cut.

Congressionally Speaking . . .

Attendance at committee meetings has been a problem for many years. Members often have multiple committee meetings or hearings scheduled at the same time and must fulfill other obligations – meet with constituents, vote on the House floor – while their committees are meeting. Thus, members often grant their committee leaders authority to cast proxy votes in their absence.

To control abuses of proxy voting, the House and Senate have adopted rules on their use. An old House rule provided that a majority of committee members must actually be present at the meeting for a committee to report legislation to the floor. If a majority were not present, a point of order could be raised against a bill when it reached the floor, which would lead the Speaker to rule a bill out of order.

But getting a majority of committee members to show up at one time and circumventing points of order can be troublesome. House Democrats moved in 1993 to minimize the problem. Their rule allowed a "rolling quorum." House Rule 11 now counts as "present" members who voted in committee even if no majority was actually present at the same time. Moreover, no point of order could be raised on the House floor unless it was raised at the appropriate time in committee.

House Republicans banned proxy voting and rolling quorums after they gained a majority in the 1994 elections. Since that time, attendance has continued to be a problem for committee chairs, some of whom have suggested returning to some form of proxy voting. Despite persistent problems with committee attendance, the rules remained intact when Democrats took over in 2007.

Furthermore, party leaders have become more involved in committee chairmanship fights and creating task forces and other forums for writing legislation.

Senate Committee Chairs

The Senate also adopted rules to provide guidelines for the conduct of committee meetings, hearings, and voting and to require committees to publish additional rules governing committee procedures. But unlike in the House, Senate chamber and party rules have never specified internal committee organization in any detail and are silent on the functions of subcommittees; indeed, most Senate committees' rules are very brief. In the majority of cases, the full committee chair is assumed to have great discretion, although even that is left unstated. For nearly all Senate full committees, the referral of legislation to subcommittees and the discharge of legislation from subcommittees remain under the formal control of the committee chair.

Senate Republican party rules specify limitations on the number and type of committees Republicans can lead. In 1995, after the Senate Republicans regained a majority, they joined their House counterparts in placing even stricter limitations on committee chairs in party rules. The Senate Republicans adopted a party rule prohibiting full committee chairs from chairing any subcommittees and further barring any Republican senator from chairing more than two subcommittees. Both rules were intended to spread chairmanships among as many senators as possible and to limit the special influence that any one senator might enjoy through multiple chairmanships. The rule soon proved to be a hardship for the party, however. On a few committees, the Republicans found themselves without a sufficient number of eligible senators to take another subcommittee chairmanship, so they began to grant waivers to the rule. Senate Democrats have not adopted similar rules.

Subcommittees

Subcommittees became more common after the Legislation Reorganization Act of 1946 consolidated committee jurisdictions and reduced the number of standing committees in both chambers. The number of subcommittees continued to grow into the 1970s, as individual committees responded to new policy problems and as members demanded their own subcommittees. Currently, of the committees with authority to report legislation, the only ones without subcommittees are the House Budget, House Administration, and Standards of Official Conduct Committees and the Senate Budget, Rules and Administration, Indian Affairs, Small Business and Entrepreneurship, Veterans' Affairs, and Intelligence committees.

THE HOUSE. In the House, the resistance of some full committee chairs to efforts to create legislative subcommittees was eventually overcome by a 1974 rule that provides that "each standing committee ... except the Committee on the Budget ... that has more than twenty members shall establish at least four subcommittees." As a result, subcommittees proliferated – over 125 subcommittees existed in 1980. Later, problems associated with the growth in the number of House subcommittees – jurisdictional squabbles between subcommittees, scheduling difficulties, and the burden of subcommittee hearings on executive officials – led the Democratic caucus in 1981 to limit the number of subcommittees. The 1981 rule was supplanted

---

Congressionally Speaking...

The first great book about Congress was Woodrow Wilson's *Congressional Government*, written in 1883 and 1884 when Wilson was a graduate student at Johns Hopkins University. He penned two frequently quoted phrases – "Congressional government is *committee government*" (emphasis added) and "Congress in session is Congress on public exhibition, whilst Congress in its committee-rooms is Congress at work." Wilson later became president of the United States.

The power of subcommittees was enhanced during the early 1970s, leading observers to look for new ways to label Congress. Political scientists Roger Davidson and Walter Oleszek characterized the House as *subcommittee government* in their 1977 book *Congress Against Itself*. Neither Davidson nor Oleszek has exhibited ambitions for high public office.

---

by a new House rule, adopted in 1993, limiting the number of subcommittees to five per committee, unless a committee maintains a subcommittee on oversight (in which case the committee may have six subcommittees). The 1993 rule permitted only two committees to exceed the subcommittee limit – Appropriations (which may have 13 subcommittees) and Government Reform (which may have seven). The rules changes adopted in 1993 required the abolition of 16 subcommittees, and additional changes introduced by the Republicans in 1995 further scaled back the number of subcommittees. Cumulatively, these changes brought the House back to the 1955 level of about 80 subcommittees. The number of subcommittees has crept up since then, reaching 101 in 2007. Contributing to this trend was a 2007 rules change granting additional exemptions to subcommittee limits to Armed Services (which may have seven), Foreign Affairs (which may have seven), and Transportation and Infrastructure (which may have six).

THE SENATE. The Senate and the Senate parties do not have formal rules on the number of subcommittees. Instead, the Senate's limits on the number of subcommittee assignments that individual senators may hold effectively restricts the number of subcommittees that can be created. In 1985, compliance with the limits on subcommittee assignments led to the elimination of 10 subcommittees. Republicans further reduced the number of subcommittees after taking majority control of the Senate in 1995. In 1997, the Senate had 68 subcommittees, down from nearly 90 ten years earlier. The number of Senate subcommittees has changed little since that time – 71 in 2007.

Checking the Power of Subcommittees in the House

In the Democratic House of the 1970s, subcommittees became very important in committee decision-making in the House. The House and the Democratic caucus adopted rules in the early 1970s that substantially weakened the ability of full committee chairs to control subcommittees. Consequently, decision-making processes within House committees became more decentralized than they had been in the 1950s and 1960s. Most legislation originated in subcommittees, the vast majority of hearings were held in subcommittees, about half of all committee staff was allocated to subcommittees, and subcommittee chairs usually served as the floor managers for legislation originating in their subcommittees. The House and Democratic party rules together created substantial uniformity across House committees in their reliance on subcommittees for initial action on legislation. The pattern in the House led some observers to label House decision making "subcommittee government."

Subcommittee government evaporated with the new Republican majority in 1995. House subcommittees were no longer guaranteed that legislation sent to their parent committees would be referred to them. In addition, as noted previously, the Republicans forced most House committees to reduce the number of their subcommittees from six to five (with exception to those committees maintaining an oversight subcommittee and those granted explicit exemptions), and they returned to full committee chairs control over subcommittee appointments and over all committee and subcommittee staff. When they cut committee budgets, a disproportionate share of the resulting staff cutbacks occurred in subcommittee staffs. Whereas subcommittee chairs once had the authority to hire one staffer, House rules now give full committee chairs the authority to determine the staff allotted to subcommittees. Subcommittee staff now constitutes less than 40 percent of all committee staff, down nearly 10 percent from the 1980s. The consequence of these changes has been the reemergence of variation across House committees in the way they use subcommittees.

It is too early to determine whether the Democratic majority elected to the House in 2006 will return to greater reliance on subcommittees for initial consideration of legislation. Early signs are that the Democratic full committee chairs are giving subcommittee chairs greater independence than did their Republican predecessors.

The Senate and its parties never adopted rules granting subcommittees the kind of independence that House subcommittees enjoyed under the Democrats in the 1970s and 1980s. The lack of formal rules empowering

subcommittees in the Senate has produced great variation among committees in their reliance on subcommittees. Several Senate committees hold no
or only a few hearings in subcommittee, and only a few Senate committees
use subcommittees to write legislation. "Subcommittee government" never
fit the decision-making processes in most Senate committees.

Committee Staff

Committees in the early nineteenth century worked without staff assistance,
which meant that committee chairs personally managed the administrative
details of committee business. However, the growing workload of the mid-
1800s rendered this practice infeasible. In 1856, the House approved committee assistance for the Ways and Means committee, and the Senate did the
same for the Finance committee. Expansion in committee assistance following this was slow; it was not until 1890 that the total number of committee
employees in both chambers exceeded 100.

The Legislative Reorganization Act of 1946 was a significant turning point
in the history of committee staffing as it established statutory provisions for
the allocation of staff. Specifically, it granted standing committees in both
chambers the authority to hire four professional staff assistants and six clerical aides. The number of professional assistants was raised to six (totaling
12 statutory positions) in 1970 by the second Legislative Reorganization
Act. In addition, committees were extended the opportunity to make annual
requests for committee staff beyond the statutory allotments. This gave way
to a rapid expansion of committee staff, particularly in the non-statutory
category (referred to as "investigative"). After the 1970 Legislative Reorganization Act, committee staffing has followed different courses in the two
chambers.

THE HOUSE. In 1974, the House increased the personnel limit to 18 professional assistants and 12 clerical aides, where it remains today. The number of
committee staff in the House exploded in the 1970s, primarily as a result of
the growth in subcommittees. While growth leveled off in the House during
the 1980s, the total number of committee staff employed continued to rise
through the early 1990s. By 1990, only one House committee had a staff
smaller than 40, while six committees had more than 100 assistants.

THE SENATE. Although growth in committee staff was more gradual in the
Senate, Senate committees, like their House counterparts, took advantage of
the 1970s procedures permitting investigative staff. However, the adoption

of a 1980 Senate resolution eliminated the distinction between statutory
and investigative staff, and moved to annual funding (changed to biennial
funding in 1985) of committee staff. As is now the practice, committees
were directed to draft budget requests to be packaged and voted on by the
chamber.

REPUBLICAN CUTS RESTORED. As they promised, the Republicans
elected in 1994 cut committee budgets and staff. House committee (full
and subcommittee) staff dropped from just over 1,700 to under 1,100; Senate committee staff dropped from nearly 1,000 to under 800. Since the mid-
1990s, House committee staff has risen to approximately 1,300, and Senate
committee staff has grown back to over 900.

Both chambers guarantee the minority party a share of the staff. Senate
rules state that the allocation of committee staff "should reflect the relative
number of majority and minority members of committees." The standing
rules of the House are less favorable to the minority than in the Senate. The
House guarantees to the minority only 10 staff members, or one-third of the
committee staff, whichever is less.

Conclusions

Committees are a central but changing feature of legislative policy making.
Changes in the role of committees are primarily the products of:

- the emergence of new and salient policy problems,
- fluctuations in the strength of congressional parties, and
- the character of the existing institutional arrangements.

When interest in an issue is narrow, the policy outcome satisfies most
members, and the issue has little impact on party fortunes, autonomous
committees are tolerated and even revered. However, when an issue is more
complex and few members are indifferent to the outcome, as appeared to
be the case more frequently in the 1970s, committees become constrained
by their parent chambers and must rely on formal procedural safeguards to
preserve their control over legislative details. When the parties' electoral fortunes are tied to the issue and the policy outcome, as happened on budget
matters in the 1980s, party leaders and their functionaries assume decision-
making responsibilities that otherwise would fan to committees.

The direction of change over the last three decades – toward less
autonomous committees and a less committee-oriented process – must not
be confused with the degree of change. The changes reported in this chapter,

particularly those in the House, appear to be quite sweeping. Many of the procedural sources of committee power seem to have been weakened. Developments affecting committee assignments, bill referrals, floor debate, conferences, and the budget process have reduced committee autonomy. Additionally, the informal norm of deference to committee recommendations certainly is much weaker today than it was in the 1950s and 1960s.

But some care must be taken in drawing inferences about these changes. Most legislation comes from a single committee in each chamber, receives few or no floor amendments, and does not require a conference. Necessary conferences are managed by conferees chosen nearly exclusively from the committee of origin. Moreover, committees have devised a remarkable variety of legislative tricks to minimize the effect of budget constraints. With the creative use of special rules and large omnibus measures in the 1980s, committees have actually recovered some of the autonomy they lost in the 1970s.

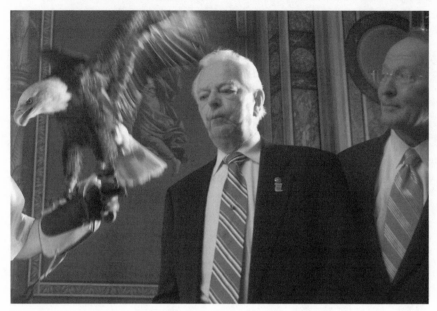

Challenger the Eagle, Sen. Robert Byrd (D-West Virginia), and Sen. Lamar Alexander (R-Tennessee) participate in the news conference announcing a resolution to name June 20, 2007 as "American Eagle Day" on Thursday, April 12, 2007. Byrd is currently the longest serving senator and is known as an expert on the rules and precedents of the Senate.

7

The Rules of the Legislative Game

CONGRESSIONAL POLITICS OFTEN HAS THE FLAVOR OF A GAME – ALBEIT A very important game – as the contending factions vie for control over public policy. The game is characterized by bargaining, procedural maneuvers, and close votes. On many issues, the outcome is uncertain. When the interests and rights of large groups in society are at stake, the game is emotionally charged. And the game is made more compelling by the personalities of the players. Members of Congress, presidents, staff aides, lobbyists, and other participants in congressional politics are ambitious people with large egos. Many of the players hate to lose. Skilled players are masters of the rules; they are proficient in strategy and tactics and take pleasure in anticipating the moves of their opponents. Their knowledge of the rules and their aptitude for strategy do not guarantee success, but can give them an advantage. Even for spectators, mastering the rules and strategy is essential to appreciating and enjoying the game.

The rules of the game change – and legislators do the changing. Each chamber of Congress is empowered by the Constitution to enact its own rules. The rules of the House of Representatives extend to more than 60,000 words, while the Senate's rules are less than half that long at around 30,000 words. The differences in the length of the rules reflect not only the differences in the sizes of the two chambers, with the larger House requiring more formalities to keep order, but also the different paths that the two chambers took at critical junctures in their parliamentary histories. The Senate, at a very early point in its history, eliminated the means to limit debate, which created the possibility of preventing a vote on a measure by refusing to stop talking. As a result, controversial changes in the rules can be blocked in the Senate. The House, in contrast, adopted a means to limit debate by a simple majority vote, which allowed even small majorities to impose new rules on that chamber. The result is that the House gradually accumulated a much larger and more detailed set of rules.

Legislative Rules in Perspective

Perhaps the most remarkable feature of the legislative process is how much it is stacked against the enactment of new law. Typically, getting a major bill passed involves attracting majority support in successive stages – first in a subcommittee, then in the full committee, then on the floor, then in conference, and then on the floor again for the conference report. This must be done in both chambers and usually requires the cooperation of both the minority and majority party leadership in the Senate and, in the case of the House, the majority party leadership and the Rules Committee. Once congressional passage is acquired, presidential approval or the support of an extraordinary majority in both chambers must be obtained. Success, then, depends on finding support from multiple groups and subgroups that are not likely to have identical policy preferences. Proponents of a new program or project usually must successfully pilot the necessary legislation through the process twice – once for an authorization bill to create the program and once for the related appropriations bill to fund the program.

Often, the members of Congress and other players in this game take the rules as they are and adjust their strategies accordingly. However, the players also seek to shape and create rules that suit their political needs, which change over time. The existing rules are seldom reevaluated in their entirety. Rather, their weaknesses or biases are considered individually and solutions are adopted piecemeal. New options, limitations, and contingencies have been added incrementally, making the rules more elaborate and altering the strategic context within which legislative factions must compete for majority support. Over the more than two centuries that Congress has been making law, a remarkably complex set of rules, further elaborated by precedents and informal practices, have evolved to shape the legislative process.

It would be a serious mistake to infer that the rules are so detailed and biased that they dictate policy outcomes. They are not. Rules are typically created to facilitate action, not determine outcomes. With a few exceptions, rules do not stipulate the issues to be considered by Congress. National and international events shape those issues, and much of the legislative struggle involves getting new issues on the congressional agenda. Moreover, rules do not determine the policy preferences of the players. Who gets elected is the most important factor in determining what policies will be favored by Congress, although interest groups, presidents, and others influence members' policy choices as well. In addition, the rules do not determine which of the interest groups, local government officials, political commentators, and others exercise the most influence on policy decisions. Larger social forces are more important than the legislative rules in this regard. Generally, the rules are not so detailed and biased that they can compensate for a scarcity of support and votes.

Nevertheless, the rules of the legislative game do matter. Some rules restrict or expand the options available to members by placing certain bills in order on the floor at certain times or by regulating the amendments that may be offered. Other rules set the decision rule – requiring a majority or supermajority for certain kinds of motions or measures – while still others specify which members have the right to make a motion or to speak at certain times. Members know that Congress's rules matter and often regret that the general public does not appreciate their importance. Robert Michel (R-Illinois), the House Republican leader from 1981 to 1994, once lamented the difficulty of attracting public attention to the plight of the minority party under House rules:

> Nothing is so boring to the layman as a litany of complaints over the more obscure provisions of House procedures. It is all "inside baseball." Even among the media, none but the brave seek to attend to the howls of dismay from Republicans [then the minority party] over such esoterica as the kinds of rules under which we are forced to debate. But what is more important to a democracy than the method by which its laws are created?

> We Republicans are all too aware that when we laboriously compile data to demonstrate the abuse of legislative power by the Democrats, we are met by reporters and the public with that familiar symptom best summarized in the acronym "MEGO" – my eyes glaze over. We can't help it if the battles of Capitol Hill are won or lost before the issues get to the floor by the placement of an amendment or the timing of a vote. We have a voice and a vote to fight the disgraceful manipulation of the rules by the Democrats, and we make use of both. All we need now is media attention, properly directed to those boring, but all-important, House procedures.[1]

Representative Michel was well aware that misconceptions about congressional rules abound. Some believe that "if there's a will, there's a way" – legislators' effort, not rules, determine outcomes. Others see congressional procedures as arcane and deeply biased against action – "the outcome is rigged by the rules." Particular rules become critical factors in shaping policy choices only in combination with the preferences of the players. If all members of Congress support a particular bill, it doesn't matter whether only a simple majority or a supermajority is required to pass it. But as divisions emerge, the particular rules under which bills are crafted and brought to a vote may influence the outcomes. The ability to offer an amendment at a crucial moment, to delay action until more support can be attracted, or to gain enactment with a simple majority rather than a supermajority can be critical to the final policy outcome.

Knowledge of the rules can be an important resource. House Energy and Commerce Chairman John Dingell (D-Michigan) once said, "If I let you write the substance and you let me write the procedure. I'll screw you every time." In both chambers of Congress, the rules and precedents are sufficiently complex that most members do not master them in their entirety. Instead, they rely on knowledgeable colleagues, staffers, the parliamentarians, and others to advise them. But a member who masters the rules is valuable to other members, more likely to be consulted, and more likely to be viewed as fit for a leadership position.

The rules governing the legislative process have two main sources: the Constitution and Congress itself. The Constitution sets a few basic but critically important rules (see Chapter 2). However, the chambers themselves are a source of rules in three ways. First, the rules adopted by the House and Senate supplement the constitutional requirements. Second, several statutes or laws passed by Congress set procedural requirements for the two chambers of Congress (although most of these allow the House and Senate to supplement or supplant the statutory requirements with their own rules). Third, the two chambers of Congress have a large body of procedural precedents, built up over their more than 200-year history, that govern many aspects of congressional operations that are not addressed elsewhere. This chapter outlines the rules that are critical to understanding legislative politics.

Beyond the Constitution: House and Senate Rules

The Constitution outlines the fundamental rules of the legislative game but leaves out important details. How legislation is to be prepared for a vote in the House and Senate is left undefined, as are the means for resolving differences between the House and Senate. The Constitution makes the vice president the presiding officer of the Senate and specifies that an elected Speaker shall preside over the House, but it does not mention the specific powers of these presiding officers. The Constitution also does not mention how the president is to decide what to recommend to Congress or the degree to which the president will rely on departments and agencies to speak for the executive branch. Moreover, the means for resolving differences between Congress and the executive branch are not discussed.

The details of legislative procedure have been filled in by the evolution of informal practices and the accumulation of recognized precedents. But in both chambers of Congress, a sizable number of formal rules have been established as well. Such rules both reflect and shape the distribution of power within Congress and between Congress and the president.

The framers of the Constitution anticipated the need for rules of procedure. The Constitution's Article I, Section 5, provides that "each house may determine the rules of its proceedings." As a result, each chamber has devised a complex set of standing rules. They concern the committee systems, procedures for amending and voting on legislation, ethics regulations for members and staff, and many other matters. It is important to keep three things in mind: (1) each chamber has its own set of rules, (2) each chamber may change its rules whenever it desires, and (3) each chamber may waive its rules whenever it desires.

Formally, the House dissolves at the end of each two-year Congress and must reestablish its rules as one of its first items of business at the start of each new Congress. In nearly all cases, this is done with a few amendments sponsored by the majority party and approved on a party-line vote. The Senate, in contrast, considers itself to be a continuous body because at least two-thirds of its members continue to serve from one Congress to the next. For that reason, the Senate's rules remain in effect from Congress to Congress unless the Senate votes to change them.

In addition to their own standing rules, the House and Senate are guided by statutes and precedents established by rulings of their presiding officers. When Congress chooses to include certain procedures in new statutes, such as the Congressional Budget and Impoundment Control Act of 1974 (see Chapter 12), these have the force of standing rules. Party rules govern such things as the selection of party leaders and committee appointments, and in some cases party rules dictate limits on the use of standing rules by party or committee leaders. Rulings of the presiding officers concern interpretations of statutory or standing rules.

The Standard Legislative Process

The standard legislative process in the modern Congress is outlined in Figure 7.1. It is called the standard process because it is patterned after the typical route legislation follows. The chambers are free to alter it for certain legislation, and they have done so with greater frequency in the last decade or two. Even the standard process involves many options that are used regularly. The standard process involves multiple stages in each chamber, followed by

FIGURE 7.1. The Standard Legislative Process for a Major Bill.

steps for resolving House-Senate differences. The Constitution stipulates that after the House and Senate agree on legislation, the president must approve or veto it, and if it is vetoed, Congress may then attempt to override the veto. The standard process is like an obstacle course in which majorities must be created at several stages among different groups of legislators.

Introduction of Legislation

The modern legislative process gives a member who is interested in enacting a new law three basic procedural options. First, she could introduce her own bill and work to gain passage in each chamber. Second, she could seek to have her ideas incorporated into legislation drafted by a committee or by other members. And third, she could offer her proposal as an amendment to someone else's legislation. She might even pursue the three options simultaneously.

Legislation may be drafted by anyone – a member and his or her staff, a committee, lobbyists, executive branch officials, or any combination of insiders and outsiders – but it must be introduced by a member and while Congress is in session. In the House, a member simply places a copy of the draft legislation in a mahogany box, the "hopper," which is located at the front of the House chamber. In the Senate, members hand their draft legislation to a clerk or gain recognition to introduce it orally from the floor. In both chambers, the chief sponsor of a measure may seek cosponsors. Legislation is designated as a bill, a joint resolution, a concurrent resolution, or a resolution, and is numbered as it is introduced (see box "Types of Legislation").

Although legislation is given a number, it may be known by several names. Each bill is required to have a formal title, which is often quite long. For example, the 2005 Energy Policy Act was "An act to ensure jobs for our future with secure, affordable, and reliable energy." But the bill is known by a more convenient, short title – 2005 Energy Policy Act. Most participants and observers simply called it the energy bill. In addition, bills often come to be known informally by the names of their chief sponsors. The Pell Act, which provided grants to college students, was named after Senator Claiborne Pell (D-Rhode Island), who fought hard for student financial aid.

Because lobbyists and other outsiders cannot introduce legislation, they search for members who are willing to champion their causes and introduce legislation they have drafted. Although they would prefer to have influential members introduce their proposals, they also seek members who have the time and interest to give their legislation some priority. The right mix is

TYPES OF LEGISLATION

There are four types of legislation. In each Congress, legislation of each type is generally numbered in the order it is introduced, although sometimes members request that specific numbers be reserved for their bills.

• **Bills** are designated H.R. (number) or S. (number). Public bills change public law. If enacted into law, public bills are published in a volume entitled *Statutes at Large* and given a public law number, such as P.L. I 11. Private bills address matters affecting individuals, such as an immigration case and, if enacted into law, are not reported in *Statutes at Large*.

• **Joint Resolutions** are designated H. J. Res. (number) or S. J. Res. (number). Most joint resolutions are the same as bills for all purposes – they change public law and, if enacted into law, are published in *Statutes at Large* and given a public law number. By tradition, certain kinds of legislation, such as special appropriations measures, are labeled joint resolutions. A special class of joint resolution is proposed constitutional amendments, which if passed by Congress do not go to the president but rather go directly to the states for ratification.

• **Concurrent Resolutions** are designated H. Con. Res. (number) or S. Con. Res. (number) and do not change public law. They concern matters affecting both chambers, such as certain changes in congressional procedures, and so must be adopted by both chambers. They sometimes are used to express the "sense of Congress" about certain issues or events.

• **Resolutions** are designated H. Res. (number) or S. Res. (number) and do not change public law. They concern matters affecting only one chamber, such as most standing rules, and so are adopted only by that chamber. They sometimes are used to express the "sense of the House" or the "sense of the Senate" about certain issues or events.

often found in a majority party member of mid-level seniority who sits on the committee with jurisdiction over the bill. Usually, gaining the sponsorship of several members willing to work together on behalf of the legislation is advantageous. Better still is a group of cosponsors who are known as serious legislators and who represent a range of views in both parties. Of course, sponsors also are sought in both chambers so that companion bills can be introduced at about the same time.

Members sometimes introduce measures "on request," as a courtesy to the president or someone else. When this is done, it is indicated next to the sponsors' names at the top of the first page of the legislation, signifying that the sponsor does not endorse the provisions of the bill. Similarly, legislation is often introduced by a committee chair on behalf of his or her committee, usually after the committee has drafted and approved the details. The chair is the formal sponsor, but the bill is recognized as a "committee bill."

Referral to Committee

After draft legislation is introduced, the Speaker of the House or the Senate's presiding officer refers it to the appropriate committee(s). In practice, the House and Senate parliamentarians inspect the content of proposed legislation and recommend referral to the committee or committees with the appropriate jurisdiction. Careful drafting of legislation may favorably influence the referral decision.

Legislation may be referred to more than one committee, an action called multiple referral, because committees sometimes share jurisdiction over the content of legislation. Multiple referral has become quite common in the House. Since 1974, the Speaker of the House has been authorized to send legislation to multiple committees. The current rule requires that the Speaker identify a "primary" committee. The Speaker may send a bill, in whole or in part, reflecting the different jurisdictions of committees, to one or more additional committees either before or after consideration by the primary committee. The Speaker also may set time limits for committee action. In recent Congresses, about one in five House measures has been multiply referred, with a higher proportion of important measures, closer to one in four, being so referred.

Most referrals are routine, but occasionally referrals can become controversial. Committee members care about referrals – staking a claim and winning a dispute over jurisdiction may expand a committee's jurisdiction and influence for years to come. Large, complex bills – such as major health care reform and telecommunications bills – often generate competition among committees with jurisdictions relevant to the legislation. Bills dealing with issues not anticipated by the existing rules governing committee jurisdictions are especially likely to stimulate competing jurisdictional claims. On some matters, the composition of the committee that receives a bill may affect the nature of the legislation it eventually reports to the floor, so bill sponsors and outside interests care about which committee receives the referral. On occasion, protracted negotiations among bill sponsors, committee leaders, and party leaders will precede introduction and referral of draft legislation.

Committee Action

Formally, committees have many options concerning how to process most of the legislation referred to them. They may approve the legislation and report it back to the parent chamber, with or without amendments; reject the measure outright; simply not consider it; or set it aside and write a new bill on the same subject. In practice, most proposed legislation does not survive committee consideration. Inaction at the committee stage dooms most legislation. In the 109th Congress (2005–2006), a fairly typical Congress, 4,920 bills and resolutions were introduced in the Senate and 8,154 were introduced in the House. But only 518 and 679 measures were reported by committees of the Senate and House, respectively – 10.5 and 8.3 percent.

Committees may send a bill to a subcommittee for initial action or hold it for the full committee to consider. Although nearly all committees have subcommittees with well-understood jurisdictions, full committee chairs have substantial discretion in deciding whether to refer measures to subcommittees or hold them for full committee consideration. Full committee chairs can also control the scheduling of meetings to expedite or delay action on a bill.

Committees and subcommittees may hold hearings to receive testimony on proposed legislation from members, administration officials, interest-group representatives, outside experts, and others. Hearings may address a general issue related to the legislation or the specifics of the legislation itself. Hearings are perhaps the most important formal information-gathering mechanism for Congress and its committees. Still, some hearings generate little but rhetoric and media coverage – members' questions turn into lengthy statements, celebrity witnesses offer scripted answers, and the television networks later replay a 20-second exchange between an antagonistic committee member and an acerbic witness. Other hearings are designed more to advertise a bill, raise issues, or draw public attention to a problem than to gather information.

If a committee or subcommittee intends to act on a bill, it normally conducts a "markup" on the legislation – a meeting at which the committee or subcommittee reviews the measure line-by-line or section-by-section and considers amendments. Committees may write their own legislation and have it introduced by their chair. When this approach is taken, the chair often proposes a "chair's mark" as the starting point for the markup. Once the markup by the full committee is complete, the measure may be reported to the floor if a majority of the committee votes to do so. Committees are free to report legislation with or without amendments or even without a recommendation that the legislation pass. But most important legislation is amended or written as a "clean" committee bill and then recommended to pass.

In the House, a bill reported to the floor from a committee must be accompanied by a document called a committee report. Senate committees are not required to write these reports but usually do. Committee reports provide the committee's justification for the bill and are usually drafted by staff members as a routine matter. Committee reports may include a statement of minority views on the legislation. On occasion, committee reports are controversial because they provide further interpretations of the bill that might guide later actions on the part of executive agencies or the courts. Committee reports sometimes help non-committee members and their aides explain complicated legislation to constituents. In the House, the Ramseyer rule (named after Rep. John Ramseyer who proposed it years ago) requires that committee reports specify all changes to existing law that the proposed legislation would make.

Circumventing Committees

Proponents of legislation opposed by a committee have a variety of means for gaining floor action on the legislation without having it reported from the committee. These mechanisms are different in the two chambers. Circumventing committees is more difficult in the House.

Circumventing Committees in the House

In the House, the options are to move to suspend the rules, to employ a discharge petition, or to gain a discharge resolution from the Rules Committee. To successfully suspend the rules and pass a bill (one motion), a member must be recognized by the Speaker to make the motion to suspend, and then a two-thirds majority must approve the motion. Because the Speaker is usually supportive of committees dominated by members of his or her own party, this approach is seldom a feasible strategy. Also, a two-thirds majority is unlikely to be obtained for a measure opposed by a committee. In recent decades, committee leaders have used the suspension process to speed floor action or avoid amendments to committee bills.

The discharge procedure allows any member to introduce a motion to discharge or extract a measure from a committee once the measure has been before the committee for 30 legislative days (that is, days on which the House meets). After the motion is filed, a discharge petition is prepared and made available for members to sign. If 218 or more members sign the petition, the motion to discharge becomes privileged business on the second and fourth Mondays of the month (except during the last six days of a session). If the discharge motion is adopted by majority vote, a motion to call up the bill for immediate consideration is in order.

Until 1993, the identity of members signing a discharge petition was not made public until the 218th signature was added. The secrecy of the signatories made it difficult to hold members accountable and undermined lobbyists' efforts to pressure members to sign. Still, both before and after the 1993 rule change, the discharge process has seldom produced House action on a bill. In fact, only 19 bills have been discharged and passed by the House since 1931. Two factors may account for this. First, committees are probably more or less in line with the House majority most of the time. Second, members may prefer to discourage a practice that could be used to discharge legislation from their own committees.

The third approach involves the Rules Committee's authority to report a privileged resolution that, if adopted, brings a bill to the floor for immediate consideration. The majority party members of the Rules Committee are appointed by the Speaker, so the committee is unlikely to use this power without the support of the Speaker. Again, the Speaker usually works to support the actions of committee majorities.

Circumventing Committees in the Senate

In the Senate, committees can be circumvented by introducing nongermane amendments to bills under consideration on the floor, by placing bills directly on the calendar for floor action, by moving to suspend the rules, and by employing the discharge procedure. Unlike the House, which requires that amendments offered to a bill be germane to the content of the bill, Senate rules are silent on the content of amendments offered to most bills. Consequently, a senator is free to offer his or her bill as an amendment to another measure pending before the Senate, thus circumventing a committee that is refusing to report the bill to the floor. There is no guarantee that a majority will support the amendment, of course, but the mechanism is very easy to employ.

Another approach is to object to the standard procedure of referring a bill to committee. Under Senate Rule XIV, a single senator may object and have a bill placed on the calendar, thus avoiding delays that might be caused by an unfriendly committee. But this action may alienate senators who otherwise might support the bill. Senators also may seek to suspend the rules, but doing this requires a two-thirds vote under Senate precedents, which makes it more difficult to use successfully than a nongermane amendment. Alternatively, a senator can move to discharge a committee, but such motions are debatable and thus can be filibustered.

Floor Scheduling

Legislation is listed, in the order it is reported from committee, on one of four calendars in the House and one of two calendars in the Senate. Each chamber has multiple mechanisms for scheduling legislation for floor consideration so that priority legislation will not get backlogged behind less important legislation. Moreover, for certain types of "privileged" legislation – such as budget and appropriations bills – the House allows committee leaders to call up the legislation directly on the floor. In both chambers, the majority party leaders assume primary responsibility for scheduling, but the two chambers have developed very different methods for setting the floor agenda.

Scheduling in the House

Minor legislation and major legislation are treated differently in the House. In recent years, minor bills have been called up most frequently by unanimous consent requests or by motions to suspend the rules. When legislation is called up by unanimous consent, there typically is no discussion. Under a motion to suspend the rules and pass a bill, debate is limited to no more than 40 minutes, no amendments are allowed (unless specified in the motion), and a two-thirds majority is required for approval. Although legislation can only be brought up under suspension of the rules on specified days (typically Monday, Tuesday, and Wednesday only), this has become a very common means for disposing of bills on the House floor. In the 109th House (2005–06), more than 900 measures were passed under suspension of the rules.

Major or controversial legislation is more troublesome. Sponsors of a major or controversial bill usually cannot obtain unanimous or even two-thirds majority support, so they go to the Rules Committee to request a resolution known as a "special rule," or simply a "rule." The following box shows a recent rule adopted by the House for a bill dealing with Federal Water Pollution Control Act. The rule provides for priority consideration of the measure by allowing the Speaker to move the House into the Committee of the Whole, where the bill may be amended (see the section on Floor Consideration). The rule limits general debate on the bill to one hour and allows only those amendments to the committee version that are listed in an accompanying report from the Rules Committee. This rule also sets aside objections (waives points of order) that may be made to the provisions of the bill or to amendments that violate House rules.

Special rules are highly flexible tools for tailoring floor action to individual bills. Amendments may be limited or prohibited. The order of voting on amendments may be structured. For example, the House can adopt a special rule known as a king-of-the-hill rule. First used in 1982, a king-of-the-hill rule provides for a sequence of votes on alternative amendments, usually full substitutes for the bill. The last amendment to receive a majority wins, even if it receives fewer votes than some other amendment. This rule allows members to vote for more than one version of the legislation, which gives them the freedom both to support a version that is easy to defend at home and to vote for the version preferred by their party's leaders. Even more important, the procedure advantages the version voted on last, which is usually the proposal favored by the majority party leadership.

If the Rules Committee grants the rule and a majority of the House supports it, the way is paved for floor debate on the bill. Since the mid-1970s, the Rules Committee has been under the direction of the Speaker. In 1975, after years of struggle to get friendly, timely rules from a Rules Committee dominated by conservatives, the House Democratic Caucus granted the Speaker the power to appoint the committee's Democratic members, subject to its approval. Because the Democrats were the majority party and insisted on firm control of the rules, they reserved nine of the 13 seats on the committee for their part – a ratio that is still in place today. Since the late 1970s, Rules Committee Democrats, often at the direction of the Speaker, have become much more creative in structuring the amendment process on the House floor.

Finally, five House committees (Appropriations, Budget, House Administration, Rules, and Standards of Official Conduct) have direct access to the floor for certain kinds of legislation. Privileged measures – such as appropriations or tax bills – are considered critical to the House as an institution. When other legislation is not pending on the floor, a member authorized by one of these committees can move for immediate consideration of a privileged measure. Special rules from the Rules Committee are the single biggest group of privileged measures. Although privileged bills do not require a special rule from the Rules Committee, their sponsors often seek one anyway to limit or structure debate and amendments or to waive a House rule that might otherwise be used to raise a point of order against the bill.

Scheduling in the Senate

Scheduling is one area, and certainly not the only one, in which the Senate is very different from the House. In some respects, floor scheduling is

Resolved. That at any time after the adoption of this resolution the Speaker may, pursuant to clause 2(b) of rule XVIII, declare the House resolved into the Committee of the Whole House on the state of the Union for consideration of the bill (H.R. 720) to amend the Federal Water Pollution Control Act to authorize appropriations for State water pollution control revolving funds, and for other purposes. The first reading of the bill shall be dispensed with. All points of order against consideration of the bill are waived except those arising under clause 9 or 10 of rule XXI. General debate shall be confined to the bill and shall not exceed one hour equally divided and controlled by the chairman and ranking minority member of the Committee on Transportation and Infrastructure. After general debate the bill shall be considered for amendment under the five-minute rule. The amendment in the nature of a substitute recommended by the Committee on Transportation and Infrastructure now printed in the bill, modified by the amendment printed in part A of the report of the Committee on Rules accompanying this resolution, shall be considered as adopted in the House and in the Committee of the Whole. The bill, as amended, shall be considered as the original bill for the purpose of further amendment under the five-minute rule and shall be considered as read. All points of order against provisions in the bill, as amended, are waived. Notwithstanding clause 11 of rule XVIII, no further amendment to the bill, as amended, shall be in order except those printed in part B of the report of the Committee on Rules. Each further amendment may be offered only in the order printed in the report, may be offered only by a Member designated in the report, shall be considered as read, shall be debatable for the time specified in the report equally divided and controlled by the proponent and an opponent, shall not be subject to amendment, and shall not be subject to a demand for division of the question in the House or in the Committee of the Whole. All points of order against such further amendments are waived except those arising under clause 9 or 10 of rule XXI. At the conclusion of consideration of the bill for amendment the Committee shall rise and report the bill, as amended, to the House with such further amendments as may have been adopted. The previous question shall be considered as ordered on the bill and amendments thereto to final passage without intervening motion except one motion to recommit with or without instructions.

simple in the Senate. Bringing up a bill is a matter of making a motion to proceed to its consideration. This is done by the majority leader, and though the motion technically requires a majority vote, it usually is approved by unanimous consent. The Senate has no committee empowered to report special rules.

What appears bizarre to many newcomers to Senate politics is that the motion to proceed is debatable and may be subject to a filibuster (see

SPECIAL RULES OF THE HOUSE

Since 1979, the House Rules Committee, in partnership with the majority party leadership, has proven remarkably creative in designing special rules to govern floor debate and amendments on major legislation. Different styles of special rules have gained informal names that are widely recognized by the members of the House. All of these creative special rules waive many standing rules of the House governing floor debate and amendments.

• *Restrictive Rules.* Three kinds of rules restricting amending activity were known before the 1980s – modified open, modified closed, and closed rules. Closed rules simply barred all amendments. Modified open rules allowed amendments except for a specific title or section of a bill. Modified closed rules barred amendments except for a specific title or section of a bill. Since the early 1980s, restrictions have come in so many combinations that these traditional categories do not capture their diversity. An example is provided in the box above.

• *King-of-the-Hill Rules.* Invented by Democrats in the early 1980s and sometimes called king-of-the-mountain rules, these rules provide that the House will vote on a series of alternative versions of a bill (substitutes) in a specified order and that the last version to receive a majority vote (no matter how large the majority on other versions) wins.

• *Queen-of-the-Hill Rules.* Invented by Republicans in 1995, these rules provide that the House will vote on a series of alternative versions of a bill in a specified order and that the version with the most votes wins. If two versions receive the same number of votes, the last one voted on wins.

• *Time-Limit Rules.* Invented by Republicans in 1995, these rules provide that all debate and amending activity will be completed within a specified period of time.

the accompanying box). That is, senators may refuse to allow the majority leader's motion to come to a vote by conducting extended debate. In fact, they may not even have to conduct the filibuster, because just the threat of doing so is usually enough to keep legislation of only moderate importance off the floor. The reason is that the majority leader usually cannot afford to create a logjam of legislation awaiting floor consideration by subjecting one measure to extended debate. Under Senate Rule XXII, breaking a filibuster is a time-consuming process that requires a three-fifths constitutional majority – if no seat is vacant, 60 senators – willing to invoke cloture. In 1994, a proposal to limit debate on motions to proceed was blocked by Republicans who threatened to filibuster the resolution providing for the change in the rules.

A good example of a bizarre filibuster was the one conducted by Senator Alfonse D'Amato (R-New York) in October 1992. D'Amato objected to the fact that a tax break for a Cortland, New York, typewriter manufacturer had been stricken from a bill in a conference committee, so he filibustered the entire bill. D'Amato held the floor for more than 15 hours, sometimes with the assistance of Senators Patrick Moynihan (D-New York) and John Seymour (R-California). Under the Senate's rules, D'Amato could not sit down or excuse himself to go to the bathroom without yielding the floor. The quality of this extended "debate," which prevented the Senate from completing its business and adjourning for the year, degenerated as time wore on. At one point, D'Amato reported:

> The young lady who works for me in my Syracuse office, Marina Twomey – her parents. She married a young boy who I ran track against in high school – went to Andrew Jackson, met Larry, he went up to Syracuse on a track scholarship, competed. And he married this lovely girl, Marina, who came from Cortland. This is how I came to know Cortland. I visited her and her family.

> Fate and life and what not, circumstances as we talk, Marina is now one of the two people – the other you know for many years, Gretchen Ralph, who used to be the leader of the symphony or the executive director- and a great community person. She and Marina Twomey run my Syracuse office. We talk about Cortland and knowing and having an affinity.[2]

By the time D'Amato gave up, the filibuster consumed a little more than 86 pages of the Congressional Record. This number was not enough to break the record established by Strom Thurmond (R-South Carolina), who spoke for more than 24 hours against a civil rights bill in 1957.

The ever-present threat of a filibuster requires that scheduling be a matter of consultation and negotiation among the majority leader, the minority leader, bill sponsors, and other interested senators. These discussions, conducted in private, often yield bargains about how to proceed and may include compromises about substantive policy matters. The agreement, which may include limitations on debate and amendments, is then presented to the Senate. It requires unanimous approval to take effect. The process contrasts sharply with the formal Rules Committee hearings and majority approval of special rules in the House.

Floor Consideration

For most minor and routine legislation that reaches the House or Senate floor, floor consideration is brief, no amendments are offered, and

---

Congressionally Speaking... The Filibuster

The term filibuster is an anglicized version of the Dutch word for "free-booter." A "filibusterer" was a sixteenth- and seventeenth-century pirate. How it came to be the Senate term for talking a bill to death in the nineteenth century is not clear. Political lexicographer William Safire notes that one of the term's first appearances was in 1854, when the Kansas-Nebraska Act was filibustered.

The current Senate Rule XXII provides for cloture (closing of debate) with the approval of a three-fifths majority of all senators present. That is, if all senators are present, at least 60 senators must support a motion for cloture to stop a filibuster. An exception is made for measures changing the Senate rules, for which a vote of two-thirds of those senators present and voting is required.

---

the legislation is approved by voice vote or by unanimous consent. On major legislation, many members usually want to speak and offer amendments, creating a need for procedures that will maintain order and expedite action. The two chambers have quite different floor procedures for major legislation.

Floor Action in the House

In the House, committee chairs write a letter to the Rules Committee chair, requesting a hearing and a special rule for major legislation they are about to report to the floor. Once a special rule for a measure is adopted, the House may resolve to convene "the Committee of the Whole House on the State of the Union" to conduct general debate and consider amendments. The Committee of the Whole, as it is usually abbreviated, consists of the full House meeting in the House chamber and operating under a special set of rules. For example, the quorum required to conduct business in the Committee of the Whole is smaller than it is for the House (100 versus 218), making it easier to conduct business while members are busy with other activities.

A chair appointed by the Speaker presides over the Committee of the Whole. The Committee of the Whole first conducts general debate on the bill and then moves to debate and votes on amendments. Legislation is considered section by section. An amendment must be relevant – germane – to the section under consideration, a requirement that is interpreted very restrictively. For example, an amendment to limit abortions cannot be considered when a bill on water treatment plants is being debated. Amendments sponsored by the committee originating the legislation are considered first for each section and are considered under the five-minute rule. That is, members are allowed to speak for five minutes each on an amendment. The special rule providing for the consideration of the measure may – and often does – alter these standard procedures.

Voting on amendments in the Committee of the Whole can take one of three forms: voice vote, standing division vote, or recorded vote. On a voice vote, members yell out "yea" or "nay," and the presiding officer determines whether there were more yeas or nays. On a standing division vote, members voting "yea" stand and are counted, followed by those voting "nay." Since 1971, it has been possible to get a recorded vote, for which each individual member's position is officially and publicly recorded. Under the current rule, a recorded vote in the Committee of the Whole must be demanded by 25 members. Since 1973, recorded voting has been done by a computerized system. Members insert an identification card into a small voting box and push a "yea," "nay," or "present" button. This system is used for recording other voting in the House as well.

Legislation cannot be passed in the Committee of the Whole, so once debate and amending actions are complete, the measure, along with any approved amendments, is reported back to the House. Special rules usually provide that the "previous question" be ordered, preventing additional debate by the House. The amendments approved in the Committee of the Whole may then be subject to separate votes; if no one demands separate votes, however, the amendments are voted on as a group. Next, a motion to recommit the legislation to committee, which by custom is made by a minority party member, is in order. If the motion to recommit is defeated, as it nearly always is, or simply not offered, the House moves to a vote on final passage.

Floor Action in the Senate

The Senate lacks detailed rules or a well-structured process for debating and amending legislation on the floor. What happens after the motion to proceed is adopted depends on whether or not unanimous consent has been obtained to limit or structure debate and amendments. In the absence of a unanimous consent agreement providing otherwise, Senate rules do not limit debate or amendments for most legislation. Debate and amending activity may go on for days. In contrast to the House, the Senate has no five-minute rule

THE CHANGING CONGRESS: "GOING NUCLEAR"

Going nuclear is a term used in the Senate to describe a strategy for limiting debate on judicial nominations and other matters. In principle, presidential nominations and treaties can be filibustered. If they are, a two-thirds majority is required to invoke cloture in order to get a vote on them. It has been argued that this practice violates the spirit of the Constitution, which provides that the president may make appointments to top executive and judicial positions with "the advice and consent" of the Senate. If the Senate cannot vote on a presidential nomination, the argument goes, it is not meeting its constitutional obligation under the advice and consent clause.

One approach to addressing filibusters is to change the cloture rule, perhaps just for nominations and treaties. However, proposals to change the cloture rule may be filibustered and would themselves require a two-thirds majority to invoke cloture. So Senate majorities have looked for another approach, an approach that Democrats and the media have described as the "nuclear option."

The idea is to get a ruling from the presiding officer (the Vice President, in all likelihood) that would establish the precedent that the Senate must vote on nominations (and maybe treaties). The proposed tactic goes like this

• A senator makes a point of order that the Constitution implies that a simple majority can bring a nomination to a vote and the presiding officer rules in favor of the point of order;

• the opposition appeals the ruling of the presiding officer to a vote of the Senate, but the senator making the point of order moves to table the appeal, a motion that is not debatable and so receives an immediate vote; and the majority votes to table the appeal and the presiding officer's ruling stands.

Why haven't Senate majorities used this tactic before to get new rules established as precedents? The primary reason is that a minority can retaliate by obstructing action on the majority's larger agenda. Partisanship would become red hot, other legislation would be filibustered, unanimous consent for routine actions would not be given, Senate action would slow to a crawl, and ultimately the majority might be blamed by the public for mismanaging the Senate. All out partisan war – going nuclear – is the likely result. In 2005, then-Senate Majority Leader Bill Frist (R-Tennessee) threatened to use the nuclear option to do away with filibusters of judicial nominations. A showdown was avoided when a group of seven Democrats and seven Republicans agreed to oppose the strategy, support votes on some of the nominations in dispute, and avoid filibusters on nominations during that Congress.

or general germaneness rule for amendments. The floor schedule becomes very unpredictable. Normally, the Senate muddles through controversial legislation with one or more unanimous consent agreements that limit debate, organize the consideration of amendments, and lend some predictability to its proceedings.

One reason consent may not be acquired for a time limitation on debate is that some senators may want to have the option of filibustering. A filibuster, and sometimes just the threat of one, will force a compromise. If a compromise is not possible, cloture must be invoked, or the majority leader will be compelled to withdraw the measure from the floor. Once cloture is invoked, 30 hours of debate are permitted (under the current rule), and germane amendments submitted before cloture was invoked can be considered. In fact, cloture is sometimes invoked to avoid the inclusion of nongermane amendments that may require embarrassing votes, complicate negotiations with the House, or risk a presidential veto.

To avoid an unanticipated filibuster, Senate floor leaders seek to learn of possible objections to their plans to bring up a bill on the floor. An informal practice has arisen in recent decades that allows senators to register their objections, usually in writing, to floor action on a bill. An objection is known as a "hold." A hold gains its bite when a majority leader refuses to bring up a measure or nomination on which a hold has been placed or when the minority leader indicates his or her objection to the consideration of a measure or nomination on the basis of a hold that has been registered. Since at least the 1970s, holds have been a source of frustration, particularly for majority leaders and bill managers, but rank-and-file senators of both majority and minority parties have voiced concerns about the practice with regularity. Making holds even more frustrating is the practice of keeping secret the identity of the senator placing a hold. While floor leaders do not always observe holds or confidentiality, the practice is difficult to avoid as long as the majority leader needs unanimous consent to take up measures and wants to avoid filibusters that would make the floor schedule unpredictable for all senators.[3]

The modern Senate does not use a committee of the whole. Floor voting can take one of three forms: voice vote, division vote, and roll-call vote. Voice and division votes are similar to those in the House, although the Senate very seldom uses division votes. The Senate does not have an electronic voting system, so recorded votes, which can be demanded by 11 senators, are conducted by a name-by-name call of the roll. The vote on final passage of a bill occurs as specified in the unanimous consent agreement or, in the absence of an agreement, whenever senators stop talking about and offering amendments.

Resolving Differences between the Chambers

The Constitution dictates that the two chambers must approve identical bills before legislation can be sent to the president. This can be accomplished in several ways. One chamber can accept a measure passed by the other. The chambers may exchange amendments until they agree on them, or they may agree to hold a conference to resolve matters in dispute and then send the bill back to each chamber for approval. For complex or controversial legislation, such a conference is the only practical approach.

Members of conference committees, known as conferees, are appointed by the presiding officers of the two chambers, usually according to the recommendations of standing committee leaders. Committee leaders take into account potential conference committee delegates' seniority, interest in the legislation, and other factors, and some committees have established traditions concerning who shall serve on conference committees, which the leaders observe. Conference committees may be of any size. Except for the large conferences held for budget measures, the average conference has roughly 24 representatives and 12 senators.

Agreements between House and Senate conferees are written up as conference reports, which must be approved by a majority of each chamber's conferees. Conference reports must then be approved by majority votes in the House and Senate. In the 109th Congress (2005–2006) only 29 conference reports were filed. Plainly, most legislation is routine and noncontroversial and therefore does not require conference action.

House and Senate Rules Compared

The procedures of the House reflect a majoritarian impulse: A simple majority is allowed to take action expeditiously and can do so easily if it is led by the majority party leadership. The House carefully follows established rules and practices, which are quite lengthy. The House makes exceptions to its most important floor procedures by granting and adopting special rules by simple majority vote. Procedures dictating internal committee procedures are elaborate. Debate is carefully limited, and the timing and content of amendments are restricted.

The rules of the Senate are relatively brief. They reflect an egalitarian, individualistic outlook. The right of individuals to debate at length and to

---

Congressionally Speaking...

The Constitution stipulates that the vice president serves as president of the Senate. The vice president retains an office in the Capitol, may preside over the Senate, and may cast a vote to break a tie. Because recent vice presidents have had a policy-making role in the administration and travel frequently, they have not used their Capitol office on a regular basis and have seldom presided over the Senate.

Eleven vice presidents never cast a vote in the Senate. In contrast, George Bush, when he was vice president between 1981 and 1989, cast seven votes, and Albert Gore, vice president under President Bill Clinton, cast two votes in 1993. The record belongs to John Adams, the first vice president, who cast 29 tie-breaking votes during the eight-year presidency of George Washington.

---

offer amendments on any subject is generally protected. Only extraordinary majorities can limit debate or amendments. For reasons of practicality, most scheduling is done by unanimous consent. The majority party usually must negotiate with minority party members to schedule floor action and to bring important measures to a vote. Consequently, Senate decision making is more informal and less efficient than House decision making.

In part, these differences (which are highlighted in Table 7.1) are due to the different sizes of the chambers. The large size of the House requires that its rules more explicitly and stringently limit participation on the floor. Scheduling floor action to suit the needs of individuals is out of the question. In contrast, Senate leaders manipulate the floor schedule through unanimous consent agreements to meet the requests of individual senators. The Senate's smaller size allows peer pressure to keep obstructionism in check. A senator who objects frequently to unanimous consent requests risks objections to consideration of his or her own bills.

The differences also reflect the unique parliamentary history of each chamber. In their earliest days, the rules of both the House and Senate contained a previous question motion. In modern times, standard parliamentary rules such as *Roberts Rules of Order* provide for a motion that, if passed, forces an immediate debate on the issue before the body. In this way, the previous question motion is a means to end debate, but in the early Congresses neither chamber used the previous question motion as a tool to end debate. The question took the form of "shall the main question be now put," which was the traditional parliamentary means of putting off discussion on a controversial measure. If the motion failed, discussion was put off; if it passed,

TABLE 7.1. Major House-Senate Differences in Rules of Practice.

House	Senate
Does not allow filibusters	Allows filibusters on most legislation
Has a general rule limiting debate	Has no general rule limiting debate
Bars non-germane amendments	Has no general rule barring non-germane amendments
Uses special rules from the Rules Committee to schedule major legislation for floor action	Relies on unanimous consent agreements to schedule major legislation for floor action
Frequently adopts restrictive special rules to limit the number of amendments and limit debate	Must rely on unanimous consent or cloture to restrict debate and amendments
Uses multiple referral frequently	Rarely uses multiple referral
Committees are not easily circumvented	Committees easily circumvented
Rules permit efficient action without minority party cooperation	Rules do not permit efficient action without minority party cooperation
Considers major legislation in the "Committee of the Whole" first	Has no Committee of the Whole
Speaker of the House empowered by House rules	Presiding officer given little power by Senate rules
Records votes by electronic device	No electronic voting system; roll calls are tabulated manually

Source: Collected by authors from House and Senate rules.

discussion continued. The early Senate rarely invoked the motion and eliminated it from its rules in 1806. The House overturned a ruling of the Speaker in 1807 that a successful previous question motion ended debate on a bill, before reversing this precedent in the face of obstruction in 1811. Thus, from 1811 forward, the House had an effective means for a majority to end debate on a bill or proposed rule change, while the Senate, bound by its lack of a previous question motion, has never been able to develop an efficient means of ending debate.

The previous question played a pivotal role in the development of House and Senate rules. With the previous question motion, House majority parties could get a vote on new rules they wanted adopted. Senate majority parties faced minority filibusters when they proposed rules that advantaged the majority. Consequently House majority parties have regularly modified and elaborated on their chamber's rules, while Senate majority parties seldom seek, let alone achieve, a change in their chamber's rules. The result is that modern House rules are several times as long as Senate rules. When the House and Senate have determined that some limitation on debate is desirable, as for budget measures and trade agreements, special provisions have been written for the Senate to guarantee that debate could be closed. But this has happened only when supermajorities favor the change and often has happened as a part of a much larger legislative package.

Not until 1917, 111 years after the Senate dropped the previous question motion from its rules, did the Senate again adopt a rule that provided a means for closing debate. Rule XXII allowed an extraordinary majority to invoke cloture – that is, to force an end to debate. The 1917 rule provided for a two-thirds majority to invoke cloture. The 1975 reform of the rule reduced the required majority to three-fifths of all elected senators (60 votes with 100 elected senators), except for matters affecting the Senate's rules, which are still subject to a two-thirds majority cloture threshold. As a result, a fairly broad base of support is still required to bring a rules change to a vote in the Senate.

Authorizing and Appropriating

Under congressional rules, most federal government programs are subject to two types of legislation: authorization bills and appropriations bills. Theoretically, an authorization bill sets the program's organization, rules, and spending ceiling, and an appropriations bill provides the money. House and Senate rules require that an authorization bill creating a federal program or agency be passed before an appropriations bill providing spending authority can be adopted. The authorization bill and the appropriations bill for each program or set of programs both follow the standard legislative process. For most programs, a new appropriations bill must be approved each year.

For example, suppose proponents of a bill creating a new financial aid program for college students managed to get the measure enacted into law. They would have taken the bill through the House Committee on Education and the Workforce and the Senate Committee on Health, Education, Labor, and Pensions. The bill would specify how the program was to be organized, how financial aid decisions were to be made, and how much – say $400 million – could be spent, at most, on the program in any one year. It is likely that the bill would authorize the program for a specific period of time – say, four or five years. A separate appropriations bill, which would include

Congressionally Speaking...

An *engrossed bill* is the final version of a bill passed by one house, including any amendments that may have been approved, as certified by the clerk of the House or the secretary of the Senate.

An *enrolled bill* is the final version of a bill as approved by both houses, printed on parchment, certified by either the clerk of the House or the secretary of the Senate (for the house that first passed it), and signed by the Speaker of the House and the president pro tempore of the Senate; it has a space for the signature of the president.

spending authority for the new program, must be passed before the program could begin operations. The House and Senate appropriations committees might decide that only $250 million should be spent on the program. If the House and Senate went along with the lower figure, the program would be limited to a $250 million budget for the next year.

In the modern Congress, jurisdiction over authorization legislation is fragmented among many standing committees. Jurisdiction over appropriations is consolidated in one appropriations committee in each chamber, although each of the appropriations committees has 13 subcommittees that do most of the work. Jurisdiction over taxes, the major source of federal revenue, falls to one tax-writing committee in each house: the House Committee on Ways and Means and the Senate Committee on Finance. Thus, power over fiscal policy is not only shared between the House, Senate, and president, it is shared among the various committees within House and Senate as well.

The system creates tensions between the congressional committees. Tax committees do not like to pass bills increasing taxes to cover spending other committees have authorized. Authorizing committees often dislike the handiwork of the appropriations committees. A small appropriation can defeat the purpose of the original authorization bill. In response, authorizing committees have pursued a number of tactics, such as including provisions for permanent appropriations for some programs (social security is one), to avoid the appropriations process.

Provisions limiting the length of authorizations are known as *sunset* provisions. In principle, sunset provisions force the authorizing committee and Congress to re-pass authorization legislation periodically, which compels the executive branch to justify the continuation of the programs and gives the authorizing committees additional influence over the executive agencies.

In recent years, many authorizations have expired but the programs have not died – sometimes out of neglect but often because of conflict over the program. Welfare reform, college student financial aid, and federal highway programs are among the dozens of unauthorized programs in recent years. These programs can continue as long as Congress passes the separate appropriations bills for them. An appropriation is possible by use of a waiver of the House rule, which may be included in the special rule under which the appropriations bills are considered on the House floor. A consequence of this practice is that the authorizing committees do not realize the special influence over the direction of these programs that was expected when the sunset provisions were first enacted.

Evolution of the Legislative Process

For most of the twentieth century, nearly all major and minor legislative measures have followed the path of the standard processes described in this chapter. The House and Senate were always free to modify their processes and have sometimes handled a bill in a special way. In the last three decades of the twentieth century, nonstandard approaches to preparing legislation for a vote have been employed with increasing frequency. By-passing committees, negotiating details in summits between congressional leaders and representatives of the president, having multiple committees consider bills, and drafting omnibus bills characterize the action on a large share of major legislation considered by recent Congresses. In fact, according to one survey of the processes used by the House and Senate on major legislation since the late 1980s, four out of five measures in the House and two out of three in the Senate were considered under some nonstandard procedure.

Unorthodox legislative procedures have been invented for many reasons. The sheer complexity of some new public policies and legislative measures forces action by many committees – and compels committee and party leaders to find new ways to piece together legislation, negotiating a bewildering array of technical provisions and working with the president to avoid a veto. The reforms of the 1970s – which strengthened the House Speaker's procedural options and reduced the power of full committee chairs – were discovered to have unanticipated uses. Perhaps most important, partisan maneuvering stimulated procedural innovations as first one party and then the other sought parliamentary advantages when pushing legislation.

Furthermore, both chambers of Congress often create new rules in response to new challenges. In some cases the House and Senate have tailored their procedures to particular kinds of legislation or specific issues. In

the last two decades, for example, Congress has created "fast-track" procedures for considering trade agreements negotiated by the executive branch
with foreign governments. These procedures limit debate and bar amendments to speed congressional approval and limit congressional second-
guessing of executive branch decisions.

An even more important class of legislation that has inspired special procedures concerns fiscal policy: decisions about federal spending, taxing, and
budget deficits and surpluses. The Congressional Budget and Impoundment
Control Act of 1974, often known simply as the Budget Act of 1974, established a process to coordinate congressional decision making affecting fiscal
policy. In the 1980s and early 1990s, skyrocketing federal deficits motivated
Congress to set tight rules constraining fiscal choices and to adopt unique
procedures for enforcing the new constraints.

In other cases, special procedures are invented for an individual bill. In
the House, special rules governing floor debate have become more complex, as have the provisions of unanimous consent agreements in the Senate.
Task forces, usually appointed by party leaders, have become an everyday
part of decision making in the House. Inter-committee negotiations guided
by party leaders sometimes occur after committees report but before legislation is taken to the floor. In these ways, the traditional committee-to-
floor-to-conference process has become a less accurate description of the
increasingly meandering route that major legislation takes through the modern Congress.

Conclusion

Rules matter. Legislative rules, whether they arise from the Constitution or
elsewhere, determine procedural advantages among the players, factions,
and parties that compete for control over public policy. The rules also are
the foundation of Congress's major organizational features, such as its leadership positions and committees, which help the institution manage a large
and diverse workload and are generally designed to serve the political needs
of its members.

The House and Senate have evolved quite different rules. Compared with
Senate rules, House rules make it more difficult to circumvent committees,
more strictly limit participation on the floor, and give the majority a greater
ability to act when confronted with an obstructionist minority. The House
is more majoritarian; the Senate is more egalitarian. The House is more
committee-oriented; the Senate is more floor-oriented.

But the rules do not determine the political and policy objectives of legislators. Those objectives are primarily the product of the electoral processes through which people are selected to serve in Congress. Campaigns and elections connect members to their constituencies and lead many members to take a local, sometimes quite parochial, outlook in legislative politics.

Above: U.S. Rep. Nancy Pelosi (D-California) swears in members of the U.S. House of Representatives after being elected Speaker of the House, becoming the first woman to hold that position, on the opening day of the legislative session on Thursday, January 4, 2006, in Washington, D.C. (Chuck Kennedy/MCT).

Below: The electronic tally board is illuminated in the United States House of Representatives chamber in the Capitol in Washington, D.C. on Thursday, January 4, 2007. The board is used to show the votes of the members when they vote electronically. Credit: Ron Sachs / CNP.

8

The Floor and Voting

W HEN THE GAVEL FELL AT 5:51 A.M. ON NOVEMBER 22, 2003, THE FINAL tally was 220–215 and the House of Representatives had passed a prescription drug benefit for senior citizens under the Medicare programs. Passage of the bill was a major victory for the House Republican leadership and President Bush, but for much of the night it looked like the bill would go down in defeat. Debate on the bill had continued until 3:00 a.m. at which time presiding officer Richard Hastings (R-Washington) announced that the House would have a 15-minute vote. At the end of 15 minutes the bill was losing by 15 votes, and after one hour, the tally stood at 216–218. By most accounts, then-Speaker Dennis Hastert (R-Illinois) was resolved to the fact that the bill would fail, but he, along with then-Majority Leader Tom DeLay (R-Texas) and others, continued to try to convince recalcitrant Republicans to vote for the bill. At 5:00 a.m., President Bush was awakened to begin calling wayward members. The combination of his encouragement and other persuasive activities was enough to secure victory. Democrats were outraged that the vote had been held open so long.

The lengthy vote on the Medicare bill was quite unusual. Votes are occasionally held open to allow straggling members to vote or in hopes of changing the outcome, but the Medicare vote set a new record. The uncertainty over the outcome is indicative of a change in the way former Speaker Hastert managed the House. Both the House and Senate have developed elaborate committee and party systems that can take much of the policy-making process off the chamber floors, but in recent Congresses, House Republicans were not hesitant to bring a bill to the floor without having a firm majority in place before hand and then doing enough "arm-twisting" to secure a majority.

During most of Congress's history, responsibility for the details of public policy rested with the standing committees. At times, power over the details

TABLE 8.1. Possible Patterns of Congressional Decision Making.

Number of units	Number of effective participants	
	Few	Many
Few	Centralized (party leadership)	Collegial (floor)
Many		Decentralized (committees)

of important bills resided in the hands of central party leaders. Most scholars have used this continuum – from decentralized, committee-oriented decision making to centralized, party-oriented decision making – to characterize the decision-making processes and distribution of power within the two houses. Everything that goes on within the House and Senate is, in principle, subject to the approval of the parent chambers in floor sessions. In principle, therefore, the details of all legislation could be written and reviewed on the chamber floors, but in modern practice, this rarely happens.

These alternatives are depicted in Table 8.1. If important decisions were made on the chamber floor, all members, in that one place, would have the opportunity to participate effectively in deliberations on all measures. In general, as we saw in Chapter 6, the modern House is more dependent on committees than is the Senate. But there have been times when central party leaders dominated the House. Thus, the House is often characterized as varying along the centralized-decentralized continuum. The Senate is more collegial – more likely to make detailed policy choices on the floor. Both committees and party leaders are important in the Senate, but relative to the House, the Senate has long been far more floor oriented. Neither committees nor party leaders have found the Senate floor predictable or controllable. These differences are obvious every day in the Capitol.

In this chapter, we report on a typical day on the House and Senate floors and explain how differences in floor procedure shape the distribution of power in the two chambers. In addition, the chapter reviews how members' records of floor voting are most commonly analyzed by political scientists, journalists, and interest groups, providing a "consumer's guide" to studies of floor voting. The chapter concludes with a review of the factors that influence the relationship between the parties, committees, and the floor.

A Typical Day on the House and Senate Floors

On a March day in 2007, a fairly typical day while Congress is in session, dozens of committees and subcommittees held morning meetings and hearings in the congressional office buildings while clerks and pages prepared for the opening of the House and Senate floor sessions. In the Senate, this meant distributing various documents to individual senators' desks, which are arranged by party (when facing the front, Democrats are on the left and Republicans are on the right) and seniority (junior members are in the back). In the House, members do not have desks or assigned seats, although, by tradition, the Democrats sit on the left and the Republicans on the right. As the clerks and pages went about their work, tourists went in and out of the galleries, some disappointed that they did not have a chance to see a debate before they hurried off to other sites in Washington. As usual, the Senate session opened before the House session – the Senate at 9:15 a.m. and the House at 10 a.m.

The Day in the House

The House session began when Speaker pro tempore Jan Schakowsky (D-Illinois) assumed the chair. The Speaker does not always preside over House proceedings. She frequently appoints other members (Speakers *pro tempore*) to take her place presiding over the House so that she can conduct business in her office or elsewhere. Typically, several members will preside during the course of the day.

The session opened with a prayer from the Reverend Thomas J. McCarthy of St. Paul Catholic Church in Salem, Ohio. The Speaker pro tempore then announced that she had examined the *Journal* of the House and announced her approval of it. Approval of the *Journal* used to require a vote of the House, but dilatory requests for votes led House Democrats to push through a rule allowing the Speaker to approve the *Journal*. A member may still demand a vote on the *Journal*, but that vote may be postponed until late in the day. Next came the Pledge of Allegiance, which has been recited since 1989. The practice was started the year the Supreme Court ruled that burning the American flag was constitutionally protected speech, and Congress responded with legislation to ban flag burning. House Republicans proposed – and the Democrats did not dare block – a House rule that required that the Pledge be recited after the prayer. After the Pledge, several members of the Ohio delegation welcomed Reverend McCarthy to the House

THE CHANGING CONGRESS: TELEVISING THE HOUSE AND SENATE

The House began televising its floor sessions in 1979. After becoming somewhat jealous of the attention given to the House, the Senate began to televise its sessions in 1986. Congressional employees operate both television systems, and the signal is made available to television networks and individual stations via satellite.

Floor proceedings are carried live on C-SPAN, the Cable-Satellite Public Affairs Network. Most cable television systems carry C-SPAN I, on which House sessions are shown. Many cable systems also carry C-SPAN II, where Senate sessions are broadcast. Many committee hearings, press conferences, and other public affairs programs are shown on C-SPAN when the House and Senate are not in session.

In both chambers, the most obvious consequence of television coverage has been an increase in floor speeches. In the House, one-minute and special-order speeches have become more numerous. One-minute speeches are made at the beginning of the day for about half an hour. Special-order speeches are made after the House finishes its regular business for the day. In 1994, House Democratic and Republican leaders agreed that special-order speeches should be limited to four hours on most days. They also began to experiment with structured, Oxford-style debates. In 1995, "reaction shots" of members on the floor were limited after members complained about being caught in unflattering shots by the floor cameras.

The Senate created a new class of speeches, the aforementioned special-order speeches, which are limited to five minutes. In addition, representatives and senators have made increasing use of large poster charts and graphs to illustrate their points for the television audience. In addition, many senators now address their chamber from the back row, some distance from their personal desks, so that the camera angle will be less steep and, in the case of male senators, will not expose their bald spots to home viewers.

and gave brief speeches on his life and accomplishments. The floor session was televised (see box "The Changing Congress: Televising the House and Senate").

The Speaker pro tempore announced that members of each party would be recognized to give one-minute speeches. The reservation of time for one-minute speeches gives legislators a brief period to address the House and the nation on any matter they choose. Frequently, members use one-minute speeches to respond to the news of the day, and they often use the opportunity to compliment or criticize the president. Occasionally, a group of members will organize themselves to emphasize a particular theme – and being outrageous or flamboyant increases the chance of getting on the evening news. On this day, there was a mix of speeches, some concerned the bill to provide more funding for military operations in Iraq, others addressed the Democrats plans for the federal budget, while others concerned less controversial topics such as prevention of veteran suicides, and honoring U.S. Marshal award winners.

After about a half hour of one-minute speeches, the Speaker pro tempore declared that the House dissolve into the Committee of the Whole House on the state of the Union for further consideration of H.R. 1227, a bill to assist in the provision of affordable housing to low-income families affected by Hurricane Katrina. The Committee of the Whole (COW) is what it sounds like, a committee of which all members of the House are members. The House often dissolves into the COW to debate and vote on amendments to bills. The quorum requirement is reduced to 100 from 218, which makes it easier to transact business. Since 1971, the House has allowed recorded voting on amendments in the COW, but the rules stipulate than any member can request that a vote be taken by the House on any amendments that pass in the COW.

Under the previously adopted special rule governing consideration of the bill, Representative Randy Neugebauer (R-Texas) was recognized to offer an amendment to the bill striking the section of the bill that would allow families to continue receiving housing vouchers after the termination of the Disaster Voucher program. Under the provisions of the special rule (see box "The Special Rule for H.R. 1227"), the amendment was debated for 60 minutes, with the time divided between Rep. Neugebauer and a member opposed to the amendment, in this case Rep. Barney Frank (D-Massachusetts). The debate centered on whether allowing hurricane victims to continue receiving housing vouchers would undermine the Section 8 public housing program. Proponents of the amendment argued that extending the vouchers was too expensive and was the wrong way to solve the region's housing problem. Opponents argued that given the level of destruction of housing in the Gulf region, there was insufficient public housing available. It was, therefore, crucial that the government not disadvantage beneficiaries of this program by putting a time limit on the voucher program.

At the conclusion of debate on the amendment, a voice vote was taken and it was announced that the amendment had failed. Rep. Neugebauer asked for a recorded vote on the amendment. House rules allow the chairperson of the Committee of the Whole to delay requests for recorded votes. This is typically done as a time-saving measure so that debate can continue on amendments. It is common practice for votes to be "stacked," that is occur

THE SPECIAL RULE FOR H.R. 1227 (ANNOTATIONS BY THE AUTHORS)

Resolved, That at any time after the adoption of this resolution the Speaker may, pursuant to clause 2(b) of rule XVIII, declare the House resolved into the Committee of the Whole House on the state of the Union for consideration of the bill (H.R. 1227) to assist in the provision of affordable housing to low-income families affected by Hurricane Katrina.

This provision gives the Speaker control over when the bill will be considered.

The first reading of the bill shall be dispensed with. All points of order against consideration of the bill are waived except those arising under clause 9 or 10 of rule X.

This provision bans points of order that might be raised against consideration of the bill on the grounds that its provisions violate some rule or precedent.

General debate shall be confined to the bill and shall not exceed one hour equally divided and controlled by the chairman and ranking minority member of the Committee on Financial Services. After general debate the bill shall be considered for amendment under the five-minute rule.

This provision sets time limits on debate. General debate – that is, debate not directed at a specific amendment – is divided so that the two bill managers control 30 minutes each. They may allocate some time to colleagues by yielding time to them. The five-minute rule refers to a standing rule of the House that governs debate in the Committee of the Whole. The Chair first recognizes the amendment's sponsor to speak for five minutes. Next a Member opposing the amendment can claim five minutes to speak in opposition. Other Members may secure five minutes for debate by offering pro forma amendments. This is done by asking the Chair "to strike the last word."

The amendment in the nature of a substitute recommended by the Committee on Financial Services now printed in the bill, modified by the amendment printed in part A of the report of the Committee on Rules accompanying this resolution, shall be considered as adopted in the House and in the Committee of the Whole. The bill, as amended, shall be considered as the original bill for the purpose of further amendment under the five-minute rule and shall be considered as read. All points of order against provisions in the bill, as amended, are waived.

These provisions provide that the Financial Services Committee's version of the bill, rather than the version originally introduced, will be the subject of floor amending activity. An amendment to the committee's version, which was considered by the Rules Committee, would be automatically adopted upon the adoption of the special rule.

Notwithstanding clause 11 of rule XVIII, no further amendment to the bill, as amended, shall be in order except those printed in part B of the report of the Committee on Rules. Each further amendment may be offered only in the order printed in the report, may be offered only by a Member designated in the report, shall be considered as read, shall be debatable for the time specified in the report equally divided and controlled by the proponent and an opponent, shall not be subject to amendment, and shall not be subject to a demand for division of the question in the House or in the Committee of the Whole. All points of order against such further amendments are waived except those arising under clause 9 or 10 of rule X.

These provisions allow consideration of amendments specified in the accompanying report, which also specifies the order of consideration and the time allowed for debate. Other amendments are prohibited. Points of order against the amendments for violating House rules or precedent are prohibited.

At the conclusion of consideration of the bill for amendment the Committee shall rise and report the bill, as amended, to the House with such further amendments as may have been adopted. The previous question shall be considered as ordered on the bill and amendments thereto to final passage without intervening motion except one motion to recommit with or without instructions.

This provision gives the minority party an opportunity to offer an amendment as "instructions." If the instructions are adopted as a part of a motion to recommit, the bill is amended and immediately considered for final passage.

Sec. 2. During consideration in the House of H.R. 1227 pursuant to this resolution, notwithstanding the operation of the previous question, the Chair may postpone further consideration of the bill to a time designated by the Speaker.

one after another, so that members who are not on the floor can vote on several items in succession. The COW then debated an amendment offered by Rep. Tom Price (R-Georgia). At the close of debate on the amendment offered by Rep. Price, recorded votes on both the Price amendment and the Neugebauer amendment were taken in succession. The Neugebauer amendment was rejected by a vote of 185–247 and the Price amendment was rejected by a vote of 96–333.

With all amendments having been considered, the COW then "rose" and the Speaker pro tempore resumed presiding over the House. The House then moved into the final stages of consideration of the H.R. 1227. Rep. Price asked for a revote on an amendment that had been adopted in the COW, which subsequently passed by a vote of 242–184. Rep. Bobby Jindal (R-Louisianna) then offered a motion to recommit with instructions that would give priority in public housing to displaced returning residents who were both "law-abiding" and employed. The motion to recommit is reserved

---

Congressionally Speaking...

On the House floor members engage in a carefully scripted language when debating on the floor. When a bill manager wishes to speak about a bill on the floor they say, "I yield myself such time as I may consume." If another member wishes to interject into debate he or she will say "Will the gentleman [gentlewoman] yield?" If the member holding the floor wishes to yield he/she will say in return, "I yield two minutes [or another block of time] to the gentleman [gentlewoman] from New Hampshire." The interjecting member will then say, "I thank the gentleman [gentlewoman] for yielding. I rise in support/opposition..." Once they have concluded they may say, "I yield back to the balance of my time." The bill manager will then begin his/her speech again with "Reclaiming my time..." This back and forth between floor managers and other members continues until the time allotted for debate is consumed.[1]

---

for the minority party or someone who is opposed to the bill "in its current form." A motion to recommit with instructions to report forthwith – the type offered by Jindal – is essentially a substantive amendment to the bill. If it is adopted, the bill does not leave the floor at all, the change is reported by the committee immediately. Rep. Jindal's motion passed by a vote of 249–176, with a majority of Democrats voting no, and a majority of Republicans voting yea. During the 12 years of Republican rule it was rare for a motion to recommit with instructions to pass against the will of the Republican Party, but in the early months of the 110th Congress, the Democrats have lost a handful of these votes. The vote on the motion to recommit is the last procedural step before the "final passage" vote on a bill. The House then passed H.R.1227 by a vote of 302–125, with all Democrats voting in favor of passage along with 72 Republicans.

Following passage of H.R. 1227, the House considered several bills under suspension of the rules. This is a procedure in which a member can ask to "suspend the rules and pass" a particular bill. Bills taken up under this procedure are allotted 40 minutes of debate and amendments are not allowed. If two-thirds of the House votes in favor, the bill is passed. This procedure is used for non-controversial bills that typically involve a cost of less than $100 million. On this day, the House considered numerous bills and resolutions under this procedure, including a resolution authorizing the use of the capitol rotunda for a Holocaust remembrance ceremony, a reauthorization of the Hawaiian Homeownership Opportunity Act, the Judicial Disclosure

THE CHANGING CONGRESS: *THE CONGRESSIONAL RECORD*

The proceedings of the House and Senate are published daily in the *Congressional Record*. The *Record* is printed overnight and distributed to Capitol Hill and to many other places, including most large libraries. Hardcover, permanent editions are published and distributed periodically.

The *Record* is much more than a report of the words spoken on the chamber floors. Introduced bills, committee meetings, and many other items are listed in the *Record* each day. The text of bills and conference reports considered on the floor is included, as are the many newspaper articles, scholarly studies, executive agency reports, and other items that members place in the *Record* by gaining unanimous consent of their house. As a general rule, the charts or graphs that members use on the floor cannot be printed in the *Record*, although tabular material may be inserted if the member receives unanimous consent.

The members' ability to alter prose reported in the *Record* after they have spoken has long been a controversial issue. Members are allowed to make non-substantive grammatical changes in their prose. As a result, some members appear far more articulate in the *Record* than they do on the floor. Statements and other insertions in the *Record* are supposed to be distinguished by a bullet (•). In the Senate, members frequently seek, and then always receive, unanimous consent to have their statements placed in the *Record* "as though read." This revision makes distinguishing what was said from what was inserted nearly impossible. Frequently, senators request that their statements be included "at the appropriate place," which is usually done so that the statement does not interrupt the discussion on a pending matter in the *Record*.

The *Congressional Record* tends to be a more faithful record of House proceedings than of Senate proceedings. Representatives frequently seek permission to "revise and extend" their remarks, so many statements reported in the *Record* were not actually read on the floor. But the House has more restrictive rules about including extraneous matter and speeches in the *Record* and requires that newspaper articles and other insertions be printed in a separate section, "Extensions of Remarks." The House also has long required that revisions or extensions that are not "a substantially verbatim" account be distinguished by a different typeface. The House adopted an even tighter rule in 1995 that limits changes to corrections of grammar and typographical errors.

Responsibility Act, and a bill to change the cost of living adjustment for veterans – with six receiving recorded votes – all passing except for the Hawaiian Homeownership Opportunity.

The House then heard a number of special order speeches – most concerning the status of the War in Iraq and what, if any, policy changes the House should adopt as part of the bill providing supplemental funding for the Iraq war. Special orders typically take place at the conclusion of other business that the House is considering that day. Members are allowed to give speeches on topics of their choice regardless of whether the speech concerns pending legislation. Members typically reserve time for special orders through the party leadership and may choose to insert the speech into the *Congressional Record* without actually delivering the speech – undelivered speeches appear in the *Extension of Remarks* section of the *Congressional Record*. The House adjourned at 1:05 a.m. until 10:00 a.m. the same morning.

The Day in the Senate

The Senate convened at 9:15 a.m. when Senator Sheldon Whitehouse (D-Rhode Island) called the Senate to order. The vice president is the president of the Senate, but tends to preside only at ceremonial occasions (for example, when the oath of office is administered to newly elected senators at the start of a Congress) and when a tie-breaking vote might be needed. The Constitution provides for a president *pro tempore* to preside in the absence of the vice president. But the president *pro tempore*, who by tradition is the most senior member of the majority party, is not able to preside on a full-time basis because of other duties. Consequently, the president *pro tempore's* staff arranges for other majority party senators, usually the most junior ones, to take turns presiding over the Senate. On this day, following the pledge of allegiance, Senator Whitehouse read a letter from the president *pro tempore*, Senator Robert Byrd (D-West Virginia), appointing Whitehouse as acting president *pro tempore*. After the prayer, Senator Kent Conrad (D-North Dakota), serving as acting majority leader in the absence of Majority Leader Harry Reid (D-Nevada), was recognized and indicated that the Senate immediately resume debate on the budget resolution for fiscal year 2008. Senator Conrad indicated that Senator John Ensign (R-Nevada) would be recognized to offer an amendment, followed by an amendment from the majority party. Senator Conrad also informed senators that there would be no recorded votes taken before 5:00 p.m. Senator Conrad also urged his colleagues to speed up debate on the budget resolution, warning them that the session could run to midnight if necessary.

Senator Ensign's amendment sought to "ensure that troops serving in harm's way remain America's top budget priority by: ensuring full funding for the Department of Defense within the regular appropriations process, reducing reliance on supplemental appropriation bills, and by improving the integrity of the Congressional budget process." Debate on the Ensign

> *Congressionally Speaking...*
>
> On the Senate floor, *quorum calls* are used to get a temporary break in the action – a time out. A senator might say, "Mr. President, I suggest the absence of a quorum," and the presiding officer will respond, "The clerk will call the roll." Technically, if a quorum is not discovered, the Senate will have to adjourn. Indeed, filibustering senators sometimes note the absence of a quorum to force senators to appear on the floor. Most of the time, however, a quorum call is used as a time out that gives absent senators time to come to the floor to offer an amendment or speak. At other times, a quorum call is used to give leaders time to work out agreements on issues or procedure.

amendment continued with several senators expressing their support or opposition. Senator Barack Obama (D-Illinois) then asked for and was granted 10 minutes to discuss the costs – both monetary and in terms of human life – of the Iraq war and to urge senators to consider these costs. The speech by Senator Obama highlights the fact that the rules of debate in the Senate are much more casual than in the House. Senators regularly ask for and receive unanimous consent to give speeches that are not related to the bill currently under consideration.

When debate on the Ensign amendment was concluded, the Senate moved on to an amendment offered by Senator Jim Bunning (D-Kentucky) concerning Social Security funding, along with several other amendments. Debate on these amendments continued until late into the afternoon, at which point the Senate moved into "morning business." Despite the name, morning business does not necessarily occur in the morning. During morning business, the Senate conducts routine business such as receiving messages from the House and the president, as well as petitions and memorials, committee reports, and bill introductions.

Following morning business the Senate moved into Executive session to consider a nominee for the post of Assistant Secretary of Preparedness and Response in the Department of Health and Human Services. The nominee was confirmed by unanimous consent. The Senate then adjourned for the day at 7:52 p.m.

House-Senate Differences

The events of this day illustrate many of the differences between the two chambers of Congress. Most of the differences are the by-product of one fact: Floor debate and amendments are governed by strict rules in the House, but are generally limited only by unanimous consent agreements or super-majority votes in the Senate. Representatives must worry that their floor amendments might not be put in order by a special rule from the Rules Committee. Once a bill is on the House floor, representatives are compelled to conform to the schedule laid out by the Speaker and the special rules. In sharp contrast, senators can introduce amendments freely, even on subjects unrelated to the bill at hand, and protect their ability to do so by objecting to requests for unanimous consent to limit amendments. Moving the Senate from amendment to amendment and from bill to bill is a constant struggle for the majority leader and bill managers. The House has a schedule that is followed in the main; scheduling in the Senate is often much like fortune telling.

Voting Procedure

By the end of that March day in 2007, the House had held 12 recorded votes, all using its computerized voting system. The Senate had held seven recorded votes, all on amendments to the budget resolution. When the Senate conducts a roll-call vote, the process is time consuming. It is an old-fashioned roll call for which a clerk calls out the individual names of the senators in alphabetical order ("Mr. Akaka ... Mr. Alexander ... Mr. Allard ... Mr. Baucus," and so on) and waits for senators to arrive on the floor and respond. After calling all of the names, the roll-call clerk starts from the beginning to call the names of senators who have not voted. The clerk is then interrupted by senators appearing during the vote to recognize them and hear their votes.

The Constitution provides that "the Yeas and Nays of the Members of either House on any question shall, at the desire of one-fifth of those present, be entered upon the Journal." This rule means that 20 senators or 87 representatives (if all members are present) may demand a vote in which each member's vote is recorded. In practice, with few members being present, usually only 11 senators or 44 representatives are required – one-fifth of a quorum, which is half of the membership of the chamber. Because the quorum requirement is not enforced unless a member makes a point of order that a quorum is not present, the presiding officer will assume that a quorum is present and order the yeas and nays based on the lower threshold. Under the rules of the House, 25 members may demand a recorded vote in the Committee of the Whole, where most votes on amendments to bills take place. The Constitution does not specify how the houses should vote in the absence of a demand for the yeas and nays.

House Voting Procedure

In today's Congress, the House votes by three means: voice vote, division vote, and recorded vote. On most motions, the presiding officer (the chair of the Committee of the Whole or the Speaker) first asks for a voice vote. He or she might say, "The question is on the amendment by the gentlewoman from Illinois. All in favor say 'aye,' all opposed say 'no.' The noes have it, and the amendment is rejected." In many cases, this is spoken so rapidly that it is obvious that the number voting each way had little to do with the announcement of the winning side. Sometimes, the issue is not controversial, and the presiding officer is merely reporting the obvious result. In other cases, the presiding officer knows that his or her announcement will make no difference because a member will demand a recorded vote on the issue.

The division, or standing, vote is used little and is virtually never decisive. Any member may demand such a vote, which is conducted by having members voting aye stand and be counted and then having members voting no stand and be counted. Only the vote tally – the number of ayes and noes – is recorded. Because few members are on the floor for debate on most matters, the result usually shows that less than a quorum of members is present (a quorum is 100 or more in the Committee of the Whole) which leads automatically to a recorded vote. Consequently, this method is seldom used any longer.

Recorded votes are conducted with the assistance of an electronic voting system and nearly always occur upon the demand of the necessary number of members after a voice vote. In the Committee of the Whole, 25 members must demand a recorded vote. (The Constitution's requirement that one-fifth of those present demand a recorded vote applies only to requests for recorded votes in the House, not in the Committee of the Whole.)

Each member is issued a voting card about the size of a credit card. To vote, a member uses his or her card in any one of the nearly 40 voting boxes scattered around the House chamber (most are attached to the back of the chamber's bench-like seats). With the card inserted, the member presses one of three buttons – yea, nay, or present – and his or her vote is recorded by the computer system. As the votes are cast, they are displayed on panels above the gallery at the front of the chamber, and the running totals can be viewed on computer terminals. Under the House rules, recorded votes take 15 minutes, although the presiding officer often holds the vote open a little longer to allow members to make it to the floor and cast their votes. On a few occasions, the Speaker has held open the vote for several minutes to find the last vote or two his or her side needed to win. The rules do permit the

Speaker to postpone votes – to "stack" votes is the jargon used – in some circumstances, such as votes on motions to suspend the rules and pass a measure. Stacked votes are cast in rapid succession in periods of five minutes each, usually near the end of a session, to allow members to vote on several matters without having to make multiple trips back-and-forth between their offices and the House floor. By the way, the record for the number of recorded votes cast without missing one belongs to Representative William Natcher (D-Kentucky), who cast 18,401 consecutive votes over 22 years before he became ill and died in 1994.

Senate Voting Procedure

The Senate, too, has voice, division, and recorded votes, but virtually no division votes are cast in the Senate because of its smaller size. On voice and recorded votes, Senate practice is quite different from House practice. On many, perhaps most, "votes," the Senate does not really vote at all. The presiding officer often brings a matter to a vote when debate appears to have ended by saying, "Hearing no further debate, and without objection, the amendment is agreed to." In this way, even the pretense of a voice vote is not observed in the Senate. Recorded roll-call votes often are ordered in advance, upon the successful demand of a senator, so no preliminary voice vote is held, as in the House.

Recorded votes in the Senate are properly called roll-call votes. The names of the senators are called out, one by one, by a clerk, and senators' responses are recorded by hand. Roll-call votes are supposed to take only 15 minutes, as stipulated by a unanimous consent agreement that the majority leader arranges at the beginning of each Congress. Many, if not most, Senate roll-call votes last longer than 15 minutes, however, to accommodate senators who need more time to make it to the floor. At times, these delays have become so burdensome that majority leaders have promised to insist that the 15-minute limit be observed, but the desire to accommodate colleagues seems so overwhelming that votes extending to 20 minutes or more remain common. Senator Robert Byrd (D-West Virginia) cast his 17,000th roll-call vote in April 2004 – a Senate record.

Changes in Floor Decision Making

On the surface, it might seem that the differences in voting procedures between the two chambers matter little. The record suggests otherwise. House voting procedures changed in the early 1970s – and with important consequences. As earlier chapters have discussed, the early 1970s was a period of remarkable change in House politics. Power devolved from full committee chairs to subcommittee chairs, many of whom were inexperienced as bill managers. Personal and subcommittee staffs were growing, which enabled more members to design and promote their own legislation. Also, a new breed of member – more media-oriented and more insistent on having a meaningful role – seemed to be flooding into Congress. In this context, the House changed the voting rules in such a way that encouraged members to pursue floor amendments more frequently and more actively.

The House voting reforms had two components. First, a new rule extended recorded voting to the Committee of the Whole. Before 1971, no recorded votes took place in the House's Committee of the Whole, where action on floor amendments takes place. That meant that members' positions on most floor amendments were not recorded. As is still the case, a roll-call vote could be demanded on amendments approved in the Committee of the Whole just before the vote on final passage of the bill, but rejected amendments could not be considered again.

Second, the electronic voting system was used for the first time in 1973. Voting "by electronic device," as they call it in the House, nearly completely replaced the old system of teller voting in the Committee of the Whole and the traditional call of the roll in the House. Teller voting was done by having members pass by tellers (members appointed to do the counting), with the yes voters to one side and the no voters to the other. The 1971 reform allowed recorded teller voting, in which members signed green (yes) or red (no) cards, deposited them in a box, and then waited for tellers to count them and turn them over to clerks, who would record each member's individual vote. This cumbersome process discouraged recorded voting in the Committee of the Whole. Automated vote counting by the electronic system allowed the Committee of the Whole and the House to complete a vote and have the results in 15 minutes.

Electronic recorded voting produced a surge in amending activity. Being able to put one's position on a particular issue on the record (and forcing one's opponents to do the same) created new incentives to offer amendments, particularly for the minority party. Electronic voting also reduced the burden imposed on colleagues by demands for recorded votes. The result, as Figure 8.1 illustrates, was an increase in the number of floor votes, most on amendments, beginning in the first Congress (the 93rd, 1973–1974) that used both electronic and recorded voting in the Committee of the Whole. By the late 1970s, the House floor began to look much more like the Senate

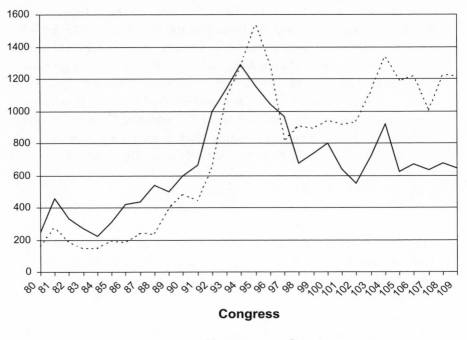

Congress

------- House ——— Senate

FIGURE 8.1. Number of House and Senate Roll Calls, 1947–2006. *Source: Data collected by the authors.*

floor than it had for a century. Longer daily floor sessions, repetitive amendments, and scheduling uncertainty had become the norm. Worse yet for the Democratic leaders, more free-wheeling amending activity made it more difficult for them to enforce deals made in committee and to hold a majority coalition together on the floor.

House Democrats sought relief in new rules and practices. In 1979, after several aborted attempts, they finally increased from 20 to 25 the number of members required to support a request for a recorded vote in the Committee of the Whole. This change seemed to have little effect on amending activity, however. A more important reaction to the increase in amendment votes was an expansion of the number of days each month in which motions to suspend the rules were in order. A motion to suspend the rules simultaneously brings a measure to the floor and passes it. No amendments are allowed and debate is limited to 40 minutes, which makes suspending the rules an attractive procedure for bill managers. Although a successful motion to suspend the rules requires a two-thirds majority, Democrats managed to increase the use of suspension motions during the 1970s, a trend that has continued.

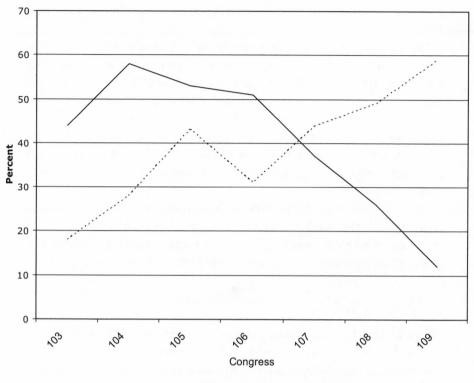

FIGURE 8.2. Restrictiveness of Special Rules, 1993–2006. *Source:* Data collected from reports of the House Committee on Rules.

The most important response by the Democrats was to have the Rules Committee design more special rules to restrict floor amendments. The change in the content of special rules in the 1980s was quite dramatic. Most special rules continued to put in order at least some, and often many, amendments (open or modified open rules), but Republicans correctly complained that many special rules had been designed to prevent all or most amendments (closed or modified closed rules). Consequently, Republicans made procedural reforms a centerpiece of the 1994 congressional campaign. As Figure 8.2 reveals, after becoming the majority party following the 1994 elections, Republicans initially kept their campaign promise to offer more open/modified open rules than had the Democrats, although there was a slight increase in the use of restrictive rules under the new Republican majority. This policy has changed dramatically in recent congresses. In 2005–2006, more than half of the special rules (59 percent) were either closed or modified closed, while only 12 percent were open or modified – a complete reversal from the last democratically controlled Congress in 1993–1994.[2]

The net result of the more than two decades of adjustments to the voting reforms of the early 1970s has been a more bifurcated process for managing legislation on the House floor. Legislation that is of little importance is not subject to amendments; it is considered under suspension of the rules or, if it is sufficiently non-controversial, it is brought up by unanimous consent and passed without a recorded vote. Legislation that is likely to attract even a few amendments is likely to be considered under a special rule that limits amending activity in some way, often to the disadvantage of the minority party.

These changes have renewed the distinctiveness of House floor decision making. While the number of House floor votes has been similar to that of the Senate in recent Congresses, House floor action is more predictable and more carefully controlled to advantage committees' legislation.

Analyzing Votes

Nearly all members participate in recorded floor votes, so floor votes offer a natural basis for comparing members' policy positions. The voting record is available in the *Congressional Record* and a variety of commercial publications. It can even be examined on personal computers through the use of THOMAS, a service of the Library of Congress (http://thomas.loc.gov). Political scientists, journalists, interest groups, challengers to incumbents, and many others have long analyzed the roll-call record for scientific, educational, and political purposes. Consequently, the use – and misuse – of the congressional voting record to make inferences about legislators is a subject that recurs in nearly every congressional campaign.

The Problems of Interpreting the Roll-Call Vote

A legislator's roll-call vote can be thought of as an act based on (1) a policy preference and (2) a decision about how to act on that preference. The policy preference may be influenced by an array of political forces – constituents, the president, interest groups, party and committee leaders, the legislator's personal views, and so on. Thus, the personal view of a legislator is not easily inferred from a roll-call vote. Moreover, whatever the basis for his or her policy preference, the legislator may hold that preference intensely or only weakly.

A member's decision about how to vote can be sincere or strategic. For example, a member may strategically vote against a bill even if she prefers the bill to no bill at all, if she believes that killing the bill will lead to action on an alternative that she will like even more. Such "strategic voting" on the first bill might lead an observer to conclude incorrectly that the member prefers the status quo to the first bill. A member also might cast a deceptive vote. An extreme example is a member who holds a strong policy preference and works hard behind the scenes to push his point of view, yet votes the other way on the floor to make the folks back home happy.

Plainly, the political and strategic character of members' policy preferences and voting choices is an obstacle to the use of roll-call votes as the basis for making claims about legislators' intentions or objections in casting a vote. But the situation is not as hopeless as it might seem. Most votes are not strategic or deceptive. They reflect the political preference of the member fairly well, which makes political sense. Members know that their votes on important issues may be used against them, so they have an incentive to cast votes that are easily explained. Besides, the number of situations that present an opportunity for strategic or deceptive voting is not nearly as large as it could be. Nevertheless, caution is required when making inferences from a particular vote.

The possibility of strategic or deceptive voting is less troublesome in analyzing summary statistics on members' voting records than it is when considering votes individually. Many voting indices summarize members' records over a large number of votes by counting the number of times that they vote in a certain way – for example, in favor of the president's position. Instances of strategic or deceptive voting are not likely to affect the scores assigned to the legislators, but skepticism is in order for scoring based on subsets of the larger voting record.

Common Voting Measures

Political scientists and journalists have relied on several indices to characterize members' voting records. The most widely reported measures are those calculated by the research department of the Congressional Quarterly (CQ), which publishes *Congressional Quarterly Weekly Report*, a news magazine that provides in-depth coverage of Congress. CQ calculates objective indicators of members' support for and opposition to the president, support for and opposition to their party's positions, and support for and opposition to the conservative coalition.

Measures of the role that party plays in members' voting decisions are the most frequently used roll-call statistics. Many of these measures are based on the party vote, which CQ defines as a vote on which a majority of Democrats oppose a majority of Republicans. The percentage of all votes that are party votes is a common measure of the degree of partisanship in the House and Senate. The historical record for party votes – sometimes called party unity votes – is demonstrated in Figure 8.3. An individual member's overall level of support for his or her party is usually determined by the percentage of times he or she has supported the party's position on party votes. CQ calls these party unity scores.

CQ's label is a little misleading. Because a party vote occurs any time a majority of one party votes differently than a majority of the other party, a party vote might occur when the parties actually differ very little. For example, a vote on which 51 percent of Democrats and 49 percent of Republicans voted yea would be a party unity vote. This result would hardly be an indication of unified parties, and party influences or differences might not have played much of a role in the outcome. Of course, any objective measure requires that some standard be used – if not a simple majority, then perhaps a two-thirds or a 90 percent majority. Thus, whereas some caution is required in using CQ's measure, it remains one of the best available for examining the frequency of party alignments in Congress over time.

CQ also analyzes congressional votes on bills for which the president has taken a position by examining the public statements of the president and administration officials. CQ calculates a success rate for the president, consisting of the percentage of such votes on which the president's position prevails. Analysts using CQ's scores must rely on the CQ staff's ability to accurately identify the votes and the president's position. They must also hope that CQ is consistent in applying its selection criteria over time. Perhaps because CQ says nothing beyond a single sentence about the president's public statements, no one has effectively challenged CQ's work on this score.

The most obvious weakness of the CQ scores is that they do not take into account the varying importance of the issues behind the votes. One way to handle this problem is to use only votes that are contested – those that show a close division. The argument is that lopsided votes – for example, 90 to 10 – are less likely to have been seen as decisive, controversial, or critical to the choices made on issues important to members. Besides, one-sided outcomes do not allow analysts to distinguish among members. Thus, analysts frequently limit their choice of votes to those with less than 75 percent, or perhaps even 60 percent, of the members voting in the majority.

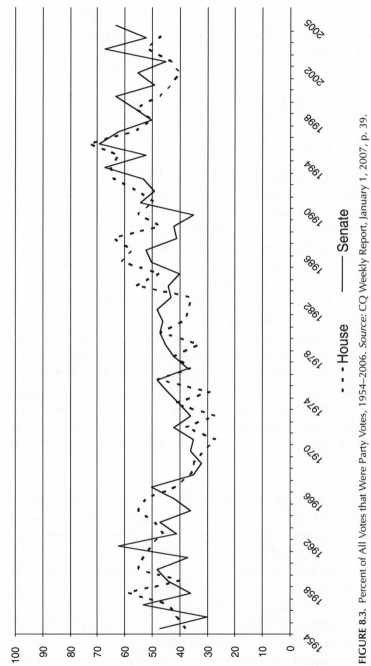

FIGURE 8.3. Percent of All Votes that Were Party Votes, 1954–2006. *Source:* CQ Weekly Report, January 1, 2007, p. 39.

- - - House   ——— Senate

CQ offers a corrective of its own by identifying 15–20 key votes every year for each chamber. The publication first identifies the year's major issues subjectively – identifying those that were highly controversial, a matter of presidential or political power, or had a great impact on the country – and then, for each issue identified, chooses the vote that was the most important in determining an outcome. CQ does not calculate scores based on these key votes, although political scientists have frequently used key votes for the construction of their own voting measures.

The Ratings Game

Dozens of interest groups regularly report ratings for members of Congress. The wide range of groups that do this includes ideological groups, farmers' organizations, environmental and consumer groups, and large labor and business associations. Not surprisingly, the ratings are used for political purposes. Most interest groups send press releases to the news media in members' home states and districts, praising their supporters in Congress and chastising their opponents. They also use their own ratings as a factor in decisions about campaign contributions. Nearly all groups use their scores to enlighten their memberships about their friends and enemies in Congress. Even incumbents and challengers advertise interest group ratings to substantiate their claims about the policy stances of the incumbents.

Interest groups' ratings of legislators are based on a limited number of votes selected by group officials. The processes by which groups select votes on which to base their ratings vary widely. Some groups do not complete their analyses until their board of directors or some other authoritative group approves the list of votes, whereas others allow low-level staff to identify the pertinent votes. Typically, groups have compiled and published their annual lists at the end of a congressional session. However, more recently some groups have begun choosing votes prior to their occurrence and sometimes even at the request of individual members or party leaders. In publicizing that a particular vote will be "scored," interest groups seek to influence wavering members to support the group's position. Upon preselecting a vote for scoring, groups will fax notices to members' offices or distribute cards prior to the vote that are imprinted with the group's logo and position on the vote. Some accounts suggest that the failure in the House to pass a comprehensive bankruptcy reform bill at the end of the 107th Congress was due in part to interest groups announcing that they would be "scoring" the vote on the special rule, which contained a provision concerning the ability of anti-abortion activists to avoid fines by filing for bankruptcy.

Groups vary in how narrowly or broadly they define their interests. The AFL-CIO, for example, includes votes in its ratings that concern issues that "affect working people who are not necessarily union members." The National Farmers Union has included votes on such issues as the MX missile, social security financing, and constitutional amendments requiring a balanced budget in its scales.

Moreover, the number of votes included in interest group scales varies widely as well. Sometimes as few as nine or 10 votes are included in an interest group's scale, which means that just one or two votes can produce great swings in the scores assigned to legislators. Groups sometimes include several votes on the same issue to give that issue greater weight in their calculations, whereas others carefully avoid doing so. And groups have been known to alter their selection of votes to get a certain scale that will benefit friends or make enemies look bad.

Further complicating the interpretation of interest groups' ratings of lawmakers is the type of votes these groups select. Quite naturally interest groups want to separate supporters and opponents, so they tend to choose important votes that show close divisions. Because legislators tend to be consistent in their policy positions, the tendency to pick votes with close divisions has the effect of repeatedly counting the same set of members as supporters and another set of members as opponents. As some critics of interest group ratings have noted, this process produces a polarized distribution of scores even when the real distribution of legislators' preferences more closely approximates a normal curve (a bell-shaped curve).

The lesson is that we should be quite skeptical of claims that legislators' interest group ratings are reliable indicators of their support for particular causes. Anyone seriously concerned about legislators' support for a cause should seek additional clues. Using the ratings of two or more groups with similar agendas is a good place to start. Sometimes, a better guide than a legislator's specific percentage rating is how that figure compares with other legislators' ratings. The legislator might have a rating of 85 percent support on a group's rating scale, but places in only the 50th percentile among all legislators on that scale. The latter often is a better indicator of where the member is positioned on the full spectrum of views on a given issue. Moreover, whenever a member's degree of commitment to a cause is at issue, we should look for corroborating evidence – bills sponsored, amendments offered, speeches made, and behind-the-scenes effort – that may be reported in the press or identified by knowledgeable observers.

Yet, interest group ratings retain their special appeal for analysts because collectively they provide a summary of legislators' policy views across a broad array of issue areas. Scholars often argue that the selection of the votes used in the ratings by knowledgeable interest group officials gives the ratings validity as measures of support for various causes. But convenience, rather than a careful judgment about the ratings' validity, seems to underlie many scholars' use of interest group ratings.

Dimensions, Alignments, and Coalitions

Given the limitations of interest group ratings, asking whether legislators' policy positions can be characterized in more objective ways is natural. They can. Political scientists have developed ways to determine the basic attitudes or dimensions that underlie voting patterns and the nature of the voting alignments in Congress (who votes with whom). Three basic concepts – dimensions, alignments, and coalitions – are important to understand.

Political scientists' techniques involve a search for consistency in the voting patterns across a set of roll-call votes. The idea is simple: If the legislators' voting behavior exhibits a discernable pattern for a set of votes, then we might assume that a particular mix of political forces were at work on members for that set of votes. A dimension of political conflict is said to be present when a certain alignment of members is visible throughout a set of votes.

For example, liberal and conservative members are often identified at opposite ends of an ideological dimension. The usual assumption is that each member holds a fairly stable ideological perspective and is guided by that perspective when deciding how to vote. Of course, members' voting behavior also may reflect the political outlook of their home state or district, the influence of party or faction leaders, and other political forces that produce an alignment of members that appears to have a liberal-to-conservative character. This is one reason politicians often resist being labeled liberals or conservatives. Some members may not even have personal views about the policies at issue on most votes and still demonstrate voting patterns that appear to fit neatly on a liberal-conservative continuum.

In principle, many dimensions of conflict may organize voting patterns, perhaps a different dimension for different sets of votes. Indeed, many scholars argue that we should expect many dimensions in congressional voting because Congress operates in a pluralistic political system, one in which a different set of interest groups and constituents wages the legislative battle on each issue. The issues may divide urban and rural Americans, producers and consumers, employers and employees, coastal- and middle-Americans, retired and not-yet-retired people, and, of course, Democrats and Republicans. The number of possible bases for conflict is large. The analyst's task is to find the important dimensions of conflict without arbitrarily limiting the search to a few of the possible alignments, such as party-based alignments.

Two schools of thought about the dimensions and alignments of congressional voting have emerged. The older school adopts the pluralistic view and emphasizes the multidimensionality of congressional voting. A newer school emphasizes the consistent presence and explanatory power of a liberal-conservative dimension. Some of the difference between the schools is due to differences in the statistical techniques they use. Part of the difference is due to differences in judgment or taste – just how much must a voting alignment vary from what is thought to be a liberal-conservative division before we count it as something else?

The difficulty of making a satisfactory interpretation is visible in an analysis of Senate votes during the 109th Congress (2005–2006). Senators' scores on two dimensions, calculated by political scientist Keith Poole, are arrayed in Figure 8.4. The horizontal dimension is related to the general liberal-conservative position on economic, tax, and spending issues; the vertical dimension separates senators according to their behavior on the very few issues that do not cleanly divide senators along liberal/conservative lines, such as free trade, immigration, and abortion. Senators with nearly identical scores on one of the dimensions often have a wide range of scores on the other dimension. However, in recent congresses the first dimension has explained more than 90 percent of the variance in roll-call voting. Party leaders, presidents, and lobbyists do not dare ignore such differences. They see important differences among members who operate in a complex world filled with conflicting pressures on legislators.

The alignment of legislators in Figure 8.4 is clearly partisan. Democratic senators are grouped in the upper left and Republicans are grouped in the lower right. We might be tempted to say that the two parties were strong coalitions on the issues confronting Congress. And yet, both parties show substantial internal variation, with some Democrats and Republicans falling closer to each other than they do to fellow partisans. Ben Nelson (D-Nebraska) and Lincoln Chafee (R-Rhode Island) are virtually

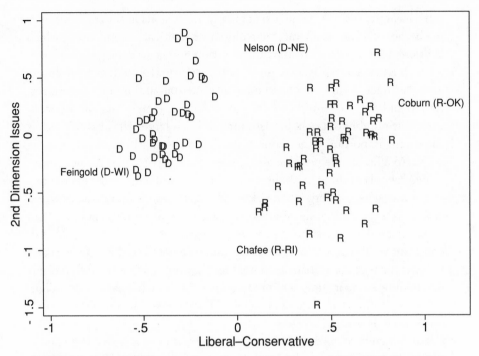

FIGURE 8.4. Ideological Alignments in the Senate, 109th Congress (2005–2006). *Source:* Data provided by Keith Poole and Howard Rosenthal, http://www.pooleandrosenthal.com.

indistinguishable on the liberal conservative dimension. Although the parties have quite different central tendencies, they simply are not tightly knit groups that keep their members from deviating from the position preferred by most party members. To be sure, party leaders and other factors tend to keep party members together, but many other forces lead party members to go their own way from time to time.

The distinction between alignments and coalitions is critical for understanding legislative politics. An alignment merely shows the distribution of policy positions among members, based on their voting behavior. But a group of members may vote the same way for different reasons, and they may vote alike only because they have similar home constituencies. They can be called a coalition only if they consciously coordinate their voting. Thus, we simply cannot determine the presence of active coalitions from voting behavior alone.

During the middle decades of the twentieth century, southern Democrats often voted with Republicans, creating policy victories for what was known as the "conservative coalition." There has been some dispute about how much coordination actually took place between Republican leaders and southern

Democratic leaders on these votes. That is, just how much of a coalition was the so-called conservative coalition? The answer seems to be that at times genuine coordination took place that affected members' voting behavior, but at most times the alignment of Republicans and southern Democrats against northern Democrats appeared without coordination as members made largely independent judgments about how to vote.

The Floor, Committees, and Parties

This chapter completes the examination of the three major features of congressional organization – the parties, the committees, and the floors. These three components combine to create the policy-making process in Congress. As we have seen, just how the components are combined varies between the two chambers and, within each chamber, over time. This is a good place to summarize the forces that lie behind those variations – the character of Congress's policy agenda, the distribution of policy preferences among members, and the institutional context.

Issue Agenda

The character of the legislative process is greatly affected by the nature of the issues that Congress confronts. As a general rule, Congress relies more heavily on committees to make policy choices when it must deal with a large number of issues and when the issues it considers are readily separable, recur frequently, or are less salient. Why? A large workload requires a division of labor so that many issues can be addressed simultaneously. A system of standing committees provides such a division of labor. If the issues are separable into distinct categories, then committees with distinct jurisdictions work well. Furthermore, if the same issues arise time and again, then fixing committee jurisdictions can be done without concern that some committees will become superfluous over time. Moreover, if most issues concern only a few members, committees are a natural place for those members to gather and make the detailed policy choices that do not interest other members.

Alignment of Policy Preferences

Because the process by which decisions are made may influence which choices are made, the contending parties and factions in Congress often seek to shape the decision-making process to their liking. Sometimes party divisions predominate; at other times, cross-party coalitions arise to make the important policy choices. When issues are salient to most members and the members of the majority party share similar policy views, the majority party may centralize policy making in the hands of its leaders. When most members care about the issues, but the majority party is not cohesive, neither committees nor majority party leaders may be trusted. Members then turn to the floor as the place where they can shape policy details.

Institutional Context

Differences in the institutional arrangements in the House and Senate are likely to cause different responses to similar changes in issue agendas and policy alignments. The Senate's rules and practices protect the rights of individual senators to offer amendments and conduct debate on the floor. Consequently, the Senate usually retains a more collegial, floor-oriented decision-making process. In contrast, the rules and practices of the House advantage the Speaker and standing committees. If the majority party is united, the Speaker tends to direct policy making with vigor; if not, the committees are more independent. As a result, House decision making is generally less collegial and less floor-oriented. Change in the House tends to come as movement along the centralized-decentralized continuum described previously.

Indeed, the constraints on floor amendments under House special rules are the product of cooperation between the traditional centers of power in the House – committees and majority party leaders. Rules Committee decisions about special rules often represent the terms of an agreement between committee and party leaders. Cohesiveness in the majority party enables agreements between committee and party leaders to gain the majority required to adopt restrictive special rules on the floor. In the Senate, the carefully preserved rights of individual members to debate and offer amendments to legislation stand in the way of committee and party leaders who might otherwise seek to structure floor action in a way that would disadvantage the minority party or individual member.

Conclusion

The floor is not only a place where the full House and Senate conduct business, it also is where the most vital stage in the policy-making process, when members exercise their equal voting rights, occurs. We have seen variations

between the House and Senate in the degree to which the details of legislation are devised on the floor, but the possible reaction of the floor to the
handiwork of committees and parties has always been a central consideration in legislative strategies. Despite similarities in the nature of floor activity
in the two chambers, we see obvious inter-chamber differences – the details
of legislation are far more likely to be determined on the Senate floor than
on the House floor.

Above: President George W. Bush pauses for an ovation during the State of the Union address on January 23, 2007. Newly elected House Speaker Nancy Pelosi (D-California) and Vice President Dick Cheney stand in the background.

Below: Sen. Charles Schumer (D-New York) (Center) speaks as (from left to Right) Sen. Bob Menendez (D-New Jersey), then-House Minority Leader Nancy Pelosi (D-California), Rep. Diana DeGette (D-Colorado), then-Senate Minority Leader Harry Reid (D-Nevada), and Jeff McCaffrey, who suffered a spinal cord injury from a traffic accident, listen during a news conference urging President George W. Bush to sign the Stem Cell Research Enhancement Act he had earlier threatened to veto. Their efforts proved futile, as Bush issued his first presidential veto on this legislation.

9

Congress and the President

U NDERSTANDING CONGRESS REQUIRES AN UNDERSTANDING OF ITS relationship with the executive branch. The basic rules of the legislative game laid out in the Constitution provide for three institutional players – the House, the Senate, and the president. Whereas the president is expected to address the needs of the nation, he can do little, particularly in domestic affairs, without Congress taking legislative action. But, the enactment of congressional legislation necessitates presidential approval, unless both chambers of Congress can muster a two-thirds majority to override a veto. Moreover, the Senate must ratify treaties negotiated by the president and must approve the president's choices for top executive and judicial posts. Interdependency, based on shared as well as separate powers, characterizes the relationship among the three institutions.

Interdependency would not be important if the House, Senate, and president held similar policy preferences on all important issues. In fact, for very good reasons they often disagree about what issues should be given priority and what should be done about them. Even when one party controls the House, Senate, and presidency, incumbents of the three institutions are not likely to have identical views. Representatives, senators, and presidents are elected on different cycles and they have diverse constituencies. The result is that they are likely to anticipate and react to somewhat different political demands and conditions.

To complicate matters, the framers left ambiguities in the Constitution about congressional and presidential functions and powers. For example, the president is instructed to appoint ambassadors and make treaties with the "advice and consent" of the Senate, yet it is unclear the specific role the Senate is to play in this relationship and how the president is to receive and account for senatorial advice. Furthermore, when the framers granted Congress the power to declare war, they did not anticipate the speed of modern military technology, which in some circumstances requires the president to make decisions about war without congressional involvement. In addition, when the framers gave the president the ability to kill a bill after a congressional adjournment by failing to take action, they were ambiguous as to what specifically constitutes an adjournment. In each case, and in many others, presidents have argued for interpretations that maximize presidential power.

The role of the president in policy making expanded during the twentieth century. Congress has delegated more power to the president and executive agencies by making general policy decisions and granting the executive branch the authority to determine the details and methods of implementing policy. Presidents have also asserted their ability to make policy through executive orders. The executive order, a presidential directive with the force of law, allows presidents to set new policy directions without the approval of Congress. Executive orders and other pronouncements, which in principle must be consistent with the Constitution and statutes, give presidents tactical advantages in setting policy and bargaining with Congress. In addition, the enhanced role of the United States in foreign affairs, and the increased importance of world events for American life, have given the president, who has important advantages over Congress in foreign affairs, a more central role.

While presidents have become more important relative to Congress in policy making over the last century, Congress has moved to strengthen its own hand. As we detail in this chapter, Congress has moved to counter the president and check the use of delegated powers to executive agencies. An expanded staff, restrictions on appropriated funds, new approaches to designing programs, and other developments have helped Congress retain a meaningful role in policy making when faced with aggressive presidents.

The President as a Legislative Player

The president is central to the legislative process, although he does not always assert himself. Many pieces of legislation do not interest the president and are routinely signed into law at the recommendation of trusted administration officials. On some issues, the president chooses to remain silent and inactive for political reasons. Yet, when the president chooses to become involved, he usually can have some influence over the outcome by threatening to use his veto power, employing his unilateral powers, and mobilizing support for his position with his considerable political resources.

The President's Formal Role

The Constitution and various federal laws clearly establish that the president is expected to recommend legislative action to Congress. This agenda-setting responsibility is complemented by the president's critical role at the end of the legislative game, for which the Constitution grants the president the authority to sign or veto legislation that has passed the two houses of Congress.

AGENDA SETTING. The framers of the Constitution expected the president to energize and focus the legislative process. Article II, Section 3 of the Constitution provides that the president "shall from time to time give to the Congress information of the state of the union and recommend to their consideration such measures as he shall judge necessary and expedient; he may, on extraordinary occasions, convene both houses, or either of them, and in case of disagreement between them, with respect to the time of adjournment, he may adjourn them to such time as he shall think proper." Of course, Congress is not required to consider matters the president brings to its attention. This is true even if the president calls a special session. Indeed, the president's powers and duties were designed to spur congressional action without giving the president coercive power over the activity of Congress or the ability to impose new laws unilaterally.

Presidents now address a joint session of Congress early in each calendar year with a speech known as the State of the Union Address. The speech is covered on live, prime-time television. It signals the president's priorities and is designed to generate support for his program. Some recent presidents have sent to Congress longer written versions of their addresses to provide more detail and rationale. Since the 1970s, a congressional leader of the opposite party has sought network television time after the speech to respond to the president. The major networks, however, have not always given opposition leaders the requested time.

Federal law requires the president to submit statements and legislation to Congress. Of particular importance is the requirement that the president submit an annual budget message and an annual economic message to Congress. The budget message, required by the Budget and Accounting Act of 1921, specifies the president's taxation and spending proposals for the forthcoming fiscal year. The economic message, prescribed by the Employment Act of 1946, provides a presidential assessment of the state of the U.S. economy and details the chief executive's economic projections

Congressionally Speaking...

Executive orders are edicts issued by the president to require or authorize some action of executive branch agencies. Some executive orders are authorized by law, but more often they are issued on the basis of the express or implied constitutional powers of the president. These presidential directives can have a significant affect on the structure of the executive branch and public policy. For instance, executive orders have been used to create new agencies, such as the Office of Homeland Security following the 9–11 terrorist attack. While most executive orders are reasonably unimportant, some have the effect of establishing an important policy by the unilateral action of the president. This was particularly true in the civil rights arena. President Harry Truman desegregated the military by executive order, and President John Kennedy created the Presidential Committee on Equal Employment Opportunity by an executive order in which the term "affirmative action" was first used in federal policy. Recent presidents have more frequently issued executive orders to achieve policy objectives without going to Congress for new legislation, often citing existing executive orders to justify additional unilateral action.

for the coming fiscal year. These messages sometimes stir controversy and often shape congressional debate over spending and tax policy each year.

Starting with President Truman in 1948, modern presidents have offered special messages providing additional detail – and often drafts of legislation – for the components of the administration's legislative program outlined by the State of the Union addresses and the budget and economic messages. The administration's legislation usually is introduced by members of the House and Senate as a courtesy to the president. Since Truman, presidents have devised time-consuming, complex processes for generating, synchronizing, and integrating legislative proposals from the bureaucracy and other sources.

The implied powers of the president under the Constitution also contribute to the president's role in agenda setting. In particular, the president's implied authority to issue regulations and executive orders to subordinates in the executive branch without the direct authorization of Congress boosts the president's ability to influence policy. This positive power becomes particularly controversial when the president seeks to interpret laws in a manner inconsistent with the expectations of members of Congress. Presidential actions often stimulate Congress to clarify its position on new legislation, if such legislation can survive a presidential veto.

While the Constitution is rather vague with respect to the powers of the executive, presidential use of executive orders is, in theory, limited. Executive orders must be linked to executive authority and must not contradict a statute passed by Congress. Throughout most of the eighteenth and nineteenth centuries, executive orders were principally used for routine administrative matters. Along with the expansion of the executive branch in the late nineteenth century and throughout the twentieth century, executive orders changed in scope. Specifically, the conventional limits on executive orders began to evaporate, giving presidents addition legislative authority.

Since the Constitution does not unambiguously define executive authority, there is incentive for presidents to explore the boundaries. Presidents can often expand executive authority when Congress chooses not to respond to executive orders that reach beyond conventional usage. Presidents have broadened the definition of executive authority by pursuing executive orders in unprecedented policy areas. In fact, executive orders have been used in recent years to appropriate funds, a power clearly specified by the constitution as belonging exclusively to Congress.

The expectation that executive orders not contradict a statute also has grown less rigid. In the 1980s, the Supreme Court, in a series of cases, upheld the right of the president to exercise executive powers provided that they do not directly challenge explicit guidelines set out by Congress in legislative form. Since it is unrealistic for legislators to spell out every detail when writing legislation, these decisions grant the president substantial flexibility in policy making. Furthermore, it is not necessarily the case that Congress will prevail when executive orders and statutes *are* directly at odds with one another. The Supreme Court has found circumstances in which an executive order or proclamation invalidates a law. In sum, the executive order has been an important instrument for expanding the president's legislative authority.

Formal constitutional rules also grant the president agenda-setting power in negotiating treaties and international agreements. Specifically, the Constitution authorizes the president to make treaties "by and with the Advice and Consent of the Senate." The executive branch customarily initiates treaties and international agreements, although the president does not have exclusive power over the treaty-making process. The president must submit treaties to the Senate and obtain ratification by a two-thirds majority vote. The Senate, however, is under no obligation to act on treaties presented by the president. Furthermore, the president is often dependent on the House for the appropriation of the necessary funds to comply with the terms of a treaty. Nevertheless, the power to determine the starting point for policy bargaining on treaties and international agreements gives the president considerable power. It is exceedingly unusual for the president's proposal to fail, and the Senate accepts a majority of treaties without change.

THE VETO POWER. The power to sign, veto, or take no action on legislation passed by Congress makes the president a critical actor in the legislative process. When the president vetoes a measure (a bill or joint resolution), he returns it to the chamber that first passed it, along with a message indicating his objection to the legislation in its present form. If the chamber that first passed the measure is capable of obtaining the votes of two-thirds of the members to override the veto, the measure is then sent to the other chamber. This chamber also must vote to override the veto by a two-thirds majority before the measure can become law.

The veto power gives the president both the ability to block legislation (subject to a possible override) and a source of leverage with legislators to gain policy concessions. Legislators must necessarily consider both a potential presidential veto and the likelihood of forming a two-thirds coalition to override a veto in their initial legislative decisions. For instance, members interested in passing some form of legislation may choose to make policy concessions to the president if they expect the president to veto their most preferred legislation and they lack sufficient numbers to orchestrate an override. It should be noted, however, that there are instances in which congressional majorities that lack enough support for an override will present the president with legislation they know the president will find unacceptable. Typically, this is a strategic maneuver with the purpose of intensifying partisan differences or forcing the president to expend valuable political capital to win a veto battle.

Congress seldom overrides a presidential veto – since 1789 Congress has overridden just four percent of all vetoes (Table 9.1). Recent presidents facing opposing majority parties in Congress have increasingly resorted to vetoes in confronting Congress. President George H.W. Bush (1989–1993) used vetoes rather successfully; only one of his 31 regular vetoes was overridden. Of the 36 regular vetoes issued by President Clinton, all during periods of divided government, only two were overridden. Presidents challenge the House and Senate with vetoes much less frequently when their parties have enjoyed majorities in both houses. While President Clinton issued a number of vetoes during Republican Congresses, he did not veto a single measure passed when Democrats had majorities in both chambers.

In some circumstances, the veto is a sign of presidential weakness. Failing to persuade Congress to pass legislation to his liking, the president resorts to a veto. For example, President Reagan in 1988 – weakened by revelations of

TABLE 9.1. Presidential Vetoes, 1947–2007.[1]

Year (Congress)	President (Party)	Total Vetoes	Regular Vetoes	Pocket Vetoes	Vetoes Overridden
1947–1948 (80th)	TRUMAN (D)	75	42	33	6
1949–1950 (81st)	**TRUMAN (D)**	**79**	**70**	**9**	**3**
1951–1952 (82d)	**TRUMAN (D)**	**22**	**14**	**8**	**3**
1953–1954 (83d)	*EISENHOWER (R)*	*52*	*21*	*31*	*0*
1955–1956 (84th)	EISENHOWER (R)	34	12	22	0
1957–1958 (85th)	EISENHOWER (R)	51	18	33	0
1959–1960 (86th)	EISENHOWER (R)	44	22	22	2
1961–1962 (87th)	**KENNEDY (D)**	**20**	**11**	**9**	**0**
1963 (88th)	**KENNEDY (D)**	**1**	**1**	**0**	**0**
1963–1964 (88th)	**JOHNSON (D)**	**8**	**4**	**4**	**0**
1965–1966 (89th)	**JOHNSON (D)**	**14**	**10**	**4**	**0**
1967–1968 (90th)	**JOHNSON (D)**	**8**	**2**	**6**	**0**
1969–1970 (91st)	NIXON (R)	11	7	4	2
1971–1972 (92d)	NIXON (R)	20	6	14	2
1973–1974 (93d)	NIXON (R)	12	11	1	1
1974 (93d)	FORD (R)	27	16	11	4
1975–1976 (94th)	FORD (R)	37	32	5	8
1977–1978 (95th)	**CARTER (D)**	**19**	**6**	**13**	**0**
1979–1980 (96th)	**CARTER (D)**	**12**	**7**	**5**	**2**
1981–1982 (97th)	REAGAN (R)	15	9	6	2
1983–1984 (98th)	REAGAN (R)	24	9	15	2
1985–1986 (99th)	REAGAN (R)	20	13	7	2
1987–1988 (100th)	REAGAN (R)	19	8	11	3
1989–1990 (101st)	GEORGE BUSH (R)	21	16	5	0
1991–1992 (102d)	GEORGE BUSH (R)	25	15	10	1
1993–1994 (103d)	**CLINTON (D)**	**0**	**0**	**0**	**0**
1995–1996 (104th)	CLINTON (D)	17	17	0	1
1997–1998 (105th)	CLINTON (D)	8	8	0	1
1999–2000 (106th)	CLINTON (D)	12	11	1	0
2001–2002 (107th)*	GEORGE W. BUSH (R)	0	0	0	0
2003–2004 (108th)	*GEORGE W. BUSH (R)*	*0*	*0*	*0*	*0*
2005–2006 (109th)	*GEORGE W. BUSH (R)*	*1*	*1*	*0*	*0*
2007 (110th, 1/1– 6/20)	GEORGE W. BUSH (R)	2	2	0	0

Democratic presidents facing a unified Democratic Congress appear in **bold**.
Republican presidents facing a unified Republican Congress appear in *italics*.
Presidents (D or R) under divided control of government appear in regular typeface.
* Congress was under unified Republican control from January 20, 2001, to June 6, 2001.
Source: Vital Statistics on American Politics (Washington, D.C.: CQ Press, 2000), entries for the 107th–110th Congresses collected by the authors.

the Iran-Contra scandal – vetoed several bills that had broad congressional support, including measures to overhaul the nation's water pollution control and highway funding programs. The vetoes were swiftly overridden.

At other times, a veto is an interim step in a longer bargaining process. That is, presidents sometimes use the veto in the hope of forcing additional concessions from Congress. An analysis of vetoed bills between 1946 and 1991 shows that Congress re-passed about 35 percent of them in a modified form. Of the re-passed bills, 83 percent became law, which reflects the success of the president in extracting policy concessions following a veto.[2]

The pocket veto deserves special mention. The Constitution allows the president to kill a bill by simply failing to sign it if Congress has adjourned within 10 days (Sundays excepted) of enacting a measure. If Congress has adjourned and therefore is not in session, its absence prevents the president from returning the bill to Congress with an official veto message. The informal name for such a veto is a pocket veto.

The pocket veto has been controversial. What counts as a congressional adjournment has been challenged in several court cases. In response to a lawsuit filed by Senator Edward Kennedy (D-Massachusetts), the Ford administration in 1976 declared that pocket vetoes would be used only after the adjournment at the end of a Congress's second session. This move limited the president's ability to use the pocket veto during vacation recesses and the adjournment period between the first and second sessions of a Congress, provided that Congress had made arrangements for receiving veto messages during the intervening periods. President Reagan, however, maintained that intersession pocket vetoes were constitutional. Although a federal district judge upheld the president's position, an appeals court reversed the decision. The appeals court ruling stands as the most definitive ruling to date. Since the Supreme Court has yet to rule directly on the issue, presidents continue to challenge the use of pocket vetoes. President Clinton, for example, used the pocket veto three times in the middle of a session.

The President's Informal Role

Formal institutions place the president firmly in the legislative game. So too do the expectations of the American public and the president's fellow partisans, as well as the presidents' own aspirations.

PARTISAN EXPECTATIONS. The president's service as the recognized leader of his party also helps position him as a player in the legislative process. Parties often are seen as a means for bridging the gap between the legislative and executive branches, and much of the responsibility of building this bridge is borne by the president. The president is expected to provide the necessary leadership to forge a national consensus out of the interests represented in the House and Senate. Furthermore, members of the president's party usually expect the president to perform in a way that reflects well on the general reputation of the party, which enhances their own electoral prospects. In this respect, the party serves as a brand-name or signal to the public. Some scholars suggest that the success of political actors is partially a function of the value of the brand name at the time of elections. Since the public's evaluations of presidential performance have a substantial effect on the electoral fortunes of the congressional parties, as exemplified in the 2006 midterm elections, rank-and-file legislators and their party leaders frequently voice their concerns to presidents about the policy and political consequences of presidential legislative programs and strategies.

The relative weakness of American political parties makes it difficult for the president to command support in Congress simply by virtue of his position as the recognized head of his party. The president does not determine who represents his party in Congress; legislators gain the ballot through primaries and are elected largely on the basis of their own efforts. The president does not select his party's leaders in the House and Senate; legislators elect their own leaders. Consequently, while the president is expected to and generally wants to take the lead in setting legislative strategy for his party, the president often must bargain with legislators of his own party over priorities and the direction of public policy.

PUBLIC EXPECTATIONS. The American people expect presidential leadership on matters of national importance. The emergence of the president as the focal point of an expanding federal government after the Great Depression and World War II was accompanied by heightened public expectations of the president. Increased media concentration on the chief executive, as well as the president's tendency to resort to public appeals for support, has contributed to the president's standing as the most visible elected official in the country. In recent decades, the American public has increasingly expected the president to take action both at home and abroad, even in the face of declining party strength and the constraints that exist because of shared power with Congress.

The president's policy objectives are determined in part by the public commitments he makes during campaigns. President George H. W. Bush's campaign pledge of "no new taxes" effectively limited his budget policy options for much of his first two years in office. When the president reneges on such public commitments, he risks losing public approval and electoral support from his various constituencies as well as from members of Congress, which is precisely what Bush experienced when he broke his campaign promise by raising taxes. While in office, the president makes innumerable public commitments as well. As presidents turn more and more to the public to mobilize public pressure on behalf of their policy preferences, presidents are increasingly constrained by the public stands they take.

The chief executive's role as a legislative player is also conditioned on public approval ratings. Members of Congress, primarily for electoral reasons, are more willing to pay heed to the legislative proposals and policy positions of a president who has the confidence of the public. A president with high approval ratings cannot, however, be expected to dominate all policy formation. High approval ratings do not translate to presidential influence on all types of legislation. Instead, scholars have found that approval ratings are related to a president's legislative influence on matters that are both salient and complex. When the public is paying little attention to an issue, legislators do not fear electoral repercussions from opposing a popular president.

PERSONAL ASPIRATIONS. Most presidents, and surely all presidents since the 1920s, have had aspirations that required they take an active role in the legislative process. Whether seeking to move the federal government into new endeavors or modify or repeal existing policy, presidents have had to work with, and often resist, Congress. Presidents' personal interests, political commitments, and circumstances beyond their control compel them to become engaged.

Presidents' Strategies

Presidential strategies for influencing legislative outcomes depend upon the political context. Although executed in a variety of ways, every recent president has confronted decisions about how to structure his legislative agenda, how to generate congressional support, how to employ the veto power, and how to control the bureaucracy in the face of competition from Capitol Hill.

Agenda Setting

Perhaps nothing affects presidential success in Congress as much as a president's decisions about what legislation to recommend to Congress, when to recommend it, and what priority to give each recommendation. Political scientist Paul Light observes that "control of the agenda becomes a primary tool for securing and extending power. Presidents certainly view the agenda as such."[3] The president's legislative choices send a signal to a wide audience – Congress, administration officials, interest groups, the media, and the public – about the president's view of the lessons of the last election, the president's policy preferences, and the president's likely priorities. The president's choices shape the strategies of other legislative players and help set expectations by which the president's own success or failure will be judged.

In most situations, the president cannot force Congress to address his proposals. Rather, he must convince members of Congress to give priority to his legislation. Members of Congress may see national problems differently, give precedence to other issues, or approach problems in a different way. The president must, therefore, motivate Congress by generating support among important members or groups of members, organized interest groups, and the general public. He may employ the full range of presidential resources available to encourage Congress to take his proposals seriously.

Except in times of national crisis, the president's ability to influence the legislative agenda is strongest at the beginning of his first term, followed, perhaps, by the beginning of the second term. At those times, the president's time horizon, public support, claim to an electoral mandate, and core congressional support tend to be most in his favor. Also at those times, opponents of the president's programs are likely to be the most disorganized and least able to counter presidential momentum. Just after a presidential election, the president's opponents are likely to be weaker in Congress, internally divided over how to change their predicament, and suffering low public esteem.

Consequently, the ability to propose legislation immediately after entering office gives the president an edge in shaping the legislative agenda. Nevertheless, a president must carefully calculate which proposals to pursue. Since some proposals may be unacceptable to Congress, a president will prefer to avoid certain defeat and the reputation of ineffectiveness that might result.

Moreover, the president must not overload Congress and his own staff with too many proposals. Congress and its committees have a finite capacity to produce major legislation quickly. And the administration has a limited ability to formulate detailed proposals, lobby Congress, and negotiate compromises in its first few months in office. The president also is unable to generate media attention and public support for more than a few proposals at a time.

Among recent presidents, Ronald Reagan appears to have used the early months of his first term most effectively. Reagan moved quickly and set his priorities carefully by defining his agenda as two major bills, one for domestic budget cuts and one for tax cuts. Although both were complex, multifaceted proposals, Reagan was successful in leading the media and the public to focus on the broad effects of his proposals. The approach allowed the Reagan administration to concentrate its resources, stimulate public pressure on Congress for widely recognized proposals, and gain legislative action in its first year in office.

Attracting Congressional Support

On important legislation, modern presidents usually pursue a mixed strategy – both quietly bargaining in Washington with members of Congress and lobbyists and more widely soliciting public support to affect legislators' estimates of the public response to their treatment of the president's proposals. In deciding how to allocate resources to inside and outside strategies, the White House takes into account how many members of Congress must be persuaded, which members must be persuaded, the strategies of the opposition, whether public opinion currently favors the president's position, the commitment of resources to other issues, and how much time the president has before Congress makes a decision. Daily, even hourly, tactical adjustments are common in the midst of a tough legislative fight.

A president's legislative strategy is often shaped by the demands of members of Congress. Congressional leaders of the president's party regularly consult with the White House and other administration officials about the substance of policy proposals and legislative tactics. In fact, recent presidents have met with their party's congressional leaders at least once a week while Congress is in session. Committee and faction leaders also press the administration to pursue certain strategies. Presidents are compelled to consider these demands so as not to jeopardize the reelection of their party's congressional membership. In addition, cooperating with important members of Congress, as well as with influential interest groups, bureaucrats, and others, may encourage these actors to employ their own resources on behalf of the administration's program.

INSIDE STRATEGIES. The inside strategy is one of bargaining. Although often seen as underhanded, presidents must frequently employ bargaining tactics to accomplish legislative objectives. This is particularly true when presidents are faced with an effective, committed opposition within Congress. Knowing when, where, and how to make a deal with the members and factions of Congress requires information and skill on the part of presidents and their legislative advisors. Successful bargaining also revolves around formal rules of the game, the composition of the Congress, public opinion, and other resources.

The cost to the president of doing business with Congress depends upon the political context. When the president is popular, legislators are more likely to be happy to be associated with the president and his program and fewer legislators will require special attention to get their votes. When the president is unpopular, the cost of attracting votes – whether by making concessions on the substance of policy proposals or in offering other incentives – will be higher.

Presidents may use the stick as well as the carrot. In 2006, Representative Peter King (R-New York) was the target of retribution after refusing to support President George W. Bush's proposal to allow a Dubai company to assume operations at six major U.S. ports. King, who was chair of the House Homeland Security committee, threatened to block Bush's port deal. In a matter of days after King issued the threat, the Pentagon notified him that it would no longer provide an aircraft and military support for his upcoming trip to Iraq – a trip that had been cleared months earlier.

OUTSIDE STRATEGIES. Observers of presidential strategies have noticed that presidents have become more reliant on outside strategies in recent decades. Twentieth-century presidents as early as Theodore Roosevelt sought public support to strengthen their hand against Congress, but only recent presidents have routinely done so. Through such activities as televised prime-time addresses, press conferences, domestic and foreign travel, exclusive interviews, timely leaks, and now television talk shows and call-in programs, presidents are increasingly cultivating external allies to strengthen their position within Washington.

"Going public," as the outside strategy is labeled by political scientist Samuel Kernell, is an attractive strategy for several reasons. First, technological advances, such as transcontinental jets and live satellite feeds, have increased the ease of reaching a wide audience. Second, campaign finance practices and declining presidential coattails have reduced legislators' dependence on support from the president and the parties. Third, the administration's advantage in information and expertise has weakened, as rank-and-file members have benefited from the diffusion of power and staff within Congress. Finally, budgetary constraints have reduced the president's supply of projects and other favors that he can use to trade with individual members.

Fundamentally, going public is about taking credit and issuing blame. With this strategy, the president seeks to increase the benefits to legislators of supporting him and to increase the electoral costs of opposing him.

The strategy breeds counterstrategies. Opposition leaders are encouraged to develop public relations strategies of their own, and, in doing so, they are motivated to propose alternatives to the president's program that the president and his supporters would be embarrassed to oppose. In this way, outside strategies encourage early public commitments by legislators, foster partisan maneuvering and grandstanding, and discourage bargaining and compromise that require a softening of positions and a sharing of credit and blame.

A high-profile appeal, such as a special televised address to the nation from the Oval Office, entails risks for a president. In general, members of Congress view this approach as an effort by the president to go over their heads. As such, presidential appeals can cause tension between Congress and the president. This strategy is particularly likely to produce resentment among members of Congress toward the president if the president's appeal creates electoral problems for them at home. Since the president cannot make such appeals frequently, he must reserve this approach for only those issues of significant importance in which his appeal is likely to generate critical support. Failure to gain more public or congressional support may damage the president's reputation, reducing his effectiveness in future legislative battles and perhaps hurting his own reelection chances. Therefore, more cautious, less publicized, and more targeted approaches, such as speaking before certain groups and calling on small groups of newspaper editors, may be preferred at times.

The Veto

The veto inserts the president into the legislative game. A threatened veto may lead congressional leaders to set aside certain legislation or to make concessions to the president before passing the legislation. Particularly when control of the Congress and presidency is divided between the parties, the veto gives the president a critical source of leverage with legislators. It has been argued that the increasing polarization of Congress has limited the president's ability to bargain directly with Congress, and therefore has elevated the relative importance of the veto within the president's arsenal.

Veto threats are relatively infrequent events, but tend to result in policy changes that are favorable to the president. Veto threats are most common when the legislation under consideration is important and the president is faced with a Congress dominated by the opposing party. One study estimates that presidents threaten to veto roughly 14 percent of important measures; this number increases to 23 percent under divided government.

The Veto Process

To veto a bill, the president signs a veto message that is sent to Congress. The message may contain the president's reasoning. The house of Congress that first passed the legislation acts first on the veto. That house may attempt an override, pass new legislation without an override attempt, or take no further action. The bill dies if a two-thirds majority is not acquired to override the veto. If the first house does override the veto, the other house also may attempt an override, pass new legislation without an override attempt, or take no further action. The bill dies if a two-thirds majority is not also acquired in that house to override the veto. New legislation may reflect concessions to the president. It must be approved by both houses and sent to the president for signature or veto.

Moreover, it appears that presidents are often quite successful in extracting policy concessions from Congress when veto threats are issued. In fact, by one approximation, roughly 90 percent of bills that encounter a veto threat are modified, to varying extents, to accommodate the preferences of the president.[4] Given the success of veto threats, why do we not see presidents issuing threats on *all* congressional proposals?

The answer to this question lies largely in the fact that successful veto threats require credibility. It would be neither feasible nor politically prudent for a president to veto all legislation, and therefore threatening to do so would result in the veto threat losing its teeth. A president that consistently fails to follow through on threats is likely to gain a reputation for bluffing.

Members of Congress are certainly not passive bystanders in the veto game. Members frequently solicit a veto threat from the administration to solidify their bargaining position on Capitol Hill. Sometimes a congressional party will bait the president with a bill that it knows he will find unacceptable. A vetoed bill can be a rallying point for the president's opposition as it seeks to generate credit for itself and blame for the president. A well-documented example of this was the 1995–96 battle over welfare reform. During this knock-down-drag-out fight between a unified Republican Congress and Democratic President Bill Clinton, Congress presented Clinton with two virtually identical successive versions of welfare reform legislation, which they suspected would be vetoed by Clinton without the possibility of generating a two-thirds majority to override the vetoes. This was largely an effort made by congressional Republicans to portray Clinton as an opponent to reform in order to create a campaign issue for the 1996 elections.

Statistically, attempts to override vetoes are associated with low presidential popularity, a strong opposition party in Congress, and bipartisan support for the legislation. Low presidential popularity and bipartisan support for the legislation also contribute to successful override attempts. Generally, highly partisan legislation, as vetoed legislation tends to be, is not overridden since supermajorities are required. Parties seldom have close to the two-thirds of the seats in both chambers needed to override a veto.

Controlling the Executive Branch

Much of the competition between Congress and the president concerns control of the executive branch agencies whose responsibility it is to implement policy. Agencies become players in the legislative game once they are established and begin to perform functions that are valuable to others. They have resources of their own to bring to the legislative battle. Much of the information and expertise about federal programs resides in the agencies. That information and expertise can be shared selectively with Congress and the White House. Agencies also have friends within the interest group community and the general public from whom they can expect support. But presidents seek to control departments and agencies. By securing control over the bureaucracy, the president is better able to manage the signals emanating from the executive branch, eliminate sources of opposition to his legislative goals, and increase the probability that old and new laws will be implemented in a manner consistent with his preferences.

An unfavorable agency policy is not always easy for Congress to change. The need for agreement among all three legislative institutions – House, Senate, and president – makes a formal legislative response difficult and perhaps impossible. Consequently, members of Congress, presidents, and the organized interests seek means other than the legislative process to control agencies. For presidents, the most direct means of control is to appoint department and agency heads who support administration policies. But appointment power is not the only presidential tool.

The central arm of the president's bureaucratic control is the Office of Management and Budget (OMB). This agency, like its predecessor, the Bureau of the Budget, constructs the president's budget proposals for the federal government. Furthermore, central clearance – the job of coordinating and approving all executive branch proposals sent to Congress – is the responsibility of the OMB. OMB responsibilities also entail scrutinizing written proposals and even preparing the congressional testimony of

---

Congressionally Speaking...

As Chief Executive, the constitution requires that the president "take care that the laws be faithfully executed." In recent years, the practice of issuing signing statements at the time the president signs legislation has raised questions about whether the president is fulfilling this constitutional obligation.

Signing statements are written declarations issued by the president that indicate to Congress how he intends to direct his administration in the implementation of the law and often to articulate constitutional limits on the implementation of certain provisions. In practice, the signing statement has become reminiscent of the line-item veto. While proponents of signing statements say that they communicate valuable information to Congress, opponents contend that they are used by presidents to pick and choose the provisions they wish to enforce or implement.

Some scholars credit President Ronald Reagan for developing the signing statement into a policy-making tool, but President George W. Bush has used signing statements with unprecedented frequency. Through January 2007, one study finds that Bush has used signing statements to challenge 1,149 provisions in 150 bills.[5] Some observers speculate that the signing statement has supplanted the veto in Bush's arsenal. The advantage of the signing statement is that it is far less visible than the veto, allowing the president greater flexibility in shaping policy out of the public eye and without creating a veto override showdown with Congress.

---

executive branch officials to ensure consistency with the president's policy goals. In addition, the OMB reviews enacted legislation to provide the president with a recommendation to sign or veto it.

In recent decades, the OMB has become more politicized and has expanded its bureaucratic control functions. By appointing aides ideologically aligned with himself to run the OMB, and by centralizing the rule-making process within the OMB, President Reagan turned the OMB into a major instrument in shaping national policy and managing relations between the administration and Congress. By executive order, Reagan authorized the OMB's Office of Information and Regulatory Affairs (OIRA) to review regulatory proposals from agencies and departments to assess their value in terms of strict cost-benefit analysis and consideration of alternatives. In reality, granting this authority to OIRA provided a means for the president to make certain that agency activity was in step with his preferences or policy objectives. On numerous occasions during the Reagan administration, OIRA intervened in agency rule making and stopped agencies from issuing congressionally mandated regulations. This intervention was principally achieved through use of return letters – a letter from the administration that returns a rule for further consideration. These requirements notably undercut the independence of agency and department heads.

Under the George H.W. Bush administration, the OMB's regulatory review functions were supplanted to some extent by the efforts of the Council on Competitiveness, also created by executive order. The council was officially located in the office of, and headed by, Vice President Dan Quayle. This organizational arrangement protected the council's inner workings from public and congressional scrutiny, to which the OMB is subject. As the administration intended, members of Congress, lobbyists, and the media found it difficult to anticipate or react to unfriendly White House efforts to interpret law and mold regulations required by law.

President Clinton did not reestablish the Council on Competitiveness, but instead returned authority to the OMB. Early in the administration, Clinton issued an executive order repealing the executive order issued by Reagan that had governed regulatory review up to that time. In general, there were few differences between the executive orders. In fact, Clinton's executive order preserved the use of cost-benefit analysis in evaluating regulatory rules and their alternatives. Clinton's executive order did, however, mandate "the primacy of Federal agencies in the regulatory decision-making process." Under the Clinton administration, this is precisely what occurred. Although OIRA maintained powers of bureaucratic oversight, it reviewed only the most salient regulatory matters. Furthermore, Clinton restructured OIRA to allow for preferred interest groups to gain greater access to the decision-making process.

Under President George W. Bush, OIRA's role in regulatory oversight has returned to a state similar to that seen under the Reagan administration. Much like Reagan, George W. Bush has used his broad appointment powers to place individuals with like ideologies in key agency positions. The president's appointment of outspoken critics of regulation to key OIRA positions has sent a message that the administration takes seriously the oversight of regulatory agencies and their proposals. In Bush's first six years, OIRA reported issuing 23 return letters, reflecting opposition to agency proposals. In comparison, during the eight years of the Clinton administration, OIRA issued only nine return letters.

In 2001, OIRA took regulatory review a step beyond return letters by implementing a new tool for oversight known as a "prompt letter." Whereas return letters require agencies to reevaluate proposed regulations, prompt letters request that agencies reconsider an existing regulation. The addition of the prompt letter gives the president greater ability to curtail regulations according to his preferences. Through 2006, OIRA reported issuing 13 prompt letters.

In early 2007, President George W. Bush signed an executive order that further strengthened his control over the regulatory activities of executive agencies. The executive order mandated that all agencies put into place a regulatory policy office to supervise the development of agency rules. Not surprisingly, the regulatory policy offices are to be run by political appointees of the president. The addition of these offices, imbedded in the agencies, effectively gives the White House another gatekeeper to monitor agency activity and to block, if not preempt, rules that are unfavorable to the administration. Presumably, Bush's decision was a reaction to the legislative difficulties anticipated between Congress and the president.

Foreign and Defense Policy

The legislative politics of foreign and defense policy are typically different from the politics of domestic affairs. Political scientist Aaron Wildavsky argues that the presidential activities associated with these policy arenas differ substantially. Moreover, the degrees of success that presidents have in foreign and domestic affairs are sufficiently different that the American presidency can be thought of as two distinct presidencies. While Wildavsky's distinction is not always useful, it is true that the rules of the game often advantage the president in foreign policy. Under the Constitution, the president more clearly takes initiative and has greater autonomy over action related to foreign and defense matters than he does in domestic affairs. He appoints ambassadors (with the advice and consent of the Senate), makes treaties (subject to the approval of a two-thirds majority in the Senate), receives the ambassadors of other countries, serves as the commander in chief of the armed forces and of state militias when they are called into the service of the federal government, and commissions the officers of the United States. Although senators have become increasingly involved in monitoring treaty negotiations and limiting presidents' reinterpretation of treaty provisions, the president largely retains control over U.S. diplomacy.

Congress is not helpless, of course. In fact, the Constitution gives Congress many resources. Because funding is required for much international activity, control of appropriations inserts Congress as a critical actor in foreign and defense policy. The Constitution also gives Congress the power to declare war, create and organize armed forces, regulate foreign commerce, and define offenses against the law of nations. Yet in practice substantial ambiguity exists about the proper role of the two branches. How much discretion is granted to the president in using troops, making minor agreements with other governments, or conducting secret negotiations is not clearly defined in the Constitution. For the most part, the courts have left it to Congress and presidents to work out their differences.

Presidents who claim broad implicit powers argue that they are free to ignore Congress on some matters of foreign and defense policy. This position has been strengthened by the increasing importance of world affairs during the twentieth century. Scientific and technological advances have integrated economies and yielded weapons of mass destruction, increasing the importance of the president's ability to coordinate U.S. policy and act with secrecy. Presidents often argue that the dangers of the modern world and the prominent role of the United States in international affairs, requires that the president be free to conduct diplomacy, launch secret operations, and even deploy armed forces as he sees fit. Several Supreme Court cases have endorsed an unfettered right of presidents to conduct foreign policy. Chief among these rulings was *United States v. Curtiss-Wright Export Corp.*, a 1936 ruling asserting that even if extensive powers over foreign affairs were not spelled out for the president in the Constitution, the president is best suited to assume those responsibilities.

Furthermore, as international affairs gained importance to the United States, control of national security was increasingly centralized and institutionalized in the White House. The 1947 National Security Act consolidated control of the military in a single Defense Department and created the Central Intelligence Agency and National Security Council. All three organizations are headed by individuals who are directly accountable to the president – the secretary of defense, the director of central intelligence, and the national security adviser. In 2004, new legislation created the position of Director of National Intelligence, appointed by the president, to supervise intelligence activities of the government and serve as the principal intelligence advisor to the president. These developments have enhanced the president's ability to collect and digest information and to act promptly without substantial congressional participation.

Moreover, public expectations of presidential leadership continue to give the president an advantage in the area of foreign policy. Because the electorate supports centralized leadership on national security matters, particularly in times of international crisis, congressional opposition to an assertive

THE CHANGING CONGRESS: EVOLVING WAR POWERS

The Constitution grants Congress the power to declare war (Article I, Section 8), but also makes the president the commander in chief of the armed forces (Article II, Section 2). Congress has formally declared war only five times – the War of 1812, the Mexican War (1846–1848), the Spanish-American War (1898), World War I (1917–1918), and World War II (1941–1945).

Presidents have used the commander-in-chief power, various treaty obligations, resolutions of the United Nations, and their implicit duty to provide for national security as grounds for committing U.S. forces abroad without a declaration of war. By one count, the United States had been involved in 192 military actions without a declaration of war by 1972. At least nine more have occurred since then, including the response to the Iraqi invasion of Kuwait in 1990 (the Persian Gulf War), the use of troops in Somalia beginning in 1992, the military efforts in Afghanistan following the events of September 11, 2001, and the conflict in Iraq beginning in 2003. Many of these commitments were very brief, and Congress had no time to respond. In other cases, such as the Vietnam War, Congress implicitly supported the president by approving the funding he requested for the effort.

The costly Vietnam War in the 1960s and early 1970s stimulated efforts in Congress to limit the war powers that presidents had assumed. In 1973, Congress enacted, over President Richard Nixon's veto, the War Powers Resolution. This law requires that the president notify Congress about any commitment of military forces within 48 hours and terminate the commitment within 60 days unless Congress approves an extension or is unable to meet. The commitment may be extended by the president for another 30 days. Congress may halt the action at any time by concurrent resolution (that is, by a resolution that does not require the president's signature).

No one seems particularly satisfied with the 1973 law. Supporters of broad presidential discretion argue that the act infringes on the president's constitutional powers; supporters of a literal interpretation of the Constitution claim that the act gives away Congress's constitutional powers by allowing the president to initiate wars. Since 1973, presidents have observed the reporting requirement, but have sought alternatives to formal congressional approval. In 1983, President Reagan and Speaker O'Neill negotiated a timetable for the involvement of U.S. Marines in Lebanon. In 1991, Congress approved a resolution that authorized President George H.W. Bush to use "all necessary means" to enforce the United Nations resolution calling for the removal of Iraqi forces from Kuwait. In 2002, Congress approved a resolution that authorized the use of force against Iraq to "defend the national security of the United States against the continuing threat posed by Iraq" and to "enforce all relevant

(continued)

THE CHANGING CONGRESS: EVOLVING WAR POWERS (*continued*)

United Nations Security Council resolutions regarding Iraq," which concerned weapons of mass destruction. In all three cases, the president avoided endorsing the constitutionality of the War Powers Resolution; in none of the cases did Congress actually declare war, but in the latter two cases Congress indicated that the terms of the War Powers Resolution requirement for congressional authorization were met.

president is unpopular with the electorate. The public is especially supportive of the president if the lives of Americans are at stake.

In the decades after World War II, the liberties given to the president to fight world communism led some observers to believe that Congress was acting as if it ought to defer to the president on matters of foreign affairs. By the early 1970s, as Congress was beginning to assert itself against presidential policies it opposed, views about congressional deference to the president began to change. However, the national consensus about Cold War policy generated a basic agreement between Congress and presidents about international affairs that effectively returned Congress to a state of greater passivity. When that consensus began to disintegrate, members of Congress looked for ways to recapture their influence. In the immediate aftermath of the terrorist attacks of September 11, 2001, however, the president was once again poised to forge the way in foreign and defense policy. With growing discontent over the war in Iraq, and an administration embroiled in controversy, the current shifting balance in power is reminiscent of the early 1970s.

The reassertion of congressional power in the early 1970s represented the beginning of a tug-of-war between congressional Democrats and White House Republicans that is still evident today. Between 1969 and 2006, there were only 10 years in which the president's party controlled both chambers of Congress. Conversely, for 20 years during that period presidents faced a unified Congress of the opposing party. Therefore, partisanship confounded matters by reinforcing institutional conflict between the branches. In addition, legislative action became increasingly central to the making of foreign policy as international economic relations, human rights, environmental problems, and other issues gained a more prominent role in this sphere of policy making. This, in conjunction with the ideological gap between Congress and the president that prevailed for the better part of this period, made deference to the president particularly costly for Congress.

Policies governing the intelligence agencies have been a prime source of conflict between Congress and the president. The tension between the branches increased significantly after the revelations of the Iran-Contra affair. In 1985 and 1986, the administration secretly sold arms to the Iranians in efforts to negotiate the release of American hostages in the Middle East. Furthermore, the administration used the profits from the arms sales to fund the Contras in Nicaragua, which violated congressional restrictions on funding and covert assistance to the Contras.

Presidents' Resources

The strategies adopted by presidents and members of Congress to influence policy outcomes are influenced by the quality and quantity of resources available to each. The president possesses numerous resources that serve to strengthen the role of the presidency in legislative politics. Some of these resources, such as constitutional powers, White House staff, information, and expertise, are relatively secure and may even expand during a president's term of office.

The president has a sizable staff operation to assist him in managing relations with Congress. The president controls the size of his White House staff, although it is subject to congressional appropriations. In recent decades, the White House staff has expanded, particularly in the offices for legislative affairs, communications, and domestic and foreign policy. In addition, presidents have expanded agencies within the larger Executive Office of the President, such as the Office of Management and Budget (OMB) and Council of Economic Advisers, to enhance their policy-making capability. These staffs help the president monitor developments on Capitol Hill, work with committees and leadership, and give the president adequate representation on legislative matters.

Congress has moved to curtail the president's discretion in managing executive office staff. In the 1970s, after the OMB had gained great importance in the development and implementation of policy, Congress required the president to receive Senate confirmation for the director of the agency as for cabinet secretaries. In the 1980s, when President Ronald Reagan was proposing cuts in domestic programs, congressional Democrats made sure that funding for White House staff was constrained as well. In 1992, House Democrats moved to eliminate funding for Vice President Dan Quayle's Council on Competitiveness to show their opposition to its role in disapproving regulations proposed by federal agencies. In general, however, presidents have been able to organize their staffs as they choose and have had adequate funding to do so.

Some resources, such as information and expertise, may increase during a presidency as experience is acquired. For example, a lack of Capitol Hill experience was a serious shortcoming of President Jimmy Carter and his top aides when he entered office in 1977. As time went on, the Carter team gained familiarity with the people and ways of doing business in Congress. But Carter also recognized the limitations of his White House staff and moved to hire more experienced people. An important element of the change was giving more responsibility to Vice President (and former senator) Walter Mondale in the planning of legislative strategies.

In contrast, the president can suffer losses of other resources while in office. One scholar called this the "cycle of decreasing influence." Party strength in Congress and public support often diminish during a president's term. Recent exceptions aside (see Chapter 3), the president's party typically loses congressional seats in midterm elections.

Public support for a president often declines during a presidential term, weakening support for the president in Congress. As President Johnson reportedly once told his staff:

> You've got to give it all you can that first year. Doesn't matter what kind of majority you come in with. You've got just one year when they treat you right and before they start worrying about themselves. The third year, you lose votes.... The fourth year's all politics.[6]

This advice, which most presidents take to heart, encourages presidents to try to move quickly on their legislative programs early in their terms.

Presidents eventually run out of time. The two four-year terms that a president may serve under the Twenty-second Amendment are a long time, to be sure, but they are shorter than the legislative careers of many members of Congress and far shorter than the time horizons of many lobbyists and most bureaucrats. In fact, the president often seems to be in more of a hurry than others in Washington. There is good reason for this. Beyond the diminishing political capital that results from typical patterns of decreasing public and congressional support associated with the natural progression of the presidency, members of Congress, lobbyists, and even bureaucrats tend to sever relations with incumbent presidents nearing the end of their office with hopes of investing in the future president. When that happens, the president loses much of his influence and may become little more than a caretaker of the White House.

LEGISLATIVE RESOURCES OF PRESIDENTS

Partisan base in Congress. The size of the House and Senate caucuses of the president's party can boost presidential success in enacting their priorities. When a president's partisans in Congress are cohesive and ideologically in step with him, the advantages offered to the president increase.

Formal powers. Presidents gain leverage with legislators by using, or threatening to use, their formal powers. The most obvious power is the power to veto legislation. In addition, the president may issue executive orders that interpret laws or regulate the behavior and decisions of executive branch agencies.

Visibility and public approval. The national media concentrate on the president. Unlike Congress, which finds speaking with one voice difficult, the president can dominate the news and manipulate the types of information Americans receive about his activities. If presidents mobilize public support for their initiatives, members of Congress must weigh carefully the costs of opposing the president.

Expertise and information. Broad policy expertise is available to the president from the agencies of the executive branch.

White House staff. The president has a large personal staff in the White House that allows the president to monitor and communicate with Congress, lobbyists, the media, and others.

Patronage and projects. Presidents and top cabinet officials use personnel appointments to assert control of the bureaucracy and to do favors for members of Congress. Modern presidents make more than 6,000 executive and judicial branch appointments. Presidents and top administration officials can influence decisions about who wins federal contracts and the location of federal installations and buildings.

National party organizations. The president effectively controls the resources of his party's national committees, which can be used to do favors for members of Congress.

Congressional Resources and Strategies

The tendency to see legislative-executive relations as a zero-sum game is strong. That is, observers tend to think that if the president is gaining power, then Congress must be losing power. This perspective is too simplistic. Both Congress and the president have gained power as the role of the federal government has expanded over the decades. Moreover, neither branch is monolithic. Within the executive branch, power has been distributed in a variety of ways between the White House, departments, and independent regulatory commissions. Within Congress, the somewhat different constitutional responsibilities of the House and Senate have meant that their power has not always shifted in the same direction. Moreover, developments that seem to affect the power of Congress adversely may enhance the power of certain members, factions, or parties within the institution. Since members of Congress and the president represent different audiences with different interests, it also may be the case the changes in the legislative-executive relationship benefit both branches even if one side appears to be reaping an advantage.

Thus, it is wise to keep in mind that Congress does not really use its resources – individual members, groups of members, and legislative parties use the institution's resources as they pursue their political goals. The exercise of congressional power is usually the by-product of the competition among members within the institution. In other words, congressional output is the result of (sometimes intense) competition between members with different preferences. Given the degree to which preferences in Congress diverge, seldom do all members consider themselves to be winners on important matters.

Congress's most fundamental resources are the formal powers granted to it by the Constitution. The ability to exercise those powers effectively depends on the human and technological resources of the institution. The membership's motivation, committee and party structures, parliamentary procedure, staffing arrangements, electronic information systems, relations with outside experts and information sources, and other factors affect Congress's performance. Congress has periodically attempted to better equip itself to compete with the expanding capabilities of the president. The legislative reorganization acts of 1946 and 1970, among many other less-extensive efforts, expanded staff, reorganized committees, and changed procedures. In sum, Congress has developed a battery of resources to support an expanding repertoire of strategies for responding to challenges from the executive branch.

Periodic Authorizations

Historically, most agencies and programs have continued indefinitely once they were created. Although they must receive annual appropriations from Congress, most of the basic laws creating and empowering agencies have been permanent. Delegating authority to an executive branch agency in such a manner increases the difficulty of retracting or altering the authority later.

SUNSET PROVISIONS TO GAIN LEVERAGE (AND FOR OTHER PURPOSES)

While the concept of the sunset provision dates back to the writings of Thomas Jefferson, its use as a legislative tool is a recent phenomenon. Sunset provisions grew in popularity when the Republicans took control of Congress in 1995. Throughout President George W. Bush's presidency, they have been a common addition to legislation. In fact, most of the bills central to Bush's legislative agenda have included clauses to terminate portions of the bills on a predetermined date. The Patriot Act as well as the tax cuts of 2001 and 2003 all included such provisions.

Sunset provisions are frequently viewed as victories for opponents to a bill because they require that a measure be reconsidered in the future. In the case of the Patriot Act, passed in 2001, the Republican leadership added sunset provisions as a concession to both Democrats and skeptical members within their party. The legislation was reauthorized in 2006 and included provisions scheduled to expire again in 2009. Senator Dianne Feinstein (D-California) declared that the sunset provisions were an "important element of the continued vigorous oversight necessary to ensure this law is carried out in an appropriate manner."[7]

Republican majorities used sunset provisions on tax cut bills for a different purpose. By making certain provisions to the bills temporary, they were able to minimize projected costs and present a more favorable long-term estimated budget. Republicans now face the reality that the tax cuts may be reversed if Congress fails to extend them when the expiration dates arrive in 2010.

After all, a new law requires the agreement of the House, Senate, and president, or, in the case of a presidential veto, a two-thirds majority in both houses of Congress.

In recent decades, Congress has moved away from permanent authorizations. When Congress enacts legislation creating a program or establishing a new policy, it may limit the lifespan of the authorization. That is, the law may include a "sunset" provision, such that new authorizing legislation must eventually be passed to keep a program or policy alive. This approach requires administration officials to return to Congress to justify the continuation of the program as well it ensures that Congress will periodically review the law underlying the program. In recent decades, periodic authorizations have been used more often by Congress to keep a rein on executive agencies. When a program must be reauthorized periodically, an agency or a president controlling the agency knows that Congress may modify the agency's authorization if its existing power is not used in a manner that is more or less consistent with Congress's preferences.

An important case is the authorization for the Department of Defense, which must be passed each year. Before the 1960s, defense programs were authorized for an indefinite period. However, throughout the 1960s and 1970s Congress gradually added more defense programs – military personnel, weapons systems, research and development, and so on – to the annual defense authorization bill. The immediate effect was to give members of the armed services committees greater influence over the activities of the Department of Defense. The long-term effect was to give all members of Congress a regular opportunity to influence the direction of defense policy. Issues such as arms control have been addressed on defense authorization bills.

Designing Agencies

In practice, much of the conflict over legislation is about the design of the agencies charged with implementing policy. The line of authority, decision-making and appeals procedures, decision-making criteria, rule-making deadlines, reporting requirements, job definitions, personnel appointment processes and restrictions, and salaries all may affect the ability of Congress, the president, the courts, and outside interests to gain favorable action by agencies. Legislators, responding to political pressures from organized interests and others, generally seek to insulate agencies from unfriendly influences, including future Congresses and presidents, and to guarantee that agencies are guided by their policy preferences. Presidents, on the other hand, generally seek to place new programs in the hierarchy of executive departments to which they can appoint politically loyal individuals to important administrative positions. Thus, congressional and presidential views about the organization and control of agencies are often in conflict.

The effort to elevate the Environmental Protection Agency (EPA) to department-level status – making the head of the EPA a member of the president's cabinet – is a good example of structural politics. Democrats in Congress sought to modify the EPA's status in 1990 to give environmental programs more priority and authority within the executive branch. The bill, passed by the House on a vote of 371 to 55, also called for the creation of a Bureau of Environmental Statistics, which was to be independent of the new department. In addition, the bill would have established a separate Commission on Improving Environmental Protection, with the purpose of coordinating the regulations of the new department and other federal agencies with environmental jurisdiction.

The independent department was designed to be insulated from political manipulation. In fact, the bill required the department to report its findings directly to Congress, without review by the OMB or the new secretary of the environment. Furthermore, the multimember commission would have added a policy-making unit outside of the president-department line of authority. The White House, which wanted a bill that would reinforce President George H.W. Bush's claim to be the "environment president," opposed the bureau and commission on the grounds that they undermined the president's line of authority over agency activities. The bill stalled in the Senate because of credible threats of a filibuster by Republicans after the administration threatened a veto.

In the next Congress, the bill passed the Senate on a voice vote after its Senate sponsors met the Bush administration's demands by folding the statistics bureau into the new department and restricting the policy-making authority of the commission. House Democrats refused to act on the Senate bill. The bill died in the House Committee on Government Operations because House Democrats wanted to deny President Bush an opportunity to claim credit for pro-environmental legislation in an election year.

The EPA bill is typical of the conflict between Congress and the president over the structure of agencies. Agreement about the general policy was not enough to guarantee enactment because the conflict over presidential control of the agency proved to be too divisive. Conflict over the control of information and personnel in this case was at least as controversial as the specification of policy. Specifically, the point of contention was whether the executive branch official controlling the information going to Congress would be responsible to the president or an independent bureau chief. The president's veto power ultimately forced concessions from Senate Democrats, but House Democrats were more concerned about the political sacrifices than about raising the EPA to cabinet status.

Structural politics is not limited to original authorizations and reauthorizations. The fight is continuous, as the issue of personnel ceilings demonstrates. In recent decades, Congress has become more specific in dictating the design of executive agencies. On occasion, administrations have undermined congressional efforts to bolster agency resources by refusing to hire or replace important personnel. The appropriations committees have responded in committee reports by specifying a minimum number of personnel for agencies, requiring reports on deviations, and insisting on a formal presidential request when an agency seeks to reduce spending with a personnel ceiling. Increasingly, Congress has imposed statutory restrictions on personnel ceilings, thus limiting the administration's control over agencies' personnel resources.

Plainly, the structure of executive agencies is the result of compromise. This give-and-take process can produce a variety of possible outcomes, ranging from agencies that are distant from the president and responsive to Congress to agencies that are firmly under the control of the executive administration. The decision of political actors to make concessions on some aspects of structural policy and not on others is principally a function of the impact that the given agency has upon preferred constituents. Members of Congress and the president are reluctant to relinquish power over an agency when the agency under consideration has a significant direct effect – either positive or negative – on constituents of interest. For example, presidents with substantial support from the corporate sector have historically been unwilling to abdicate control of the EPA, especially when Congress has incentives to expand environmental regulation.

The Power of the Purse

A major congressional strategy for controlling policy and its implementation involves Congress's "power of the purse" – the constitutional provision that "no money shall be drawn from the treasury, but in consequence of appropriations made by law." Since laws must originate in Congress, the legislative body can refuse to appropriate funds for certain purposes or condition the use of funds upon certain stipulations. Thus, the authority over appropriations gives Congress the ability to shape the actions of the executive branch in a manner consistent with congressional preferences. Certainly, conditioning appropriations upon specific activity explicitly mandates behavior consistent with the will of Congress. Even the threat that appropriations for an agency or program will be reduced or eliminated may achieve the same end.

In the field of foreign and military affairs, the power of the purse is often the only effective tool for Congress to influence policy. Congress's ability to restrict the uses of appropriated funds is well supported by court decisions, giving Congress a clear avenue of response to a president who asserts broad constitutional powers. By forbidding the executive branch from spending federal monies for certain purposes, Congress can prevent the president from pursuing a policy it opposes. Alternatively, Congress may withhold funds for some purpose favored by the president to gain leverage with the president on another matter. Of course, there often are political constraints on exercising this power. Stripping funds from programs or agencies that serve a vital purpose, but have deviated from the wishes of Congress, may not be popular.

Committee Reports

Committees often make clear their expectations about the implementation of programs in the reports that are required by House and Senate rules to accompany legislation when it is sent to the floor. Reports usually indicate the objectives of the legislation and sometimes interpret the language used, both of which may guide rule-making decisions by agencies. At times, committee reports indicate that the committee "clearly intends," "expects," or even "anticipates" that an executive branch official or agency will or will not do something. Earmarks for specific projects are sometimes listed in committee reports. Although they are not legally binding, committee reports often guide courts when they seek to interpret ambiguous statutory language. More important, reports make explicit the expectations of important members of Congress who will influence future legislation affecting an agency.

Packaging Strategies

The Constitution requires that the president have an opportunity to sign or veto legislation passed by Congress, but it does not indicate the size or format of the legislation Congress presents to the president. For example, a variety of items are often included in one bill to facilitate bargains among members of Congress, the president, and other interested parties. By using their ability to package legislation, members of Congress may encourage or discourage a presidential veto.

Congress exacts considerable power from its ability to package multiple measures and present the president with a single take-it-or-leave-it offer. When several bills or aspects of bills are combined into one package that includes legislation both favored and opposed by the president, Congress reduces the president's capacity to control national policy. Because the president does not have the formal authority to strike from a bill those provisions that he finds unfavorable, he is forced to make a difficult decision. Issuing a veto means losing, at least temporarily, those provisions of the legislation that he does find satisfactory. Of course, a packaged proposal that does encounter a veto may result in Congress losing valued provisions as well.

The advantages and disadvantages of packaging can be seen in the use of omnibus continuing resolutions (known as CRs), which combine two or more regular appropriations bills for the coming fiscal year into one giant package. CRs are required when Congress and the president fail to appropriate bills enacted before the beginning of a new fiscal year. If the president vetoes the bill that contains the funding for some executive agencies and no new bill is enacted, those agencies must shut down. Hence, the president needs to weigh carefully how effective a veto would be. Congress also risks losing measures packed into a CR that provoke the president's opposition. For example, Representative John Dingell's attempt in 1987 to codify in the CR the "fairness doctrine" governing broadcasters (a bill previously vetoed by President Reagan) was dropped from the bill after Reagan drew attention to its inclusion in the CR. The bundling strategy on these bills and other "must pass" legislation – such as bills to raise the federal government's debt ceiling – thus have the potential to help Congress reassert influence over the legislative game.

Recent presidents have promoted the line-item veto as a means to combat Congress's packaging strategies in appropriations bills. Adopting the line-item veto, an authority held by 43 state governors, would allow the president to strike out individual provisions nestled in individual or omnibus spending bills. However, creating a line-item veto would require a constitutional amendment. The Supreme Court ruled the line-item veto as passed by Congress in 1996 unconstitutional.

Presidential Nominations

The Senate is given a special opportunity to influence the administration every time the president nominates someone for a top executive branch post. Beyond judges, ambassadors, and "other public ministers and consuls," the Constitution allows Congress to determine by law who must stand for confirmation by the Senate. Currently, the Constitution and public law subject about 3,000 civilian executive branch positions to confirmation by the Senate (see the accompanying box "Congressionally Speaking..."). Judicial nominations and confirmations are considered in Chapter 10. In addition, the promotions of all military officers are submitted to the Senate.

The Senate tends to defer to the president on executive branch appointments, particularly on positions below the cabinet level. This is not to say, however, that the president's appointments go unchecked. In fact, in 1989 President George H.W. Bush's first nominee for secretary of defense, former senator John Tower, was rejected by the Senate largely because of concerns about the senator's private behavior. The president swiftly moved to nominate House Republican Dick Cheney, a choice calculated to be far more

Congressionally Speaking...

The Constitution and many statutes require that the president submit the names of certain appointees to the Senate for confirmation. The Constitution also allows the president to make a *recess appointment* when the Senate is not in session. A recess appointment is good until the end of the next session of Congress, which could be more than a year in duration. Presidents have used recess appointments to avoid the regular confirmation process, but they usually announce their intention to forward a regular nomination to the Senate at the time appointments are made. Because recess appointments are a way for the president to circumvent, at least for a short while, the authority of the Senate, this practice can and does create animosity.

President George W. Bush has employed the recess appointment with greater frequency than his two predecessors, but appears to be lagging slightly behind President Ronald Reagan. In his first six years as president, George W. Bush made 167 recess appointments, whereas President Bill Clinton made 140 over two terms and President George H.W. Bush made 77 in his single term. Reagan, on the other hand, made 240 recess appointments during his eight years in office.[8]

acceptable to the Senate. In 1993, President Bill Clinton's first nomination for attorney general was withdrawn when it was discovered that the nominee, Zoe Baird, had hired illegal aliens as household help. He eventually appointed Janet Reno, a Florida prosecutor, who was quickly approved by the Senate. According to the Senate Historical Office, Baird became the fifth cabinet-level nomination to be withdrawn by a president. Only 10 cabinet-level nominees have been rejected.

Occasionally Congress acts to require that certain executive officials be subject to Senate confirmation. In 1973, Congress required the president to receive Senate confirmation on appointments to director of the OMB. In 1986, Congress extended their authority by requiring that the president also receive Senate confirmation on appointments to head OIRA. When Congress approved legislation to create the Department of Homeland Security in 2002, the new secretary of the department automatically became subject to Senate confirmation.

Moreover, Congress may, and does, get involved in executive branch personnel matters beyond Senate action on presidential nominations. Congress is able to specify in law the qualifications required of presidential appointees, and it may even grant department heads, rather than the president, the authority to appoint certain officials. Congress also may limit the ability of the president or agency heads to dismiss employees. In these ways, Congress may seek to insulate certain executive branch officials from White House pressure.

Oversight

A member of Congress dissatisfied with agency performance or with presidential directives to an agency can choose from several oversight strategies to try to bring the bureaucracy into line. Oversight strategies centered on formal hearings include routine congressional hearings, which regularly bring agency heads in front of congressional committees, special hearings designed to draw attention to a disputed policy or agency action, and more dramatic investigations, such as the Watergate hearings in 1973 and 1974 and the 1987 Iran-Contra hearings. The highly publicized Watergate and Iran-Contra hearings earned historic fame uncharacteristic of more common oversight efforts.

Less formal methods of monitoring and influencing agency behavior include written and telephone communications with agency officials, discussions during informal office visits, and timely public statements. Such approaches can be useful in congressional efforts to increase agency responsiveness to the interests of Congress. Although a considerable amount of bureaucratic oversight occurs within the committee forum, there are oversight mechanisms available to members that are independent of committees. Members seeking to influence agency actions in their districts also have recourse to informal visits and more formal inquiries conducted by staff. Often, members acting on behalf of communities in their district will pressure agency officials to respond to local concerns. For example, individual members frequently push the Environmental Protection Agency to investigate hazardous waste sites or to initiate cleanups in their districts. At other times, members will compel the administration not to act in their district when agencies have the potential to adversely affect preferred constituents.

Some observers have distinguished between "police-patrol" and "fire-alarm" oversight. Under police-patrol oversight, Congress pursues routine, systematic surveillance of executive branch agencies on its own initiative. In contrast, fire-alarm oversight is more decentralized. Instead of initiating and maintaining patrols, Congress develops a system that lets others pull their local alarms. Citizens, interest groups, or the media trigger alarms and spur

THE IRAN-CONTRA AFFAIR

A Lebanese newspaper reported in early November 1986 that the Reagan administration had been engaged in trading arms to Iran for release of hostages held by Islamic extremists in Lebanon. When Attorney General Edwin Meese later that month uncovered a memo outlining the diversion of profits from the arms sales to the Nicaraguan Contras, a series of executive and congressional investigations ensued. Together, these events sparked the biggest scandal of President Reagan's two terms in office and helped precipitate Reagan's marked decline in popularity and influence.

An investigation by special House and Senate panels into the Iran-Contra affair uncovered a remarkable series of events, in which officials of the Reagan administration lied to Congress and helped subvert normal democratic decision-making processes. The Reagan administration essentially pursued private policies that were in direct conflict with public policy objectives. On one hand, the administration's public policies were to ban arms shipments to Iran and to make no concessions for the release of hostages. On the other hand, the administration pursued private policies of selling sophisticated missiles to Iran and trading weapons to get the hostages back. Although Reagan originally told a special investigatory commission that he approved the shipments, he later reversed this statement. Finally, he testified that he could not remember whether or not he had approved the shipments.

Reagan's advisors admitted to directing the covert arms transactions and the subsequent attempts to divert the profits to the Contras. Furthermore, they confessed to concealing and, at times, outwardly lying about the activities to Congress. The arms sales violated laws requiring that such transactions be reported to Congress. Even though a series of Boland amendments were in place at the time prohibiting military or paramilitary assistance to the Contras, national security staff under the guidance of Lt. Colonel Oliver North and National Security Advisor John Poindexter secretly assumed direction and funding of the Contras' military efforts. Denied funds by the U.S. Congress for the Contras, the National Security Council (NSC) staff sought illicit funding from foreign countries and private citizens, and turned over much of the operation to arms merchants Richard Secord and Albert Hakim. Their private "enterprise" accumulated approximately $10.6 million, carrying out covert U.S. policies with private funds entirely unaccountable to Congress.

In the end, more hostages were taken and the military situation in Nicaragua worsened. But the policy failures pale in comparison to the failure of democratic and constitutional processes at the heart of the affair.

members of Congress to respond to certain agency decisions. Members may prefer fire-alarm oversight because it is more cost-efficient and because it allows them to claim credit for acting when the alarm bells ring.

Yet police-patrol oversight appears to have become more common since the early 1970s. Fiscal constraints may have led members to turn away from legislation for new programs and instead to focus on overseeing the implementation of established programs. Expanded committee staffs and the independence of subcommittees, some devoted exclusively to oversight activities, have also facilitated more conventional oversight. Furthermore, the centralization of the executive branch's regulatory process in the OMB and the Council on Competitiveness motivated members to pursue formal oversight hearings more aggressively. Partisan rivalries when there is divided party control of Congress and the White House have motivated legislators to be more aggressive in their oversight activities.

Congress has increasingly turned to the Government Accountability Office (GAO) to assist with oversight. The GAO is an agency of Congress and is authorized to examine any federal agency. It gives members of Congress the option of having its expert, non-partisan staff conduct an investigation of executive branch performance without a large commitment of time on the part of members or their staff. The duties of the GAO were expanded under the Legislative Reorganization Act of 1970, and since then the GAO has significantly increased the range and number of its audits and analyses of program effectiveness.

In recent decades, Congress has more frequently required the president and executive agencies to provide written reports on their actions and performance. In some cases, the requirement is designed to ensure the timely receipt of information – for example, just before Congress must reauthorize a program. In other situations, Congress demands that an agency conduct a special study of a problem and report the results. Executive branch officials often complain that they spend too much time writing reports that few members, if any, read. From Congress's perspective, however, the exercise is another aspect of police-patrol oversight that shifts the burden to agencies themselves.

Beginning in 1978, police-patrol oversight was extended by the creation of offices of inspectors general within major departments and agencies. Inspectors general are given substantial independence from political appointees and agency heads, are authorized to conduct wide-ranging audits and investigations, and are required to submit their reports directly to Congress. With few exceptions, Congress has looked favorably upon having a full-time, on-site bureaucratic oversight mechanism.

Police-patrol oversight also is reflected in Congress's intensified scrutiny of "reprogramming" by agencies. Congress usually appropriates funds for executive branch activities in large lump-sum categories, with the understanding that the funds will be spent in accordance with the more detailed budget justifications that agencies submit each year. Frequently, variation from the budget justifications – reprogramming – is deemed prudent or even necessary because of changing conditions, poor estimates, or new congressional requirements. Agencies and the White House, however, have occasionally taken advantage of reprogramming discretion to spend money for purposes not anticipated – or even opposed – by Congress. Congress has responded by establishing more and more requirements, such as demanding advanced notification of reprogramming actions and even requiring prior approval by the appropriate committees.

National security is an area in which Congress's ability to oversee the executive branch and publicize what it learns is somewhat limited. Several committees, including the appropriations, national security, and intelligence committees, receive classified information from executive agencies and hold hearings on classified matters in executive sessions. Committee reports from hearings or investigations are cleared with executive agencies and frequently must exclude materials that the agencies determine should remain classified. In 2004, as a part of a large intelligence reform package, Congress assigned the Public Interest Declassification Board (PIDB), comprised of members appointed by both Congress and the president, to resolve disputes between Congress and executive agencies about classified material that Congress wishes to publish.

Legislative Veto

A congressional strategy of disputed constitutionality is the use of the legislative veto. A legislative veto is a provision written into legislation that delegates authority for certain actions to the president or agencies, subject to the approval or disapproval of one or both houses of Congress, certain committees, or even designated committee leaders. The legislative veto gives Congress a way to check executive branch action without having to pass new legislation that would require presidential approval. Congress can, then, avoid writing detailed legislation by delegating rule-making power to the executive branch, and still retain the final say over executive decisions.

Legislative vetoes may, at first glance, appear to be a strategy used exclusively by congressional players against the president. The origins of the legislative veto, however, convey a different story. In 1932, Congress and

President Herbert Hoover reached an agreement on executive branch reorganization that included the first legislative veto. The compact delegated reorganization powers to the president, provided that Congress did not disapprove his plan within 60 days. The agreement effectively gave the president wide latitude in exercising powers delegated to him, but it also gave Congress a chance to control those actions without having to enact another law. The provision seemingly benefited both Congress and the president by expanding the powers of the president, but giving Congress an opportunity to nullify those decisions.

The Supreme Court eventually saw it differently and declared legislative vetoes unconstitutional in 1983 in *Immigration and Naturalization Service* v. *Chadha*. The majority of the Court noted that some legislative vetoes circumvent constitutional requirements that legislative actions be passed by both chambers. Perhaps more important, the Court said, legislative vetoes violate the constitutional requirement that all measures subject to congressional votes be presented to the president for signature or veto. The Court's position was evident: If Congress wants to limit executive branch use of delegated authority, it must pass new legislation by the traditional route.

Congress has devised no consistent strategy to replace the legislative veto. At times, Congress has written more detailed legislation or committee reports, added new procedural requirements for agencies, or turned to sunset provisions. At other times, it has turned toward informal agency-committee spending agreements, which require agencies to notify certain committees before they act. Although advance notification requirements have been upheld by the courts, committees actually retain an implicit form of veto under these arrangements. Specifically, agencies encountering opposition from the committees that fund them are not likely to proceed with their original plans out of fear of reprisal when their authorizing and appropriations legislation is next before Congress.

Despite the Court's 1983 ruling, Congress has continued to add legislative vetoes to new laws. In just over a year after the Chadha decision, an additional 53 legislative vetoes were enacted into law. By the completion of the 105th Congress (1997–1998), more than 400 new legislative vetoes had been enacted. New forms of legislative vetoes are still being attempted and, in some cases, enacted. These efforts reflect the desire of Congress, the president, and the executive agencies to find mutually acceptable ways to balance the delegation of power with checks on the use of that power. The president and agency officials know that courts would rule in their favor if they chose to challenge legislative vetoes, but they often agree to comply with them because legislative vetoes are a necessary condition for the latitude that accompanies them.

A convenient inference is that the Supreme Court's 1983 decision had little practical effect on inter-branch relations. Such an inference is premature and probably incorrect. A scholarly review of inter-branch relations in the foreign policy arena indicates that the 1983 decision eliminated an important means for resolving conflict. Where Congress and the executive branch are in serious disagreement, the executive branch appears unwilling to accept even symbolic legislative veto provisions, and Congress seems unwilling to delegate power that the executive branch seeks. Thus, changing the rules of the game seems to have affected the ability of the branches to identify cooperative strategies.

Conclusion

This review of congressional and presidential strategies suggests how dynamic and complex the relationship between the legislative and executive branches has become. As political conditions have evolved, senators, representatives, presidents, and bureaucrats have devised new and sometimes ingenious strategies to influence policy outcomes. Dissatisfaction with the likely or realized outcomes of the game has often yielded institutional innovations, such as expanding the responsibilities of the OMB, creating the line-item veto, expanding the use of executive orders, and creating legislative vetoes. Incrementally, the web of statutes, court rulings, and informal understandings produced by this process of innovation has made inter-branch relations more complex. On the whole, the separation of powers between Congress and the president has become less clearly defined with the expansion of the president's legislative powers and Congress's administrative capabilities. What keeps the system operating is a minimal level of agreement among the House, Senate, and president, or at least an understanding that compromise is essential to prevent complete gridlock.

The three-institution legislative game of the House, Senate, and presidency generates cooperation and conflict as the policy preferences and political interests of officeholders vary across issues and over time. However, the requirement that the three institutional players agree before new law can be made, in the absence of sufficient congressional support to override a veto, leads to exploitation of extra-statutory tactics and often necessitates informal accommodation. Accommodation is frustrating to players set on gaining outright victories, and it often is possible only after a long struggle. Furthermore, accommodation produces unstable results. New Congresses and presidents seeking new strategies to meet their own political needs frequently alter the state of the institutions. Consequently, relations between the branches seldom remain in equilibrium for long.

Above: Judge John Roberts takes the oath before his testimony at the Senate Judiciary Committee on his nomination to become the Chief Justice of the Supreme Court on September 12, 2005. **Below:** Judge Samuel A. Alito, left, and his family are escorted to the East Room of the White House by United States President George W. Bush, right, for his swearing in as Associate Justice of the United States Supreme Court in Washington, D.C. on February 1, 2006. Credit: Ron Sachs / CNP.

10

Congress and the Courts

S UPREME COURT NOMINATIONS WERE AT THE CENTER OF ATTENTION IN THE summer of 2005. Sandra Day O'Connor announced her intentions to resign on July 1, 2005 creating the first vacancy on the Supreme Court in 11 years. Then, before O'Connor's seat could be filled, Chief Justice William Rehnquist lost his battle with thyroid cancer on September 3, 2005. Rehnquist's death created a second vacancy on the Supreme Court and gave President George W. Bush an opportunity to shape the ideological direction of the Court for a generation. Chief Justice Rehnquist was often considered a reliably conservative vote, while O'Connor was considered to be the "swing" justice who often cast the deciding vote in bitterly divided 5–4 decisions. President Bush first nominated John Roberts, a judge on the D.C. Circuit Court of Appeals, to replace O'Connor, but following Rehnquist's death, Bush nominated Roberts to become the new Chief Justice. Roberts was considered to be a "home run" of a nominee with impeccable credentials and qualifications. Conservatives were sure he would be a reliable vote on their side, while liberals could find little in his record to warrant opposing him. Roberts played his part well in his confirmation hearings as he repeatedly showed off his intellect all the while proclaiming judicial modesty, best exemplified in his opening statement where he declared:

> Judges are like umpires. Umpires don't make the rules; they apply them. The role of an umpire and a judge is critical. They make sure everybody plays by the rules. But it is a limited role. Nobody ever went to a ball game to see the umpire. Judges have to have the humility to recognize that they operate within a system of precedent, shaped by other judges equally striving to live up to the judicial oath.

Roberts easily won Senate confirmation by a vote of 78–22, which then focused the nation's attention on who President Bush would nominate to

replace Justice O'Connor – the first female justice to serve on the Supreme
Court. Bush first nominated White House Counsel Harriet Miers, a long-
time ally and loyal soldier in the Bush administration. Unlike Roberts, Miers
immediately came under fire from politicians of all political stripes. Conservatives questioned whether or not she was conservative enough, given her
apparent support for abortion rights in her earlier work as an attorney, while
others questioned her qualifications given that she had never worked as a
judge or served in any posts that would have appeared to prepare her for
the job. Both sides questioned whether President Bush put cronyism above
finding the best nominee for the post. Miers eventually asked to have her
name withdrawn from consideration citing, among other factors, the growing opposition to her nomination.

Bush quickly named a new nominee – 3rd Circuit Court Judge Samuel
Alito – who was cut from the same model as Chief Justice Roberts. Alito
was eminently qualified, having spent 15 years as a judge, and was thought
to be a judicial conservative – in fact, many compared him to current Justice
Antonin Scalia. Alito found the Senate much less receptive to his nomination
than it had been to Roberts. Alito endured grueling confirmation hearings –
that once brought his wife to tears – and an attempted filibuster on the
Senate floor before eventually winning confirmation by a vote of 58–42.

The battle over judicial nominees such as Roberts, Miers, Alito, and scores
of lower court nominees has raged in the past two decades at least in part
because the House, Senate, and president are not the only institutional
players in the policy-making game. Federal judges serve, as Justice Roberts
stated, as "umpires" in encounters between players in the legislative and
executive arenas and help determine the boundaries of each institution's
powers. In separation-of-powers cases, for example, judges often draw lines
between the two branches and specify the constitutional powers on each
side. Judges also consider the scope of legislative powers generally, including the scope of congressional power to investigate the executive branch and
where the line between federal and state jurisdictions should be drawn.

The courts are not simply umpires in the legislative game, however. They
are both political and legal institutions. In the past generation, judges have
increasingly contributed to making policy – not merely interpreting statutes
already enacted. Growth of judicial activism since the 1970s and the reactions to judicial activism are an important part of the story of relations
between Congress and the courts.

Congress is not a quiet bystander to the decisions of the courts. Most
important areas of law are the product of interaction between the legislative institutions (Congress and the president) and the courts. The legislative

institutions have a number of ways to influence, at least indirectly, the decisions the courts make, as Congress and the president determine the composition of the courts. The president nominates judges and the Senate must
confirm the nominees. Moreover, the size of the Supreme Court and lower
courts, the organization and funding for the federal court system, and the
Supreme Court's jurisdiction with respect to appeals from lower courts are
determined by law, making them subject to the legislative process controlled
by the House, Senate, and president. More directly, Congress and the president anticipate and react to court rulings. They sometimes comply with,
ignore, or even reverse judicial decisions. They may speed, slow, or even
exclude court consideration of certain matters in the way they write law.
This chapter takes up each of these subjects – the courts as umpires, the
courts as policy makers, and congressional resources and strategies.

Courts as Umpires

The Constitution implicitly grants to the Supreme Court the power to
declare actions of state and federal legislatures and executives unconstitutional. This authority inserts the court into the dynamics of the legislative
game. First exercised in *Marbury* v. *Madison* in 1803, the power of *judicial
review* – the ability to declare laws unconstitutional – gives the courts a say
in the enactment of new legislation.

Most cases come to the courts when a private party, sometimes an interest
group, challenges the constitutionality of an act of Congress after an executive agency seeks to implement or enforce the act. Occasionally, members
of Congress file suit against the executive branch for its failure to implement laws in a manner consistent with the members' expectations. In fact,
members have apparently been plaintiffs in suits filed against the executive branch in more cases during the past two decades than in all previous
decades. Issues of great importance are appealed from lower courts to the
Supreme Court, although this process might take years after the original
enactment of the legislation.

As Figure 10.1 shows, the Supreme Court has overturned federal laws at
an uneven pace over its history. Before 1865, only two statutes were overturned. Indeed, for much of its history the Supreme Court has exercised its
review powers only intermittently. Intense legislative-judicial conflict is relatively infrequent, occurring in the two decades around the New Deal (1920s
and 1930s) and in the two most recent decades. Even then, historically the
majority of laws overturned by the Court are actually minor or relatively
unimportant, yet this tendency has changed in recent years as the Court has

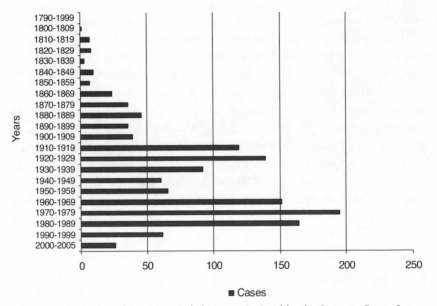

FIGURE 10.1. Number of Provisions Ruled Unconstitutional by the Supreme Court. *Source:* Lawrence Baum, *The Supreme Court*, 9th edition. Washington, D.C.: Congressional Quarterly Press.

taken on high-profile legislation such as the Violence Against Women Act and the Religious Freedom and Restoration Act.

In this section, two types of cases involving the interpretation of the Constitution are discussed: cases involving the separation-of-powers between Congress and the executive branch and cases concerning the scope of congressional powers. The section concludes with a discussion of the role of courts as umpires in disputes about the meaning of statutes.

Separation-of-Powers Cases

In the decades before the 1970s, court involvement in separation-of-powers cases was uncommon. Because Congress was relatively deferential to the executive branch, fewer encounters were likely to provoke conflict over the powers of each branch. That situation changed dramatically during the Nixon administration (1969–1974) and in the following years when Congress moved to reassert itself.

President Richard Nixon asserted broad presidential powers in his conflict with a Congress controlled by the Democrats. The most conspicuous conflict was Nixon's battle with Congress over federal spending. Nixon claimed a right to withhold funds from executive agencies – a process called impoundment – even after the appropriations legislation was enacted into law. For example, Nixon impounded funds appropriated for sewage treatment plants administered by the Environmental Protection Agency. The impoundments were frequently challenged in the courts and Nixon usually lost. In 1973 and 1974 alone, only six of more than 50 cases upheld the president's position on impoundments in any way. Most of the decisions were made at the U.S. district court level and were not appealed by the administration to higher courts. In the sewage-treatment case, the Supreme Court ruled that the president was obligated to follow the law and allocate the funds.

In the 1980s, partisan dissension between the Republican White House and the Democratic House continued to drive each branch to the courts for redress against the perceived excesses of the other branch. For most of the Reagan and G. H. W. Bush presidencies, the Supreme Court followed a "doctrinal notion of separated powers" – the view that a sharp line can be drawn between executive and legislative powers. Three particularly revealing decisions in which the Court decided against Congress were *Immigration and Naturalization Service v. Chadha* (1983), *Bowsher v. Synar* (1986), and *Clinton v. City of New York* (1998). These decisions merit attention in light of the ways in which the Court refereed contentious encounters between the branches.

In the *Chadha* decision, the Supreme Court ruled 7 to 2 that the legislative veto (see Chapter 9) was unconstitutional. According to the Court, Congress was to present bills to the president, who had the sole power to veto them. Arguments that the legislative veto was a workable means of extending authority to the executive short of formal enactment of a law were rejected. Still, the ban on legislative vetoes has largely been ignored by Congress, with more than 400 legislative vetoes enacted into law after Chadha – often with the agreement of the executive branch.[1] Although the *Chadha* decision has forced Congress to be more creative in crafting provisions that give the legislature a potential veto, the response to the decision shows the weakness of the Court as an umpire when Congress and presidents agree on mutually beneficial ways to distribute power between themselves.

The Supreme Court's decision in *Clinton v. City of New York* (1998), striking down the line-item veto, demonstrated that the Court will enforce the separation of powers between Congress and the President even when the two branches are not in conflict. In 1996 Congress passed and President Clinton signed the line-item veto, which gave the President the power to remove or veto specific spending or tax breaks from bills while signing the underlying bill, with the law taking effect after the presidential election of 1996. Presidents had long sought this power to control federal spending, while many in Congress were eager to let the President help control it and take the blame for cutting popular programs. In striking down the line-item

veto, the Court ruled that allowing the modification of a bill before signing
it violated the constitutionally prescribed legislative process, specifically the
"presentment" clause of Article I. President G. W. Bush and many members
of Congress have expressed their desire to reenact a version of the line-item
veto, but the Court's ruling has made it clear that it will guard the constitutionally prescribed separation-of-powers.

The Court's responsibility to referee separation of powers conflicts is
also put into perspective by the narrowness of many of its rulings. Despite
the breadth of disagreement between Congress and the president on many
separation-of-powers cases, the Court often confines itself to fairly narrow
questions. In *Bowsher v. Synar*, the Court again tried to maintain a strict
boundary between the branches, claiming that the framers of the Constitution provided for a "separate and wholly independent Executive Branch."
But in this challenge to the constitutionality of the Gramm-Rudman-
Hollings deficit-reduction law (see Chapter 12), the Court ruled only on
a fairly narrow, technical point. That provision gave the comptroller general
(the head of the General Accountability Office) the authority to determine
the size of spending cuts required when the federal deficit exceeded a specified level. Because the comptroller general could be removed by Congress,
the Court ruled that executive duties could not be assigned to this position. The Court ignored more complex questions about the appropriate budgetary responsibilities of the two branches and instead focused on the nar-
rower legal question of removal powers as they concerned the comptroller
general.

Congressional Powers

The courts also referee the legislative game by their involvement in questions
of congressional powers. Although Article I of the Constitution specifies in
some detail the powers of Congress, the Supreme Court has often ruled on
whether certain acts of Congress are permissible. In contrast, the Supreme
Court has heard relatively few cases on Congress's authority over its internal affairs. On questions of membership qualifications, Congress's ability to
punish its members, and speech privileges of members, the Court has generally given Congress a good deal of leeway. A few examples show how difficult
the issues can be and how much the role of the courts as umpire can change
in particular areas of the law.

THE COMMERCE CLAUSE. The most frequent way that the courts have refereed legislative politics is by interpreting the limits of congressional power

under the Constitution. Perhaps the best examples are Supreme Court rulings that interpret the commerce clause of the Constitution (Article I, Section 8). The commerce clause allows Congress to enact legislation that regulates interstate commerce, and it has been used by Congress to regulate many aspects of American life that are related, however indirectly, to interstate commerce. Over the years, the Supreme Court has decided many cases that affect the limits of what activities are related to interstate commerce. As the national economy became more integrated and as Congress sought to establish more uniform policies for the nation in the late 1800s and early 1900s, congressional powers under the commerce clause became a controversial issue.

In the late 1800s and early 1900s, the Supreme Court took a narrow view of interstate commerce. If an activity concerned production or manufacturing, concerned only intrastate exchange, and did not directly affect interstate commerce, the Court tended to protect it from federal regulation. This interpretation greatly limited the ability of Congress and the president to respond to the rapidly changing national economy. In fact, the Court's narrow view of the commerce clause led it to strike down Franklin Roosevelt's New Deal legislation in the early 1930s, which was enacted in response to the Great Depression. After Roosevelt requested, but failed to get, congressional approval to enlarge the Court so that he could change the balance of opinion on the Court, two justices changed their views on the commerce clause, and the Court reversed itself on several major decisions.

Since the 1930s, step-by-step, the Court has allowed Congress to determine what activities are related to interstate commerce. In the 1980s and early 1990s, the Court upheld laws that ban threats and extortion to collect on loans, set minimum wages for employees of state and local governments, and prohibited age discrimination by agencies of state government. Until recently, Court action appeared to erase the line between intrastate and interstate commerce and leave very broad powers for Congress under the commerce clause.

In 1995, led by conservative justices, the Supreme Court changed the direction of 70 years of rulings in favor of congressional discretion to determine the breadth of the commerce clause. In *United States v. Lopez*, the Court struck down a 1990 law that prohibited anyone from knowingly carrying a firearm in a school zone. The government argued that Congress had implicit authority, from its ability to interpret the commerce clause, to regulate firearms for such a public purpose. The Court ruled that nothing in the commerce clause or other constitutional provisions authorizes Congress to regulate such behavior, absent compelling evidence that the presence of firearms in school zones had an adverse effect on interstate commerce.

The Court continued its efforts to set limits on Congress's ability to stretch the commerce clause by striking down parts of the Violence Against Women Act in *U.S. v. Morrison* (2000). The 5–4 ruling invalidated a portion of the statute allowing women who were victims of sexual assault to sue their attackers in federal court. Congress had granted women this power citing numerous studies indicating that fear of violence had a chilling effect on the mobility of female students and employees. The majority opinion in *U.S. v. Morrison* held that Congress's attempt to regulate crimes against women in this manner could, "obliterate the Constitution's distinction between national and local authority" while the dissent held that Congress had adequately demonstrated the link between violence against women and interstate commerce.

The conservative majority that had seemed intent on limiting the power of Congress under the commerce clause splintered in *Gonzales v. Raich* (2005). The case dealt with whether or not the federal government could prohibit states from enacting laws sanctioning the use of medicinal marijuana. The government argued that the Controlled Substances Act – a law regulating the use of drugs such as marijuana – did not allow the use of the drug for medicinal purposes. The defendants argued that the Controlled Substances Act was unconstitutional because the drug was homegrown, did not cross state lines, and was not sold; hence did not involve interstate commerce. A 6–3 majority of the Supreme Court disagreed, finding that Congress did have the power to regulate medicinal marijuana under the commerce clause, signaling a backtracking in the Court's tightening of Congress's powers under the commerce clause.

POWER TO INVESTIGATE. One area in which the courts have been more active in interpreting congressional powers has been Congress's power to investigate. Although the power to investigate is not mentioned explicitly in the Constitution, investigatory authority has traditionally been considered an implied power of Congress. In general, the authority to acquire information is usually seen as necessary for the proper functioning of a legislature. For example, the investigative and contempt powers of the English Parliament are exempt from judicial review. Although most investigations by the U.S. Congress are carried out without ending up in court, the Supreme Court has on occasion reached some rather controversial decisions about the scope of congressional investigatory authority. In particular, the Court has refereed cases contesting the subjects Congress can investigate and the rights that congressional witnesses retain. The Court originally took a narrow view of congressional investigative and contempt authority in *Kilbourn v. Thompson*, decided in 1881. In overturning the arrest of Hallet Kilbourn, who refused to provide information to the House about certain real estate deals, the Supreme Court limited Congress's ability to investigate private matters. The Court also delineated several principles concerning the proper scope of congressional powers to investigate. Specifically, the Court limited the scope of congressional authority to matters on which Congress could legitimately legislate and on which the chamber had indicated its intent to legislate.

Those standards stood for nearly 50 years, until the Supreme Court broadened congressional authority in *McGrain v. Daugherty* in 1927. The Court ruled that Congress had no general power to investigate private matters, but the Court extended the scope of congressional authority to any subject of *potential* legislation. The Court also affirmed Congress's power to compel private individuals to testify. Still, the Court did reserve for individuals the right to refuse to answer certain questions if they were not pertinent to the general investigation. Reserving a right for individuals to refuse to testify was to become central to Senator Joseph McCarthy's investigations of subversive activities in the 1950s.

In the 1950s and 1960s, the Warren Court moved to protect the right of private individuals to refuse to answer questions, based on their Fifth Amendment privilege against self-incrimination *(Watkins v. United States,* 1957; *Bernblatt v. United States,* 1959). *Watkins* concerned the rights of persons convicted of contempt of Congress for failing to answer questions about their association with the Communist Party that were posed by the House Un-American Activities Committee. In this case, the Court ruled that the committee did not have a sufficiently well-defined legislative purpose to justify requiring an individual to respond to questions. Chief Justice Earl Warren, writing for the Court, noted that "there is no congressional power to expose for the sake of exposure."

REGULATING CAMPAIGN SPENDING. In overturning parts of campaign finance legislation passed in 1974, the Supreme Court ruled in *Buckley v. Valeo* (1976) that Congress cannot limit individual or group expenditures in a political campaign when those expenditures are made independently of a particular candidate or party. The Court said that the First Amendment of the Constitution, which guarantees freedom of speech, prevents the government from regulating political speech – in this case, speech funded by an individual on her own behalf.

The Court said that limitations on campaign expenditures, as for any restraint on political speech, are constitutional only if some compelling government interest exists. The determination of what constitutes a compelling interest requires the courts to exercise discretion and judgment. In this case, the Supreme Court decided that the goal of limiting the electoral influence of wealthy individuals or groups was insufficient and ran directly counter to the intent of the First Amendment. The Court reached a different conclusion in a case regarding the constitutionality of the 1974 law restricting the amount of money that political parties could spend directly on behalf of candidates. In reversing a previous decision by a circuit court, the Supreme Court held in *FEC v. Colorado Republican Federal Campaign Committee* (1996), that coordinated spending by political parties was not protected by the First Amendment and thus could be constitutionally regulated. Further, a majority of the Court found that there was a compelling government interest in regulating the spending activities of political parties. The Supreme Court upheld Congress's most recent attempt to regulate campaign finance, the 2002 Bipartisan Campaign Reform Act, in *McConnell v. FEC* (2003). As we describe in detail in Chapter 3, the Court allowed Congress to ban soft money and set restrictions on issue advocacy ads placed on television.

The Politics of Statutory Interpretation

When courts act as umpires in the legislative game, they often make judgments about the meaning of statutes. The imprecision of language, inconsistencies among various laws adopted at different times, and evolving circumstances to which a statute must be applied guarantee that the courts will face difficult decisions about the interpretation of laws. Compounding matters is that the legislators and presidents responsible for drafting legislation may have disagreed about the legislation's meaning or even deliberately left certain provisions vague to smooth over differences among themselves that would have been obstacles to enactment. Judges, when asked to resolve disputes about the interpretation of statutes, may affect the direction of public policy and sometimes alter the strategies of legislators, presidents, and others who care about policy.

Judges and legal scholars have developed several approaches to interpreting statutes, each reflecting a different view about how Congress functions, how legislative outcomes are reached, and how capable judges are of understanding congressional intent. The most traditional approach to interpreting statutes relies on the "canons of statutory construction." The canons outline for judges how to interpret the language of laws and are often stated in Latin.

For example, one canon – *inclusio unius est exclusio alterius* – means that the inclusion of one thing indicates the exclusion of another. Other canons apply to specific subjects. For example, the "rule of lenity" stipulates that statutes that make certain conduct unlawful and impose penalties must be construed to apply narrowly to the conduct specified.

Unfortunately canons often conflict and there is no canon to help judges choose the appropriate canon. One school of legal scholars advocates that judges determine the objective or purpose of the statute and then deduce the outcome most consistent with the law's purpose. Another school insists that judges should determine how legislators, motivated by the special interests influencing them, would decide a question if asked to do so. Yet others contend that judges should be free to interpret and reinterpret statutes as the societal or legal context changes. Not surprisingly, some scholars argue that judges should refuse to resolve ambiguities and insist that they be resolved in the legislative process.

Perhaps the most important issue in statutory interpretation is being waged over the relevance and content of legislative histories. A few purists argue for strict construction of statutes. Rather than turning to committee reports and floor debates to interpret legislative intent, supporters of this approach urge courts to restrict themselves to the "plain meaning," or intrinsic meaning, of a statute's text. This view seems to be gaining support in the federal judiciary. Its most prominent proponent is Supreme Court justice Antonin Scalia.

In practice, most judges still gladly accept guidance from committee reports, the record of floor debate, statements of bill or amendment sponsors, presidential messages, and other documented evidence of the intent of a bill's authors. Yet, because legislative histories often encapsulate conflicting views, they are not straightforward guides to statutory interpretation for judges. Further, members of Congress can try to add things to the legislative history to influence the decisions of judges. Most judges seem willing to exercise some judgment about which views should be considered most authoritative. Some effort has been made in recent years to improve communication between the federal judiciary and Congress so that problems of statutory interpretation can be minimized.

In recent years, a majority of justices on the Supreme Court have begun to look more carefully at legislative histories in the context of federalism cases. In striking down major provisions of the Americans with Disabilities Act, the Violence Against Women Act, and the Religious Freedom and Restoration Act, and upholding provisions of the Family and Medical Leave Act, the Court has cited legislative histories extensively in their opinions. The

---

Congressionally Speaking...

Members frequently attempt to establish a clear record about how certain provisions of a bill should be interpreted. One way of doing this is to discuss the provisions in the *committee report* that accompanies the bill. Committee reports provide the background and justification for the bill and its provisions and often provide detailed sections on the meaning of key words or phrases. They are drafted by committee staffs and approved by committees, sometimes after long debate. Members also engage in *colloquies* – scripted exchanges on the floor among two or more members to clarify the interpretation of a bill or an amendment. Colloquies, of course, are transcribed in the *Congressional Record*, where judges, executive branch officials, and others can find floor statements.

In recent years, presidents have used *signing statements*, issued at the time they sign legislation, to offer their interpretation of controversial provisions. These statements send a message to administrative agencies about the interpretation of the law. Courts have not yet placed much weight on signing statements in their reading of legislative histories. They have tended to place greater weight on *veto statements* when the veto is not overridden by Congress and the legislation is modified in the direction suggested by the president.

Court in these cases has used the content of legislative histories to determine whether or not Congress has generated a record of mistreatment of individuals by the States. The Court has reasoned that a substantial legislative record is necessary for Congress to abridge states' Eleventh Amendment protection against lawsuits in order to enforce the equal protection clause of the Fourteenth Amendment. This new line of reasoning by the Court has altered the balance of power between Congress and the States, and raised new questions about the quality and content of legislative deliberation, such as what standards of evidence Congress should be held to in demonstrating the need for new laws.

Members, lobbyists, and administrations often anticipate that legislative history may be important when issues are taken to the courts. Sometimes, the language of committee reports is the subject of as intense a fight as the bill language itself. For example, after the House Energy and Commerce Committee voted to approve a major overhaul of clean air laws in 1990, it took nearly a month for committee staff to hammer out report language that was acceptable to all sides. On most matters, carefully prepared statements by committee chairs and bill sponsors are made on the floors of the two chambers to give weight to a particular interpretation of major provisions of legislation and to set a record that judges cannot easily ignore.

Judges as Policy Makers

Although the courts' primary role is to serve as an umpire for disputes about legislative authority and procedure, the relationship between courts and the legislative institutions is more complex than that. In recent decades, federal judges have been seen as policy makers – as players, not just umpires. At times, judges have even moved aggressively to place themselves at the center of political disputes. But in many areas, Congress and the president have encouraged courts' policy-making activities in the legislation they have enacted.

The assertiveness of the Warren Court in the 1950s in addressing racial desegregation marked a considerably more active and aggressive involvement of the courts in national policy making. Although the Burger Court impeded somewhat the extent of judicial involvement in policy making, the Rehnquist Court was the most "activist" ever (see Figure 10.1).

In the 1970s and 1980s, the mix of liberal, conservative, and moderate judges on the Supreme Court further fueled the expansion of court involvement in policy making. Reading statutes broadly and sometimes creatively enabled the two sides to sidestep controversial constitutional issues, which as a by-product expanded court involvement in the creation of national policy. In lower courts, judges often found that they were much less likely to evoke criticism from the Supreme Court if they misread statutes than if they misread the Constitution.

Judicial activism was reinforced by legislative activism on the part of Congress and the president. The wave of legislation between the mid-1960s and mid-1970s created new civil rights, broadened eligibility for welfare and health benefits, established new consumer rights, and set new public health, safety, and environmental standards. Much of the legislation required administrative agencies to design new regulations. Other legislation required agencies to account formally for additional factors in making their decisions. And some new laws were enacted that assigned the executive branch the duty to achieve certain policy goals. At the same time, new and often complex procedures were imposed on agencies by new legislation – the Freedom of Information Act, the Privacy Act, Government in the Sunshine Act, and other legislation. These procedural requirements were designed to open agency decision making to public scrutiny, protect individual rights, and ensure that agency officials heard all interests and views.

Although the role of the courts in the administrative process is, in part, the result of judges' assertiveness, it is much more than that. The creation of new substantive and procedural rights is often the direct product of interest group politics. Interest groups that lack confidence in decisions by regulatory agencies often view litigation as an alternative route for securing favorable policy outcomes. The type of agency decisions that are reviewable by courts, the actions courts may take, the parties who have standing to sue, and other issues are subject to the give-and-take of legislative politics.

The result is that courts are often left to enforce new rights and procedures, determine whether certain factors were given adequate weight in decisions, and evaluate the effectiveness of agency strategies for achieving specified goals. On the procedural side, judicial review sometimes encourages or even requires agencies to elaborate decision-making processes in ways unanticipated by Congress. Political scientist William Gormley[2] notes that

> by stressing the need for due process and by defining due process very broadly indeed, many federal courts have encouraged administrative agencies to adopt cumbersome procedures when handling individual cases, such as welfare or social security cases. A similar development in rule-making review has stimulated the growth of "hybrid ruling-making" procedures, including opportunities to cross-examine witnesses and other procedural guarantees. In practice, hybrid rule-making often benefits special interest groups, who need little additional protection. That is because such groups can afford the legal representation that hybrid rule-making requires.

The courts have often taken the step from procedural matters to the substance of agency decisions. In some cases, the law provides explicitly for the appeal of agency decisions to the courts. For example, the law requiring public schools to provide education for children with disabilities provides appeals to give local groups a chance to challenge federal, state, and local decisions affecting education in their communities. In such cases, courts are called on to judge what constitutes adequate education. In doing so, the courts are asked to direct public policy, even to influence the spending priorities of government.

In other cases, lawsuits pursued by affected parties or interest groups unhappy with agency decisions have led courts to make policy judgments. Gormley explains:

> Citing the "hard look doctrine" popularized by the late Judge Howard Leventhal, [courts] have insisted that agencies take a hard look at the available evidence, engage in reasoned decision-making, and give careful consideration to alternatives. All of this sounds rather innocuous. In practice, however, the hard-look doctrine enables judges to substitute their judgment for that of administrative officials who possess far greater technical expertise.

Thus, by applying judicially derived doctrine for situations in which agencies have been delegated substantial policy-making discretion, the courts sometimes have become policy makers themselves.

The question of why Congress has tended to devolve quasi-legislative powers to agencies and the courts remains. Plainly, institutional politics has become quite complex. Some commentators argue that members of Congress often use the agencies and the courts to avoid difficult choices and political blame. Members, according to this view, often are unable or unwilling to resolve their differences, so they give up and leave legislation ambiguous or include contradictory provisions, a practice which sometimes leaves interested parties no option but to take the matter to court. Other observers note that Congress and the courts have largely been willing allies in the expansion of the federal bench into the legislative arena. Unwilling to trust agency regulators under Republican administrations, Democratic majorities in Congress repeatedly turned to the courts to help put teeth into increasingly complex and detailed legislation in the 1970s and 1980s. Yet other analysts emphasize the influence of interest groups to whom Congress and the president are responding when they approve legislation.

Each of these interpretations seems to fit at least some major legislation. Members of Congress have certainly tried to use the courts when they have lacked the political support to secure policy goals through legislation. As just discussed, failed efforts by members to enforce the War Powers Resolution in the courts show the limits of enticing the courts to resolve political controversies. But Congress's tendency to draw the courts into the policy arena also reflects the cumbersome nature of legislating under divided government. Unable to procure favorable outcomes from regulators, members of Congress and organized groups have deliberately sought the assistance of the courts in battling administrators.

Congressional Resources and Strategies

Congress has formidable tools for dealing with an unfriendly federal judiciary. The framers of the Constitution left several tools for Congress and the president to check the actions of the courts. Lifetime tenure of federal judges is intended to provide some autonomy to the courts, as is the prohibition against reducing the compensation of judges. But neither Congress nor the president has been willing to give a free hand to the federal judiciary. Congress has used its constitutional authority to impeach federal judges, change the number of judges and courts, set the courts' budgets, and alter the appellate jurisdiction of the Supreme Court. Perhaps most familiar to even casual observers of American politics, the president and Congress frequently struggle over appointments to the federal bench.

In addition, Congress has responded legislatively to court decisions. Congress often enacts new legislation that is adapted to court rulings. For example, in 1993 Congress enacted the Religious Freedom and Restoration Act – a direct refutation of the Court's decision in *Oregon v. Smith* (1990), which dealt with religious practice and federal unemployment benefits. When Congress objects to a court's interpretation of a law, Congress sometimes passes a new bill that clarifies its intentions. In some cases, Congress adjusts the new legislation to take into account a court's ruling about the constitutionality of certain kinds of provisions. In recent years, several bills have been introduced in Congress to remove federal court jurisdiction from certain policy areas. And, of course, Congress may propose a constitutional amendment to overrule the courts' interpretation of an existing provision.

Congress and the Structure of the Federal Judiciary

The Constitution vests judicial power in the Supreme Court but grants to Congress the authority to establish inferior courts when it chooses. The size, budget, and appellate jurisdiction of the Supreme Court, as well as the structure, size, budget, and jurisdiction of lower courts, are determined by law and are therefore subject to the normal legislative process. In addition, Congress is authorized by the Constitution to create what are known as Article I courts, or legislative courts – the military courts, tax court, customs courts, and bankruptcy courts. These courts are located in either the executive or judicial branches, the judges are appointed by the president with Senate confirmation, and the judges serve fixed, limited terms.

Partisan politics has been an ever-present condition in Congress's handling of the judiciary. The first major effort to structure the courts for political purposes occurred in 1801, when the defeated president John Adams and his Federalist supporters in Congress created new circuit court judgeships to be filled with Federalists. The effort to influence the character of the federal bench failed, however, when the new Republican Congress repealed the act and abolished the judgeships. Even though Congress postponed the next meeting of the Supreme Court to prevent it from hearing a challenge to its repeal, the Court upheld Congress's power to repeal the Federalists' Judiciary Act of 1801 a year later.

Congress has only once limited the jurisdiction of the Supreme Court. In 1868, striking down parts of Reconstruction legislation in 1866, the court was scheduled to hear another case on Reconstruction law – the Habeas Corpus Act, which concerned the rights of individuals held in detention. Anticipating that the Court would use the occasion to find all Reconstruction laws unconstitutional, Congress enacted a law to prevent the

Court from hearing cases related to the Habeas Corpus Act. The Supreme Court, incidentally, backed down from any confrontation with Congress when it upheld the constitutionality of the repeal of its jurisdiction a year later.

With the exception of the Reconstruction-era episode, efforts to curb the Supreme Court's jurisdiction have failed. This result is not too surprising. After all, the House, Senate, and president, or two-thirds of both houses of Congress, must agree to legislation curbing Court jurisdiction before it is enacted. Nevertheless, members of Congress continue to introduce bills that would restrict the jurisdiction of the Supreme Court or all federal courts. Between 1975 and 2002, according to one count, 132 bills were introduced to limit the federal judiciary's jurisdiction in some way. While none of these efforts were successful, and none have been since then, many members see them as an opportunity to demonstrate to judges that Congress can limit jurisdiction, and these efforts are often popular with constituents.

Congress also has had a mixed record in efforts to control the Supreme Court by changing its size. In the nineteenth century, Congress used its power over the size of the Court several times to exert pressure on the Court and to help change its ideological shape. Although Presidents James Madison, James Monroe, and John Quincy Adams each claimed that a growing nation needed a larger Supreme Court (that started with just six members), Congress did not change the Court's size until 1837. Even then, it postponed the change to nine members until the last day of President Andrew Jackson's term that year. Later, by increasing the size of the Court to ten justices, Congress gave President Abraham Lincoln an opportunity to solidify a pro-Union majority on the Court. Soon thereafter, Congress reduced the number of justices from ten to eight to prevent President Andrew Johnson from filling any vacancies. When Johnson's successor, Ulysses S. Grant, took office, Congress changed the number of justices to nine, where it has remained.

The best-known attempt to influence Supreme Court decisions by altering its size was the "court-packing" plan of President Franklin Roosevelt. Roosevelt, disturbed by rulings that struck down important parts of his New Deal legislation, proposed in 1937 that the Supreme Court be expanded from nine to 15 justices so that he could appoint new justices and change the balance of opinion. Congressional resistance, as well as a series of Supreme Court decisions more favorable to Roosevelt's New Deal legislation, led Roosevelt to drop his plan. But the uproar over the Roosevelt plan has had a chilling effect on other presidents and Congresses that might have pushed legislation to alter the size of the Court for political purposes.

The Senate and Judicial Nominations

The shared power of appointment remains the primary means by which senators and presidents influence federal courts. Needless to say, the president and the Senate do not always agree on what course federal courts ought to take. Historically, this battle was largely fought over presidential nominations to the Supreme Court, with the nominations of Judge Robert H. Bork in 1987 and Judge Clarence Thomas in 1991 standing out as particularly controversial. As we explore in the following section, recent years have seen the controversies extend to appointments to the lower courts.

LOWER COURT NOMINATIONS. Senators of a president's party typically have had a great deal of influence over the president's appointments to federal district courts and the courts of appeal (see box "The Changing Congress"). These senators usually play an active role in the nominating process by suggesting acceptable candidates to the administration. But only a few senators usually play an active role in Senate deliberations considering judicial appointments at the district level. Unlike nominations to the Supreme Court, and more recently circuit courts, which elicit much broader interest, district court seats generally draw fairly localized interest from the Senate body. In most cases, the Senate's Judiciary Committee staff studies lower-court nominees, receives reports from the American Bar Association and the Federal Bureau of Investigation, and routinely recommends approval to the full Senate, which confirms the nominees with little or no discussion.

The record of judicial appointments during the Reagan and G. H. W. Bush presidencies continued the pattern of routine approval for most nominees, but with the addition of a few very controversial cases. During the course of the Reagan and G. H. W. Bush presidencies, more than 460 appointments were made to appeals and district courts, meaning that by the end of the Bush administration, more than 70 percent of sitting federal judges had been appointed during the Reagan and Bush years. These appointments have produced a much more conservative federal bench. Although the Democrats controlled the Senate for more than half the period, they largely acquiesced to presidential preferences for more conservative, younger, white federal judges. Not until the few months before the 1992 presidential election did Senator Joseph Biden (D-Delaware) and the Judiciary Committee take a more aggressive stance against the administration's nominees, apparently emboldened by the possibility that Democrat Bill Clinton would win the presidency. After suggesting that he would be more selective about which

THE CHANGING CONGRESS: "REVERSE FILIBUSTER" HIGHLIGHTS INCREASED PARTISANSHIP ON JUDICIAL NOMINEES

Lacking a majority on the Senate Judiciary Committee, Senate Democrats in 2003 refused to allow a floor vote on some of President G. W. Bush's lower court nominees. Senate Republicans, who had the slimmest of majorities in the 108th Senate (51), were short of the 60 votes needed to invoke cloture, or end debate, on these nominees. Although they pursued several options to change Senate rules regarding filibusters on judicial nominees, Senate Republicans remained frustrated by their inability to gain up or down votes on some judicial nominations. In an attempt to raise public awareness of the impasse on these nominations, in November 2003 Senate Republicans staged a 39-hour continuous debate seeking to highlight Democratic obstruction. The marathon debate, labeled a "reverse filibuster" by its organizers, was ironic in that it used extended debate to highlight real or threatened obstruction by some members of the Democratic Party. Senate Republican leaders hoped that the event would attract enough publicity to increase public pressure on Senate Democrats to agree to vote on the stalled nominees and would increase public support for their efforts to reform the filibuster rule.

Instead, the event turned into political theatre, with lots of melodrama, but nothing of substance accomplished. Republicans labeled the session a "Justice for Judges" marathon, complete with T-shirt and signs bearing the slogan, while Democrats countered with a large sign emblazoned "168–4" – representing the number of Bush's judges confirmed (168) and the number blocked (4). Cots were set up for tired senators, beer was provided for the reporters covering the event, Democrat Tom Harkin posted a sign reading, "I'll Be Home Watching 'The Bachelor'," and a filibuster bingo game was unveiled. At the end of the marathon session, it did not appear that much had changed; none of the judges in question received a vote in the Senate, and there was no noticeable public outcry. In fact, one of the police officers standing guard outside the Senate summed up the likely opinion of most members of the public, stating: "I could see if it was something important like the budget or Iraq, but who cares about judicial appointments?"

Bush nominees would receive hearings before the election, Biden and the Judiciary Committee slowed down the pace of confirmation hearings for appellate court appointments.

When Bill Clinton assumed the presidency, he had 99 seats on the federal bench to fill – seats that observers expected would be filled by a greater proportion of minorities and women than were those filled by Bush and Reagan. With a Democratic majority in the Senate during his first two years in office, Clinton was successful in getting rapid confirmations. But after the

---

Congressionally Speaking...

Senatorial courtesy is the practice of conferring with senators of the president's party whenever a vacancy in a position subject to presidential appointment is located within the senators' state. The practice applies to vacancies in federal district courts. For many years, senators could exercise a virtual veto over appointments affecting their states. The practice rests on the willingness of the Senate and its Judiciary Committee to refuse to act on nominees opposed by those senators. It gives senators a form of patronage with which to reward political friends.

Senatorial courtesy is institutionalized through the use of *blue slips* – blue sheets of paper sent out by the Judiciary Committee asking senators from a nominee's home state his or her opinion of the nominee. A home state senator who objects to a nominee will often write on the blue slip that the nominee is "personally offensive." This practice has existed since the early 1910s, with negative blue slips usually meaning that the Judiciary Committee will not act on a nominee. While not always the case today, a negative blue slip usually makes confirmation of the nominee extremely difficult.

Republicans took majority control of the Senate in 1995, the speed of Senate confirmations declined markedly. In 1998, Chief Justice William Rehnquist complained about the slow pace, noting that 101 judicial nominees had been confirmed in 1994 but only 17 were confirmed in 1996 and 36 in 1997.

Many vacancies had gone unfilled for more than 18 months, with some going up to four years between nomination and confirmation. Senate Judiciary Committee Chairman Orrin Hatch (R-Utah) insisted that the Republican Senate had been just as responsive as the Democrats had been for President G. H. W. Bush, and the battle has continued into the administration of G. W. Bush. In all, the confirmation rate for lower court judges has declined markedly in the past two decades, going from 90 percent in the Carter administration to less than 75 percent in the Clinton administration. Presidents Clinton and G. W. Bush have seen only around 50 percent of their circuit court nominees receive Senate confirmation.

The influence of partisanship in appointment to the lower courts is clear. More than 90 percent of nominees to the lower courts are affiliated with the party of the president nominating them. Moreover, lower-court nominees in the fourth year of a four-year presidential term are much less likely to be confirmed than are nominees sent to the Senate in other years, and the confirmation process typically takes much longer when the Senate and presidency are controlled by different parties. At the end of a president's term, senators of the opposition party often prefer to leave judgeships vacant until they see which party wins the presidency. If their party wins the presidency, the new president can submit new names – presumably more to their liking.

SUPREME COURT NOMINATIONS. As the Miers/Alito spectacle described in the introduction points out, Supreme Court nominations are not routine. Unlike the appointment process for district court seats, presidential nominations to the Supreme Court garner a much broader spectrum of interest across the Senate. In fact, lower court nominees are often screened more carefully if they are thought to be potential Supreme Court nominees. After a president makes a nomination, the Senate Judiciary Committee has the nominee complete a lengthy questionnaire, orders its staff to conduct an extensive background investigation on the nominee, receives an evaluation from the American Bar Association, and then holds several days of hearings. Recently interest groups have actively lobbied senators and generated publicity for the groups' views. The administration, which sometimes discusses a list of possible nominees with senators in advance of the nomination, coaches the nominee in preparation for the hearings.

The outcomes of Supreme Court confirmation efforts hinge on numerous factors. First, the partisan makeup of the Senate matters. When the president's party has been in the majority, close to 90 percent of nominees have been confirmed. In contrast, during times of divided government, only 59 percent of nominees have been approved by the Senate. Second, the timing of the nomination also has implications. Not only does partisanship in Congress tend to increase in election years, but the president's influence in the legislative arena usually declines during the course of his term in office. Presidents also appear to be more successful when they make public statements on behalf of their nominees. Overall weakness of a president clearly affects his ability to get a nominee approved by the Senate. Reagan nominated Robert Bork in 1987 after the revelations of the Iran-Contra scandal had significantly weakened the president's standing in Congress and public approval. Bork was turned down by the Senate.

Timing is important from other perspectives as well. Many argue that senators up for reelection give greater weight to public opinion than do senators who do not face reelection in the near future. But most senators appear to take into account the qualifications and ideological outlook of nominees. The greater the distance from his or her own positions and the less qualified the nominee, the lower the probability of a senator's voting in favor of the president's choice. The appearance of one or more of these factors – partisan balance, presidential popularity, lateness in presidential term, ideological

placement, or nominee qualifications – increases the likelihood of conflict in
the Senate during the confirmation process. On many confirmation votes,
individual senators are also likely to be influenced by constituency concerns.
In the case of Thurgood Marshall and Clarence Thomas's nominations to
the Court, state racial composition had a determinative effect on votes by
senators representing states with large African American populations.

The Senate has failed to confirm only 26, or about 20 percent, of presidents' nominations to the Supreme Court. Twentieth-century presidents
have had better luck than their predecessors, but even recent presidents have
stumbled. President Lyndon Johnson was forced to withdraw two nominations, two nominees of President Richard Nixon were rejected, President
Reagan withdrew one nomination and one nominee was rejected, and both
Presidents G. H. W. and G. W. Bush withdrew one name. Two nominations
deserve special mention: President Reagan's nomination of Robert Bork,
which was rejected by the Senate, and President G. H. W. Bush's nomination of Clarence Thomas, which was approved by a narrow margin, 52 to 48.

In 1987, President Reagan faced a Democratic Senate when he nominated Judge Bork, then a judge on the U.S. Court of Appeals for the District of Columbia and a former solicitor general and law school professor.
Bork's longstanding and well-published opposition to affirmative action and
the established ruling on abortion, along with his judicial activism, stimulated an extraordinary and influential effort by civil rights groups and others
to prevent his confirmation by the Senate. Interest in his nomination stimulated unprecedented scrutiny by the media – the media even reported Bork's
videotape rentals. The Senate voted 58 to 42 against his confirmation.

Four years later, President Bush nominated Clarence Thomas, also a sitting judge on the U.S. Court of Appeals for the District of Columbia, and a
former chair of the Equal Employment Opportunity Commission (EEOC).
Thomas had relatively little judicial experience: He had been on the appeals
court for only 18 months and had never argued a case before a court. The
American Bar Association's review committee rated him "qualified" on their
three-point scale (highly qualified, qualified, and not qualified), with two
members of the committee voting "not qualified," making Thomas the only
Supreme Court nominee rated by the Bar Association to receive such a
weak evaluation. Thomas had a record of commitment to conservative views
on many issues, leading liberal groups to mobilize against him and drawing
tough questions from the liberal Democrats on the Judiciary Committee.

Nevertheless, Thomas's confirmation seemed likely until the eve of the
scheduled vote by the full Senate. National Public Radio reported that
a complaint of sexual misconduct against Thomas had been disclosed to

Judiciary Committee staff and noted in an FBI report, although it had not been mentioned in the initial committee hearings. The committee reopened the hearings to listen to the testimony of Anita Hill, a University of Oklahoma law professor who had worked for Thomas at the EEOC. At the hearings, she repeated her charges against Thomas. He responded, and the committee heard character witnesses for both Thomas and Hill, all before a very large national television audience.

After Thomas was confirmed by the full Senate by a vote of 52–48, the committee and the Senate were criticized for the manner in which they had conducted the hearings. Senator Arlen Specter ran into difficulty in his 1992 reelection bid because of the way he had grilled Professor Hill. In response to the criticism, Senator Biden announced changes in Judiciary Committee practice guaranteeing that all information received by a committee and its staff would be placed in the nominee's FBI file to ensure all senators access to FBI reports and provide for closed briefings for all senators so that any charges against nominees, if there were any, could be reviewed. And, in a conspicuous move to make sure that any sexism on the committee would be held in check, two women – Senators Dianne Feinstein (D-California) and Carol Moseley-Braun (D-Illinois) – were appointed to the committee in 1993.

Congress and the Impeachment of Judges

Under the Constitution, judges "shall hold their offices during good behaviour," but the House is empowered to bring and vote on impeachment charges against judges. If a judge is impeached by the House, the Senate conducts a trial on the charges. A two-thirds vote of the senators present is required to convict and remove a judge – the same number required for removing a president from office. Removal of a judge by House impeachment and Senate conviction is rare. Over the course of the history of the federal bench, no Supreme Court justice has been removed from office by Congress. In 1804, Republicans tried to impeach Justice Samuel Chase on several charges, but they failed to get a two-thirds vote to convict. Thirteen lower federal judges have been impeached by the House, and only seven have been convicted by the Senate. Of the seven judicial convictions, three have occurred since 1986.

Congress's impeachment power has not proven to be a source of leverage over the courts. Even the threat of impeachment has only once been credited with inducing a change in Supreme Court membership: Justice Abe Fortas resigned in 1969 after revelations of questionable financial practices.

Impeachment trials do pose certain challenges for a Senate already having trouble managing its time and discharging its duties. Any trial procedure involving the full Senate inevitably distracts the Senate from its legislative agenda. To address this problem, the Senate moved in 1986 to form a special 12-member committee to gather and review evidence on behalf of the full Senate.

Legislative Responses to the Courts

Interaction between Congress and the courts does not necessarily end with judicial action. Congress can, of course, use its traditional legislative powers to respond to court decisions. For example, after the Supreme Court decided in 1988 that burning the U.S. flag in protest of government policy should be afforded First Amendment protection as a form of political speech, Congress eventually enacted a statute designed to strip flag burning of its constitutional protection. In another case, Congress overrode a presidential veto to reverse a Supreme Court decision concerning sex discrimination in colleges and universities.

But successful reversals of unpopular Supreme Court decisions are not automatic. On some occasions, efforts to reverse decisions pass one chamber and get stalled in the other. Other efforts often get stymied at the committee level, after hearings are held on possible legislation to reverse the decision.

Studies show that Congress responds to about one-third of these Supreme Court moves to nullify a federal law. Why? The three-institution legislative game makes a response to the Court difficult. All three institutions must agree, or at least two-thirds of both chambers must agree, to any legislative response. If the committees with jurisdiction over the affected legislation recognize that gaining the approval of the House, Senate, and president is impossible, they may choose to take no action. Nevertheless, Congress sometimes does respond to court decisions. Several factors appear to motivate congressional efforts to respond to court decisions. One study emphasizes the important role of public opinion in motivating Congress to act. If the majority of public opinion is in favor of action by Congress, the probability of a congressional response increases dramatically. Salience of the issue to organized interest groups, sometimes indicated by the participation of groups in the case before the Supreme Court, also appears to influence congressional decisions to respond. In many cases, however, members seem to have been motivated to take preliminary steps to respond to demands, but they did not push the legislation to the point of passage.

Not surprisingly, Congress is also more likely to respond to Supreme Court decisions when invited to do so by judges on the bench. On occasion, the Court rules that although particular provisions are unconstitutional, Congress could remedy the problem by rewriting the provision. In effect, the Supreme Court outlines the boundaries of what changes would be considered constitutional. Such guidance by the courts markedly increases the chances that Congress will undertake efforts to respond to or reverse the nullifying decision. Judicial invitations to review give a different cast to relations between Congress and the courts. Far from the conflict that many normally assume exists when the Court overturns a federal law, these invitations to reverse reflect a more cooperative relationship between the branches.

Amending the Constitution

A frequent response of members to court decisions is to propose a constitutional amendment. Since the Supreme Court's decision in *Roe* v. *Wade* (1973), for example, many members have supported a constitutional amendment that would reserve to the states the power to regulate abortions. The constitutional requirement that an amendment receive the support of two-thirds of both chambers before it is sent to the states for ratification sets a high threshold that has seldom been met. Only four amendments to the Constitution were adopted in direct response to Supreme Court decisions: the Eleventh Amendment, on the ability of citizens of one state to bring suit against another state; the Fourteenth Amendment, on the application of the first 10 amendments to the states; the Sixteenth Amendment, on the federal income tax; and the Twenty-sixth Amendment, on the right of 18-year-olds to vote. Recently, President Bush has advocated a constitutional amendment that would ban marriage between two individuals of the same sex, in response to same-sex marriage laws in Massachusetts and other states. As of this writing, the proposed amendment has not passed either chamber of Congress and many states themselves have moved to ban same-sex marriages.

Conclusion

The courts occupy a critical, but often overlooked, place in forming national policy. The roles played by the courts vary widely – from separation-of-powers umpire to congressional overseer and partner in policy making.

Relationships between the branches clearly depend on the rules of the game. But those rules, as we have seen, are themselves often the product of political battles. The rules of the policy-making process can be ambiguous, and this ambiguity gives the courts an opening into the legislative game. As a result, members of Congress have an incentive to watch over the actions of courts carefully and, on occasion, to enlist judges in their campaigns against a recalcitrant executive branch.

Judges, however, are not always willing to take the bait. Sometimes, the courts smell a political contest and send the dispute back to congressional players to resolve themselves. Other times, judges simply define respective powers of each contending actor and set boundaries for future interactions between the players. Although Congress and the president can shape the membership of the bench, other congressional tools rarely give members enough leverage over the courts to limit judicial independence and discretion. When the courts have chosen to enter the policy process, however, major changes in policy making have often occurred. Whether expanding procedural rights of individuals or forcing executive agencies to work more assiduously to follow congressional intent, federal courts in recent decades have made inroads into the legislative arena. Attention to the interactions of judges, legislators, and executives thus markedly affects our understanding of how separate branches are indeed sharing power to shape national policy.

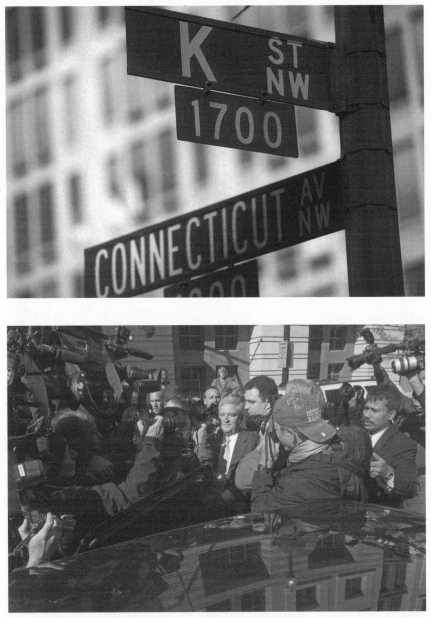

Above: A photograph of a street sign identifying K Street, the Washington, D.C., thoroughfare known for being the nation's epicenter of lobbying firms.
Below: Former Rep. Bob Ney struggles to get to his car outside the U.S. District Court in Washington after pleading guilty to making false statements and conspiracy to commit fraud, making him the first member of Congress to be convicted in association with the wide-ranging Jack Abramoff lobbying scandal.

11

Congress, Lobbyists, and Interest Groups

THE FIRST AMENDMENT TO THE CONSTITUTION PROVIDES THAT CONGRESS may make no law abridging the right of the people to petition the government for a redress of grievances. Court rulings interpret the Amendment broadly to include organized and paid representatives of the people, therefore limiting Congress's ability to regulate lobbying. In practice, interest groups and their lobbyists are a very important means by which the public conveys their expectations and demands to Congress. Nevertheless, Americans believe that members of Congress are beholden to special interests and lobbyists. A 2004 survey conducted by the Center on Congress at Indiana University found that only 49 percent of the public believes that congressional representatives have their constituents' interests in mind when casting roll call votes; over 63 percent of citizens believe that representatives are mindful of special interests when making policy decisions.[1] A 2006 CBS/*New York Times* survey found that 75 percent of Americans agreed that most members of Congress are more interested in serving special interest groups than the people they represent.[2]

These contrasting views – lobbyists are essential to democracy and yet reviled by the public – give interest groups and lobbyists an uneasy place in congressional politics. In earlier chapters, we have noted that representation of organized interests is a rapidly growing industry in Washington. In this chapter, we reemphasize this theme, discuss the evolving strategies of interest groups, and review the limited efforts of Congress to regulate lobbying. Congress, in accordance with the Constitution, has been able to put in place only minimal regulations on lobbying. As an alternative, Congress has placed more severe restrictions on legislators, as it is allowed to do, in their relations with organized interests. Restrictions on campaign contributions from organized interests were detailed in Chapter 3. In this chapter, we concentrate on developments in the legislative strategies of groups and lobbyists.

The Expanding Community of Lobbyists and Interest Groups

Lobbyists have been present since the first Congresses. The wide reach of federal policy and Congress's central role in shaping it motivates many citizens, organized groups, and lobbyists to converge on Washington (see box "Congressionally Speaking..."). Congress's internal decision-making processes are largely responsible for this. Reliance on committees and subcommittees for writing the details of most legislation gives outsiders many points of contact with legislators and staff. Even congressional parties are quite permeable. Many legislators influence party strategies through their participation in party caucuses, committees, and task forces. If legislators can be influenced, so too can party strategies. The vast institutional partitioning of Congress (i.e., bicameralism, parties, committees, subcommittees, etc.) gives lobbyists more opportunities for influence than they find in most other national legislatures. The more complex the legislative process and the more places that interests can be protected, the more valuable the experienced lobbyist is to the average citizen.

Generalizing about lobbyists is difficult. Some lobbyists are officials of organized interest groups such as the U.S. Chamber of Commerce, the Sierra Club, and the National Cable Television Association. Other lobbyists are lawyers, former members or staff of Congress, or public relations specialists who have their own lobbying firms that are hired by interest groups, corporations, or other organizations to represent their interests, sometimes on a specific bill or issue. Many lobbyists work for universities and colleges, state and local governments, and even foreign governments that seek to influence federal policy. Frequently, lobbyists are citizens who have made the trip to Washington to make their case in person. As discussed later in this chapter, important legal distinctions are made between those hired to lobby for a person or organization and concerned citizens that lobby on their own behalf.

Most interest groups represent occupational or organizational communities. Occupational groups include organizations representing doctors, teachers, accountants, and even association executives. Government employees have many specialized interest groups – the American Association of State Highway and Transportation Officials, for example. Many, perhaps most, interest groups are associations comprised of organizations. Most trade associations, such as the American Petroleum Institute, the Association of American Railroads, and the National Association of Wholesaler-Distributors, represent corporations in a particular sector of the economy. But associations representing member unions, universities, local governments, and other organizations are important as well. The Association of American Universities and the National League of Cities are prominent examples.

Congressionally Speaking...

Lobbyist is a term that referred originally to reporters waiting in the lobby of the British House of Commons to speak to members of Parliament. In the mid-nineteenth century, the term came to be used for people seeking to influence legislators and soon gained quite negative connotations because of the money and other resources with which lobbyists plied legislators.

Today, a lobbyist has a more technical meaning in federal law – someone who is paid to communicate with Congress on behalf of others. And lobbyists now see themselves as specialized professionals. They even have their own professional association, the American League of Lobbyists.

Citizens' groups compose about 20 percent of the interest group community. Their members generally are individuals rather than representatives of organizations or institutions. Political scientist Jack Walker observed that these groups usually arise in the wake of broad social movements concerned with such problems as the level of environmental pollution, threats to civil rights, or changes in the status of women. Citizens' groups include Citizens for Tax Justice, Common Cause, the National Association for the Advancement of Colored People, the National Organization for Women, and Ralph Nader's Public Citizen.

Citizens' groups often are created by political entrepreneurs operating with the support of wealthy individuals, private foundations, or elected political leaders who act as their protectors, financial supporters, and patrons. It is common to see a few individuals bearing much of the cost of group formation. Such an arrangement is often essential to overcoming the numerous obstacles associated with collective action.

The greatest dilemma that interest groups encounter in the formation process is that of free riders – individuals who consume the benefits of a public good without paying a fair share of the costs of its production. All groups seek to attract members by appealing to a sense of obligation to support a cause, but often that is not enough to attract and retain members. Some groups overcome this problem by offering selective benefits restricted to those who contribute. For example, members of the AARP (formerly the American Association of Retired Persons but now using just the initials) receive a variety of benefits including discounts on airfare, car rentals, hotels, and cruises, as well as reasonably priced legal services and health care. Others offer special events, club memberships, or other social benefits to attract members.

The size of the lobbying and interest group community has expanded tremendously in recent decades. The *Encyclopedia of Associations* listed more than 22,400 organizations in 2003, which marks a more than 50 percent increase in the number of interest groups since 1980 and an almost 400 percent increase since 1955.[3] The most rapid documented growth in interest groups occurred between the 1960s and 1980s, during which many federal programs were created and expanded. During this period, the interest group community became significantly more diverse as well. Along with the rapid expansion and diversification of the interest group community came a proliferation of organizations settling in Washington. A 1982 survey of 2,800 organizations that had lobbying offices in Washington found that 40 percent had been created since 1960 and an additional 25 percent since 1970.[4] One analyst found that the number of Washington offices for trade associations – the National Association of Manufacturers and the National Independent Retail Jewelers, for example – nearly tripled from about 1,200 in 1960 to 3,500 in 1986. Even greater proportionate growth in the number of corporations with offices in Washington occurred in the same period.[5]

Since the 1990s, the size of the interest group community has remained relatively stable. Nevertheless, the number of groups with Washington representation continues to grow, which points to the significance of lobbying in modern day politics. Today, nearly 5,000 organizations have some kind of representation in Washington. In 2007, the privately published directory *Washington Representatives* listed more than 18,000 "persons working to influence government policies and actions" – a number that has more than quadrupled since the early 1970s.[6] Even with these soaring numbers, it appears that there is no shortage of demand for their services. Between 2000 and 2005, by one account, D.C. lobbyists increased their fees to new clients by as much as 100 percent.[7]

Many factors have contributed to the proliferation of the interest group community and lobbying activity. Among the most important factors is the rapid social and economic change characteristic of recent decades. The expanding role of federal programs and regulation motivated individuals, firms, and local governments to organize and lobby. A series of social movements, such as civil rights, women's rights, environmental protection, and consumer rights, swept the country, redefined the nation's policy agenda, and spawned lasting interest groups. And organization spurred counter-organization. For example, Planned Parenthood was challenged by the National Right to Life Committee. The consequence of organization and counter-organization was the proliferation of strongly issue-oriented citizens' groups and greater diversity in the kinds of groups found in Washington.

While citizens' groups have changed the contours of Washington lobbying, the interest group community remains dominated, at least numerically, by business groups. By one estimate, 70 percent of organized interests in Washington are business groups. Nevertheless, the growth of citizens' groups does mean that business interests are more likely to be challenged and challenged successfully.

An enlarged middle class and technological advances also contributed to the growth of the Washington interest group community. The middle class has become an important base of support for occupational and citizens' groups that depend on membership dues and other contributions for financial support. Technological advances in communications and computer-generated mailings have facilitated the growth of groups that require support from the general public. Also, advances in communication and transportation have made it more convenient and affordable for groups to headquarter in Washington, far from concentrations of their members.

Finally, the federal government is responsible for directly stimulating the creation of some groups and underwriting their costs of operations. Much of the domestic legislation of the 1960s and 1970s required some kind of citizen participation in executive agency rule making or provided for the creation of community-based groups. Many interest groups representing citizen, environmental action groups, and legal and health care organizations for the poor were stimulated by these public policies. Indeed, the activists running many of the new social programs vigorously promoted the creation of new organizations to represent their clients' interests. In other cases, federal agencies encouraged the formation of groups to facilitate communication between the agencies and the sector they served and to build a base of support for their own programs and budgets. Additionally, as federal domestic programs expanded, many more citizens' groups received grants or contracts from the federal government to conduct studies or perform services for executive agencies.

The enlarged community of lobbyists and interest groups has altered the political environment of members of Congress in important ways. The most obvious effect is that the expanded lobbying community has increased the diversity and intensity of demands placed on members of Congress. Issues of even modest importance are more likely to generate conflict among groups, and no one group is as likely to dominate policy making as was often the case at mid-twentieth century. There is now greater uncertainty about the mix of organized interests that will seek to influence congressional action and hold members accountable for their individual actions.

Developments in Interest Group Strategies

Influencing Congress involves much more than gaining the votes of individual members. Lobbyists work hard to find legislators who are willing to

FAMILY MEMBERS AS LOBBYISTS

A recent trend among organized interest groups is to hire the relatives of key congressional members and their top aides as lobbyists on a variety of issues. A 2005 study of the 94 members of the House and Senate appropriations committees and their 250 top staffers found that spending bills reflected the lobbying efforts of family members. Specifically, the study found 30 instances in which a relative lobbied for money in an appropriations bill that his or her family member or family member's boss helped write. In 22 of these cases, the relative was successful in obtaining funds – a total of roughly $750 million in projects.

Examples of such activity abound. In 2006, for instance, Senator Byron Dorgan (D-North Dakota) fought fervently to maintain the federal estate tax. It was later reported that the life insurance industry, a leading proponent of the estate tax, had employed Dorgan's wife as a lobbyist since 1999. That same year, Senator Elizabeth Dole (R-North Carolina) was an outspoken advocate of President George W. Bush's unpopular proposal to allow a Dubai company to assume operations at six major U.S. ports. Unbeknownst to most at the time was the fact that her husband, former senator Bob Dole, had been hired to lobby on behalf of the same company.

Critics have argued that using family members in such a manner creates a significant conflict of interest. A provision of the Senate's 2007 lobbying reform bill (S. 1) addresses this matter. It stipulates that a member and his or her staff are prohibited from having any official contact with any relative of the member who is a registered lobbyist. An exception is granted to the spouse of a member who has served as a registered lobbyist at least one year prior to the member's election or at least one year prior to marrying the member. Should this bill be passed into law, only one senator, Senator Kent Conrad (D-North Dakota), is affected by this rule. As of the time of this writing, the House has not taken equivalent action.

To avoid generating controversy, however, many of the members have publicly adopted policies that prohibit family members from lobbying their office and staff.

Source: Based on information from Matt Kelley and Peter Eisler, "Relatives Have 'Inside Track' in Lobbying for Tax Dollars," *USA Today*, October 17, 2006; John Solomon, "Lawmakers' Lobbying Spouses Avoid Hill Reforms," *Washington Post*, January 17, 2007.

champion their causes. Lobbyists need members to introduce their proposals as legislation, to offer amendments in committee and on the floor, and to help them get issues on, or keep issues off, the agendas of committees and subcommittees.

Moreover, lobbyists spend more time gathering, digesting, and reporting information to their clients than they do trying to influence Congress. They help their clients anticipate and track legislative developments that are difficult for people not experienced in congressional politics to follow. Because congressional politics and federal policy are so much more complex and important than they were a few decades ago, corporations and other organizations need the assistance of experienced insiders to observe and interpret congressional activity that might affect their interests. A good lobbyist seeks to develop access to well-placed members and staff on Capitol Hill to meet the demands of his or her clients for information.

Lobbyists employ a wide range of techniques, which have evolved as lobbyists have adapted to changes in technology, society, and Congress. The empowerment of House subcommittees in the 1970s, the greater individualism in the membership, and expansion of congressional staffs since the mid-twentieth century have forced lobbyists to develop relationships with more members and staff and follow the activity of more committees and subcommittees. At the same time, developments in electronic communications and computers have enabled lobbyists and interest groups to reach people throughout the country with ease.

These developments have stimulated important changes in the way lobbyists do their work. Many observers of Washington politics have noted the change from inside lobbying, or face-to-face efforts to influence a few important legislators, to outside strategies, or public relations efforts to generate public support for special interest causes. Perhaps more accurately, outside strategies have supplemented the old-style inside strategies that once dominated Washington lobbying.

Inside Lobbying

The more traditional form of lobbying – inside lobbying – involves personal contact between a lobbyist and members of Congress. Successful lobbyists use access to important decision makers, a network of contacts, mastery of the process, policy expertise, Washington experience, and money to develop strong ties to legislators and their staffs. Their success often depends on their being able to phone a prominent member of Congress, get the call returned promptly, and gather critical intelligence about when an issue will be raised or which member is wavering on an important provision. An aide to a former House Speaker characterized the work of the inside lobbyist this way:

> They know members of Congress are here three nights a week, alone, without their families. So they say, "Let's have dinner. Let's go see a ballgame." Shmooze

with them. Make friends. And they don't lean on it all the time. Every once in a
while, they call up – maybe once or twice a year – ask a few questions. Call you
up and say, "Say, what's Danny [Rostenkowski, chair of the House Ways and
Means Committee] going to do on this tax-reform bill?" Anne Wexler [a former
official in the Carter White House, and now a lobbyist] will call up and spend
half an hour talking about left-wing politics, and suddenly she'll pop a question,
pick up something. They want that little bit of access. That's what does it. You
can hear it. It clicks home. They'll call their chief executive officer, and they've
delivered. That's how it works. It's not illegal. They work on a personal basis.[8]

Career Washingtonians – former members, former executive branch officials, and even some family members of prominent public officials who have
developed personal friendships with members and their staffs – are greatly
advantaged in direct lobbying. Former members are particularly advantaged
because they retain special privileges of access on Capitol Hill – access to the
House and Senate floors, gyms, and dining rooms. They also benefit from the
political and policy expertise gained from service in Congress, a certain visibility in Washington and in the country, and their established contacts with
people and organizations with money. In 2006, the Center for Responsible
Politics identified 155 registered lobbyists as former members of Congress.

Former congressional staff aides and federal employees share many of the
advantages and knowledge enjoyed by former members, so they also make
ideal lobbyists. In 2000, for instance, the pharmaceutical industry, a powerful
interest in Washington, hired a total of 625 Washington lobbyists, nearly half
of whom were formerly employed in either congressional offices or other federal positions.[9] Many of these individuals developed numerous and strong
connections while working on the Hill. One study finds that of the more than
1,600 bills that the top 20 drug corporations and the industry's two trade
groups – PhRMA and the Biotechnology Industry Organization – reported
lobbying between 1998 and 2004, more than 50 percent of those bills were
sponsored by members who had been lobbied by their former staff aides.[10]
Because staff aides and federal employees develop contacts and skills that
make them attractive to law firms, corporations, and lobbying firms, many
individuals enter jobs on the Hill with the intent of going to these other
more lucrative positions (see box "Limits on Lobbying after Leaving Capitol
Hill").

Beyond personal relations, money and information are essential ingredi-
ents of successful inside strategies. Money, of course, can be used as an
outright bribe, though it seldom is any longer. But money has been a vital
asset to gaining access to legislators. In recent years, money has allowed
lobbyists to arrange for members to take trips to exclusive resorts to attend

LIMITS ON LOBBYING AFTER LEAVING CAPITOL HILL

The exchange of personnel between high-level public and private sector positions is commonly referred to as the *revolving door*. Upon leaving their positions within government, former members of Congress as well as congressional staffers and employees of the federal government frequently enter private sector positions to serve as lobbyists. Furthermore, it is often the case that individuals in top positions within industries are called upon to fill key roles within the government, such as agency directors.

The heightened access that former members, congressional staffers, and federal employees have does not, however, go unchecked. As established by the Lobbying Disclosure Act of 1995 (LDA), former members of Congress are banned from lobbying Congress for one year, known as a "cooling off period." There has been a recent push to increase the cooling off period to two years. Congressional staff whose salaries are at least 75 percent of the salaries of members (or $123,900 in 2006) are, for the duration of one year, prohibited from lobbying the committee or members for whom they worked. The Senate has implemented its own rule banning *all* departing Senate staff from lobbying their former employing entity for one year. Former members and senior staff are prohibited from lobbying the executive branch on behalf of another party for one year as well.

conferences or charity functions that are also attended by lobbyists and corporate leaders, to host outings to golf courses, ball games, and concerts, and to sponsor lunches, dinners, and receptions in Washington (see box, "Golf According to Jack (Abramoff, that is)"). Such activities are sometimes labeled "social lobbying" because they facilitate the development of personal loyalties between lobbyists and members. The House rules changes passed in 2007 severely constrain gifts of this variety, although there are loopholes that will inevitably be exploited. As of the time of this writing, the Senate has not imposed analogous restrictions. But money allows lobbyists to do more than simply dole out goodies. With adequate financial means, lobbyists are also able to acquire other resources, such as the assistance of policy experts, which are often critical in dealing with legislators and their staffs.

The most obvious, and perhaps most important, use of money is for campaign contributions. Some lobbyists are able to make considerable contributions themselves. And many are in a position to orchestrate contributions from numerous political action committees and wealthy individuals to maximize their influence with a few legislators.

Just how much influence is exercised through campaign contributions is an open question. Most campaign contributions appear to flow to members

GOLF ACCORDING TO JACK (ABRAMOFF, THAT IS)

In May 2000, then-House Majority Whip Tom DeLay (R-Texas) took a 10-day vacation to Great Britain coordinated by lobbyist Jack Abramoff. DeLay, his wife, and two aides, stayed at lavish hotels, ate at the best restaurants, went to the theater, and took a four-day side trip to play golf at the historic links at St. Andrews golf course. DeLay's financial disclosures reported that the $70,000 trip was paid for by a nonprofit conservative organization, the National Center for Public Policy Research. It was later discovered that a Native American tribe and a gambling services company that had hired Abramoff had each contributed $25,000 to the National Center for the purpose of the trip. Large portions of the trip were found to have been paid with a credit card under Abramoff's name.

House ethics rules permit members and their staff to have travel expenses paid for only when travel is connected to official business and only by organizations directly connected to the trip. House ethics rules also prohibit travel paid for by registered lobbyists. Finally, rules require that members accurately report the cost of a trip and the names of the people and organizations that paid for it. Given the facts that were uncovered, the trip was in violation of each of these rules. To make matters worse, email correspondences later confirmed that DeLay's office was aware of the infractions and was perhaps even concerned "if someone starts asking questions."

While we cannot be certain what DeLay's motivations were in making policy decisions, we do know that following the trip DeLay helped kill legislation opposed by the tribe and the gambling services company that were represented by Abramoff.

Sources: Jeffrey Smith, "DeLay Airfare Was Charged to Lobbyist's Credit Card," *Washington Post,* April 24, 2005; James V. Grimaldi and Jeffrey Smith, "Gambling Interests Funded DeLay Trip," *Washington Post,* March 12, 2005; John Solomon, "E-mails: DeLay Staff Knew Lobbyist Paid for Golf Trip," *The Associated Press,* May 7, 2006.

who already support the positions of the contributors – the money follows the votes, the saying goes. But measuring the influence of campaign contributions is very difficult. Some contributions are intended to encourage members to remain inactive, or at least not to challenge policies favored by groups. Other contributions are designed to generate action at less visible stages of the legislative process – to offer an amendment in a subcommittee markup, to hold to a policy position in private negotiations in conference, and so on. Of course, members in key positions, such as party leaders or committee chairs, attract substantial contributions. In his first two years as House speaker, Dennis Hastert (R-Illinois) received more than double the contributions he had in the previous Congress ($1.0 million in 1997–1998 and $2.4 million in 1999–2000).

Despite the difficulties in gauging the influence of campaign contributions, few doubt that contributions are an important link between members and those lobbyists who can generate large sums for the members' campaigns. We can infer from interest group behavior that there are returns to making contributions. In recent years, members have increasingly called upon lobbyists to organize fundraising activities on their behalf. Lobbyists often do not dare refuse, because they fear losing access that they have worked so hard to gain.

Information is a critical resource for the lobbyist engaged in inside lobbying. Legislators appear to have an insatiable desire for information about the policy and political consequences of their actions. Political scientists David Austen-Smith and John R. Wright contend that legislators are imperfectly informed about constituency preferences and, therefore, lobbyists provide an important source of information. Furthermore, they argue that competition among interests induces truthful behavior from the interest groups. Lobbyists who develop a reputation for having reliable information at hand are called on more frequently by legislators and are more likely to gain the access necessary for exercising influence. Of course, the amount of technical information a professional lobbyist is likely to have is limited, so success depends on having a network of contacts in research institutes, universities, executive agencies, corporations, or wherever expertise relevant to the lobbyist's interests is found. In fact, many lobbying firms and interest groups hire technical specialists such as lawyers and social and physical scientists so that they can provide timely information to decision makers and even conduct original research of their own.

Outside Lobbying

The most dramatic change in the lobbying business in recent decades has been the increase in outside, or grassroots, lobbying. Rather than relying solely on Washington lobbyists to make appeals on behalf of a cause, groups often attempt to mobilize their membership or the general public to generate outside pressure on members of Congress. Successful mobilization of members' constituents increases the stakes for members by increasing the likelihood that their actions will have electoral consequences. The survey of lobbying groups reported in Table 11.1 shows that more than 80 percent of groups inspired letter-writing or telegram campaigns, 80 percent mounted grassroots lobbying efforts and prodded influential constituents to contact

TABLE 11.1. Percent of Interest Groups that Reported Using a Lobbying Technique.

Testify at hearings	99
Contact government officials directly to present your point of view	98
Engage in informal contacts with officials – at conventions, over lunch, etc.	95
Present research results or technical information	92
Send letters to members of your organization to inform them about your activities	92
Enter into coalitions with other organizations	90
Attempt to shape the implementation of policies	89
Talk with people from the press and the media	86
Consult with government officials to plan legislative strategy	85
Help draft legislation	85
Inspire letter-writing or telegram campaigns	84
Mount grassroots lobbying efforts	80
Have influential constituents contact their congressman's office	80
Make financial contributions to electoral campaigns	58
Publicize candidates' voting records	44
Run advertisements in the media about your position on issues	31

Source: TABLE (Adapted) – "Percent of Interest Groups That . . ." from *Organized Interest and American Democracy* by Kay Lehman Schlozman and John T. Tierney, 150. Copyright © 1986 by Kay Lehman Schlozman and John T. Tierney. Reprinted by permission of HarperCollins Publishers, Inc.

their congressional representatives, and about one-third ran advertisements in the media about their positions on the issues.

Technology and money have driven innovations in outside lobbying. Throughout the history of Congress, groups of people from around the country have converged on Washington to demand action on their programs. Improved means of transportation have increased the frequency with which groups mobilize their members or the general public for marches, special lobbying days, and other events in Washington that are designed to heighten congressional interest and support for their causes. Mass marches have always been the necessary strategy of large groups without the money and experienced Washington lobbyists essential to execute effective inside strategies. But today, many groups, even well-established groups, bring large numbers of people from around the country on special occasions to pressure members of Congress.

By the 1970s, computer-generated mailings allowed groups to send "legislative alert" letters to group members or targeted groups in the general public to stimulate an avalanche of mail and waves of phone calls to congressional offices. Members of Congress soon learned to identify and discount orchestrated letter-writing campaigns. Nevertheless, as lobbyist Bill Murphy observes, "The congressman has to care that *somebody* out there in his district has enough power to get hundreds of people to sit down and write a postcard or a letter – because if the guy can get them to do *that*, he might be able to influence them in other ways. So, a member has no choice but to pay attention."[11] At a minimum, a member must worry that those same constituents could be motivated, by the same means used to stimulate their letter writing, to contribute their money to or cast their votes for a member's opponent.

Today's lobbyists take outside strategies several steps further. For example, Washington-based firms have adapted telemarketing strategies to congressional politics. Working from computer-generated lists of Americans likely to support a particular point of view, telephone operators dial homes, ask a few questions, and then transfer the call to the appropriate congressional offices so that constituents' views can be registered with their representatives and senators. Particular geographic constituencies can be targeted to maximize the pressure on a few members of Congress.

The internet also serves as a valuable, low-cost resource for interest groups looking to engage the public. Large-scale email campaigns have become a common grassroots strategy among organized interests. And considering the minimal cost of the approach, the returns tend to be sizeable. In one instance, an email campaign organized by the National Education Association (NEA) encouraged public education advocates to pressure members of Congress to back a class-size reduction and a 15 percent increase in education funding – an ambitious proposal. The effort prompted 20,000 emails and resulted in a 12 percent increase in the education budget.

Media advertising has become an increasingly integral part of lobbying strategies. Most advertising of this variety is intended to increase the visibility of an issue or cause and shape opinion in the general public. For the most part, the media ads are designed and produced by the same people who produce election campaign ads. One group, the U.S. Chamber of Commerce, produces its own television programs that are shown on local stations throughout the country. It uses its production and satellite facilities to link its Washington studios (which are just one block from the White House) with corporate sponsors.

A particular advantage of outside lobbying is that there are few registration and disclosure requirements. Under current law, organized interests and representatives of organized interests that engage exclusively in grassroots lobbying are not obligated to register as lobbyists or file any disclosure

GRASSROOTS VS. ASTROTURF

New technologies and strategies have greatly expanded efforts to influence members of Congress by generating an avalanche of phone calls and letters to Capitol Hill. A type of grassroots lobbying, the new contrivances have been labeled astroturf lobbying.

Sometimes the new strategies are too obvious to succeed. For example, a group called the Health Care Coalition had operators call small business owners who were likely to be affected by an amendment pending in the House, tell them that the amendment would be bad for managed health care, and then offer to connect them to the office of the member from their district. Dozens of calls were targeted at critical members.

In another case, hundreds of telegrams were dumped onto the floor of the House Commerce Committee to show public opposition to a telecommunications bill. Perhaps thousands more were sent directly to members. Suspicious congressional aides discovered that many of the telegrams were sent without the signatories' permission by a group called the Seniors Coalition. The public relations firm in charge of the effort blamed shoddy work by a mass marketing subcontractor. Some of the signatories proved to be deceased.

Source: Juliet Eilperin, "Dingell Takes on Bogus Mailgram," *Roll Call*, October 16, 1995, 1, 20. Reprinted by permission.

statements. Disclosure of grassroots lobbying is only triggered by participation in direct, or inside, lobbying. Groups that have limited lobbying ambitions may, therefore, adopt grassroots strategies to avoid undue reporting burdens. This loophole has, however, led to the emergence of massive grassroots lobbying organizations whose practices go largely unchecked.

Legislators are likely to discount communications that are orchestrated by organized interests, but they cannot ignore such communications altogether. After all, if constituents can be motivated to write or call legislators, they might be motivated by the same means and by the same groups to vote for or against legislators in the next election. Indeed, the messages sent to legislators' offices sometimes explicitly warn about the senders' voting intentions.

Plainly, Washington lobbying has become very much like running an election campaign. Robert Beckel, a lobbyist who was Walter Mondale's 1984 presidential campaign manager, explains:

> What we do is take campaign techniques and go out to the districts of these guys in Congress and organize the districts like a campaign. What we can do is get some real honest-to-goodness back-home pressure. We do a lot of subcontract

work for lobby firms who say "We got a real problem with Congressman X on this issue." And so we'll go into his district, and because we invariably know a lot of people in every district in the country, we'll find somebody who in a sense becomes a campaign manager for us. And we go to work on the congressman.[12]

The growing importance of outside strategies has led to the proliferation of "full-service" lobbying firms. These large firms combine traditional insider lobbyists with policy experts, specialists in public relations, graphic arts, and electronic media, speechwriters, fundraisers, communications and computer technicians, and pollsters. The model is Hill & Knowlton Public Affairs, a firm with more than 180 employees that boasts its own broadcast studio. The firm includes former members of Congress, staff assistants, and executive officials from both parties. Firms, like Hill & Knowlton, with the capacity to effectively employ both inside and outside strategies must determine the mix of strategies that will position them to best meet their goals. According to political scientists Marie Hojnacki and David Kimball, organized interests are likely to use inside lobbying to target allies in committee, so as to influence the content of legislative proposals. Outside lobbying, on the other hand, has the broader goal of maintaining and expanding the base of legislative support, and, therefore, is used to influence members irrespective of their policy position. Outside lobbying, however, has less potential to affect meaningful policy change (also see box, "The Choice of Strategies").

Coalitions

Whatever an interest group's mix of inside and outside strategies, it seldom stands alone in major legislative battles. Many coalitions are created for specific issues and then disappear once congressional action on certain legislation is complete. Other coalitions are more enduring. Some coalitions have formal names; others do not. Coalitions are a means for pooling the resources of lobbyists and groups. They also are a means for lobbyists and groups to demonstrate a broad base of support for their cause and to make their effort appear to be as public-spirited as possible. Some coalitions are the creation of lobbyists looking to manufacture a new client.

An impressive example of an interest group coalition was the Archer MSA (medical savings account) Coalition, which played a prominent role in shaping the 2003 Medicare Prescription Drug, Improvement, and Modernization Act. The coalition was comprised of 49 interest groups, including such notable organizations as the American Medical Association (AMA) and the Christian Coalition of America. It was a vocal proponent of tax-preferred health savings accounts (HSAs). Although there was some resistance to the

THE CHOICE OF STRATEGIES

In effort to learn more about interest group strategies, political scientist Jack Walker conducted a detailed survey of the top officers in 734 national interest groups. Walker found that:

most groups adopt a preferred style of political action early in their histories, and, when these early choices are made, group leaders naturally emulate the tactics being employed at that time by the most successful groups. Once either an inside or outside strategy becomes the association's dominant approach, it is very difficult to move in a new direction. Choices made early in the history of a group establish a strategic style that restricts innovation, largely because political strategies are so intertwined with other basic organizational decisions.

Not surprisingly, Walker discovered that groups facing organized opposition to their goals tend to more aggressively pursue both inside and outside strategies than do other groups. Outside strategies, however, are more frequently the choice of groups with many local chapters or subunits, citizens' groups, and groups from the non-profit sector (local governments, universities, non-profit professions, and so on). Inside strategies are more likely to be the choice of groups representing business and groups that have established large central office staffs, usually in Washington.

Source: Based on information from Jack L. Walker, Jr., *Mobilizing Interest Groups in America: Patrons, Professions, and Social Movements* (Ann Arbor: University of Michigan Press, 1991), 103–121; quote from 119–120.

inclusion of HSAs among Republicans, the coalition made its presence felt. The final version of the legislation included the HSAs and passed by narrow margins in both chambers, handing the Archer MSA Coalition a major victory.

Much remains unanswered about interest group coalitions. There is, for instance, no clear-cut answer for why coalitions emerge when they do. There is a tremendous amount of variation across issues in terms of the number and size of coalitions that form. Scholars have suggested that the emergence of coalitions is systematically related to such factors as issue conflict and salience. There is, however, only tentative support for these hypotheses. Also somewhat of a mystery is whether interest groups are more successful than acting alone. While the Archer MSA Coalition appears to have been successful in 2003, not all coalitions are so fortunate. Moreover, there were interest groups that acted alone on the Medicare legislation, such as the AARP (formerly the American Association of Retired Persons), that also were successful in achieving their policy objectives. One study of coalition success found that a mere 58 percent of coalitions accomplished any of their goals.[13] This

lackluster rate could reflect some of the disadvantages to coalition formation – namely, greater collective action problems to overcome. While the
comparative advantages of belonging to a coalition are not entirely clear,
there is some evidence that coalition formation leads to greater success when
seeking to defend the status quo.

Legislators Influencing Organized Interests

The path of influence between lobbyists and members is a two-way street.
Plainly, lobbyists seek to influence outcomes in the legislative process by
persuading at least a few members to support or even champion their cause
that would not have done so otherwise. But legislators often want something
from lobbyists, too. And since lobbyists want to cultivate or maintain good
relations with key legislators, they are often quite responsive to legislators'
demands. Legislators frequently pressure interest groups to generate campaign contributions for them. They ask lobbyists for assistance in attracting
support from other legislators, the public, or others on issues not directly of
concern to the lobbyists. Legislators may enlist the support of lobbyists on
matters before the executive branch or encourage lobbyists to take action
in the courts. Lobbyists may resist these pressures. After all, the requests
may not be compatible with other objectives the lobbyists pursue. But lobbyists must assess how important the legislator is, or will be in the future, to
their groups' or their personal interests. Ignoring senior party and committee
leaders can come at a significant cost.

When congressional Republicans gained majority party status in 1995,
GOP leaders launched a project to pressure Washington lobbying firms to
hire Republicans for top positions. Called the K Street Project, Republican
leaders tracked the party affiliation of Washington lobbyists and rewarded
those that were loyal. With like-minded individuals in key lobbying positions,
congressional Republicans could limit the power of opposing interests. With
unified control of Congress and the White House between 2000 and 2006,
lobbying firms had to stay in the good graces of Republicans if they wished
to exert influence over legislative outcomes. Whereas lobbying firms have
historically hired lobbyists from both parties to accommodate changes in
party control, there is reason to believe that lobbying firms predicted lasting Republican dominance. This, along with the strict oversight of the K
Street Project, led many lobbying firms to pass up Democrats for important
lobbying positions. In 2004, the Capitol Hill newspaper, *The Hill*, reported
that "retiring House Democrats are feeling a cold draft from K Street as
they seek post-congressional employment at lobbying firms, trade groups

and corporations. By contrast, K Street is aggressively courting GOP law-makers who have announced their retirements."[14]

Things began to change in the months leading up to the 2006 elections, as lobbying firms sensed a Democratic takeover of one or both houses of Congress. The same firms that, months earlier, had shunned Democrats were now embracing them with open arms. The eventual Democratic victory led to a rush to hire Democratic lobbyists. One prominent lobbyist reported that the average annual salary for Republican lobbyists plummeted 50,000 dollars upon the election returns. Shortly after taking control, House and Senate Democrats addressed the practices of the K Street Project that had burdened them for the past decade. House rules were adopted that prohibit members from influencing "on the basis of partisan political affiliation an employment decision or employment practice of any private entity." The lobbying reform bill passed by the Senate in January 2007 contains the identical language, although it was not enacted by the time of this writing.

Regulating Lobbying

Modern lobbying is remarkably clean and ethical, at least when compared with lobbying during most of American history. In the nineteenth century, lobbyists ran gambling establishments to put legislators in their debt and openly paid members for representing their interests on Capitol Hill. With few (recent) exceptions, the retainers and bribes are gone. In fact, lobbyists now have their own professional code of ethics.

At various points throughout history, congressional, journalistic, and criminal investigations have exposed remarkably corrupt lobbying practices, but on only a few occasions did Congress or either house impose any restrictions on lobbying. In 1876, for example, Congress for the first time required that lobbyists register, but the rule was in effect for only one Congress. Congress did not pass its first comprehensive lobbying regulations until 1946, when the Federal Regulation of Lobbying Act was adopted as a part of the Legislative Reorganization Act.

The central feature of the 1946 law was the requirement that people who solicit or receive money for the purpose of influencing legislation must register with the clerk of the House or the secretary of the Senate. Lobbyists were required to file quarterly reports on the money they received for and spent on lobbying. The authors of the 1946 act hoped that disclosure of lobbyists' clients and legislative purposes would put members, reporters, and the public in a better position to evaluate lobbyists' influence.

The law proved to be unenforceable. In 1954, the Supreme Court ruled in *United States* v. *Harriss* that the registration and reporting requirements applied only to those persons who are paid by others to lobby, who contact members directly, and whose "principal purpose" is to influence legislation. The Court argued that the First Amendment to the Constitution, which prohibits Congress from making a law that abridges the right "to petition the Government for a redress of grievances," limits Congress's ability to regulate an individual's right to represent him or herself before Congress and to organize others with the intent of influencing Congress. By confining the force of the 1946 act to those lobbyists whose principal purpose is to influence legislation, the Court created a large loophole for anyone who wanted to claim that influencing legislation was not his or her principal purpose.

Interest in creating meaningful registration and reporting requirements was renewed in the early 1990s. Ross Perot gave great emphasis to the influence of "special interests" in his 1992 presidential campaign. Perot's theme was reinforced by television reports about members' all-expenses-paid trips to vacation resorts where they fraternized with lobbyists. In response to the heightened public scrutiny of the relationship between lobbyists and members of Congress, a large number of members elected for the first time in the 1990s had promised to reduce the influence of special interests in Washington. The result was the consideration of significant lobbying reforms.

In late 1995, Congress enacted new legislation designed to close some of the loopholes in the 1946 law. The new law, titled the Lobbying Disclosure Act of 1995 (LDA), extends the 1946 law that covered only people who lobbied members of Congress, to also include those who seek to influence congressional staff and top executive branch officials. The LDA formally defines a lobbyist as:

> Any individual who is employed or retained by a client for financial or other compensation for services that include more than one lobbying contact [Defined as any oral or written communication (including an electronic communication) to a covered executive branch official or a covered legislative branch official that is made on behalf of a client], other than an individual whose lobbying activities constitute less than 20 percent of the time engaged in the services provided by such individual to the client over a six month period.

Anyone who is hired to lobby a covered public official and spends 20 percent or more of his or her time in paid lobbying, must register with the clerk of the House and the secretary of the Senate within 45 days of being hired or making the first contact, whichever is earlier. Individuals who receive $5,000 or less in a six-month period and organizations that spend less than $20,000 in a six-month period do not have to register. Therefore, average citizens simply looking to have their voices heard are not required to register. Lobbyists are required to file semiannual reports that disclose who their clients are, the general issue area they were hired to influence, and a good faith estimate of the total amount paid by clients. Lobbyists for foreign governments or organizations must register. The registration requirement excludes grassroots lobbying, such as efforts to persuade people to write members of Congress.

The LDA more than doubled the number of registered lobbyists. Among the newly registered were a variety of lobbying coalitions – organized groups of lobbyists, associations, and lobbying firms – that had not been registered under the old law. Separately, the House and Senate adopted rules limiting lobbyists' gifts to members and staff. Until recently, the House and Senate rules banned gifts valued at more than $50, including meals and entertainment. Gifts from any one source could not exceed $100 in value for a year, with gifts under $10 excluded from the calculation. Gifts from family members and gifts of token value (T-shirts, mugs) were also excluded. In addition, chamber rules permitted privately funded trips but banned travel paid for directly by a lobbyist.

In recent years, the public has witnessed an inordinate number of lobbying scandals. In March 2006, former Representative Randall "Duke" Cunningham (R-California) was convicted of accepting $2.4 million in bribes primarily from defense contractors in return for securing contracts. In May 2006, the FBI raided the home of Representative William Jefferson (D-Louisiana) to find $90,000 in his freezer. The government claims that Jefferson took in excess of $400,000 in bribes. In October 2006, former Representative Bob Ney (R-Ohio) pled guilty to accepting gifts in exchange for favorable action on behalf of convicted lobbyist Jack Abramoff's clients. The election outcomes were, at least in part, a reaction to the many scandals.

After gaining new House and Senate majorities in the 2006 elections, the Democrats espoused significant ethics and lobbying reform. House Democrats did so immediately by including ethics and lobbying reforms in the chamber rules. House rules now ban all gifts from lobbyists and entities that employ lobbyists, while previous limits still apply for nonlobbyists. Perhaps the most drastic change in rules is with respect to travel – no doubt inspired by former representative Tom DeLay. Representatives and their staff are not permitted to accept privately financed travel from lobbyists or entities that employ lobbyists. Moreover, representatives and their staff are prohibited from traveling with lobbyists present on any segment of the trip. The rules do allow travel for one day and one night to locations where there is minimal lobbyist involvement. Representatives may also have travel expenses compensated for trips to colleges and universities.

In August, 2007, the House and Senate approved the Honest Leadership and Open Government Act that amended the LDA of 1995 in several important ways. The law requires quarterly instead of semiannual filing of lobbying disclosures reports, provides for electronic filing, and disclosure by registered lobbyists of all past executive and congressional employment. Lobbyists' required reports must identify all earmarks they have requested on behalf of their clients. For former senators, the law bans directly lobbying in the Senate for two years after leaving office. The law prohibits legislators and staff whose spouses are lobbyists from having "lobbying contact," which is defined in the law, with their spouses. Legislators are prohibited from negotiating private employment as a lobbyist until after his or her successor is elected and must file disclosure forms about negotiations about any other private employment. The law sharply limits privately funded trips, requires reimbursement at the charter rate for the use of corporate jets, imposes a ban on gifts from lobbyists to legislators and their staffs. The new law also requires the Secretary of the Senate and the Clerk of the House to maintain certain lobbying disclosure information in an electronic data base, available to the public free of charge over the Internet, and to make lobbying activity reports available for public inspection over the Internet within 48 hours after such report is filed.

Members' Groups and Legislative Service Organizations

Groups of members frequently coalesce or even formally organize to pursue specific political interests. In fact, informal groups of members have been prominent features of Washington politics since the early Congresses. In the early nineteenth century, members tended to find lodging in boarding houses where they found like-minded colleagues. Informal but conspicuous intra-party factions, such as southern Democrats, have been quite important from time to time. And state delegations, particularly those of the larger states, have been the building blocks for coalitions throughout the history of Congress. Two developments of recent decades have altered the character of membership groups.

The first is that intra-party factions developed formal organizations with formal memberships, elected leaders, staff, offices, and even membership dues. The prototype, and still the largest such group, is the Democratic Study Group (DSG). The DSG was formed in 1959 by House Democratic liberals to counter the strength of the conservative coalition of Republicans and southern Democrats. The services of the DSG – especially issuing and scheduling reports – eventually became so highly valued that nearly all Democrats joined and contributed dues to take advantage of the group's work. Nevertheless, the DSG remains the organizational focal point for liberal activists in the House.

Since the 1970s there has been a remarkable increase in the number of single-issue caucuses. Today there are over 200 such caucuses, and many have bipartisan memberships. The Congressional Arts Caucus and the Congressional Sportsmen's Caucus formed to promote certain public funding for the arts and to oppose many proposed regulations on fire arms, respectively; regional interests are promoted by the Northeast-Midwest Congressional Coalition and the Congressional Western Caucus. Both constituency concerns and personal circumstances provide a foundation for the Congressional Black Caucus, the Congressional Hispanic Caucus, and the Congressional Caucus for Women's Issues. District economic interests are reflected in the Congressional Coastal Caucus, Congressional Steel Caucus, and the Congressional Tourism and Travel Caucus.

Caucuses, now officially called congressional members organizations in the House, are a way for members to become involved in and demonstrate a commitment to a particular cause or issue that falls outside of the scope of their regular committee duties. This is particularly true in the House, where most members are limited to two committee assignments. In fact, about 90 percent of caucuses are found in the House. In most cases, a caucus is a basis for publicizing a cause or an issue and building policy coalitions within Congress. Outside interest groups seeking to cultivate congressional support for their interests have stimulated the creation of many congressional caucuses.

Until recently, many caucuses were formally recognized in the House as "legislative service organizations," or LSOs, and were subject to audits and a few regulations. LSOs were controversial because they received dues from members' office accounts and gained office space in the House office buildings. Critics charged that this practice allowed money from office accounts to be spent indirectly for purposes, such as dinners, for which office account funds cannot be spent directly. Moreover, many LSOs bridged the gap between interest groups and congressional caucuses by creating foundations and institutes with close ties to both external groups and internal caucuses. In the view of some critics, the ability of lobbyists and interest groups to contribute money to these new foundations was just another way for special interests to support travel and social events for members and congressional staff participating in the work of the foundations. These critiques of LSOs paved the way for the second significant development in membership groups in recent decades.

The newly elected Republican majority of 1995 fundamentally changed the character of membership groups by banning LSOs. Membership groups lost several special privileges – the ability to receive dues paid from official budgets and office space in House buildings. Slowly, congressional member organizations, or CMOs, replaced LSOs and are granted more limited privileges. Members of CMOs may jointly pay for staff and other functions, but they do not pay dues for separate staff and activities. Dozens of member organizations have been created and, among other activities, serve to advertise legislators' interests in subjects important to key groups in their districts and states.

The Influence of Lobbyists and Interest Groups

Even experienced and insightful watchers of the lobbying and interest group community have mixed views about the influence of special interest lobbying. A popular view in the 1950s and 1960s was that policy making was dominated by "subgovernments" or "iron triangles" – tightly bound sets of interest groups, executive agencies, and committees. According to this view, cozy relationships among lobbyists, bureaucrats, and members prevented other interests from influencing policy choices and implementation. The subgovernments perspective was always recognized as an overly stylized view, but it captured an important feature of Washington politics: In many policy areas, only a few groups, agencies, and members took an interest in the issues, so they dominated the policy choices that were made.

The classic case of subgovernment policy making was mid-twentieth century agriculture policy politics. Generally, only those agriculture groups directly affected by certain federal commodities programs, the Agriculture Department bureaus that ran the programs, and a few members sitting on the agriculture committees of Congress took an active interest in farm policy. Those groups, bureaucrats, and members interested in the various farm commodities assisted each other in gaining congressional approval of the periodic legislation that supported federal programs. Although federal taxpayers paid for these programs, the costs were not so high as to breed resistance. And the lack of conflict among agriculture sector groups and decision makers helped keep others from paying attention.

Many political scientists responded to the subgovernments' perspective by noting the special conditions that allow a subgovernment to develop and dominate policy making. The most important feature is little conflict. Conflict among the interested groups and members would encourage the contending forces to recruit supporters from a broader range of groups, legislators, executive branch officials, and even the general public. Expanding the scope of the conflict in this way usually alters the balance of forces and the policy outcome. The low level of conflict, in turn, is the product of the concentrated benefits and widely distributed costs of some programs. The beneficiaries are motivated to organize and lobby to protect their interests, and the fairly small burden on taxpayers stimulates little opposition. But the number of people affected by policy choices, distribution of costs and benefits, and the scope and intensity of conflict varies greatly across policy areas. The result is significant variation in the role of groups in shaping policy choices.

Political scientist Hugh Heclo noticed that policy areas once dominated by subgovernments had lost their insular character by the 1970s. Heclo coined the term *issue networks* to capture the more diverse, mutually antagonistic, and fluid character of the lobbying and interest group community found in many policy areas. Many factors contributed to the change. In the 1960s and 1970s, new citizens' groups, many of which were by-products of broad-based social movements, challenged established groups. Groups representing economic interests proliferated, partly in response to new government policies and regulations, which led to a fragmentation of Washington representation in many policy areas that were once dominated by just one or two groups. In addition, congressional reforms made Congress more open, accessible, and democratic, which encouraged new groups to lobby and stimulated more members of Congress to champion the cause of once-neglected interests.

Analysts are divided over the political implications of the expansion of the interest group community and the breakdown of subgovernments. Tierney and Schlozman emphasize the continuing numerical advantage of business-oriented groups. They also observe that the explosion of interest group activity has

> introduced a potentially dysfunctional particularism into national politics. If policymakers in Congress are forced to find an appropriate balance between deference to the exigencies of the short run and the consideration of consequences for the long run, between acquiescence to the clearly expressed wishes of narrow groups that care intensely and respect for the frequently unexpressed needs of larger publics, the balance may have shifted too far in the direction of the near-term and the narrow.[15]

Political scientist Robert Salisbury disagrees. He insists that the large number of corporate lobbyists and the tremendous resources of business groups should not lead us to conclude

> that business interests or even self-serving groups invariably prevail. The total system of policy advocacy is far broader than the array, vast as it is, of organized interest groups. Every holder of public office – indeed, every candidate for public office – is or may be an advocate of some policy alternatives. Members of

CONGRESS, LOBBYISTS, AND INTEREST GROUPS

Congress do not wait passively for lobbyists to persuade them one way or the other; they too are advocates, as are the more prominent members of the administration, the editorialists and commentators in the mass media, the academic pundits and writers, and a host of other citizens who write letters, attend rallies, argue with each other, and generally make their views known on policy questions of the day.[16]

Besides, Salisbury contends, most business-group resources are devoted to monitoring government activity important to business decisions rather than to influencing policy choices.

It seems fair to say that Tierney and Schlozman's critical view is more widely shared among sophisticated observers of congressional politics than is Salisbury's more forgiving perspective. Nevertheless, Salisbury's note of caution is important. Lobbyists and interest groups are not the only source of pressure on members, nor are they the only important source of change in the nature of congressional politics. Communications and transportation technologies, electoral campaigns, the structure of the legislative process, the distribution of power within Congress, and other factors affect the balance of forces influencing congressional policy choices as well.

Conclusion

Lobbyists and interest groups are among the most controversial and least well-understood features of the legislative game. They appear to be both an essential part of the representation of interests before Congress and a potential source of bias in the policy choices made by Congress. Generally, they direct members' attention to narrow and parochial issues that might otherwise not be addressed. Whatever their consequences, the relationship that lobbyists and interest groups have with members of Congress has changed markedly over the years. In particular, transformations in Congress have caused lobbyists and interest groups to evolve. They are now:

- A much larger and more diverse community than just a few decades ago,
- more professional, with increasingly developed infrastructures,
- a more central player in congressional elections, both in terms of direct contributions and advocacy efforts, and
- better able to provide legislators with quick and accurate information.

These developments have sensitized the general public about the influence of special interests and produced new efforts to regulate lobbyists and lobbying.

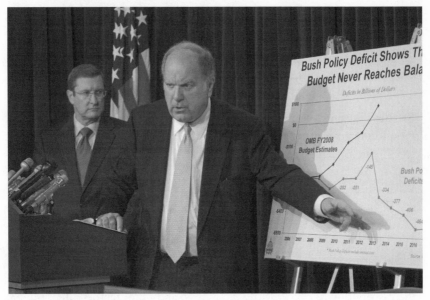

House Budget Committee Chairman John Spratt (D-South Carolina) points at a line graph during a press conference with Senate Budget Committee Chairman Kent Conrad (D-North Dakota).

12

Congress and Budget Politics

THE FEDERAL BUDGET IS OFTEN THE CENTER OF CONGRESSIONAL
politics. For fiscal 2007, the federal government's spending exceeded
$2.8 trillion, approaching $10,000 for every American.[1] While many people are bored to tears when the details of spending and tax policy are discussed, the budget reflects fundamental choices about the role of government in American life. Action on the annual budget tends to generate the
most partisan fights in Washington. The twists and turns of budget politics
have strongly influenced winners and losers in elections, shaped the political
careers of the most prominent politicians, reshaped congressional decision-
making processes, and altered the distribution of power within Congress.

Federal budgeting since the 1970s has been a roller coaster ride. Beginning in the late 1970s and continuing for more than a decade, presidents
and Congress struggled with annual deficits. In fiscal year 1992, the federal
government spent about $290 billion more than it received from taxes and
other revenues. To pay the interest on the debt that had accumulated over
the years (nearly $4 trillion by that point), the federal government spent a
little more than $200 billion – about 14 percent of its $1.5 trillion budget for
fiscal year 1992. By 1998, the budget picture had improved markedly. Fiscal
year 1998 ended with a small surplus, and annual surpluses were achieved in
the three following years. Deficits returned by late 2001 during an economic
recession. The fight against terrorism and the war in Iraq prompted increases
in defense and homeland security spending, while tax cuts enacted in 2001
and 2003 cut into revenues. Deficits were looming again by 2002 and have
continued until through to the present – a deficit of nearly $300 billion was
projected for fiscal 2007.

During the past four decades, political battles stimulated by budget deficits have produced a series of procedural innovations in the way Congress
drafts the budget. In the 1970s and early 1980s, the process was modified

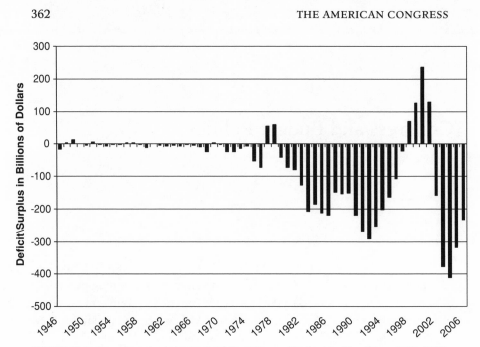

FIGURE 12.1. Annual Surplus (+) or Deficit (–) in Billions of Dollars, for Fiscal Years 1946–2006. *Source: Congressional Budget Office.*

to force congressional committees to write legislation that would either reduce spending or raise more revenue. Since then, the emphasis has been on enforcing multiyear budget plans. Each new effort to enforce deficit and spending agreements was a response to legislators, whose votes were often pivotal to passing budget legislation, to take credible action against deficits.

This is an important story. Step-by-step, the changes in rules reshaped the congressional decision-making process, contributed to heightened partisanship, and shifted the relative power of party and committee leaders. Cumulatively, these changes proved so important that they warrant special attention in this chapter.

Overview of the Federal Budget

Figure 12.1 shows the history of the federal deficit since the end of World War II. In the aftermath of the war, the federal government managed small annual budget surpluses about as often as it experienced budget deficits. In the 1960s, small deficits were the norm. Deficits crept upward during the 1970s and became a dominant issue in the 1980 presidential campaign, which ended with the election of the Republican candidate, Ronald Reagan, and a Republican majority in the Senate. During the 1980s and early 1990s,

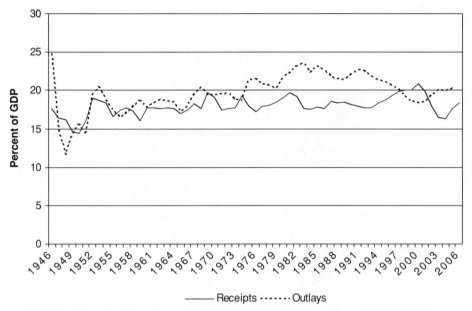

FIGURE 12.2. Federal Receipts and Outlays as a Percent of Gross Domestic Product, Fiscal Years 1946–2006. *Source:* Office of Management and Budget.

the deficit never came close to dropping back to the level experienced in 1980, Jimmy Carter's last year as president. The deficit contracted a little in the mid-1980s, but returned to a pattern of continued growth thereafter. President Clinton confronted this situation when he entered office in 1993. Clinton left office after surpluses had returned and his successor, George W. Bush, served while deficits expanded.

The federal deficit must be seen in the context of the overall size of the U.S. economy, which has grown a great deal in the last half century. Figure 12.2 shows the size of federal expenditures and revenues as percentages of the gross domestic product (GDP), an annual measure of all of the goods and services produced in the United States. The figure demonstrates that federal revenues as a percentage of GDP have been fairly stable since World War II, seldom reaching 20 percent of GDP. It also shows that the deficit since 2002 is due to both higher spending and lower revenues.

The increase in federal outlays that has put spending over 20 percent of GDP in most years since the early 1980s is due to both defense and domestic spending. Higher defense spending accounted for about half of the overall increase in expenditures between 1979 and 1983 and again after 2001. Most of the rest of the increase – and nearly all of it since the mid-1980s – is due to the rising cost of entitlement programs.

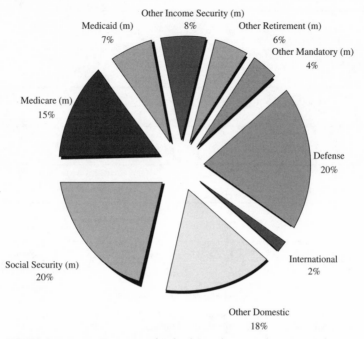

FIGURE 12.3. Major Categories of Federal Spending, Fiscal 2006. Mandatory programs desig-nated with (*m*), others are discretionary. *Source: Congressional Budget Office.*

Entitlements are provisions in law that guarantee individuals certain benefits if they meet eligibility requirements. The spending is considered *mandatory* – unless Congress changes the law it must provide the required funding. In contrast, for *discretionary* programs, year-to-year spending is not dictated by eligibility requirements but rather is determined by Congress. Social security, Medicare (health care for the elderly), Medicaid (health care for the poor), veterans' benefits, and other income-security programs such as pensions are examples of entitlement programs with mandatory spending. Defense, education, environmental protection, medical research, and space programs are examples of discretionary spending. Entitlements have grown so much that they now account for about 60 percent of federal expenditures, as Figure 12.3 shows.

Creating a Congressional Budget Process: 1974

In the early 1970s, interest in budget reform was spurred by chronic deficits and political tensions between the Democratic Congress and a Republican president. In retrospect, the deficits of that period seem small, but they were unprecedented for a time without a declared war. The shortfall was largely

Congressionally Speaking . . .

The *fiscal year* for the federal government begins on October 1 and runs through September of the following year. For example, fiscal year 2008 starts on October 1, 2008, and ends on September 30, 2009. Thus, Congress aims to have spending and tax bills for the next fiscal year enacted by October 1 of each year. The president proposes a budget in February, leaving Congress less than eight months to act on it. Failure to pass bills that approve spending for federal agencies, called *appropriations bills*, may force a shutdown of some government agencies. In most such cases, Congress passes *continuing resolutions*, which are joint resolutions of Congress that authorize temporary spending authority at the last year's level or at some percentage of that level.

the result of new and expensive domestic initiatives (President Lyndon Johnson's Great Society program) and the Vietnam War. Promising to gain control of the budget, Republican Richard Nixon won the 1968 presidential election and then proceeded to engage in intense battles with the Democratic Congress over spending and taxes. These battles motivated Congress to strengthen its own budget-making capacities by adopting the Congressional Budget and Impoundment Control Act of 1974, usually called the Budget Act of 1974.[2]

The Budget Act created a process for coordinating the actions of the appropriations, authorizing, and tax committees. Each May, Congress would pass a preliminary budget resolution setting nonbinding targets for expenditures and revenues. During the summer, Congress would pass the individual bills authorizing and appropriating funds for federal programs, as well as any new tax legislation. Then, in September, Congress would adopt a second budget resolution, providing final spending ceilings. This resolution might require adjustments to some of the decisions made during the summer months. Those adjustments would be reflected in the second resolution, and additional legislation, written by the proper committees, would then be drafted to make the necessary changes. This process of adjustment was labeled "reconciliation," to reflect the need to reconcile the earlier decisions with the second budget resolution. The reconciliation legislation was to be enacted by October 1, the first day of the federal government's fiscal year.

The Budget Act provided for two new committees, the House and Senate Budget Committees. The budget committees write the budget resolutions and package reconciliation legislation from various committees ordered to adjust the programs under their jurisdiction. The Congressional Budget Office (CBO) was created by the act to provide Congress with nonpartisan, expert analyses of the economy and budget.

The Budget Act also modified Senate floor procedures in a critical way. The act barred nongermane amendments and set a limit of 20 hours on debate over budget resolutions and reconciliation legislation. These rules mean that budget measures cannot be loaded with extraneous floor amendments or killed by a Senate filibuster. However, the rules did not restrict the kinds of provisions committees could write into budget measures. Consequently, the door was left open for committees to include in reconciliation bills legislation unrelated to spending cuts. This became a common practice once reconciliation bills became a central feature of the budget-making process in the 1980s.

Reducing the Discretion of Committees: 1980 and 1981

The new budget process worked smoothly during its first four years, primarily because congressional Democrats did not use budget resolutions to constrain or compel action from appropriations, authorizing, or tax committees. But in 1979 and 1980, the last two years of the Carter administration, escalating deficits spurred a search for new means to control spending. An effort in 1979 to include reconciliation instructions to committees in the second budget resolution ended in failure, in part because of resistance from some committees to reducing spending on programs under their jurisdiction. Confronting projections of a rapidly rising deficit and a reelection campaign in 1980, President Carter and Democratic congressional leaders agreed to include reconciliation instructions in the first budget resolution, adopted in May. That is, they decided to order some committees to report legislation that would reduce spending at a point in the process before the usual authorization and appropriations legislation was considered. This switch meant that the initiative would shift from the various authorizing committees to the budget and party leaders, who together with administration officials would devise the reconciliation instructions. The innovation worked. The 1980 reconciliation legislation reduced the deficit by $8.2 billion, through a combination of spending cuts and tax increases. Strangely, the term reconciliation was and still is used, even though it ostensibly refers to the process of reconciling the decisions of the summer months with the second budget resolution.

Republicans learned from the experience of the Carter years and used reconciliation instructions to force much deeper cuts in domestic programs

IMPOUNDMENT

During the early 1970s, the Nixon administration began to cut off funds for programs opposed by the president. That is, the president unilaterally stopped spending for programs for which funds had been appropriated by law. The practice, known as *impoundment*, created a constitutional crisis. Many members of Congress charged the president with violating his constitutional responsibility to see that the laws are faithfully executed. The courts agreed, for the most part, although some programs had been irreparably harmed by the time a court had ruled on the issue.

Congress responded in its 1974 budget reforms by providing for two types of impoundments – rescissions and deferrals. To withhold funds permanently for a particular purpose (make a rescission), a president would have to gain prior approval from both houses of Congress. To temporarily delay spending (make a deferral), a president would only have to notify Congress, and the president could defer spending unless either house specifically disapproved.

In 1983, the Supreme Court ruled that the legislative veto was unconstitutional because it allowed Congress to check an executive action without passing a regular bill. The ruling implied that the deferral process of the 1974 reforms was unconstitutional. Congress responded in 1987 by formally limiting the deferral authority to routine administrative matters.

Rescission authority continues to be used but it has involved only a very small fraction of total federal spending. Between 1976 and 2005, presidents requested nearly $73 billion in rescissions but Congress approved only about $25 billion.

once they took over the White House and the Senate after the 1980 elections. The Republicans managed to gain adoption of reconciliation instructions and pass a reconciliation bill that cut spending for fiscal year 1982 by about $37 billion.

Figure 12.4 illustrates how the inclusion of reconciliation instructions in the first budget resolution has altered the budget process. Reconciliation, authorization, and appropriations legislation now proceed simultaneously, so there is no need for a second budget resolution.

Sequestration: 1985 and 1987

The savings achieved by the 1981 reconciliation bill were more than offset by a large tax cut enacted in separate legislation that year, continued increases in entitlement spending, and the budget crisis which intensified in the early 1980s. A tax increase in 1982 – initiated by Senate Republicans and quietly

FIGURE 12.4. Steps in Budget Process.

accepted by President Reagan – helped reduce the deficit a little, but it was not enough to change its long-term upward trajectory.

In 1985, a trio of senators – Republicans Phil Gramm (Texas), Warren Rudman (New Hampshire), and Democrat Ernest Hollings (South Carolina) – pushed a seemingly irresistible amendment to a debt-ceiling bill, establishing the amount of outstanding debt the federal government is permitted to carry. The Gramm-Rudman-Hollings proposal was adopted as the Balanced Budget and Emergency Deficit Control Act of 1985. It provided for reducing the deficit by $36 billion in each of the following five years, so that the deficit would drop from about $ 172 billion in fiscal year 1986 to zero in fiscal year 1991. If Congress failed to meet any year's deficit target by more than $10 billion, as determined by the comptroller general (who headed the General Accounting Office, now called the Government

Accountability Office), across-the-board cuts in spending would be ordered by an amount necessary to reduce the deficit to the specified level. This process of withholding a certain percentage of funding from programs was called "sequestration." Sequestration, it was argued, would be so distasteful to lawmakers that Congress and the president would be motivated to find a way to reduce the deficit without triggering the automatic cuts. If Congress and the president failed to do the job, sequestration would do it for them.

To reinforce this deficit-reduction scheme, the 1985 law barred floor amendments to budget resolutions and reconciliation measures that would raise the projected deficit beyond specified levels. A point of order could be made against any ineligible amendment. But the Senate had a history of overruling its presiding officer on points of order and dozens of popular nongermane amendments were proposed to the reconciliation bill considered in the fall of 1985. Senator Robert Byrd (D-West Virginia) therefore proposed, and the Senate approved, a new rule that provided that the presiding officer's ruling on the germaneness of an amendment to a reconciliation bill could not be overturned unless a three-fifths majority agreed. The "Byrd rule" reinforced the 1974 Budget Act's restrictions on floor amendments and debate and made Senate rules governing the content of budget measures and amendments to them even more restrictive than those in the House.

On paper, Congress and the president met the deficit targets in the next three fiscal years. But, in each case, this goal was accomplished through a remarkable combination of creative accounting and absurdly optimistic estimates about the economy, future demands on federal programs, and the next year's revenues. "Blue smoke and mirrors" became the catch phrase used to describe federal budgeting. As a result of this budgetary legerdemain, the actual deficit in fiscal 1988 turned out to be $155 billion rather than the targeted $108 billion.

In the fall of 1987, another debt-ceiling bill presented an opportunity to restart the Gramm-Rudman-Hollings process. Congress attached to the bill a new set of targets, this time moving the zero-deficit deadline back from 1991 to 1993. The measure also made it more difficult for the Senate to waive the deficit targets, by requiring a three-fifths rather than a simple majority vote. But many observers, including stock market investors, thought that merely restarting the Gramm-Rudman-Hollings process was woefully inadequate, a view that appeared to contribute to a crash in the stock market in October 1987.

The crisis of the stock market crash and the November 20 sequester deadline propelled Congress and President Reagan to reach a new agreement.

Congressionally Speaking . . .

Only a few congressional rules are known by the name of their original author. One of them is the Byrd rule, named after Senator Robert C. Byrd (D-West Virginia), the former majority leader and former Appropriations Committee chair.

The *Byrd rule* bars extraneous matter from reconciliation bills. A provision is considered to be extraneous if it does not change spending or revenues, concerns issues that lie outside of the jurisdiction of the committee reporting it, or leads to a net increase in spending or decrease in revenues for the years beyond those covered by the bill. In addition, strangely, any change in social security, Washington's political sacred cow, is considered a violation of the Byrd rule.

The rule is enforced by points of order raised by senators from the floor and upheld by a ruling of the chair, who depends on the advice of the Senate parliamentarian. The Senate may overturn the ruling of the chair as long as 60 senators agree. If a point of order is successful, either through a ruling of the presiding officer or by a vote, the entire bill falls. The rule gives a sizable minority the ability to force certain kinds of provisions from reconciliation bills. It is one of the few places in which Senate rules are more restrictive than House rules.

The agreement was unique because it provided separate spending ceilings for defense and non-defense spending for a two-year period – fiscal 1987 and 1988. This compromise allowed the Reagan administration to end with a truce with Congress on the budget. Neither party was eager to continue the battle into the election year of 1988.

PAYGO: 1990

The partisan war over the budget resumed in 1989, the first year of the Republican George H. W. Bush administration. By late 1989, it was clear that the Gramm-Rudman-Hollings procedure had been a failure. Instead of a $100 billion deficit, as targeted in the 1987 Gramm-Rudman-Hollings Act, the deficit turned out to be a record $221 billion because of a slumping economy. The Gramm-Rudman-Hollings procedure was shown to have a major weakness: the absence of a means for forcing further reductions during a fiscal year for which the original deficit estimates had been too optimistic.[3]

The 1990 budget package set a new direction for enforcing agreements, as indicated by its title – the Budget Enforcement Act (BEA). The 1990

BEA focused on spending limits rather than deficit reduction *per se*. For fiscal years 1991 to 1993, the BEA provided for three categories of non-entitlement spending (defense, international, and domestic) and established spending ceilings for each. These ceilings were to be adjusted for inflation each year so that economic conditions would not make them more or less onerous. If a category's ceiling was exceeded, sequestration would apply only to programs within that category – thus, this process is called categorical sequestration. "Firewalls" were established; that is, it became a violation of the rules to transfer funds between the three categories. In this way, Republicans would not fear a raid on defense funding to increase domestic spending, and Democrats did not have to worry about transfers in the opposite direction.

The 1990 BEA added teeth to the budget-making process by requiring that all tax and direct spending legislation be deficit-neutral. That is, if a bill cut taxes or increased spending, it also would have to provide fully offsetting tax increases or spending cuts. This pay-as-you-go mechanism – known as PAYGO – was enforced by a provision allowing any member to raise a point of order against a bill on the grounds that it was not deficit-neutral. If a bill that was not deficit-neutral were to sneak through, a sequester on spending in the appropriate category would be applied.

The PAYGO focus on spending ceilings rather than deficit-reduction targets meant that Congress and the president had given up on the Gramm-Rudman-Hollings approach. Of course, if the economy slumped and revenues declined, the deficit would go up even if the spending ceilings were obeyed. But if the economy performed better than expected, spending would be controlled as expected, revenues would flow into the Treasury faster than expected, and the increased revenues would reduce the deficit.

The 1990 budget deal made it more difficult for authorizing and tax committees to propose new policy initiatives. Legislation that would create a new program that entailed spending would have to provide for spending cuts somewhere else. Tax-writing committees could not propose legislation to grant tax breaks to some groups or industries unless they increased taxes or cut spending for other programs under their jurisdiction. The net winners under the 1990 rules seemed to be the appropriations committees. Although they had to operate under the spending ceilings, the ceilings were viewed as reasonably generous, given the programs that had to be funded, and would be adjusted for inflation. The appropriators also had substantial flexibility on how to set priorities within the broad categories.

Unfortunately for President Bush, deficits shot upward in 1991 and 1992, despite the fact that domestic discretionary spending was constrained. The economy did not perform well, which reduced revenues over those two years by nearly $90 billion from what had been predicted in 1990. The slow economy contributed to increased spending on entitlements – particularly Medicare, Medicaid, and farm price supports – outside of the discretionary spending ceilings. Unanticipated expenditures for the Persian Gulf War and disaster aid to help Florida and Hawaii recover from hurricanes added to the deficit. The 1992 deficit of $290 billion was nearly $140 billion larger than the deficit in 1989, Bush's first year in office. Bush failed to win election to a second term.

Deficit-Reducing Trust Fund and Entitlement Review: 1993

Congress demonstrated remarkable creativity in devising new rules and processes for budgeting during the 1970s, 1980s, and early 1990s. But the impressive array of budgetary enforcement devices – reconciliation, sequestration, points of order, spending ceilings, PAYGO, and firewalls – did not seem to improve the bottom line. Deficits were never put on a downward path during the Reagan and Bush administrations, as the major deficit-reduction packages had promised. By the time Bill Clinton was sworn in as president in January, 1993, the public was deeply cynical about federal budgetary politics, the annual deficit was at a record high, and the deficit was a major obstacle to the new president's other policy objectives.

Entitlement spending, particularly health care spending, spurred large annual increases in the budget. As Figure 12.5 demonstrates, the escalating costs of health care programs posed serious threats to deficit control. The major government health care programs, Medicare and Medicaid, are entitlement programs for the elderly and the poor. Cutting those programs entails either reducing the number of eligible people, which is an unpopular option, or cutting payments to hospitals, doctors, and state governments. Reducing payments, however, leads hospitals and doctors to shift their costs to people with private insurance, thereby increasing the cost of health care for everyone else.

Domestic programs that do not involve entitlements – most education, law enforcement, transportation, housing, energy, research, construction, and space programs – have declined as a percentage of GDP since 1980. Most federal programs were cut or frozen, in terms of constant dollars, during the 1980s. In most cases, further cuts would mean a basic change in the direction of public policies that are popular or have strong constituencies. Moreover, defense spending has been on a downward path for several years.

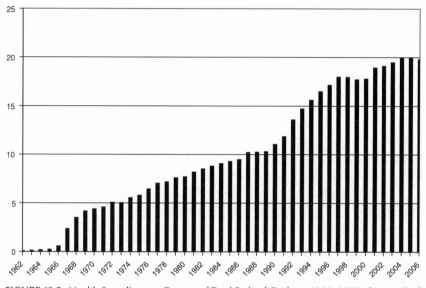

FIGURE 12.5. Health Spending as a Percent of Total Federal Outlays, 1962–2006. *Source: Budget of the United States Government,* Fiscal Year 2007, Historical Tables.

In 1993, President Clinton sought increases for some domestic programs, cuts in others and in defense, and some tax increases, all in the hope of reducing the deficit by $500 billion over five years. The Democrats decided to move budget measures at a more rapid pace and to incorporate Clinton's proposed tax increases in the reconciliation bill. Placing the tax increases in the reconciliation bill had important advantages for the Democrats. Selling never-popular tax increases might be easier as a part of a larger deficit-reduction package. Furthermore, reconciliation instructions to committees set deadlines on reporting legislation. This change meant that the two tax-writing committees, House Ways and Means and Senate Finance, could not indefinitely delay the tough decisions about taxes. And just as important, reconciliation bills are subject to a 20-hour limit on debate in the Senate, which protects them from filibusters and nongermane amendments. These special budget procedures meant that Republican opponents of the tax legislation could not delay Senate action.

The administration's plan ran into serious difficulty with conservative Democrats and, as had happened in previous years, the president's plan was adopted only once. New procedural devices – a deficit-reduction trust fund and a mandatory review of entitlement spending – were invented to satisfy legislators who lacked confidence in the legislation's goals. The trust fund plan provided that an amount equal to the projected deficit reduction from the bill be placed in a trust fund that could be used only to pay maturing public debt obligations, thereby reducing the national debt. The trust fund innovation proved insufficient to satisfy many conservative Democrats, however, so an agreement was reached between Democratic leaders and leading conservatives to make highly privileged legislation to address entitlement spending if such spending ultimately exceeded levels specified in the budget bill. In this way, the conservatives were assured that Congress would consider more serious entitlement reform if the budget plan proved too optimistic. With this agreement in place, a sufficient number of the Democrats supported the reconciliation bill for it to pass, 219 to 213. No Republicans voted for it, and 38 Democrats still voted against it.

After the Senate passed its version of the bill, the conference committee negotiations on the bill occurred almost entirely among Democrats. Their problem was a common one for the Democrats – how to keep liberals satisfied with commitments for domestic spending without raising taxes to the point that the party's conservatives would object. To make matters worse, a deadline of sorts loomed for approving the bill. The August recess was scheduled to begin at the end of the week of August 2. The Democrats did not want their internal divisions to delay the recess and give Republicans an opportunity to score political points by claiming that the Democrats had failed to end gridlock in Washington. Protecting the party's public image, as well as its policy objectives, appeared to motivate the Democratic leaders, and the conference's many staff assistants labored through several nights to produce the 1,800-page conference report.

As House and Senate leaders began to reveal the compromises they were making on various details of the conference report, some conservative Democrats who had supported the reconciliation bill indicated their intention to vote against the conference report. To appease at least some of them, President Clinton acted unilaterally to add credibility to the promise that the new tax revenues would be used to reduce the deficit rather than to increase spending. By executive order, he created the deficit trust fund and established an entitlement review process to measure whether legislators were abiding by the budget plan's requirements. Moreover, the House would adopt, as a part of a special rule for the conference report, a requirement that it act on new legislation to address any overages in entitlement spending when they occur. No provisions were made to bind the Senate to the same process, but House action on entitlement spending in future budget resolutions would force the Senate to confront the issue.

Even with these last-minute concessions, the outcome eventually turned on the vote of a freshman member, Marjorie Margolies-Mezvinsky, a Democrat from a Republican-leaning district just outside Philadelphia. She had voted against the president's position on the budget resolution and on passage of the House bill, but reportedly she had promised her support if her vote turned out to be pivotal – no doubt hoping it would not be. Early in the 15-minute period for the vote, Margolies-Mezvinsky cast a no vote. But with no time left in the vote, the Democrats had only 216 votes – two votes short of a majority – so the Speaker held the vote open. Ray Thorton (D-Arkansas), who had not yet voted, signed a red voting card to vote no. Only if both Margolies-Mezvinsky and Pat Williams (D-Montana) changed their votes to yes would the conference report pass. Williams was a 14-year veteran Democrat from Montana who had made the same promise as Margolies-Mezvinsky. Williams changed his vote first, and then all eyes fell on Margolies-Mezvinsky, who was being ushered to the front desk by a group of colleagues. The Republicans chanted, "Goodbye, Marjorie," referring to her reelection prospects if she voted against them. She signed a green card to vote yes, and the Speaker gaveled the vote closed.

Margolies-Mezvinsky spent the next few days explaining her vote. She appeared on local television and radio; was interviewed on National Public Radio, the *MacNeil/Lehrer News Hour*, and CNN's *Moneyline*; and immediately aired radio ads in her district to explain her vote. Her explanation was that she had extracted an important promise from the president. Minutes before the vote, she was called to the phone to talk to the president. Asked what it would take to get her vote, she told the president that she wanted a high-level conference for a serious discussion of cutting entitlement spending. Clinton agreed, so she agreed to vote yes. The next week, Secretary of Health and Human Services Donna Shalala traveled to Philadelphia to discuss plans for the conference. The full conference finally took place in December, with the president in attendance. Margolies-Mezvinsky lost her bid for reelection in 1994.

The Senate outcome came down to the decision of Senator Bob Kerrey, a Nebraska Democrat. Kerrey, who had acquired the nickname "Cosmic Bob" during his failed 1992 presidential bid, frustrated the White House because there were no particular provisions or promises of future action that he was looking for that could be used to get him to vote yes. Several talks with Clinton did not clarify Kerrey's position. Finally, hours before the Senate vote, Kerrey went to the Senate floor to announce his decision in favor of his party. He said, in part, "President Clinton, if you are watching now, as I suspect you are, I tell you this: I could not and should not cast a vote that brings down your Presidency. You have made mistakes and know it far better than I. But you do not deserve, and America cannot afford, to have you spend the next sixty days quibbling over whether or not we should have this cut or this tax increase." His Democratic colleagues rose in applause. The Republicans watched in silence. With Kerrey staying with his party, another tie vote was ensured. Once again Vice President Gore cast the deciding vote, and the conference report was approved, 51 to 50.

Tax Bill Certification: 1995–1996

Budget legislation became the central battleground for the new Republican majorities elected to the House and Senate in 1994. In 1995, the Republicans failed to gain congressional approval of a constitutional amendment to require an annually balanced budget, but in 1996 they gave the president the line-item veto for spending bills (although it was later struck down by the courts). In the interim, the Republicans pursued a strategy that they thought would compel the president to accept a budget reconciliation bill representing a far different mix of spending and taxing priorities than those contained in the 1993 bill. They failed miserably. The result contributed to the demise of Speaker Newt Gingrich's House career and bolstered President Clinton's chances for reelection in 1996. It also proved to be a lesson about political brinksmanship that congressional majority parties would carry into future Congresses.

In designing their budget resolution and reconciliation bill in 1995, the congressional Republican majorities largely ignored the proposals of the Clinton administration. They combined the goal of achieving a balanced budget by 2002 – which had been jettisoned in the fight over the 1993 bill – with a plan to cut taxes by $245 billion over seven years, which meant that federal spending had to be cut deeply. They sought to limit Medicaid spending and to give the states administrative responsibility for the program, stem the growth of Medicare, eliminate three executive departments (the Departments of Education, Commerce, and Energy), cut welfare spending, limit environmental regulations, and eliminate dozens of federal programs.

Procedural innovations were once again used to help bridge policy differences. Many senators were concerned that the deep tax cuts proposed would undermine the effort to balance the budget. To gain their support for the budget resolution, a provision was included that required the Finance Committee to wait to mark up tax cut provisions for the reconciliation bill until the Congressional Budget Office had officially certified that the bill would actually balance the federal budget by 2002. In this way, a nonpartisan staff arm of Congress, the CBO, had to approve estimates of the long-term effects of the budget package *before* a committee could act on the budget package.

By the time Congress approved the budget resolution, in the early summer of 1995, the House Republican leadership had devised a strategy that they hoped would gain the president's signature for their reconciliation bill, which would incorporate their spending and tax legislation. The Republicans would refuse to pass two critical sets of legislation – appropriations bills and a debt-ceiling increase – until the president agreed to approve their reconciliation bill. Failure to enact appropriations bills would force many departments to shut down at the end of the fiscal year (at midnight on September 30). Failure to increase the debt ceiling when needed would force the government to stop borrowing and possibly default on its debt obligations. The ceiling would be reached sometime in the fall. The strategy was predicated on the assumption that the Republican budget plan would be popular with the public. The Republicans' view, articulated by Speaker Gingrich, was that the president would not dare to shut down federal services or allow the government to default on its loans and would feel compelled to sign their legislation.

As the October 1 deadline approached, talk of the "train wreck" that would occur if the appropriations bills were not enacted began to dominate Washington. The reconciliation bill was due on September 22, but that date slipped by as Republicans struggled to resolve differences within their own ranks and finish writing the huge bill. Unfortunately for the Republicans, public enthusiasm for their budget plan had weakened. By November 13, Congress had failed to pass any appropriations bills or the reconciliation bill and the debt ceiling was about to be reached. The need for the debt-ceiling bill was eased when administration found ways to juggle money in trust funds to create cash for the government to continue to pay its debt-service obligations.

The Republicans remained eager to force a showdown with the president. They passed an extension of appropriations authority through December 15 and a temporary debt-ceiling increase measure extending the government's borrowing authority to December 12. The debt-ceiling bill included provisions that prevented the president from juggling the trust funds and would revert the debt ceiling to its previous level on December 12. The continuing resolution was designed to be unpalatable to the president – it reduced spending in the affected agencies to just 60 percent of the previous year's level and canceled a scheduled reduction in Medicare premiums.

To the Republicans' surprise, Clinton vetoed both bills. As the administration knew, the Republicans lacked the two-thirds majority in each house required to override a presidential veto. The result was a shutdown of the unfunded federal agencies, forcing about 800,000 "nonessential" federal

MAJOR DEVELOPMENTS IN THE BUDGET PROCESS, 1974–2007

1974 Congressional Budget and Impoundment Control Act

Created the modern budgeting process, established the budget committees, and provided for congressional review of presidential rescissions and deferrals.

1980 Reconciliation Bill

Provided that (for the first time) reconciliation be used at the start of the budget process. Committees were required to forward legislation drafted specifically to reduce spending as required by the first budget resolution.

1985 and 1987 Gramm-Rudman-Hollings Bill

Set fixed annual targets for deficit reduction and established a sequestration process to bring spending down to levels required to meet targets.

1990 Budget Enforcement Act

Dropped the fixed deficit targets of the Gramm-Rudman-Hollings approach and replaced them with caps on spending in domestic, defense, and international budgetary categories; pay-as-you-go rules for spending and revenues; and restrictions on loans and indirect spending.

1993 Omnibus Budget Reconciliation Act

Modified spending priorities and extended the enforcement provisions of the 1990 act through 1998.

1996 Balanced Budget Act

Modified spending priorities, extended the enforcement provisions of the 1993 act through 2002, and projected a balanced budget in fiscal year 2002.

2002

PAYGO enforcement provisions allowed to expire.

2007

PAYGO rule adopted; rules requiring sponsors of earmarks to be identified; House rule provides a "trigger" that establishes a point of order against tax-cut legislation that does not require that the OMB certify that the tax cuts cost less than $179.8 billion through fiscal 2012 or more than 80 percent of any surplus projected for 2012 at the time.

workers to be furloughed. Additional accounting moves made the veto of the debt-ceiling bill inconsequential, but the shutdown caused by the veto of the continuing resolution proved politically costly – for the Republicans. Although the Republicans blamed the shutdown on Clinton's unwillingness to bargain, the public blamed the Republicans over Clinton by a two-to-one margin. The fact that Republicans had made their strategy so conspicuous but still didn't have a reconciliation bill ready to pass hurt their cause. Worse yet for the Republicans, the president's willingness to take a stand enhanced his popularity with the public, giving the president a stronger bargaining position. The Republicans had misjudged Clinton's willingness to veto the bills and had badly miscalculated the general public's response.

Scrambling to determine what to do next, the Republicans adopted another continuing resolution – which ended a six-day shutdown – and soon approved a conference report on the reconciliation bill. It was expected that the reconciliation bill would be vetoed as well, so the issue was how to conduct negotiations to find a version acceptable to the president and to both houses of Congress. The second continuing resolution included a new feature: It stipulated that the president and Congress must agree to a plan to balance the federal budget within seven years – by 2002 – using economic estimates provided by the Congressional Budget Office. The Republicans viewed the commitment to a balanced budget as a large victory, but the details of a new budget plan were yet to be negotiated.

Partisan rhetoric sharpened. Differences between the parties over the reconciliation bill continued to concern the size of spending cuts in domestic programs and the size of tax cuts. A handful of regular appropriations bills passed and received presidential approval, but several others remained unfinished by December 15, again forcing a shutdown of many federal agencies, this time involving approximately 260,000 workers. House Speaker Gingrich and Senate Majority Leader Bob Dole appeared to be willing to pass another continuing resolution, but hard-line House Republicans made it plain that they would not support another resolution. Before they would agree to fund certain federal agencies, they wanted concessions from the president that the president was simply unwilling to grant. The result was that this shutdown lasted 21 days.

News stories of hardships suffered by government workers over the holidays worsened the standing of the congressional Republicans in the polls. By the first week of January, Clinton's poll ratings were heading up, and the Republicans were eager to pass continuing resolutions. In fact, they passed three measures – one narrow appropriations bill, to keep the most popular programs funded through September 1996; a second appropriations bill, to fund a couple of other programs through March 15; and a continuing resolution to keep the remaining programs and agencies open until January 26. Meanwhile, deep divisions among Republicans concerning the efficacy and political costs of their strategy began to emerge.

The debt ceiling loomed on the horizon yet again. The financial adjustments that had allowed the administration to avoid defaulting on the country's debt obligations were just about exhausted. To avoid being blamed for playing games with the debt ceiling, Republican leaders wrote President Clinton that they intended to increase the debt ceiling when required. No progress had been made on the reconciliation bill by January 26, however, so another continuing resolution was enacted. It was now four months after the start of the fiscal year, and still no budget was in place. The process for drafting a budget for the next fiscal year began on February 5, when the president submitted his budget proposals to Congress. Plainly, those proposals meant little in the absence of a budget for the current fiscal year.

Just before March 15, for the fifth time since September of the previous year, a continuing resolution was passed to avoid a shutdown of federal agencies, this time for only a week. This practice of passing short-term continuing resolutions went on for several more weeks. Eventually, late in the evening of April 24, nearly seven months late and after a total of 14 limited spending bills and short-term continuing resolutions, the president and congressional Republican leaders agreed on a budget. The next day, Republican leaders rushed through to passage an appropriations bill to fund government agencies for the rest of the fiscal year. Compromise spending and tax cuts were quickly enacted.

Dropping and Reinstating PAYGO Rules: 1997–2007

With the 1996 budget plan in place, the Republicans did not challenge President Clinton on the budget again; instead, they turned to tactical fights on individual appropriations bills. They had no interest in repeating the political disaster of the 1995–1996 budget fight. Many Republican conservatives did not like Speaker Gingrich's willingness to compromise with Clinton, but, at least in the Speaker's view, there was little to be gained by laying down more ultimatums for the president. By the end of 1997, a strong economy, which yielded both reduced spending and increased tax revenues, had cut the deficit much faster than expected. In fact, a balanced budget was achieved in 1998, four years earlier than predicted in the 1996 budget. The large strategic moves of deficit politics were replaced with the less visible, tactical moves of surplus politics, with congressional Republicans and the Democratic president fighting over the details of appropriations bills.

Partisan differences caused four straight years of gamesmanship with appropriations bills. Sparring over spending details routinely led to delays in passing appropriations bills, which required that Congress pass numerous continuing resolutions. Moreover, when agreement was finally reached, compromises often extended over several appropriations bills and many extraneous measures that were packaged in large omnibus appropriations bills. In 1998, for example, eight of the 13 regular appropriations bills and over 30 non-appropriations measures were included in the omnibus appropriations bills for fiscal 1999. In 2000, 21 continuing resolutions were adopted before an omnibus appropriations bill was passed a few days before Christmas. That bill included the provisions of three regular appropriations bills, some new emergency spending, and non-appropriations legislation on Medicare, Medicaid, medical savings accounts and other tax provisions, immigration, and commodities regulation. This multidimensional bill represented many bargains and reflected members' realization that it was the last opportunity to address some issues before that Congress ended.

The political tables had turned in Washington after Republican President George W. Bush was elected in 2000. Bush was in office for less than a year when the 9–11 terrorist attack occurred. The subsequent airline and New York subsidies, homeland security, war on terrorism, and Afghan and Iraqi wars cost many hundreds of billions for the federal government, contributing to the creation of the first deficit after four years of surpluses. A prolonged recession and spending on national security contributed to the deficits, as did a tax cut enacted in 2001 when surpluses were still projected.

In February 2003, President Bush proposed a budget deficit of over $300 billion for fiscal 2004. He proposed more tax cuts, some of which were opposed by at least a few Senate Republicans, and some spending increases. The administration argued that much of the tax proposal and some of the spending hikes were needed to boost the economy. The proposals, if adopted, would require Congress to adjust spending ceilings in the budget enforcement mechanisms.

The return of deficits was accompanied by failure to pass appropriations bills on time. From 2001 through 2004, most appropriations bills were not enacted until after the October 1 deadline and most were wrapped into large omnibus bills. For example, in 2002, when the appropriations bills for fiscal 2003 were considered, no appropriations bill was enacted by October 1 and eventually 10 continuing resolutions were adopted. Democrats argued that Republicans deliberately delayed action on a few of the bills so that Republicans would not have to cast potentially embarrassing votes just before the 2002 election. Not until January 2003, more than four months after the bills were due to be passed and after a new Congress was in place, did the House and Senate pass an omnibus bill that incorporated 11 of the 13 regular appropriations bills. Conference committee negotiations over the bill were not complete until February – six months late and halfway through the fiscal year. The Republican Congress passed all appropriations bills in 2005 and 2006 before adjourning, although many were passed long after the October

382

THE BATTLE OVER EARMARKS

In early 2006, Republicans found themselves embarrassed by the volume of earmarks, totaling about $20 billion, that were included in a supplemental appropriations bill, which President George W. Bush threatened to veto. Earmarks are provisions to fund individual projects that are championed by individual members, often in collaboration with outside interests and lobbyists. Republican leaders passed the bill only after promising earmark reform. The promised reform included a requirement that the names of earmarks' sponsors be made public. Members of the Appropriations committees believed that they were being singled out for earmarks when members of the tax-writing committees used legislation to write into law narrow provisions for tax breaks or tariff protection. As a consequence of the bad publicity for the bill and other developments, particularly a lobbying scandal, Republicans started but never completed work on an ethics reform bill that addressed earmarks.

House Democrats, after gaining a majority in the 2006 elections, incorporated earmark reform, including provisions that Republicans invented but did not adopt in the previous Congress. In response to the reform, House committees must keep a record of requests for earmarks. Critics of the reform approved of requirements requiring the publications of sponsors' names but preferred that floor votes could be guaranteed on individual earmarks. The Senate developed similar rules but put them in a bill that has not been enacted as of this writing.

The reform appeared to limit the number of earmarks, but legislators and lobbyists looked for ways to circumvent the new requirements. Lobbyists reported that they put more effort into persuading executive branch officials to include specific projects in the president's budget requests so that legislators would not have to file requests with committees. Executive officials also would be lobbied to use their discretion to favor certain projects after receiving appropriations.

deadline, but, facing difficult choices in the 2006 election year, leaving work on nine of 11 appropriations bills incomplete after they lost their House and Senate majorities.

The new Democratic majority of 2007 reinstated PAYGO rules having scored political points against Republicans in the 2006 campaign for letting the deficit drift upward. The Democrats did not include a sequestration process so the process lacked the tough enforcement mechanism that was included in the 1990, 1993, and 1996 versions. Instead, they included only a point of order, which could be waived by approving a special rule, for a bill or amendment that increased the deficit. Republicans complained that the new rule would make it easy for Democrats to block extension of tax cuts, enacted in 2001 and 2003. Republican and President Bush's opposition prevented adoption of a similar rule in the Senate, where a filibuster was possible and a veto override was unlikely.

Both houses moved to put in place new rules governing earmarks, the term used to describe funding for specific projects. The rules do not ban earmarks but rather require the disclosure of the name of the legislator sponsoring each project, publication of a justification for the project, and certification that the project does not benefit the legislator or his or her spouse. In addition to spending on construction projects, the rule applies to tax and tariff provisions geared to individual firms or organizations.

Conclusion

The history of budgetary politics discussed in this chapter illustrates several important features of congressional politics that have been recurrent themes throughout this book:

1. Legislative outcomes in the United States are the product of a three-player legislative process in which the House, the Senate, and the president must negotiate and reach compromises. In the budget battles described in this chapter, differences in policy preferences among the three institutional players, combined with the necessity of gaining the consent of all three, produced compromised efforts to reduce the deficit and procedural innovations designed to force other players to act.

2. The president is a central player in congressional politics. When the president proposes a change in direction in budget policy, it usually changes Congress's agenda. The president's proposals may be set aside by the majority party in Congress, as they were initially in 1995. Doing so entails great political risks, however. For the party controlling the White House, the president, not the party's congressional leaders, tends to be the chief strategist for the party.

3. Rules matter. The constitutional requirement of a two-thirds majority in each house to override a presidential veto prevented the majority party in Congress from imposing its budget priorities in 1995 and 1996. Statutory limits on appropriations authority and the debt ceiling proved vital. The Senate rule that prevents extraneous amendments from being attached to budget bills (the Byrd rule) limited the options of House and Senate committees. Also, enforcement provisions included in previous budget agreements were essential to crafting compromises that the players could trust would be honored. Except

for the basic rules outlined in the Constitution, all of these rules were subject to change and became a part of the debate over budget policy.

4. The Budget Act, and how the different players made use of it, altered the traditional relationship between the parent houses and their committees. Historically, committees had taken the initiative in setting the policy agenda and designing legislation within their jurisdictions. The new budget process, however, allowed top party and budget leaders to present comprehensive budget resolutions to the parent houses and required committees to produce legislation, after the fact, that they most certainly would not have drafted had they been left to their own discretion.

5. The rules of the legislative game are changed by the players. The players often turned to new procedural rules to guarantee that promises critical to achieving a compromise would be kept in the future. New enforcement mechanisms were invented on several occasions to convince key groups of legislators that uncertainties about the future would not work to their disadvantage.

6. Elections have clear and powerful effects on policy making. In the history described in this chapter, elections produced realignments in the preferences of key players – the president and members of Congress – concerning budgetary policy. Divided party control of the House, Senate, and White House was the direct product of elections and shaped the players' strategies in basic ways. Less significant, but clearly present, were the effects of election timing. On several occasions, approaching elections tended to dampen partisanship and encourage compromise on the part of the party with the greater public relations problem. In addition, public opinion polls, which are taken as a gauge of the potential electoral consequences of political events and policy positions, appeared to alter players' strategies on many occasions.

7. Parties are the primary building blocks for creating voting coalitions, but party discipline is far from perfect. Leaders of both the Democratic and the Republican parties, when they were in the majority in Congress, first attempted to satisfy enough fellow party members to create a majority before soliciting support from the other party. In the end, voting on the budget plans, which typically encapsulated the major policy priorities of the majority party, was very partisan. Those party members who voted against the position of their own party leaders were criticized but ultimately faced no formal punishment.

8. Party leaders are important players in Congress, but they are not all-powerful. In the budget negotiations described in this chapter, the

distribution of power within Congress showed a fairly centralized pattern that was partly the result of the rules governing the budget process and partly a reflection of the need for high-level negotiations to work out differences of great importance to the parties and the two branches. The large differences in the two parties' budgetary policy preferences and each party's fairly great internal cohesiveness encouraged party leaders to be assertive strategists on behalf of their party. But party leaders, it appears, were more than mere agents of their parties. They focused agendas, made good and poor tactical decisions, and shaped their parties' images with the general public in ways that had consequences for the eventual legislative outcome. Some reliance on party leaders is inevitable, given the difficulty of producing collective action among the dozens of members in each of the four congressional parties. Still, as was most obvious in the 1995–1996 budget battle, even the most aggressive leader is constrained by what his or her party colleagues are willing to accept in terms of strategy and policy.

9. Committees play a central role in the legislative process, but their influence is not constant. Budgetary politics since the late 1970s has tended to push key decisions up to central budget and party leaders and to reduce the independence of committees and their chairs. And yet, it is important to qualify this important consequence of budgetary politics by observing that committees were still responsible for writing the details of most of the legislative provisions of budget packages, even if they were highly constrained by agreements negotiated elsewhere. Even when the top party leaders and administration officials were hammering out the overall shape of the budget deals, most of the language of the budget packages was written by committees, and hundreds of specific policy provisions were negotiated by committee representatives.

The importance of parties, leaders, and committees in congressional policy making will continue to be shaped by the alignment of members' policy preferences, the nature of the issues, and the inherited rules of the game. Perceptions and preferences about budgetary issues are particularly important because of the pervasive effect of the budget on policy initiatives throughout the government. If budget issues begin to lose salience as the deficit fades from memory, then more policy initiatives originating from interest groups and creative members may rejuvenate the committees.

Appendix

Introduction to the Spatial Theory
of Legislating

Much of congressional politics has geometric characteristics. When we speak of most Democrats as liberals, most Republicans as conservatives, and some legislators as moderates, we have in mind an ideological or policy spectrum – a line or dimension – along which we can place legislators. In recent Congresses, the parties have been sharply divided, with very little overlap between the parties. Figure A-1 illustrates this for the 109th Congress (2005–2006) for senators. Using a statistical technique, senators were scored on the basis of their overall voting record in the Congress. Democrats and Republicans were concentrated on opposite sides of the spectrum, creating one of the most polarized Senates in history.

Legislators' policy positions also can be represented in two or more dimensions, when appropriate. In Figure A-2, senators' policy positions are identified in two dimensions for a debate on an immigration reform bill in 2006. Their locations are identified with the help of a statistical analysis of their votes on about three dozen amendments and other motions that were considered on the Senate floor. The most significant issue during the debate concerned the standards for allowing illegal immigrants to gain legal entry to the United States. Senators who opposed special arrangements for reentry lined up on the far right, while senators who favored standards that would ease reentry for work or citizenship were located on the left (the horizontal dimension). Other issues, such as the ceiling on the number of legal immigrants allowed, were debated, too, and sometimes divided senators differently than the votes related to the treatment of current illegal immigrants (the vertical dimension). Democrats tended to favor both standards that facilitated reentry and larger quotas, while Republicans were split on reentry standards and tended to favor smaller quotas.[1]

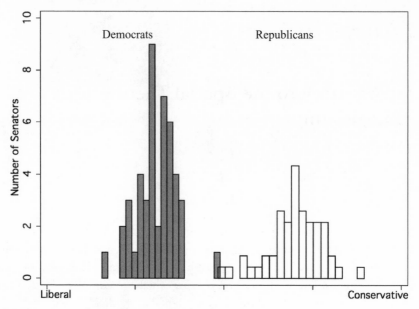

FIGURE A-1. Distribution of Senators on Liberal-Conservative Dimension, 2005–2006 (Democrats on left; Republicans on right). *Source:* Optimal Classification scores; www.voteview.com.

Basic Concepts for Analyzing a Legislative Body

Political scientists have taken advantage of geometric representations to develop spatial theories of legislative politics. The theories provide a way to conceptualize the location of legislators, policy alternatives, and policy outcomes. Like all scientific theories, spatial theories are based on assumptions that allow us to draw inferences about expected behavior. With a few assumptions about legislators, the policy space, and the rules governing

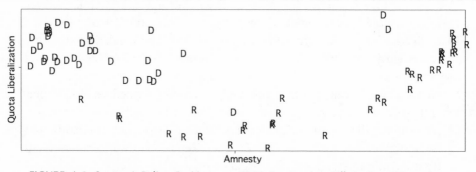

FIGURE A-2. Senators' Policy Positions on 2006 Immigration Bill in Two Dimensions (Democrats, D; Republicans, R). *Source:* Optimal Classification scores on Senate votes related to S2611, 109th Congress.

FIGURE A-3. Illustration of the Median Voter Theorem.

decisions, we can deduce remarkably useful and usually intuitive propositions about the location of legislative outcomes. Non-intuitive predictions are particularly useful because they often yield insights that even the close observer of legislative politics might overlook.

Preferences and the Policy Space

Spatial theories assume the legislators, presidents, and other players have preferences about policy outcomes. Preferences may reflect personal beliefs or political influences. The preferences are assumed to be consistent. For example, if a legislator prefers policy *A* over policy *B* and also prefers *B* over *C*, then she favors *A* over *C* (transitive preferences, we say). When a legislator's preference are depicted geometrically, as in the figures, it is usually assumed that alternatives that are closer to the legislator's ideal point are preferred to more distant points (a Euclidean policy space, we say). Furthermore, it is assumed that each legislator chooses a strategy that she believes will yield the best possible outcome – that is, minimizes the distance between her ideal point and the outcome.

Simple Majority Rule and the Median Voter Theorem

Spatial theorists define "institutions" as a set of rules that govern decision making. Rules may concern who has the right to participate, the "weight" that each participant has in determining the outcome, the way in which policy proposals are constructed, the order in which policy proposals are considered, the standard for a final decision, and so on. Here, we assume that each legislator has the right to cast one vote and, to begin, that a simple majority of legislators is required for a proposal to be adopted.

In Figure A-3, a small legislature with five legislators is illustrated. With a simple majority decision rule, a winning majority will always include legislator C. As the median legislator, C can join two other legislators – to the left with A and B, to the right with D and E, or in the middle with B and D – to form a three-vote majority. Of course, larger majorities could form, but they will always include C. A spatial theorist would say that C is pivotal – C must be included in a majority and so can demand that the outcome be located at her ideal point. The *median voter theorem*, which we will not formally prove

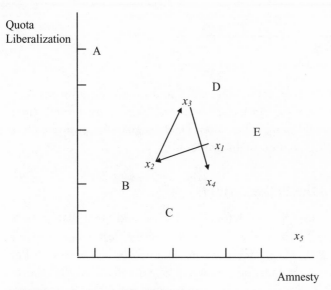

FIGURE A-4. Illustration of the Chaos Theorem.

here, provides that if C's position is adopted it cannot be defeated by another proposal. A corollary is that if two alternatives are presented, a majority will always prefer the alternative closer to the median legislator.

The median voter theorem means that when a median exists we can predict the outcome by knowing only the median legislator's ideal point. Spatial theorists refer to the stable prediction of the median outcome as an *equilibrium*. When a new legislature is elected, a new median location would lead us to predict a change in the outcome. That is, a new equilibrium is expected.

Multidimensional Spaces and the Chaos Theorem

A multidimensional policy space, such as the one in Figure A-4, creates important complications for predicting legislative outcomes. No legislator is the median on both dimensions. C is the median on the amnesty dimension but E is the median on the quota liberalization dimension. What is the expected outcome? In fact, political scientists have demonstrated mathematically that in most cases there is no single predicted outcome, no equilibrium, as there is in the unidimensional case.

A thought experiment will demonstrate an important point. Let us assume that current policy is located at x_1. Legislator B might propose a policy at x_2 and would win the support of A and C, both of whom are closer to x_1 than to x_2 and so would join B to form a majority to vote for x_2 and defeat x_1. But then D might offer x_3 and win the support of A and E. This process can continue indefinitely with a new majority of three forming at each step. If the rules allow a continuous flow of new proposals, there is no single outcome that cannot be defeated by some other proposal. This illustrates the *chaos theorem*. The theorem provides that, as a general rule, we cannot expect a stable outcome from simple majority rule in two (or more) dimensions.

Agenda Setting, Structure-Induced Equilibria, and Political Power

The chaos result – or majority rule cycling – may seem surprising. Legislatures regularly make final decisions without endless cycling through proposals. Why that is the case is the subject of a vast literature in political science. We do not want to review the complexities here, but three important points about legislative politics need to be understood.

First, legislative rules may not allow multidimensional proposals or may limit the number of proposals that may be considered. Such rules would limit the range of possible outcomes and make those outcomes more predictable. If only unidimensional proposals may be considered, the median voter theorem applies and majority rule chaos is avoided. Theorists use the label *structure-induced equilibria* for constraints on outcomes that are imposed by the rules. Thus, even if legislators' preferences are multidimensional, the rules may generate median outcomes by either limiting the range of proposals that are allowed or imposing unidimensionality on the proposals that may be considered.

Second, special influence over the agenda, either granted under the rules or gained through informal means, may control the alternatives subject to a vote and further limit the possible outcomes. A Speaker or presiding officer may be able to limit who is recognized to offer a motion. A coalition of legislators, such as members of the majority party, may agree to support only those proposals that a majority of the coalition endorses, thus limiting the set of proposals that can win majority support.

Three, introducing a proposal that creates a new dimension can transform a situation that would produce a median outcome into one with no predictable outcome. A legislator who dislikes the median outcome might be motivated to offer a proposal on an issue that divides his colleagues in a new way in order to avoid the certain, but undesirable outcome. The original median legislator would be motivated to create an agenda that prevents the proposal on the new issue from being considered.

In practice, then, rules and legislative strategies can contract or expand the range of possible outcomes. Real politics is often played in this way. Political scientists have studied many of the consequences of a variety of rules and

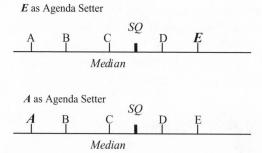

FIGURE A-5. Illustration of the Effect of the Status Quo and an Agenda Setter, the Unidimensional Case.

strategies, but continue to pursue research on the relationship between rules, strategies, and outcomes.

The Status Quo and Agenda Setting

A legislature often inherits policy from past legislatures. In most cases, the inherited policy, which we call the *status quo* (*SQ*), remains in place until a new policy is adopted. That is, the *SQ* is the default outcome if it is not defeated by a new proposal. The set of proposals that can defeat the *SQ* is called the *win set of SQ*. When there are no proposals that can defeat the *SQ*, we say that the win set is empty and predict that the outcome will remain at *SQ*.

The effect of the *SQ* on legislative strategies is important and intuitive. In Figure A-5, five legislators are arrayed on a single dimension. In the figure's top panel, let's assume that no proposal can be considered unless legislator E approves, but if a proposal is offered it can be amended. E, of course, wants the outcome at her own ideal point and might make a proposal there. However, A, B, or C might offer an amendment to move the outcome away from E and to the other side of *SQ*. Such an amendment would win a majority and E would be worse off than if he left the policy at *SQ*. Consequently, we would expect E to refuse to make an initial proposal. In this case, the agenda setter, E, protects the status quo. In contrast, in the lower panel in Figure A-5, legislator A is the agenda setter. Because A prefers the median's position over the *SQ*, A is willing to allow the legislature to consider a proposal and have it amended to C, the expected outcome.

Thus, the location of the status quo relative to the median determines the agenda setter's strategy. With the same agenda setter and median, different issues can generate different outcomes – the median or the *SQ*.

The same logic applies to the multidimensional case, as in Figure A-6. Legislators will support a proposal that improves on the status quo, *SQ*. In

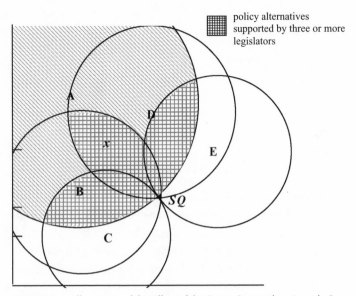

policy alternatives
supported by three or more
legislators

FIGURE A-6. Illustration of the Effect of the Status Quo and an Agenda Setter, the Multidimensional Case.

the figure, these *preferred-to* sets are denoted by the partial or full circles. For example, within the shaded circle centered on legislator A is the preferred-to set for A. The double shaded areas are the sets of locations preferred by at least three of the five legislators over *SQ*. Because points in the double shaded areas attract majority support for a proposal over the *SQ*, they define the win set of *SQ*. A large number of locations will not defeat *SQ* so majority rule narrowed the possible outcomes considerably. But, in this two-dimensional space, the win set includes a wide range of possibilities, many of which are less preferred to the *SQ* by one or two of the legislators. A, B, and D might agree to an outcome at *x*, which would make C and E worse off than leaving the policy at *SQ*.

Bicameralism, Separation of Powers, Agency Decisions, and Legislative Outcomes

Bicameralism

In the previous section, we considered a single legislative body. Congress and many other legislatures are bicameral, and usually require that a majority of each chamber approve legislation before it is sent to the president or chief executive. Spatially, this means that we must consider the relationship between the outcomes in the two chambers.

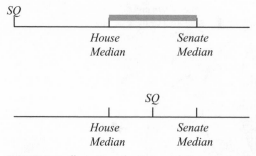

FIGURE A-7. Illustration of a Bicameral Outcome in One Dimension.

In unidimensional space, shown in Figure A-7, the outcome would be negotiated between the House and Senate medians. If both medians favor some of the same proposals over SQ, as they do in the top panel, they will negotiate an outcome among the range of proposals that they both prefer to SQ. If SQ falls between the two medians so that each house median prefers SQ to anything the other house would prefer to SQ, as in the figure's lower panel, the houses will not agree to a new policy and the outcome will be SQ.

In multidimensional space, as depicted in Figure A-6, we would define the bicameral win set as the intersection of the win sets in the two houses. We do not show that situation here. The overlap in the win sets for the two houses can be very small or very large. Little overlap greatly narrows the range of possible outcomes. Large overlap creates the possibility that a conference committee charged with finding compromise legislation will be able to exercise great discretion in determining the location of the final bill and still be able to attract majority support in both houses for the final version.

The President and the Veto

Under the Constitution, the president may veto legislation and a veto can be overridden only with the support of a two-thirds majority in each house of Congress. The threshold of a two-thirds majority in each house makes it necessary to appeal to more legislators than the requirement of a simple majority for initial approval of legislation. In our five-legislators illustrations, this means attracting the support of four of the five legislators (three of five would be less than the two-thirds required).

The president will veto any legislation that makes him worse off than SQ. In one dimension, several possibilities arise. In Figure A-8, the president's ideal point is P and the House and Senate medians are M_H and M_S, respectively. The two houses of Congress negotiate a bill at B somewhere between their medians. The president prefers SQ to B so he vetoes the bill. Both

FIGURE A-8. Illustration of Upholding a Presidential Veto, in One Dimension.

House and Senate medians would like to override the veto but they must gain the support of two thirds of their colleagues. V_H and V_S are the *veto pivots*. That is, they are the legislators who are the leftmost members of the two-thirds majority that is required to override a veto. Without their support for the bill over the SQ, the veto cannot be overridden. In this case, V_H prefers SQ to B and so votes against the override. SQ is the outcome. Thus, the general rule is that a presidential veto will kill a bill whenever at least one of the veto pivots is on the same side of SQ as the president.

Other scenarios are easy to understand without illustration. Whenever the chamber medians are on the same side of SQ as the president, the president will sign the bill with a veto. Whenever V_H and V_S are on the same side of SQ opposite the president (not shown), the two houses of Congress can override the veto of the president.

As always, the multidimensional case is more complicated but it is still easy to visualize. In Figure A-9, there are two regions in which four of the five legislators of one house would favor the bill over the SQ. Consequently, a veto would be overridden any time the president vetoes a bill that is located in those regions. The bill also would have to be located in similar regions in the other house for both houses to override a president's veto. A bill that is located in the *veto win set of SQ* is one for which a veto can be overridden in both houses.

Plainly, the two-thirds majority requirement for a veto override shrinks the region of bill locations that can survive a veto to one that is smaller than the region of bill locations that can receive simple majority support in both houses. The implication is that the threat of a veto requires more careful negotiations within Congress and may have implications for legislators who win and lose. In Figure A-9, for example, the bill at x_2 survives a veto but a bill at x_1 does not, although both would receive simple majority support. But the outcome at x_2 is less favorable to legislators A and D and more favorable to B and C.

Agency Decisions

Political scientists often think of executive branch agencies as having policy preferences of their own. Staffed by people who have personal or

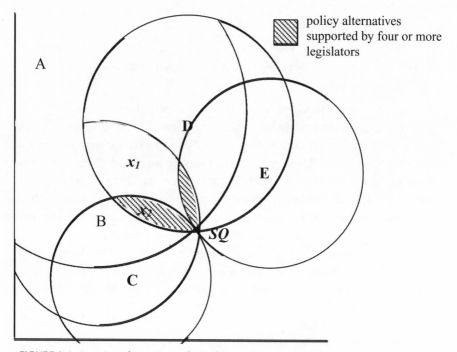

A

policy alternatives
supported by four or more
legislators

D

x_1

E

B

SQ

C

FIGURE A-9. Location of Veto Override Coalitions, the Multidimensional Case.

professional experience in a policy field, agencies are likely to devise rules
and regulations that implement law in a manner that reflects their own preferences. Congress and presidents may seek to control the independence of
agencies, but agency officials know that it may not be easy for Congress
and the president to enact new legislation to place additional constraints on
them. After all, new legislation requires the approval of the House, Senate,
and president, or, in the case of a veto, a two-thirds majority in both houses.
This is a high threshold. If a House majority, Senate majority, or president
favors the direction an agency is taking, it can block legislation that would
place new constraints in statute. (We have reported on other congressional
strategies in Chapter 9.)

The strategic setting of agency decision making can be treated spatially,
as we do in Figure A-10. To simplify, we characterize the House and Senate
as having specific locations in multidimensional space just as the president
does. If an agency took action to move a policy from a_1 (the current policy)
to a_2, the Senate would like the move and block any effort by the House to
enact legislation to require that the policy be returned to a_1. In this case,
the agency, knowing that the Senate will protect its move, is free to shift
policy without fear that the law will be changed. In contrast, if the agency

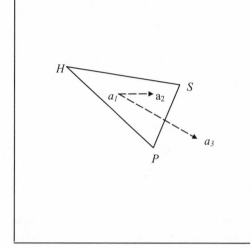

FIGURE A-10. Illustration of Agency Discretion, in Multidimensional Space.

sought to move policy as far as a_3, all three of the policy-making institutions would be better off by enacting legislation located on the line between S and P.

These scenarios demonstrate that the autonomy of an agency is limited to the range of policy moves that will not generate a new law. The farther apart the House, Senate, and president, the greater the discretion the agency enjoys. In fact, the triangle formed by the House, Senate, and president defines the limits of agency discretion. Any move that yields policy inside or to the edge of the triangle will be defended by at least one of the House, Senate, or president. Any move outside of the triangle will stimulate new legislation.

Advanced Theory and the Limits of Spatial Theory

We have presented a rudimentary introduction to the spatial theory of legislative politics. Political scientists have extended the theory in many directions. They have developed additional theory on the conditions that limit the range of possible outcomes under majority rule, explored the effect of agenda control rules that advantage parties or committees, and considered the effects of different assumptions about legislators' preferences and decision rules. We encourage our readers to pursue these important subjects elsewhere.

Spatial theory is not the ultimate theory of legislative politics. The spatial theorist assumes that legislators' policy preferences are known and invariant and theorizes only about how they motivate strategies. The determinants of legislators' policy preferences are beyond the scope of spatial theory.

The effects of nonpolicy motivations, such as the desire for reelection or to serve in the majority party, also are beyond the scope of spatial theory. Such motivations may be the overriding consideration in some circumstances. A legislator whose bill is rejected by the House of Representatives might be seen as a loser by some observers, but she may benefit from favorable press coverage and an appreciative home constituency for putting up a good fight. A legislative majority that fails to override a presidential veto may use the issue in a campaign to get more fellow partisans elected in the next Congress. Winning and losing in politics is sometimes hard to judge, at least in the short term.

Nevertheless, spatial theory is a powerful tool for predicting behavior and legislative outcomes. It often establishes a baseline expectation for outcomes against which the effects of other considerations can be measured. We can better judge the effects of persuasion by party leaders or presidents once we have a prediction for the outcome expected on the basis of legislators' prior policy preferences. It also shows that policy preferences and parliamentary rules often do not yield very specific predictions and define sometimes large ranges of possible outcomes that can be influenced by other political forces at work. Most important, spatial theory yields important insights about the effects of institutions – the rules of the game – that are so transparent in legislative decision making.

Notes

1. The American Congress

1. Paul Boller, *Congressional Anecdotes* (New York: Oxford University Press, 1991), 18.
2. Norman J. Ornstein, "Congress Inside Out: Here's Why Life on the Hill Is Meaner Than Ever," *Roll Call*, September 20, 1993, 27.
3. Robert A. Dahl, "Americans Struggle to Cope with a New Political Order That Works in Opaque and Mysterious Ways," *Public Affairs Report* (Institute of Governmental Studies, University of California, Berkeley, September 1993), 1, 4–6.
4. Robert H. Salisbury, "The Paradox of Interest Groups in Washington – More Groups, Less Clout," in *The New American Political System*, 2nd ed., ed. Anthony King, 203–229 (Washington, D.C.: American Enterprise Institute, 1990). For an analysis of the effects of these developments on Congress, see Barbara Sinclair, *The Transformation of the U.S. Senate* (Baltimore: Johns Hopkins University Press, 1989), 57–64.
5. See Theodore J. Lowi, "Toward a Legislature of the First Kind," in *Knowledge, Power, and the Congress*, ed. William H. Robinson and Clay H. Wellborn, 9–36 (Washington, D.C.: Congressional Quarterly Press, 1991).
6. Lawrence C. Dodd, "Congress and the Politics of Renewal: Redressing the Crisis of Legitimation," in *Congress Reconsidered*, 5th ed., ed. Lawrence C. Dodd and Bruce I. Oppenheimer, 426 (Washington, D.C.: Congressional Quarterly Press, 1993).
7. David E. Price, "Comment," in *Knowledge, Power, and the Congress*, 128.
8. Quoted in Helen Dewar, "Senate Bows to Braun on Symbol of Confederacy," *Washington Post*, July 23, 1993. Also see *Congressional Record*, July 22, 1993: S9256.
9. Ruth Shalit, "A Star Is Born," *The New Republic*, November 15, 1993: 19.
10. Richard F. Fenno, Jr. *Learning to Govern: An Institutional View of the 104th Congress* (Washington, D.C.: Brookings Institution, 1997). On the consequences of alternating party control of Congress, also see Lawrence C. Dodd and Bruce I. Oppenheimer, "Congress and the Emerging Order: Conditional Party Government or Constructive Partisanship?" in *Congress Reconsidered*, 6th ed., 390–413.
11. "Capitol Hill's Uncertainty Principle," *National Journal*, November 2, 1996: 2365.

2. Representation and Lawmaking in Congress

1. Robert S. Weissberg, "Collective vs. Dyadic Representation in Congress," *American Political Science Review* 72 (1978): 535–547.
2. Jane J. Mansbridge, *Beyond Adversarial Democracy* (Chicago: University of Chicago Press, 1983).
3. Calvin Jillson and Rick K. Wilson, Congressional Dynamics: Structure, Coordination, and Choice in the First American Congress, 1774–1789 (Stanford: Stanford University Press, 1994).
4. Gordon S. Wood, *The Origin of the American Republic, 1776–1787* (New York: Norton, 1969).
5. Wood, *Origin of the American Republic*, 197–255. Also see George Tsebelis and Jeannette Money, *Bicameralism* (New York: Cambridge University Press, 1997), 15–43, for a comparison of bicameral systems.

4. Members, Goals, Resources, and Strategies

1. David E. Price, *The Congressional Experience: A View from the Hill* (Boston: Little, Brown, 1973), 146.
2. Quoted in Craig Winneker, "That Was The Year That Was...Whew!" *Roll Call*, December 21, 1992, 15.
3. As quoted in Deering and Smith, *Committees in Congress*, 67.
4. Richard F. Fenno, Jr., *The Making of a Senator: Dan Quayle* (Washington, D.C.: Congressional Quarterly Press, 1989), 29.
5. From Neil MacNeil, *Forge of Democracy: The House of Representatives* (New York: D. McKay, 1963), 141.
6. Adapted from Richard F. Fenno, Jr., *Home Style: House Members in Their Districts* (Boston: Little, Brown, 1978), 1–30.
7. Michael J. Malbin, *Unelected Representatives: Congressional Staff and the Future of Representative Government* (New York: Basic Books, 1980), 5.
8. Tim Whitmire, "N.C. Republican Switched Vote on CAFTA," *Associated Press*, July 29, 2005.
9. Rob Christensen, "Hayes is CAFTA Foe no Longer; Textile Heir Casts Key Vote in House," *The News & Observer*, July 29, 2005.
10. John W. Kingdon, *Congressmen's Voting Decisions*, 2nd ed. (New York: Harper & Row, 1981), 96.
11. Richard F. Fenno, Jr., *The Emergence of a Senate Leader: Pete Domenici and the Reagan Budget* (Washington, D.C.: Congressional Quarterly Press, 1991), 134.
12. A report on the Senate aides' responses can be found in Steven S. Smith, "Informal Leadership in the Senate," in *Leading Congress*, ed. John Kornacki (Washington, D.C.: Congressional Quarterly Press, 1990), 71–83. Most respondents were members' legislative directors or administrative assistants.

13. Press release, "U.S. Senator Dan Quayle: Effective Leadership for Indiana," November 3, 1986.

5. Parties and Leaders

1. *Majority and Minority Leaders of the Senate*. U.S. Senate No. 91–20 (Washington, D.C.: Government Printing Office, 1969), 13.

6. The Standing Committees

1. Joel D. Aberbach, *Keeping a Watchful Eye: The Politics of Congressional Oversight* (Washington, D.C.: Brookings Institution, 1990), 35.
2. Eric Pianin and Guy Gugliotta, "Large Influx of Freshmen to Fuel Major Reorganization," *Washington Post*, November 8, 1992.
3. Joel D. Aberbach, "What Has Happened to the Watchful Eye?" *Congress and the Presidency* 29 (2002): 3–23.
4. Bryan D. Jones, Frank R. Baumgartner, and Jeffery C. Talbert, "The Destruction of Issue Monopolies in Congress," *American Political Science Review* 87, no. 3 (1993): 657–671.
5. Ben Pershing, "Buyer Challenges Smith for Veterans Affairs," *Roll Call*, January 4, 2005, 1, and Ben Pershing, "'Team Players' Boosted in GOP," *Roll Call*, January 10, 2005, 1.

7. The Rules of the Legislative Game

1. Robert H. Michel, "The Minority Leader Replies," *Washington Post*, December 29, 1987, A14.
2. *Congressional Record*, October 5, 1992, S16894.

8. The Floor and Voting

1. Information taken from "Pocket Guide to Common Parliamentary Phrases in the House of Representatives." Congressional Research Service.
2. Some rules do not affect amending activity, so percentages do not sum to 100.

9. Congress and the President

1. Charles M. Cameron and Nina Fischman, "Veto Bargaining," Columbia University, mimeo, March 1993.

2. Paul Light, *The President's Agenda*, revised edition (Baltimore: Johns Hopkins University Press, 1991), 2.

3. Charles M. Cameron, *Veto Bargaining: Presidents and the Politics of Negative Power* (New York: Cambridge University Press, 2000), 188.

4. Citing a study by Christopher Kelley, Charlie Savage, "House Panel Probing Bush's Record on Signing Statements," *The Boston Globe*, February 1, 2007.

5. As quoted in Light, *President's Agenda*, 13.

6. *Congressional Record*, February 16, 2006: S1402.

7. Henry B. Hogue, "Recess Appointments: Frequently Asked Questions," CRS Report, Congressional Research Services, September 10, 2002; Henry B. Hogue, "Recess Appointments: Frequently Asked Questions," CRS Report, Congressional Research Services, January 16, 2007.

10. Congress and the Courts

1. William T. Gormley, Jr. "The Bureaucracy and its Masters: The New Madisonian System in the U.S." *Governance*, January 1991, 10–11

2. *Ibid.*

11. Congress, Lobbyists, and Interest Groups

1. Edward G. Carmines, Jessica C. Gerrity, and Michael W. Wagner, "How the American Public Views Congress: A Report Based on the Center on Congress' 2004 Public Opinion Survey," Report from the Center on Congress at Indiana University (2005).

2. CBS New/*New York Times Poll* conducted September 15–19, 2006. Available at http://www.pollingreport.com/congress.htm#misc.

3. Burdett A. Loomis and Allan J. Cigler, "The Changing Nature of Interest Groups," in *Interest Group Politics*, 6th ed., ed. Allen J. Cigler and Burdett A. Loomis (Washington D.C.: Congressional Quarterly Press, 2002), 12; Frank Baumgartner, "The Growth and Diversity of US Associations, 1956–2004," Working Paper.

4. Kay Lehman Schlozman and John T. Tierney, *Organized Interests and American Democracy* (New York: Harper & Row, 1986), 74–82.

5. Jeffrey M. Berry, *The Interest Group Society*, 2nd ed. (Glenview, IL: Scott, Foresman, 1989), 20–21.

6. Zina L. Watkins, "Lobbyists and Interest Groups: Sources of Information," CRS Report, Congressional Research Services, February 5, 2007; Fred R. Harris, *Deadlock or Decision: The U.S. Senate and the Rise of National Politics* (New York: Oxford University Press, 1993), 64.

7. Jeffrey H. Birnbaum, "The Road to Riches is Called K Street," *The Washington Post*, June 22, 2005.

8. Hedrick Smith, *The Power Game* (New York: Ballantine Books, 1988), 232.

9. "The Other Drug War: Big Pharma's 625 Washington Lobbyists," *Public Citizen's Congress Watch*, July 2001.

10. M. Asif Ismail, "Drug Lobby Second to None: How the Pharmaceutical Industry Gets its way in Washington," Special Report from the Center for Public Integrity, July 7, 2005.

11. Quoted in John T. Tierney and Kay Lehman Schlozman, "Congress and Organized Interests," in *Congressional Politics*, ed. Christopher J. Deering (Chicago: Dorsey Press, 1989), 212.

12. Smith, *The Power Game*, 240–241.

13. Christine Mahoney and Frank Baumgartner, "When To Go It Alone: The Determinants and Effects of Interest-Group Coalitions," Working Paper.

14. Hans Nichols, "K Street Freezes out Dems," *The Hill*, September 15, 2004.

15. Tierney and Schlozman, "Congress and Organized Interests," 216.

16. Robert H. Salisbury, "Putting Interests Back into Interest Groups," in *Interest Group Politics*, 3rd ed., ed. Allan J. Cigler and Burdett A. Loomis (Washington, D.C.: Congressional Quarterly Press, 1991), 382–383.

12. Congress and Budget Politics

1. The most current budget figures and estimates are available in the current budget projections section of the Congressional Budget Office's website, http://www.cbo.gov.

2. On the developments leading up to the enactment of budget reform in 1974, see Allen Schick, *Congress and Money: Budgeting, Spending and Taxing* (Washington, D.C.: The Urban Institute, 1980), 17–81.

3. On the 1989 budget battle, see Lawrence J. Hass, *Running on Empty: Bush, Congress, and the Politics of a Bankrupt Government* (Homewood, IL: Business One-Irwin, 1990).

Appendix. Introduction to the Spatial Theory of Legislating

1. Figure A-2 is drawn to show greater variance on the first dimension, which explains far more the variance in voting behavior than the second dimension.

Suggested Readings

1. The American Congress: Modern Trends

Burrell, Barbara C. *A Woman's Place Is in the House*. Ann Arbor: University of Michigan Press, 1994.

Carroll, Susan J. *The Impact of Women in Public Office*. Bloomington: Indiana University Press, 2001.

Cooper, Joseph, ed. *Congress and the Decline of Public Trust: Why Can't the Government Do What's Right*. Boulder: Westview Press, 1999.

Dodson, Debra L. 2006. *The Impact of Women in Congress*. Oxford; New York: Oxford University Press.

Gertzog, Irwin N. *Women and Power on Capitol Hill: Reconstructing the Congressional Women's Caucus*. Boulder: Lynne Reinner Publishers, 2004.

Hibbing, John R., and Elizabeth Theiss-Morse. *Congress as Public Enemy*. Cambridge: Cambridge University Press, 1995.

Hibbing, John R. *Congressional Careers: Contours of Life in the U.S. House of Representatives*. Chapel Hill: University of North Carolina Press, 1991.

Kean, Thomas H., Lee Hamilton, and Benjamin Rhodes. *Without Precedent: The Inside Story of the 9/11 Commission*. 1st ed. New York: Alfred A. Knopf, 2006.

Lawless, Jennifer L., and Richard Logan Fox. *It Takes a Candidate: Why Women Don't Run for Office*. Cambridge; New York: Cambridge University Press, 2005.

Loomis, Burdett A. *The New American Politician: Ambition, Entreprenuership, and the Changing Face of Political Life*. New York: Basic Books, 1988.

Mann, Thomas E., and Norman J. Ornstein. *The Broken Branch: How Congress is Failing America and How to Get It Back on Track*. Oxford; New York: Oxford University Press, 2006.

Mayhew, David R. *America's Congress: Actions in the Public Sphere-James Madison through Newt Gingrich*. New Haven: Yale University Press, 2000.

Mikulski, Barbara. et al. *Nine and Counting: The Women of the Senate*. William Morris and Company, 2000.

Ornstein, Norman J., Thomas E. Mann, and Michael Malbin. *Vital Statistics on Congress, 2001–2002*. Washington, D.C.: AEI Press, 2002.

Rosenthal, Cindy S., ed. *Women Transforming Congress*. Norman: University of Oklahoma Press, 2002.

Schaffner, Brian F, Wendy J. Schiller, and Patrick J. Sellers. "Tactical and Contextual Determinants of U.S. Senators' Approval Ratings." *Legislative Studies Quarterly* 28, no. 2 (2003): 203–223.

Schwindt-Bayer, Leslie A., and Renatto Corbetta. "Gender Turnover and Roll-Call Voting in the U.S. House of Representatives." *Legislative Studies Quarterly* 29, no. 2 (2004): 215–229.

Shepsle, Kenneth. "The Changing Textbook Congress," In *Can the Government Govern?*, edited by John E. Chubb and Paul E. Peterson. Washington, D.C.: Brookings Institution Press, 1989.

Sinclair, Barbara. *The Transformation of the U.S. Senate*. Baltimore: Johns Hopkins University Press, 1989.

Swain, Carol. *Black Faces, Black Interests: The Representation of African Americans in Congress*. Cambridge: Harvard University Press, 1993.

Swers, Michele L. *The Difference Women Make: The Policy Impact of Women in Congress*. Chicago: University of Chicago Press, 2002.

The Year of the Woman: Myths and Reality, edited by Elizabeth Adell Cook, Sue Thomas, and Clyde Wilcox. Boulder: Westview, 1994.

Thomas, Sue. *How Women Legislate*. New York: Oxford University Press, 1994.

Tolchin, Susan, and Martin Tolchin. *Glass Houses: Congressional Ethics and the Politics of Venom*. Boulder: Westview Press, 2003.

Whitby, Kenny J. *The Color of Representation: Congressional Behavior and Black Interests*. Ann Arbor: University of Michigan Press, 1998.

2. Representation and Lawmaking in Congress: The Constitutional and Historical Context

Anderson, Thorton. *Creating the Constitution: The Convention of 1787 and the First Congress*. University Park: Pennsylvania State University Press, 1993.

Barclay, John M. *Constitution of the United States of America with the Amendments thereto: To Which are Added Jefferson's Manual of Parliamentary Practice, The Standing Rules and Orders for Conducting Business in The House of Representatives and Senate of the United States and Barclay's Digest of the Rules of Proceeding in the House of Representatives of the United States*. Washington, D.C.: Government Printing Office. 1860, 1863, 1867, 1868, 1872.

Bates, Ernest S. *The Story of Congress: 1789–1935*. New York: Harper and Brothers, 1936.

Bessette, Joseph M. *The Mild Voice of Reason: Deliberative Democracy and American National Government*. Chicago: University of Chicago Press, 1994.

Binder, Sarah. "Dynamics of Legislative Gridlock, 1947–96." *American Political Science Review* 93 (1999): 519–534.

Byrd, Robert C. *The Senate, 1789–1989. Vol. 4. Historical Statistics, 1789–1992*. 100th Congress, 1st session.S. Doc. 100–20. Washington, D.C.: Government Printing Office, 1993.

Cooper, Joseph. *Congress and its Committees: A Historical Approach to the Role of Committees in the Legislative Process*. New York: Garland Publishing, Inc., 1988.

Cooper, Joseph. *The Origins of the Standing Committees and the Development of the Modern House*. Houston: William Marsh Rice University, 1970.

Currie, David P. *The Constitution Congress: The Federalist Period, 1789–1801*. Chicago: University of Chicago Press, 1997.

Davidson, Roger, and Walter Oleszek. *Congress Against Itself*. Bloomington: Indiana University Press, 1977.

Devins, Neal, and Keith E. Whittington. *Congress and the Constitution*. Durham: Duke University Press, 2005.

Fenno, Richard, Jr. *The United States Senate: A Bicameral Perspective*. Washington, D.C.: American Enterprise Institute, 1982.

Grant, J. Tobin, and Thomas J. Rudolph. "The Job of Representation in Congress: Public Expectations and Representative Approval." *Legislative Studies Quarterly* 29, no. 3 (2004): 431–445.

Haynes, George H. *The Election of Senators*. New York: Henry Holt and Company, 1906.

Haynes, George H. *The Senate of the United States: Its History and Practice*. 2 vols. Boston: Houghton Mifflin, 1938.

Jefferson, Thomas. *A Manual of Parliamentary Practice for the Use of the Senate of the United States*. First Edition 1801 With Annotations by the Author. Washington, D.C.: Samuel Harrison Smith, 1801. Reprint, Washington, D.C.: Government Printing Office (page references are to the reprint edition), 1993.

Jillson, Calvin, and Rick Wilson. *Congressional Dynamics: Structure, Coordination, and Choice in the First American Congress, 1774–1789*. Stanford: Stanford University Press, 1994.

Morgan, Donald. *Congress and the Constitution*. Cambridge: Harvard University Press, 1966.

Polsby, Nelson W. *How Congress Evolves: Social Bases of Institutional Change*. Oxford; New York: Oxford University Press, 2004.

Rakove, Jack N. *Original Meanings: Politics and Ideas in the Making of the Constitution*. New York: Vintage, 1997.

Riker, William H. "The Senate and American Federalism." *American Political Science Review* 49, no. 2 (1955): 452–469.

Rothman, David J. *Politics and Power: The United States Senate, 1869–1901*. Cambridge: Harvard University Press, 1966.

Schickler, Eric. *Disjointed Pluralism*. Princeton: Princeton University Press, 2001.

Schiller, Wendy. *Partners and Rivals: Representation in U.S. Senate Delegations*. Princeton: Princeton University Press, 2000.

Swift, Elaine K. *The Making of an American Senate: Reconstitutive Change in Congress, 1787–1841*. Ann Arbor: University of Michigan Press, 1996.

Wilson, Woodrow. *Congressional Government: A Study in American Politics*. Boston: Houghton Mifflin Company, 1885 [1985].

Wilson, Woodrow, and Walter Lippmann. *Congressional Government: A Study in American Politics*. Mineola, NY: Dover Publication, 2006.

Wirls, Daniel, and Stephen Wirls. *The invention of the United States Senate*. Baltimore: Johns Hopkins University Press, 2004.

Young, James S. *The Washington Community, 1800–1828*. New York: Columbia University Press, 1966.

Zelizer, Julian E. 2006. *On Capitol Hill: The Struggle to Reform Congress and Its Consequences, 1948–2000*. 1st pbk. ed. Cambridge; New York: Cambridge University Press.

U.S. Senate History Website.

http://www.senate.gov/pagelayout/history/g_three_sections_with_teasers/origins.htm

3. Congressional Elections and Policy Alignments

Abramowitz, Alan I., and Jeffrey Segal. *Senate Elections*. Ann Arbor: University of Michigan Press, 1992.

Baretto, Matt A., Gary M. Segura, and Nathan D. Woods. "The Mobilizing Effect of Majority-Minority Districts on Latino Turnout." *American Political Science Review* 98, no. 1 (2004): 65–76.

Biersack, Robert, John Green, Paul Herrnson, Lynda Powell and Clyde Wilcox. *The Financiers of Congressional Elections: Investors, Ideologues, and Intimates*. New York: Columbia University Press, 2003.

Brady, David W. *Critical Elections and Congressional Policy Making*. Stanford: Stanford University Press, 1988.

Burden, Barry, and David Kimball. *Why Americans Split Their Tickets: Campaigns, Competition, and Divided Government*. Ann Arbor: The University of Michigan Press, 2002.

Campbell, James E. *The Presidential Pulse of Congressional Elections*. Lexington, KY: University of Kentucky Press, 1993.

Canon, David T. *Race, Redistricting, and Representation*. Chicago: University of Chicago Press, 1991.

Canon, David. *Race, Redistricting, and Representation: The Unintended Consequences of Black Majority Districts*. Chicago: University of Chicago Press, 1999.

Citrin, J, Eric Schickler, and John Sides. "What if Everyone Voted? Simulating the Impact of Increased Turnout in Senate Elections." *American Journal of Political Science* 47, no. 1 (2003): 75–90.

Corrado, Anthony, Thomas E. Mann, and Trevor Potter, eds. *Inside the Campaign Finance Battle: Court Testimony on the New Reforms*. Washington, D.C.: Brookings Institution Press, 2003.

Currinder, Marian L. "Leadership PAC Contributions Strategies and House Member Ambitions." *Legislative Studies Quarterly* 28, no. 4 (2003): 551–577.

Dion, Douglas. *Turning the Legislative Thumbscrew*. Ann Arbor: University of Michigan Press, 1997.

Dwyer, Diane, and Victoria Farrar-Meyers. *Legislative Labyrinth: Congress and Campaign Finance Reform*. Washington, D.C.: Congressional Quarterly Press, 2000.

Fenno, Richard, Jr. *Congress at the Grassroots: Representational Change in the South, 1970–1998*. Chapel Hill: University of North Carolina Press, 2000.

Fenno, Richard, Jr. *Senators on the Campaign Trail: The Politics of Representation*. Norman: University of Oklahoma Press, 1996.

Fiorina, Morris P. *Congress: Keystone of the Washington Establishment*, 2nd ed. New Haven: Yale University Press, 1989.

Fowler, Linda, and Robert McClure. *Political Ambition: Who Decides to Run for Congress*. New Haven: Yale University Press, 1989.

Glazer, Amihai, and Bernard Grofman. "Two Plus Two Plus Two Equals Six: Tenure of Office of Senators and Representatives, 1953–1983." *Legislative Studies Quarterly* 12, no. 4 (1987): 555–63.

Gronke, Paul. *The Electorate, the Campaign, and the Office: A Unified Approach to Senate and House Elections*. Ann Arbor: University of Michigan Press, 2000.

Gross, Christian, and Antoine Yoshinaka. "The Electoral Consequences of Party Switching by Incumbent Members of Congress, 1947–2000." *Legislative Studies Quarterly* 28, no. 1 (2003): 55–76.

Herrnson, Paul S. *Congressional Elections: Campaigning at Home and in Washington*, 3rd ed. Washington, D.C.: Congressional Quarterly Press, 2000.

Jacobson, Gary C. *The Politics of Congressional Elections*. 6th ed. New York: Longman, 2004.

Jacobson, G. and S. Kernell. *Strategy and Choice in Congressional Elections*. New Haven: Yale University Press, 1983.

Jacobson, Gary, Samuel Kernell, and Jeffrey Lazarus. "Assessing the President's Role as Party Agent in Congressional Elections: The Case of Bill Clinton in 2000." *Legislative Studies Quarterly* 29, no. 2 (2004): 159–184.

Jones, David R., and Monika L. McDermott. "The Responsible Party Government Model in House and Senate Elections." *American Journal of Political Science* 48, no. 1 (2004): 1–12.

Kahn, Kim F., and Patrick J. Kenney. *The Spectacle of U.S. Senate Campaigns*. Princeton: Princeton University Press, 1999.

Kazee, Thomas, ed. *Who Runs for Congress? Ambition, Context, and Candidate Emergence*. Washington, D.C.: Congressional Quarterly Press, 1994.

Lewis-Beck, Michael, and Tom Rice. *Forecasting Elections*. Washington, D.C.: Congressional Quarterly Press, 1992.

Lipinski, Daniel L., William T. Bianco, and Ryan Work. "What Happens When House Members 'Run with Congress'? Consequences of Institutional Loyalty." *Legislative Studies Quarterly* 28, no. 3 (2003): 413–429.

Maestra, Cherie, Sarah Fulton, L. Sandy Maisel, and Walter Stone. "When to Risk It? Institutions, Ambitions, and the Decision to Run for the U.S. House." *American Political Science Review* 100 (2) (2006):195–208.

Magleby, David B., J. Quin Monson, and Kelly D. Patterson. *Electing Congress: New Rules for an Old Game: Real Politics in America*. Upper Saddle River, NJ: Pearson Prentice Hall, 2007.

Maisel, L. Sandy. *From Obscurity to Oblivion: Running in the Congressional Primary*. Knoxville: University of Tennessee Press, 1982.

Mann, Thomas E. *Unsafe at Any Margin: Interpreting Congressional Elections*. Washington, D.C.: American Enterprise Institute Press, 1978.

Nelson, Candice J., David A. Dulio, and Stephen K. Medvic. *Shades of Gray: Perspectives on Campaign Ethics*. Washington, D.C.: Brookings Institution Press, 2002.

Peterson, David, *et al.* "Congressional Response to Mandate Elections." *American Journal of Political Science 47*, no. 3 (2003): 411–426.

Stone, Walter, L. Sandy Maisel, and Cherie Maestas. "Quality Counts: Extending the Strategic Politician Model of Incumbent Deterrence." *American Journal of Political Science 48*, no. 3 (2004): 479–495.

Sulkin, Tracy. *Issue Politics in Congress*. Cambridge; New York: Cambridge University Press, 2005.

Tate, Katherine. "Black Opinion on the Legitimacy of Racial Redistricting and Minority-Majority Districts." *American Political Science Review 97*, no. 1 (2003): 45–56.

Thurber, James. ed. *The Battle for Congress: Consultants, Candidates, and Voters*. Washington, D.C.: Brookings Institution Press, 2000.

West, Darrell M. *Air Wars: Television Advertising in Election Campaigns 1952–1996*. Washington, D.C.: Congressional Quarterly Press, 1997.

Wolfensberger, Donald. *Congress and the People: Deliberative Democracy on Trial*. Baltimore: Johns Hopkins University Press, 1999.

Websites:

Federal Election Commission. http://www.fec.gov/

Census Bureau (Districts and Apportionment).
   http://fastfacts.census.gov/home/cws/main.html

4. Members, Goals, Resources, and Strategies

Abramson, Paul, John Aldrich, and David Rohde. "Progressive Ambition Among United States Senators: 1972–1988." *Journal of Politics 49*, no. 1 (1987): 3–55.

Baker, Ross K. *Friend and Foe in the U.S. Senate*. New York: Free Press, 1980.

Bianco, William. *Trust: Representatives and Constituents*. Ann Arbor: University of Michigan Press, 1994.

Cain, Bruce, John Ferejohn, and Morris Fiorina. *The Personal Vote: Constituency Service and Electoral Independence*. Cambridge: Harvard University Press, 1987.

Canon, David. *Actors, Athletes, and Astronauts: Political Amateurs in the United States Congress*. Chicago: University of Chicago Press, 1990.

Cook, Timothy E. *Making Laws and Making News: Media Strategies in the U.S. House of Representatives*. Washington, D.C.: Brookings Institution Press, 1989.

Davidson, Roger H. *The Role of the Congressman*. Indianapolis: Bobbs-Merrill, 1969.

Dodd, Lawrence C. 1977. "Congress and the Quest for Power," edited by L.C. Dodd and B. Oppenheimer. *Congress Reconsidered*. New York: Praeger.

Fenno, Richard, Jr. *Going Home: Black Representatives and Their Constituents*. Chicago: University of Chicago Press, 2003.

Fenno, Richard, Jr. *Home Style: House Members in Their Districts*. Boston: Little, Brown, 1978.

Fowler, Linda, and Robert McClure. *Political Ambition: Who Decides to Run for Congress?* New Haven: Yale University Press, 1989.

Fox, Harrison, Jr., and Susan W. Hammond. *Congressional Staffs: The Invisible Force in American Lawmaking*. New York: Free Press, 1977.

Lee, Frances E., and Brice I. Oppenheimer. *Sizing Up the Senate: The Unequal Consequences of Equal Representation*. Chicago: University of Chicago Press, 1999.

Lee, Frances E. "Bicameralism and Geographic Politics: Allocating Funds in the House and Senate." *Legislative Studies Quarterly* 29, no. 2 (2004): 185–213.

Loomis, Burdett. *The New American Politician*. New York: Basic Books, 1988.

Matthews, Donald. *U.S. Senators and their World*. Chapel Hill: University of North Carolina Press, 1960.

Miller, Warren E., and Donald E. Stokes. "Constituency Influence in Congress." *American Political Science Review* 57, no. 1 (1963): 45–56.

Parker, Glenn R. *Homeward Bound: Explaining Changes in Congressional Behavior*. Pittsburgh: University of Pittsburgh Press, 1986.

Price, David E. *The Congressional Experience: A View from the Hill*, 2nd ed. Boulder: Westview Press, 2000.

Rocca, Michael S. "Military Base Closures and the 1996 Congressional Elections." *Legislative Studies Quarterly* 28, no. 4 (2003): 529–550.

Wawro, Gregory. *Legislative Entrepreneurship in the U.S. House of Representatives*. Ann Arbor: University of Michigan Press, 2000.

Websites:

Current Representatives. http://www.house.gov/house/MemberWWW.shtml

Current Senators.

http://www.senate.gov/general/contact_information/senators_cfm.cfm

Congressional Budget Office. http://www.cbo.gov/

Government Accountability Office. http://www.gao.gov/

5. Parties and Leaders

Aldrich, John, and David Rohde. "The Transition to Republican Rule in the House: Implications for Theories of Congressional Politics." *Political Science Quarterly* 112, no. 4 (1997): 541–567.

Aldrich, John, Mark Berger, and David Rohde. "The Historical Variability in Conditional Party Government, 1877–1994." In *Parties, Procedure and Policy: Essays on the History of Congress*, edited by D. Brady and M. McCubbins. Stanford: Stanford University Press, 2002.

Aldrich, John H. *Why Parties? The Origin and Transformation of Political Parties in America*. Chicago: University of Chicago Press, 1995.

Ansolabehere, Stephen, James Snyder, Jr., and Charles Stewart III. "The Effects of Party and Preferences on Congressional Roll Call Voting." *Legislative Studies Quarterly* 26, no. 4 (2001): 533–572.

Bawn, Kathleen. "Congressional Party Leadership: Utilitarian versus Majoritarian Incentives." *Legislative Studies Quarterly* 23, no. 2 (1998): 219–243.

Brady, David, David Epstein, and Mathew McCubbins, eds. *Party, Process, and Political Change in Congress*. Stanford: Stanford University Press, 2002.

Burden, Barry C., and Tammy N, Frisby. "Preferences, Partisanship, and Whip Activity in the U.S. House of Representatives." *Legislative Studies Quarterly* 29, no. 4 (2004): 569–590.

Caro, Robert A. *The Years of Lyndon Johnson: Master of the Senate.* New York: Alfred A. Knopf, 2002.

Connelly, William, Jr. and John Pitney. *Congress' Permanent Minority? Republicans in the U.S. House.* Lanham, MD: Rowman and Littlefield, 1994.

Cox, Gary, and Mathew McCubbins. *Legislative Leviathan: Party Government in the House.* Berkeley: University of California Press, 1993.

Cox, Gary W., and Mathew D. McCubbins. *Legislative Leviathan: Party Government in the House.* 2nd ed. Cambridge; New York: Cambridge University Press, 2007.

Cox, Gary W., and Mathew D. McCubbins. *Setting the Agenda: Responsible Party Government in the U.S. House of Representatives.* Cambridge: Cambridge University Press, 2005.

Forgette, Richard. "Party Caucuses and Coordination: Assessing Caucus Activity and Party Effects." *Legislative Studies Quarterly* 29, no. 3 (2004): 407–430.

Frohman, Lewis, Jr., and Randall Ripley. "Conditions for Party Leadership: The Case of the House Democrats." *American Political Science Review* 59, no. 1 (1965): 52–63.

Gamm, Gerald, and Steven S. Smith. "The Dynamics of Party Government in Congress." In *Congress Reconsidered*, 7th ed., edited by Lawrence C. Dodd and Bruce I. Oppenheimer. Washington, D.C.: Congressional Quarterly Press, 2001.

Gamm, Gerald, and Steven S. Smith. "The Emergence of Senate Party Leadership," in *Senate Exceptionalism*, edited by Bruce I. Oppenheimer. Columbus: Ohio State University Press, 2002.

Hasbrouck, Paul D. *Party Government in the House of Representatives.* New York: Macmillan, 1927.

Hess, Stephen. *The Ultimate Insiders.* Washington, D.C.: Brookings Institution Press, 1986.

Jacobson, Gary C. "Party Polarization in National Politics: The Electoral Connection," in *Polarized Politics: Congress and the President in a Partisan Era*, edited by J. Bond and R. Fleischer. Washington, D.C.: Congressional Quarterly Press, 2000.

Jenkins, Jeffrey, and Charles Stewart III. "Out in the Open: The Emergence of *Viva Voce* Voting in House Speakership Elections." *Legislative Studies Quarterly* 28, no. 4 (2003): 481–508.

Jones, Charles O. *The Minority Party in Congress.* Boston: Little, Brown, 1970.

Jenkins, Jeffrey A., Michael H. Crespin, and Jamie L. Carson. "Parties as Procedural Coalitions in Congress: An Examination of Differing Career Tracks." *Legislative Studies Quarterly* 30 (3) (2005): 365–89.

Kolodny, Robin. *Pursuing Majorities: Congress Campaign Committees in American Politics.* Norman: University of Oklahoma Press, 1998.

Lawrence, Eric, Forrest Maltzman, and Steven S. Smith. Who Wins? Party Effects in Legislative Voting. *Legislative Studies Quarterly* 31 (1) (2006):33–69.

Lebo, Matthew J., Adam J. McGlynn, and Gregory Koger. Strategic Party Government: Party Influence in Congress, 1789–2000. *American Journal of Political Science* 51 (3) (2007).

Maltzman, Forrest. *Competing Principals: Committees, Parties, and the Organization of Congress*. Ann Arbor: University of Michigan Press, 1997.

Manley, John F. *The Politics of Finance*. Boston: Little, Brown, 1970.

Nokken, Timothy, and Keith Poole. "Congressional Party Defection in American History." *Legislative Studies Quarterly* 29, no. 4 (2004): 545–568.

Peabody, Robert. *Leadership in Congress: Stability, Succession, and Change*. Boston: Little, Brown, 1976.

Peters, Ronald M. *The American Speakership: The Office in Historical Perspective*, 2nd ed. Baltimore: Johns Hopkins University Press, 1997.

Ripley, Randall B. *Majority Party Leadership in Congress*. Boston: Little, Brown, 1969.

Rohde, David W. *Parties and Leaders in the Postreform House*. Chicago: University of Chicago Press, 1991.

Sinclair, Barbara. *Legislators, Leaders, and Lawmaking: The U.S. House of Representatives in the Postreform Era*. Baltimore: Johns Hopkins University Press, 1995.

Sinclair, Barbara. *Majority Leadership in the U.S. House*. Baltimore: Johns Hopkins University Press, 1983.

Sinclair, Barbara. *Party wars: Polarization and the Politics of National Policy Making, The Julian J. Rothbaum distinguished lecture series; v. 10*. Norman: University of Oklahoma Press, 2006.

Smith, Steven S. Parties and Leadership in the Senate. In *The Legislative Branch*, edited by P. J. Quirk and S. A. Binder. New York: Oxford University Press, 2005.

Smith, Steven S. *Party Influence in Congress*. New York: Cambridge University Press, 2007.

Smith, Steven S., and Gerald Gamm. 2001. "The Dynamics of Party Government in Congress." In *Congress Reconsidered*, edited by Lawrence C. Dodd and Bruce I. Oppenheimer. Washington, D.C.: Congressional Quarterly Press.

Strahan, Randall. 2007. *Leading Representatives: The Agency of Leaders in the U.S. House*. Baltimore: Johns Hopkins University Press.

Taylor, Andrew J., and Norman J. Ornstein. *Elephant's Edge: The Republicans as a Ruling Party*. Westport, CT: Praeger Publishers, 2005.

Websites:

House Party Leaders & Organizations.
http://www.house.gov/house/orgs_pub_hse_ldr_www.shtml

Senate Party Leaders & Organizations.
http://www.senate.gov/pagelayout/senators/a_three_sections_with_teasers/leadership.htm

6. The Standing Committees

Aldrich, John, and David W. Rohde. "The Republican Revolution and the House Appropriations Committee." *Journal of Politics* 62, no. 1 (2000): 1–33.

Baumgartner, F., B. Jones, and M. MacLeod. "The Evolution of Legislative Jurisdictions." *Journal of Politics* 62, no. 2 (2000): 321–349.

Crombez, Christophe, Keith Krehbiel, and Tim Groseclose. "Gatekeeping." *Journal of Politics* 68 (2) (2006): 322–334.

Davidson, Roger H. "Subcommittee Government: New Channels for Policy Making." In *The New Congress*, edited by Thomas Mann and Norman Ornstein. Washington, D.C.: American Enterprise Institute Press, 1981.

Deering, Christopher J., and Steven S. Smith. *Committees in Congress*, 3rd ed. Washington, D.C.: Congressional Quarterly Press, 1997.

Evans, C. Lawrence, and Walter Olezsek. *Congress under Fire: Reform Politics and the Republican Majority*. Boston: Houghton Mifflin, 1997.

Evans, C. Lawrence. *Leadership in Committee: A Comparative Analysis of Leadership Behavior in the U.S. Senate*. Ann Arbor: University of Michigan Press, 1991.

Fenno, Richard, Jr. *Congressmen in Committees*. Boston: Little, Brown, 1973.

Fenno, Richard, Jr. *The Power of the Purse*. Boston: Little, Brown, 1966.

Frisch, Scott A., and Sean Q. Kelly. *Committee Assignment Politics in the U.S. House of Representatives*. Norman: University of Oklahoma Press, 2006.

Goodwin, George. *The Little Legislatures: Committees of Congress*. Amherst: University of Massachusetts Press. 1970.

Hall, Richard I. *Participation in Congress*. New Haven: Yale University Press, 1996.

Kiewiet, D. Roderick, and Mathew McCubbins. *The Logic of Delegation: Congressional Parties and the Appropriations Process*. Chicago: University of Chicago Press, 1991.

King, David. *Turf Wars: How Congressional Committees Claim Jurisdiction*. Chicago: University of Chicago Press, 1997.

Krehbiel, Keith. *Information and Legislative Organization*. Ann Arbor: University of Michigan Press, 1991.

Longley, Lawrence, and Walter Oleszek. *Bicameral Politics: Conference Committees in Congress*. New Haven: Yale University Press, 1989.

Mayhew, David R. *Congress: The Electoral Connection*. New Haven: Yale University Press, 1974.

McConachie, Lauros G. *Congressional Committees: A Study of the Origins and Development of Our National and Local Legislative Methods*. New York: Thomas Y. Crowell, 1898.

Schickler, Eric, Eric McGhee, and John Sides. "Remaking the House and Senate: Personal Power, Ideology, and the 1970s Reforms." *Legislative Studies Quarterly* 28, no. 3 (2003): 297–331.

Shepsle, Kenneth. *The Giant Jigsaw Puzzle*. Chicago: University of Chicago Press, 1978.

Smith, Steven S. *Call to Order: Floor Politics in the House and Senate*. Washington, D.C.: Brookings Institution Press, 1989.

Strahan, Randall. *New Ways and Means: Reform and Change in a Congressional Committee*. Chapel Hill: University of North Carolina Press, 1990.

Vander Wielen, Ryan. Conference Committees and Bias in Legislative Outcomes. Ph.D. Dissertation, Political Science, Washington University, St. Louis, 2006.

Websites:

House Committees. http://www.house.gov/house/CommitteeWWW.shtml

Senate Committees.
http://www.senate.gov/pagelayout/committees/d_three_sections_with_teasers/committees_home.htm

Historical Committees. http://web.mit.edu/17.251/www/data_page.html#1

7. The Rules of the Legislative Game

Adler, E. Scott. *Why Congressional Reforms Fail*. Chicago: Chicago University Press, 2002.

Bach, Stanley, and Steven S. Smith. *Managing Uncertainty in the House of Representatives: Adaptation and Innovation in Special Rules*. Washington, D.C.: Brookings Institution Press, 1988.

Alexander, DeAlva S. *History and Procedure of the House of Representatives*. Boston: Houghton Mifflin, 1916.

Beeman, Richard R. "Unlimited Debate in the Senate: The First Phase." *Political Science Quarterly* 83, no. 3 (1968): 419–34.

Binder, Sarah. "Partisanship and Procedural Choice: Institutional Change in the Early Congress, 1789–1823." *Journal of Politics* 57, no. 4 (1995): 1093–1118.

Binder, Sarah. *Minority Rights, Majority Rule: Partisanship and the Development of Congress*. Cambridge, U.K.; New York: Cambridge University Press, 1997.

Binder, Sarah. "Parties and Institutional Choice Revisited." *Legislative Studies Quarterly* 31 (4) (2006): 413–532.

Binder, Sarah, and Steven S. Smith. *Politics or Principle? Filibustering in the United States Senate*. Washington, D.C.: Brookings Institution Press, 1997.

Burdette, Franklin L. *Filibustering in the Senate*. Princeton: Princeton University Press, 1940.

Foley, Michael. *The New Senate: Liberal Influence on a Conservative Institution, 1959–1972*. New Haven: Yale University Press, 1980.

Lawrence, Eric D. *Essays on Procedural Development in the U.S. Congress*. Ph.D. Dissertation, University of Minnesota, 2004.

Oleszek, Walter J. *Congressional Procedures and the Policy Process*. 7th ed. Washington, D.C.: CQ Press, 2007.

Roberts, Jason M. Minority Rights and Majority Power: Conditional Party Government and the Motion to Recommit in the House. *Legislative Studies Quarterly* 30 (2) (2005): 219–34.

Shepsle, Kenneth, and Barry Weingast. "When Do Rules of Procedure Matter?" *Journal of Politics 46*, no. 1 (1984): 206–221.

Sinclair, Barbara. *Unorthodox Lawmaking: New Legislative Processes in the U.S. Congress*, 2nd ed. Washington, D.C.: Congressional Quarterly Press, 2000.

Tiefer, Charles. *Congressional Practice and Procedure*. Westport, CT: Greenwood Press, 1989.

Wawro, Gregory, and Eric Schickler. *Filibuster: Obstruction and Lawmaking in the U.S. Senate, Princeton Studies in American Politics*. Princeton, NJ: Princeton University Press, 2006.

Wolfensberger, Donald. *Congress and the People: Deliberative Democracy on Trial*. Washington, D.C.: Woodrow Wilson Center Press, 2000.

Websites:

House Rules. http://www.house.gov/rules

Senate Rules.
http://www.senate.gov/reference/reference_index_subjects/Rules_and_Procedure_vrd.htm

Library of Congress (Thomas). http://thomas.loc.gov/

Bill Process (brief). http://www.house.gov/house/Tying_it_all.shtml
Bill Process (long). http://thomas.loc.gov/home/holam.txt

8. The Floor and Voting

Anderson, William, Janet Box-Steffensmeier, and Valerie Sinclair-Chapman. "The Keys to
    Legislative Success in the U.S. House of Representatives." *Legislative Studies Quarterly*
    28, no. 3 (2003): 357–386.
Arnold, R. Douglas. *The Logic of Congressional Action*. New Haven: Yale University Press,
    1990.
Bach, Stanley, and Steven S. Smith. *Managing Uncertainty in the House of Representatives:
    Adaptation and Innovation in Special Rules*. Washington, D.C.: Brookings Institution
    Press, 1988.
Binder, Sarah, and Steven S. Smith. *Politics or Principle? Filibustering in the United States
    Senate*. Washington, D.C.: Brookings Institution Press, 1997.
Calvert, Randall, and Richard F. Fenno, Jr. "Strategy and Sophisticated Voting in the Sen-
    ate." *Journal of Politics 56*, no. 2 (1994): 349–376.
Clausen, Aage. *How Congressmen Decide*. New York: St. Martin's Press, 1973.
Clinton, Joshua, Simon Jackman, and Douglas Rivers. "The Statistical Analysis of Roll Call
    Data." *American Political Science Review* 98, no. 2 (2004): 355–370.
Loomis, Burdette, ed. *Esteemed Colleagues: Civility and Deliberation in the U.S. Senate*.
    Washington, D.C.: Congressional Quarterly Press, 2001.
Frantzich, Stephen, and John Sullivan. *The C-SPAN Revolution.* Norman: University of
    Oklahoma Press, 1999.
Gamm, Gerald, and Steven S. Smith. "Last Among Equals: The Presiding Officer of the
    Senate." In *Esteemed Colleagues: Civility and Deliberation in the United States Senate*,
    edited by B. Loomis. Washington, D.C.: Brookings Institution Press, 2000.
Jackson, John, and John Kingdon. "Ideology, Interest Group Score, and Legislative Votes."
    American Journal of Political Science 36, no. 3 (1992): 805–823.
King, David C., and Richard L. Zeckhauser. "Congressional Vote Options." *Legislative
    Studies Quarterly* 28, no. 3 (2003): 387–411.
Kingdon, John W. *Congressmen's Voting Decisions*, 3rd ed. Ann Arbor: University Of Michi-
    gan Press, 1989.
Krehbiel, Keith. *Pivotal Politics: A Theory of U.S. Lawmaking*. Chicago: University of
    Chicago Press, 1998.
Poole, Keith T. *Spatial Models of Parliamentary Voting, Analytical methods for social research*.
    Cambridge; New York: Cambridge University Press, 2005.
Poole, Keith, and Howard Rosenthal. *Congress: A Political-Economic History of Roll Call
    Voting*. New York: Oxford University Press, 1996.
Poole, Keith T., Howard Rosenthal, and Keith T. Poole. *Ideology and Congress*. New
    Brunswick, NJ: Transaction Publishers, 2007.
Roberts, Jason M., and Seven S. Smith. "Procedural Contexts, Party Strategy, and Condi-
    tional Party Voting in the U.S. House of Representatives: 1971–2000." *American Journal
    of Political Science 47*, no. 2 (2003): 305–317.

Smith, Steven S. *Call to Order: Floor Politics in the House and Senate*. Washington, D.C.: Brookings Institution Press, 1989.

Websites:

Library of Congress (Thomas). http://thomas.loc.gov

Roll-Call Voting Data, NOMINATE Scores. http://www.voteview.com

Recent Roll-Call Voting Data, Raw Voting Files.
http://web.mit.edu/17.251/www/data_page.html#3

House Committee on Rules. http://www.house.gov/rules/

9. Congress and the President

A Question of Balance: The President, the Congress, and Foreign Policy, edited by T. Mann. Washington, D.C.: Brookings Institution, 1990.

Aberbach, Joel D. *Keeping a Watchful Eye: The Politics of Congressional Oversight*. Washington, D.C.: Brookings Institution Press, 1990.

Barrett, David M. *The CIA and Congress: The Untold Story from Truman to Kennedy*. Lawrence, Kan.: University Press of Kansas, 2005.

Binder, Sarah. "The Dynamics of Legislative Gridlock, 1947–1996." *American Political Science Review* 93, no. 3 (1999): 519–533.

Binder, Sarah. *Stalemate: Causes and Consequences of Legislative Gridlock*. Washington, D.C.: Brookings Institution Press, 2003.

Binkley, Wilfred. *President and Congress*. New York: Knopf, 1947.

Bond, Jon, and Richard Fleisher. *The President and the Congress in a Partisan Era*. Washington, D.C.: Congressional Quarterly Press, 2000.

Bond, John, and Richard Fleisher. *The President in the Legislative Arena*. Chicago: University of Chicago Press, 1990.

Brady, David W., and Craig Volden. *Revolving gridlock: politics and policy from Jimmy Carter to George W. Bush. 2nd ed, Transforming American politics*. Boulder, CO: Westview Press, 2005.

Cameron, Charles. *Veto Bargaining: Presidents and the Politics of Negative Power*. Cambridge: Cambridge University Press, 2000.

Collier, Kenneth E. *Between the Branches: The White House Office of Legislative Affairs*. Pittsburgh: University of Pittsburgh Press, 1997.

Ripley, Randall, and James Lindsay, eds. *Congress Resurgent: Foreign and Defense Policy on Capitol Hill*. Ann Arbor: University of Michigan Press, 1993.

Dodd, Lawrence C., and Richard Schott. *Congress and the Administrative State*, 2nd ed. Boulder: Westview, 1994.

Edwards, George C. *At the Margins: Presidential Leadership of Congress*. New Haven: Yale University Press, 1989.

Epstein, David, and Sharon O'Halloran. *Delegating Powers: A Transaction Cost Politics Approach to Policy Making Under Separate Powers*. Cambridge: Cambridge University Press, 1999.

Fenno, Richard F., Jr. *Divided Government*. New York: Allyn & Bacon, 1995.

Fiorina, Morris P. *Divided Government*, 2nd ed. Needham Heights: Allyn & Bacon, 1996.

Fisher, Louis. *Congressional Abdication on War and Spending*. College Station: Texas A&M University Press, 2000.

Fisher, Louis. *Constitutional Conflicts Between Congress and the President*, 4th ed. Lawrence: University Press of Kansas, 1997

Fisher, Louis. *The Constitution Between Friends: Congress, the President, and the Law*. New York: St. Martin's, 1978.

Fisher, Louis. *The Politics of Shared Power: Congress and the Executive*. College Station: Texas A&M Press, 1998.

Foreman, Christopher J., Jr. *Signals from the Hill: Congressional Oversight and the Challenge of Social Regulation*. New Haven: Yale University Press, 1988.

Gilmour, John B. *Strategic Disagreement: Stalemate in American Politics*. Pittsburgh: University of Pittsburgh Press, 1995.

Hersman, Rebecca K.C. *Friends and Foes: How Congress and the President Really Make Foreign Policy*. Washington, D.C.: Brookings Institution Press, 2000.

Hinckley, Barbara. *Less Than Meets the Eye: Foreign Policy Making and the Myth of the Assertive Congress*. Chicago: University of Chicago Press, 1994.

Jones, Charles O. *Separate but Equal Branches: Congress and the Presidency*, 2nd ed. New York: Chatham House, 1999.

Kernell, Samuel. *Going Public: New Strategies of Presidential Leadership*. Washington, D.C.: Congressional Quarterly Press, 1986.

Krehbiel, Keith. *Pivotal Politics: A Theory of U.S. Lawmaking*. Chicago: University of Chicago Press, 1998.

Lindsay, James. *Congress and the Politics of U.S. Foreign Policy*. Baltimore: Johns Hopkins University Press, 1994.

Light, Paul. *The President's Agenda*. Rev. ed. Baltimore: Johns Hopkins University Press, 1991.

Lowenthal, Mark M. *Intelligence: From Secrets to Policy*. Washington, D.C.: Congressional Quarterly Press, 1999.

Mayer, Kenneth R. *With the Stroke of a Pen: Executive Orders and Presidential Power*. Princeton: Princeton University Press, 2001.

Mayhew, David. *Divided We Govern: Party Control, Lawmaking, and Investigating: 1946–1990*. New Haven: Yale University Press, 1992.

McCarty, Nolan. "The Appointments Dilemma." *American Journal of Political Science 48*, no. 3 (2004): 413–428.

Mezey, Michael L. *Congress, the President, and Public Policy*. Boulder: Westview, 1989.

Moe, Terry. "An Assessment of the Positive Theory of 'Congressional Dominance.'" *Legislative Studies Quarterly 12*, no. 4 (1987): 475–520.

Moe, Terry. "The Presidency and the Bureaucracy: The Presidential Advantage." In *The Presidency and the Political System*, edited by M. Nelson, 425–457. Washington, D.C.: Congressional Quarterly Press, 2003.

Neustadt, Richard E. *Presidential Power*. New York: John Wiley and Sons, 1980.

Peterson, Mark A. *Legislating Together: The White House and Capitol Hill from Eisenhower to Reagan*. Cambridge: Harvard University Press, 1990.

Spitzer, Robert J. *President and Congress: Executive Hegemony at the Crossroads of American Government*. New York: McGraw Hill, 1993.

Thurber, James, ed. *Rivals for Power: Presidential-Congressional Relations*. Washington, D.C.: Congressional Quarterly Press, 1996.

Wayne, Stephen J. *The Legislative Presidency*. New York: Harper, 1978.

Wildavsky, Aaron. "The Two Presidencies." In *Perspectives on the Presidency*, edited by A. Wildavsky. Boston: Little, Brown, 1975.

Websites:

White House and Executive Agencies. http://www.whitehouse.gov/government/

10. Congress and the Courts

Abraham, Henry J. *Justices, Presidents, and Senators: A History of the U.S. Supreme Court Appointments from Washington to Clinton*. Lanham: Rowman and Littlefield, 1999.

Barnes, Jeb. *Overruled?: Legislative Overrides, Pluralism, and Contemporary Court-Congress Relations*. Stanford: Stanford University Press, 2004.

Berger, Raoul. *Congress v. The Supreme Court*. Cambridge: Harvard University Press, 1969.

Binder, Sarah, and Forrest Maltzman. "The Limits of Senatorial Courtesy." *Legislative Studies Quarterly* 29, no. 1 (2004): 5–22.

Cameron, Charles, Albert Cover, and Jeffrey Segal. "Senate Voting on Supreme Court Nominees: A Neoinstitutional Model." *American Political Science Review* 84, no. 2 (1990): 525–534.

Carson, Jamie L, and Benjamin A. Kleinerman. "A Switch in Time Saves Nine: Institutions, Strategic Actors, and FDR's Court-Packing Plan." *Public Choice* 113 (2002): 301–324.

Cohen Bell, Lauren. *Warring Factions: Interest Groups, Money, and the New Politics of Senate Confirmation*. Columbus: Ohio State University Press, 2002.

Frickey, Philip, and Seven S. Smith. "Judicial Review, the Congressional Process, and the Federalism Cases: An Interdisciplinary Critique." *The Yale Law Journal* 111, no. 7 (2002): 1707–1756.

Geyh, Charles Gardner. *When Courts and Congress Collide: The Struggle for Control of America's Judicial System*. Ann Arbor: University of Michigan Press, 2006.

Hoekstra, Valerie J. *Public Reaction to Supreme Court Decisions*. New York: Cambridge University Press, 2003.

Katzmann, Robert A. *Courts and Congress*. Washington, D.C.: Brookings Institution, 1997.

Lovell, George I. *Legislative Deferrals: Statutory Ambiguity, Judicial Power, and American Democracy*. New York: Cambridge University Press, 2003.

Maltzman, Forrest, James F. Spriggs, and Paul J. Wahlbeck. *Crafting Law on the Supreme Court: The Collegial Game*. New York: Cambridge University Press, 2000.

Moraski, Byron J., and Charles R. Shipan. "The Politics of Supreme Court Nominations: A Theory of Institutional Constraints and Choices." *American Journal of Political Science* 43, no. 4 (1999): 1069–1095.

Shipan, Charles R. *Designing Judicial Review: Interest Groups, Congress, and Communications Policy*. Ann Arbor: University of Michigan Press, 1997.

Solberg, Rorie L. Spill. and Eric S. Heberlig. "Communicating to the Courts and Beyond: Why Members of Congress Participate in *Amici Curiae*." *Legislative Studies Quarterly* 29, no. 4 (2004): 591–610.

Urofsky, Melvin I. *Money and Free Speech: Campaign Finance Reform and the Courts*. Lawrence, KS: University Press of Kansas, 2005.

Yalof, David. *Pursuit of Justices: Presidential Politics and the Selection of Supreme Court Nominees*. Chicago: University of Chicago Press, 1999.

Websites:

Supreme Court. http://www.supremecourtus.gov

Federal Court System. http://www.uscourts.gov/

Supreme Court Opinions. http://www.findlaw.com/casecode/supreme.html

11. Congress, Lobbyists, and Interest Groups

Biersack, Robert, Paul Herrnson, and Clyde Wilcox, eds. *After the Revolution: PACs, Lobbies, and the Republican Congress*. Boston: Allyn & Bacon, 1999.

Austen-Smith, David, and John R. Wright. "Counteractive Lobbying." *American Journal of Political Science* 38, no. 1 (1994): 25–44.

Austen-Smith, David, "Campaign Contributions and Access." *American Political Science Review* 89, no. 3 (1995): 566–581

Balla, Steven J., and John R. Wright. "Interest Groups, Advisory Committees, and Congressional Control of the Bureaucracy," *American Journal of Political Science* 45, no. 4 (2001): 799–812.

Baumgartner, Frank, and Beth Leech, "The Multiple Ambiguities of 'Counteractive Lobbying.'" *American Journal of Political Science* 40, no. 2 (1996): 521–542.

Birnbaum, Jeffrey, and Alan S. Murray. *Showdown at Gucci Gulch: Lawmakers, Lobbyists, and the Unlikely Triumph of Tax Reform*. New York: Random House, 1987.

Caldeira, Greg, and John R. Wright, "Lobbying for Justice: Organized Interests, Supreme Court Nominations, and United States Senate." *American Journal of Political Science* 42, no. 2 (1998): 499–523.

Cater, Douglas. *Power in Washington*. New York: Random House, 1964.

Cigler, Alan J., and Burdette A. Loomis, "Always Involved, Rarely Central: Organized Interests in American Politics." In *Interest Group Politics*, 6th ed., edited by Alan Cigler and Burdette Loomis. Washington, D.C.: Congressional Quarterly Press, 2002.

Campbell, Colton, and John S, Stack, Jr., eds. *Congress Confronts the Court: The Struggle for Legitimacy and Authority in Lawmaking*. Lanham, MD: Rowman and Littlefield, 2001.

Dexter, Lewis A. *How Organizations Are Represented in Washington*. Indianapolis: Bobbs-Merrill, 1969.

Hall, Richard L. and F.W. Wayman. "Buying Time: Moneyed Interests and the Mobilization of Bias in Congressional Committees." *American Political Science Review* 84, no. 3 (1990): 797–820.

Hammond, Susan W. *Congressional Caucuses in National Policymaking.* Baltimore: Johns Hopkins University Press, 1997.

Hansen, John Mark. *Gaining Access: Congress and the Farm Lobby, 1919–1981.* Chicago: University of Chicago Press, 1991.

Heclo, Hugh. "Issue Networks and the Executive Establishment." In *The New American Political System,* edited by Anthony King. Washington, D.C.: American Enterprise Institute Press, 1978.

Hojnacki, Marie, and David C. Kimball. "Organized Interests and the Decision of Whom to Lobby in Congress." *American Political Science Review* 92, no. 4 (1998): 775–790.

Cigler, Allan, and Burdette Loomis, eds. *Interest Group Politics,* 6th ed. Washington, D.C.: Congressional Quarterly Press, 2002.

Loomis, B. and A. Cigler. "The Changing Nature of Interest Groups." In *Interest Group Politics,* 6th ed. Washington, D.C.: Congressional Quarterly Press, 2002.

Lowi, Theodore J. *The End of Liberalism.* New York: Norton, 1979.

Lupia, Arthur and Mathew McCubbins. "Who Controls? Information and the Structure of Legislative Decision Making." *Legislative Studies Quarterly* 19, no. 3 (1994): 361–384.

Mackenzie, G.C., with Michael Hafken. *Scandal Proof: Do Ethics Laws Make Government Ethical?* Washington, D.C.: Brookings Institution Press, 2002.

McCubbins, Mathew, and Thomas Schwartz. "Congressional Oversight Overlooked: Police Patrols versus Fire Alarms." *American Journal of Political Science* 28, no. 1 (1984): 59–82.

McCubbins, Mathew, Roger Noll and Barry Weingast. "Administrative Procedures as Instruments of Political Control." *Journal of Law, Economics and Organization* 10, no. 2 (1987): 243–277.

McCune, Wesley. *The Farm Bloc.* New York: Doubleday, Doran, and Company, 1943.

Moe, Terry M. "Control and Feedback in Economic Regulation: The Case of the NLRB." *American Political Science Review* 79, no. 4 (1985): 1094–1116.

Olson, Mancur. *The Logic of Collective Action: Public Goods and the Theory of Groups.* Cambridge: Harvard University Press, 1965.

Ornstein, Norman, and Shirley Elder. *Interest Groups, Lobbying, and Policymaking.* Washington, D.C.: Congressional Quarterly Press, 1978.

Salisbury, Robert H., et al. "Who You Know Versus What You Know: The Uses of Government Experience for Washington Lobbyists." *American Journal of Political Science* 33, no. 1 (1989): 175–195.

Salisbury, Robert H. "An Exchange Theory of Interest Groups." *Midwest Journal of Political Science* 13, no. 1 (1969): 1–32.

Schlozman, Kay, and John Tierney. *Organized Interests and American Democracy* New York: Harper & Row, 1986.

Shipan, Charles R. *Designing Judicial Review: Interest Groups, Congress, and Communications Policy.* Ann Arbor: University of Michigan Press, 2000.

Truman, David. *The Governmental Process,* 2nd ed. New York: Knopf, 1971.

United States. Congress. Senate. Committee on Homeland Security and Governmental Affairs. 2006. *Lobbying Reform: Proposals and Issues: Hearing Before the Committee on*

Homeland Security and Governmental Affairs, United States Senate, One Hundred Ninth Congress, Second Session, January 25, 2006. Washington, D.C.: Government Printing Office.

Walker, Jack L., Jr., *Mobilizing Interest Groups in America*. Ann Arbor: University of Michigan Press, 1991.

Wright, John R. *Interest Groups and Congress: Lobbying, Contributions, and Influence*. Boston: Allyn & Bacon, 1996.

Websites:

Federal Election Commission. http://www.fec.gov/

House Lobbying Disclosure. http://clerk.house.gov/pd/index.html

Senate Lobbying Disclosure.
    http://www.senate.gov/pagelayout/legislative/g_three_sections_with_teasers/
    lobbyingdisc.htm

12. Congress and Budget Politics

Farrier, Jasmine. *Passing the Buck: Congress, the Budget, and Deficits*. Lexington: University Press of Kentucky, 2004.

Keith, Robert, and Allen Schick. *The Federal Budget Process*. New York: Nova Science Publishers, 2003.

Krutz, Glen S. *Hitching a Ride: Omnibus Legislating in the U.S. Congress*. Columbus: Ohio State University Press, 2001.

LeLoup, Lance T. *Parties, Rules, and the Evolution of Congressional Budgeting*. Pullman, WA: Washington State University, 2005.

Rubin, Irene S. *Balancing the Federal Budget*. New York: Chatham House, 2003.

Schick, Allen. *Congress and Money*. Washington, D.C.: Urban Institute Press, 1980.

Schick, Allen. *The Federal Budget: Politics, Policy Process*. Rev. ed. Washington, D.C.: Brookings Institution Press, 2000.

Sinclair, Barbara. *Unorthodox Lawmaking: New Legislative Processes in the U.S. Congress*, 2nd ed. Washington, D.C.: Congressional Quarterly Press, 2000.

Index

Note to index: An *f* following a page number denotes a figure on that page; a *t* following a page number denotes a table on that page.

Iran-Contra affair, 167, 179, 272–274, 301, 327
Iron triangles, 357–359
Issue networks, 358

Jackson, Andrew, 323
Jefferson, Thomas, 33
Jefferson, William, 4, 354
Jeffords, James, 18, 135
Jindal, Bobby, 243
Johnson, Andrew, 323
Johnson, Lyndon, 82, 133, 143, 290
Johnson rule, 188
Joint Committee on Atomic Energy, 167
Joint Committee on Printing, 167
Joint Committee on Taxation, 165–167, 188
Joint Committee on the Library, 167
Joint Economic Committee, 165
Joint resolutions, 214
Judicial activism, 319–321, 328
Judicial appointments, 41–42, 324, 327–329
Judicial review, 41–42, 309–310
Judiciary Act of 1801, 322
Judiciary branch. *See* Courts
Judiciary Committee, 178, 324–325
Judiciary Committee, Senate, 324

K Street Project, 351–352
Katz, Jonathan, 73
"Keating Five" affair, 3
Kennedy, Edward, 274
Kennedy, John F., 82, 270
Kern, John, 46
Kernell, Samuel, 279
Kerrey, Bob, 375–376
Kilbourn, Hallet, 315
Kilbourn v. Thompson, 315
Kim, Jay, 3
Kimball, David, 349
King, Peter, 279
King Caucus, 129
King-of-the-hill rules, 220, 222
Kingdon, John, 112–114

Lampson, Nick, 56
Larson, John, 187
Lawmaking. *See* Representation/lawmaking
Leaders, 129–136
  Democrats/Republicans in House, 1995–2007, 146, 147*f*
  Democrats/Republicans in Senate, 1995–2007, 146, 147*f*
  of earlier era, 157

House party leaders, 136–143
  House floor leader, 141
  House whips/whip organizations, 141–143
  majority floor leader, 141
  minority floor leader, 141
  Speaker of the House (*See* Speaker of the House)
  term limits, 140
  individualistic, 155–156
  influence within Congress, 108–109
  major responsibilities of, 131–135
  campaigning, 134
  coalition building, 132
  enhancing public reputation of party, 133–134
  as intermediary with president, 132–133
  managing floor, 132
  organizing party/chamber, 135
  resources for, 145–152
  formal rules, 146–148
  information, 150–151
  media access, 151–152
  party strength, 146
  staff, 152
  tangible rewards, 149
  selecting, 135–136
  selecting subcommittee chairs, 196–197
Senate party leaders
  majority floor leaders, 143–145
  minority floor leaders, 144
  Senate floor leaders, 143–145
  Senate party leaders, 143–145
  Senate whips/whip organization, 144–145
  term limits, 144
  seniority system and, 193–196
  term limits for, 138
  top leaders, 110th Congress, 131, 131*t. See also* Parties
Leadership political action committee, 8
Legislative assistant (LA), 111
Legislative correspondent (LC), 111
Legislative director (LD), 111
Legislative Reorganization Act of 1946, 49–50, 179, 200, 203
Legislative Reorganization Act of 1970, 50–51, 179, 203, 302
Legislative service organizations (LSOs), 356–357
Legislative veto, 303–305, 311
Less autonomous committees, 24

Small Business and Entrepreneurship
  Committee, Senate, 200
Smith, Chris, 196
Smith, Nick, 3
Social lobbying, 343
Social Security program, 364
Soft money, 61
Spatial theory of legislating, 387–398
  advanced theory/limits of spatial theory,
    397–398
  agency decisions, 395–397
  agency discretion, in multidimensional
    space, 396–397, 397f
  agenda setting, structure-induced
    equilibria, and political power,
    391–392
  basic concepts for analyzing legislative
    body, 388–389
  bicameral outcome in one dimension,
    394f
  bicameralism/separation of powers/agency
    decisions/legislative outcomes
    bicameralism, 393–394
  chaos theorem, 390f
  chaos theorem and multidimensional
    space, 390–391
  distribution of Senators on
    liberal-conservative dimension,
    2005–2006, 387, 388f
  equilibrium, 390
  majority rule cycling, 391
  median voter theorem, 389, 389f, 390
  preferences and policy space, 389
  president and veto, 394–395
  Senator policy position, 387
  Senator policy position on 2006
    Immigration Bill, 388f
  simple majority rule and median voter
    theorem, 389–390
  status quo and agenda setting, 392–393
  status quo and agenda setting,
    multidimensional case, 393f, 394
  status quo and agenda setting,
    unidimensional case, 392f, 393–394
  structure-induced equilibria, 391
  upholding presidential veto, one
    dimension, 395, 395f
  veto override coalitions, multidimensional,
    395, 396f
Speaker of the House
  formal powers, 137–140
  formal powers, reinforcement of, 146–148,
    157, 185

procedural power of, in wake of terroist
    attacks, 36
  resignations, 125, 136, 139
  selection of, 127, 129–131, 136
  term limits, 140
Speaker pro tempore, 36
Special Committee on Aging, Senate, 188
Special-order speeches, 240
Special rules, 160, 219–220, 222, 224,
    252–254
  example of, 242–243
  to limit floor amendments, 184
  restrictiveness of, 1993–2006, 252, 253f
Special/select committee, 167, 179
Specter, Arlen, 195
Spending ceilings, 231, 365, 370–371, 381
Standards of Official Conduct Committee,
    House, 200, 220
Standing committees, 43, 164. See also
    Committees
Standing/division votes, 250
Standing rules, 146
State of the Union Address, 269
Steering and Policy Committee, 196
Steering committees, 187, 196
Structural politics, 294–295
Subcommittees, 200–203
  in House, 200–201
  in House, checking power of, 202–203
  selecting chair, 196–197
  in Senate, 201
Subgovernments, 357–359
Sunset provisions, 293
Sunshine rules, 182–183
"Super A" committee, 188
Supreme Court
  court-packing and, 323
  on legislative veto, 304, 311
  on line-item veto, 311–312
  nominations to, 307–308
  on presidents right to conduct foreign
    policy, 286
  size of, 323. See also Courts; specific
    decisions
Swing ratio, 72

Task forces, 176–177
Tax, poll, 57
Tax bills, origin in House of Representatives,
    37
Tax cuts, 23, 277–278, 293, 361, 367, 376,
    379–380, 382
Tax evasion, 3–4